RENOVATING MARRIAGE

Toward New Sexual Life=Styles

ROGER W. LIBBY and
ROBERT N. WHITEHURST

With articles by JESSIE BERNARD ● GORDON CLANTON ● LARRY and JOAN CONSTANTINE ● RUSSELL FORD ● ROBERT and ANNA FRANCOEUR ● BRIAN GILMARTIN ● JOHN S. KAFKA ● DAVID KUSISTO ● PHYLLIS LYON ● JOHN McMURTRY ● DEL MARTIN ● RONALD MAZUR ● MERVYN MILLAR ● LONNY MYERS ● ROBERT RIMMER ● RUSTUM and DELLA ROY ● ROBERT G. RYDER ● PEPPER SCHWARTZ ● CHARLES VARNI ● CAROLYN WELLS ● MERVIN WHITE

Consensus Publishers, Inc.
255 Rose Street
Danville, California 94526

RENOVATING MARRIAGE:
Toward New Sexual Life Styles

Copyright © 1973 by Consensus Publishers

Printed in the United States of America. All rights reserved. This book, or any part thereof, may not be reproduced in any manner whatsoever without the written permission of Consensus Publishers, Inc., 255 Rose, Dannville, California 94526

Acquisition: Joseph L. Dana

Editor: Helen M. Friend

Cover and Design: John Bookout

Library of Congress Catalog Card Number: 73-75232
International Standard Book Number: 0-87998-008-7

ACKNOWLEDGMENTS

We appreciate permission to use the following material:

"Monogamy: A Critique." Reprinted from THE MONIST, Volume 56:4 Las Salle, Illinois with the permission of the publisher and the author.

"Is Monogamy Outdated?" This article first appeared in THE HUMANIST Mar/Apr. 1970 and is reprinted by permission.

"Infidelity: Some Moral and Social Issues." Reprinted from SCIENCE AND PSYCHOANALYSIS, Volume XVI, THE DYNAMICS OF WORK AND MARRIAGE by permission of the author and Grune & Stratton, Inc.

"The Double Standard and People's Liberation" and "Beyond Jealousy and Possessiveness." From THE NEW INTIMACY: OPEN-ENDED MARRIAGE AND ALTERNATIVE LIFESTYLES by Ronald Mazur to be published in the fall of 1973 by Beacon Press. Copyright © 1973 by Ronald Mazur; reprinted by permission of the publisher.

"Lesbian/Woman." From LESBIAN/WOMAN by Del Martin and Phyllis Lyon. Copyright © 1972 by Del Martin and Phyllis Lyon. Published by Glide Publications, San Francisco. By permission of Bantam Books, Inc. All rights reserved.

Excerpt from Marshall Berman's review of *Relations in Public*. © February 27, 1972 by The New York Times Company. Reprinted by permission.

We would like to give recognition for the able assistance and support of the many people who were instrumental in helping us get this book into final form. We would most like to express appreciation to Joe Dana of Consensus Publishers, Inc. for his patient help. Dr. Eleanor Lewis, who did much of the final proofing, was instrumental in calling to our attention the many ways in which our sexist biases crept into our writing styles.

We appreciate the effort of several students at the University of Windsor who helped gather data for two of the chapters written by Whitehurst. Last, but most importantly, we wish to thank our typists, Kay Rice and Mary Goundry, the designer, John Bookout and editor Helen Friend.

ABOUT THE CONTRIBUTORS

JESSIE BERNARD is the most famous female family sociologist in the country, if not the entire world. She has published many books and articles, including *The Future of Marriage, Sex Games,* and *Marriage and Family Among Negroes*. She is professor emeritus, Pennsylvania State University, and a resident of Washington, D.C.

GORDON CLANTON is an Assistant Professor at Rutgers University. He is currently writing a book dealing with the ethics of sexual behavior.

LARRY CONSTANTINE has been a computer programmer and is publishing a book on computer programming. With JOAN CONSTANTINE, he initiated the Multilateral Relations Project, using their own money to conduct a longitudinal study on a national sample of group marriages. Data from this research is the basis for the book *The Group Marriage* (Macmillan, 1973). Together, the Constantines have written numerous articles on group marriage which have appeared in both scientific journals and popular magazines.

RUSSELL FORD is the pseudonym of an English Professor who has written many articles in the fields of literature and sexuality. Under that name he has edited a collection of articles from *Screw* magazine, to which he is a regular contributor.

ANNA FRANCOEUR has a Master's degree from New York University and has taught both in high school and college. She has contributed many key insights and ideas to her husband's writings.

ROBERT FRANCOEUR is Associate Professor of experimental embryology and social biology at Fairleigh Dickinson University. He is author of *Utopian Motherhood: New Trends in Human Reproduction* and of *Eve's New Rib: Twenty Faces of Sex, Marriage, and Family.*

BRIAN GILMARTIN is completing his doctoral dissertation for a degree in sociology at the University of Iowa. He has a major interest in sex research methodology and marriage and the family.

JOHN S. KAFKA, M.D. is a psychiatric consultant to the Family Development section of the National Institute of Mental Health. He has collaborated with his N.I.M.H. colleagues in writing many family research articles.

DAVID KUSISTO is a graduate student in the Department of Sociology at Washington State University. His major professional interest is in the area of sex research.

RUSTUM ROY, born in India and now a Professor in the Department of Chemistry at Pennsylvania State University, has been active in radical Christian movements in the eastern United States. With DELLA ROY, he is author of *Honest Sex* (1968).

ROBERT G. RYDER is Chief of the Family Development section of the National Institute of Mental Health. He is the author of many articles based on his research at N.I.M.H.

PEPPER SCHWARTZ is Assistant Professor of Sociology at the University of Washington, Seattle. She is co-author of *Women at Yale* and is a major figure in Sociologists for Women in Society and other Women's Liberation groups.

CHARLES VARNI is a doctoral candidate in the Department of Sociology, Washington State University, where he specializes in the study of deviance, social psychology, and ethnomethodology.

CAROLYN WELLS is a graduate student at Washington State University.

MERVIN WHITE is Assistant Professor of Sociology, Washington State University. He has collected much data from a random sample of college students in an on-going longitudinal study of their sexual attitudes and reported behavior. His special areas of interest include research methods and deviant behavior.

ROBERT N. WHITEHURST is a member of the Department of Sociology at the University of Windsor, Canada. He is affiliated with the American and Canadian Sociological Societies, the Ohio Valley Sociological Society, the American Marriage and Family Counsellors, and a newly formed Canadian group, The Group for the Advancement of Family Research. He is co-editor (with Lester Kirkendall) of *The New Sexual Revolution* and author of a number of articles which have appeared in professional journals. His current research is in the counter-culture family alternatives movement, especially in changing male-female roles involving freedom and autonomy in long-term relationships.

To those—regardless of race, creed, or color—who have fought and continue the good fight for freedom. We offer our support for all who struggle in good faith and contend with a hopeful spirit.

Contents

Introduction, Roger W. Libby	3

I
The State of Sex and Monogamy — 17

A. Monogamy

1. Hot and Cool Sex: Fidelity in Marriage, Robert T. and Anna K. Francoeur — 19
2. The Monogamous Ideal and Sexual Realities, Robert N. Whitehurst — 38
3. Monogamy: A Critique, John McMurtry — 48
4. Is Monogamy Outdated? Rustum and Della Roy — 59
5. Infidelity: Some Moral and Social Issues, Jessie Bernard — 75
6. The Contemporary Experience of Adultery: Bob and Carol and Updike and Rimmer, Gordon Clanton — 95

B. Alternatives to Monogamy

7. Extramarital and Co-marital Sex: A Review of the Literature, Roger W. Libby — 116
8. Some Personal and Social Characteristics of Mate-Sharing Swingers, Brian G. Gilmartin and Dave V. Kusisto — 146
9. Contexts of Conversion: The Case of Swinging, Charles A. Varni — 166

10. Sexual Aspects of Group Marriage, 182
Larry L. and Joan M. Constantine
11. Apollonians and Dionysians: Some
Impressions of Sex in the Counter-Culture, 192
Mervyn Millar

II
Sexual Freedom for Whom? 209
12. Female Sexuality and Monogamy, 211
Pepper Schwartz
13. The Double Standard and
People's Liberation, 227
Ronald Mazur
14. Group Sex and Sexually Free Marriages, 240
Russell Ford
15. Lesbian/Woman, 254
Del Martin and Phyllis Lyon

III
Views of Future Participants 267
16. Youth Views Marriage: Some Comparisons
of Two Generation Attitudes of
University Students, 269
Robert N. Whitehurst
17. Student Attitudes Toward Alternate
Marriage Forms, 280
Mervin White and Carolyn Wells
√ 18. Notes on Marriages in the Counter-Culture, 296
John S. Kafka, M.D., and Robert G. Ryder

IV
Marriage: Emergent Futures 307
19. Changing Ground Rules and Emergent
Life-Styles, 309
Robert N. Whitehurst
20. Beyond Jealousy and Possessiveness, 321
Ronald Mazur

21. Being in Bed Naked with You Is the Most Important Thing in My Life,   332
Robert H. Rimmer
22. Marriage, Honesty, and Personal Growth (Reflections on upper-middle-class urban marriages),   345
Lonny Myers, M.D.

Epilog, Roger W. Libby   361

RENOVATING MARRIAGE

TOWARD NEW SEXUAL LIFE-STYLES

INTRODUCTION

Roger W. Libby

Whenever someone introduces into a conversation the fact that they are married, or about to marry, the ensuing dialogue as well as certain modifications in the behavior of the other speakers will make obvious a number of current stereotypes of the meaning of marriage. It is commonly assumed, for instance, that everyone *knows* what marriage means and that everyone accepts the image of a monogamous, sexually exclusive marriage as a reality for all couples who have any claim to being happily married. The symbolic wedding bands for men and diamond rings for women clearly indicate the exclusivity of the "love" relationship with no sanction for any extra-marital sex. In recent years, however, social change and new realities appear to counter this romanticized image of marriage. As this change is reflected through social science and the mass media, Americans are being forced to take another look at marriage with an eye to potentially *renovating* and redefining these relationships so that one has a range of permissible marital and sexual life-styles to choose from.

One of the contributors to this book, Jessie Bernard, has observed:

> Whether or not such relations are more frequent . . . a trend toward acceptance is unmistakable . . . a conception of marriage which tolerates, if it is not actually sympathetic with, extramarital relations is on its way,

and . . . provision for sexual varietism is almost standard in male blueprints for the future. The time is not far off when this desideratum of husbands' marriages may also be achieved. (1972:24)

One goal of this book is to challenge the assertion that Americans behave monogamously—to reveal the discrepancy between the single publicized image of monogamous bliss and the reality of many "marriages" with a range of ground rules, expectations, and behaviors. It is important to note that social scientists have barely begun to understand the nature of marriage, partly because they have been complacent about the monogamous image as reflecting cultural realities. Countless Americans are—and have for some time been—experimenting with alternatives to traditional monogamy, but they have been given few guidelines or assistance in this search by the mass media, schools, home, church, or other social institutions or groups. We hope readers will find in the following pages some ideas worth considering in a continuing re-evaluation of marriage, regarding it as a process rather than as a stereotyped and static state.

No one concept of marriage is appropriate for all people, nor are all people suited to marriage—of *any* style. Indeed, there are those who should remain single, and many more who should avoid the responsibility of parenthood. We are advocating democratic pluralism in this book—the choice to live a life-style of your own making without interference from those who tend to make others' lives their business. This is basically the philosophy of the Virgins Liberation Front in New York City—a group started to keep virgins from being harassed at cocktail parties merely because they chose *that* life-style. Since its inception, the virgins have been joined by swingers, those in group marriages, homosexuals, and others who believe in the freedom to be left alone. Specifically, we advocate clear thinking and the right to try out what pleases you rather than try to live by the mores of another age. Just as people differ in their personalities, needs, and goals, so must marriage vary for those who choose to marry. To attempt to fit all married people into the monogamous mold is to expect the impossible. It is no small wonder that the romanticized idea of satisfying all emotional and sexual needs in one relationship for a lifetime fails the test of reality soon after the honeymoon, and it is not surprising that an increasing proportion of married people "cheat" or seek divorce as an escape from marital disillusionment.

Marriage: Panacea for All Personal, Sexual and Social Problems?

Richard Udry has aptly described the typical American view of marriage:

> Americans believe in marriage above all. They marry earlier, remain unmarried less often, and remarry after divorce more frequently and more rapidly than people of any other industrialized nation. They look to their marital relationship for their greatest satisfaction in life. (1971:2)

It is likely that all but two to three percent of the younger generation will marry sometime—and most at an early age. Does this mean marriage is successful? Or happy? There is a ring of truth to the cartoon where the bride turns brightly to her husband and says: "Darling! Our first marriage!" The serially monogamous marital system we've created with an increasing divorce rate and with much frustration and confusion is not what most Americans have expected from marriage. And yet many Americans blame the individuals involved for marital unhappiness or failure, rather than focusing attention on the social structure or differing needs of individuals.

A long list of studies on marital happiness and unhappiness would seem to sum up marriage as a relatively poor situation for women. Traditionally the wife must understand and cater to the husband far more than the husband must cater to the wife. Women consistently evaluate their marriages lower than do their husbands. Aided by the mass media, a new consciousness is apparent among women—a consciousness of their inferior status in traditionally defined marital roles, including the sexual role. After reading reports of the research conducted by Masters and Johnson, women seem to be asking more stridently for their emotional and sexual needs to be met. Of course, husbands are not always so happy either—both members of the couple may be mutually disillusioned.

Once the woes of marriage are recognized, one might ask: is communication the problem? Are most marital problems "solved" by open, honest communication? No, communication is not the only important ingredient in marriage. Spouses can communicate well and still feel hostile toward each other or fail to meet each other's needs. In many cases, spouses simply do not share similar goals, or one or both spouses may have changed their goals during the marriage and now find the relationship no longer adequate. While selective communication may be one key to a happy marriage (there appears to be a fine line between honesty and insensitivity), there are some inadequacies it cannot make up for.

Americans expect that marriage will provide the "good life"—and that all emotional and sexual needs will be satisfied in the companionate marriage where spouses are supposedly equals who share everything. Conflict is generally seen as inappropriate and destructive to marriage, rather than a potentially constructive process leading to greater understanding and a more creative marriage with expanding growth potential. If people never argue, they are taken to be happily married. This assumption has been challenged in recent years by many writers, including George Bach, Jetse Sprey, William Lederer and Don Jackson, and Carl Rogers. Conflict theory may well be a popular approach applied more and more to the family by researchers and theorists.

All one must do to find that American marriage is not all it is purported to be is pick up a contemporary marriage text such as *The Social Context of Marriage* by Richard Udry, which emphasizes how much we *don't* know about marriage. Contradictory research findings and a lack of research sensitive to marital realities is evident in such a text. The myth has it that we will love each other more after years of marriage—yet the reality is often otherwise, as shown by the use of strategic threats such as: "If you don't stop running around with other women, I'll divorce you, and I've told my mother so." And yet, typically "infidelity" is unknown (or can't be proven) to the spouse who wears blinders with rationalizations or naive beliefs such as "My spouse wouldn't do something like *that!*" After reading a text such as Udry's one would realize there are at least five types of marriages—from conflict-habituated marriages to intimate, vital, or total marriages. Based on Cuber and Harroff's typology (1965) and research, utilitarian marriages are most common. We can speak of "dating and rating" and the "marriage market" and mean *just* that! We are in the market for the best "deal" we can find, so we can share in the good life. Somehow Americans expect that marriage will *provide* this good life, and they won't have to *create* it.

Some marry to get away from an unhappy home life. Perhaps one or both parents were alcoholics or they did not love each other or their children. Some marry to seek freedom—something that has eluded them in relationships with their parents, teachers, ministers and other socialization agents. Others are "forced" to marry due to a pre-marital pregnancy or obvious insecurities. To these people marriage is seen as the answer to all personal, sexual, and social deficiencies.

The Emergence of Legitimacy of Choice of Sexual Life Styles

Ira Reiss (1973) has stated that the legitimization of choice of sexual standards and behavior through the media is a major social reality which is having a profound effect on judgments about what is moral. The purposes of this book include the exploration of alternatives and encouragement of responsible research on alternatives to monogamy.

While there undoubtedly are some who feel free within monogamy, it is not accurate to say that most people *choose* this marital model as an ideal. Some undoubtedly select such a model (at least visibly) because they either are not imaginative enough to pursue alternatives or are afraid to verbalize their fantasies and feelings to even their closest friends. The mass media ultimately will be the liberators as the media make choices both visible and viable. Nicholas Johnson, FCC Commissioner, has written in *The Humanist* that "The choice you'll never know is the choice you'll never make. Many Americans are not sufficiently informed of the alternatives to make an intelligent choice of the life they most want." (p. 16)

It is very likely that many so-called monogamous, sexually exclusive marriages are far from what they *appear* in that a "contract" has been negotiated between the spouses for some variety of co-marital or open marriage. While such contracts may not be written or legal, they are nevertheless real and active in situationally defining what a couple agree is appropriate emotional and sexual sharing with others. As Susan Edmiston states in her *Ms.* magazine article entitled "How to Write Your Own Marriage Contract":

> ... writing ... a contract may seem a cold and formal way of working out an intimate relationship, but often it is the only way of coping with the ghosts of 2,000 years of tradition lurking in our definitions of marriage. (p. 67)

Jetse Sprey (1969) concludes that sexuality is emerging as an expression of the individual personality which is autonomous from marriage, the family and parenthood—which leaves sexuality as an integral part of the self, rather than something that suddenly appears at puberty or after marriage. Thus, one may retain a sense of one's own sexual self within as well as outside the pair-bond relationship in marriage. Some who are experimenting with various alternative sexual life-styles are more public about their particular choice than are others who fear they will receive negative feedback from people who are significant to them. With the emergence of books such as Bob Rimmer's *The Harrad Experiment* and later novels, *Open Marriage* by Nena and George O'Neill, *Becoming Partners* by Carl Rogers, and *John and Mimi* by John and Mimi Lobell, couples who have been secretly practicing some alternative to traditional marriage may become more vocal about their marital style.

Carl Rogers emphasizes the importance of experimenting with alternatives to marriage and the family as we've known them. He states:

> ... Marriage and the nuclear family constitute a failing institution, a failing way of life. No one would argue that these have been highly successful. We need laboratories, experiments, attempts to avoid repeating past failures, exploration into new approaches. ... Unheralded and unsung, explorations, experiments, new ways of relating, new kinds of partnerships are being tried out, people are learning from mistakes and profiting from successes. They are inventing alternatives, new futures, for our most sharply failing institutions, marriage and the nuclear family. (p. 212)

Rogers is realistic enough to realize that most Americans do not experiment with variations of sexually exclusive marriage which are openly agreed upon. The image of "fidelity" is still tied directly to sexual expression legitimate only within monogamous marriage.

Better Dead Than in Bed?

Most Americans conceive of extramarital sex (EMS) as adultery and therefore as morally bankrupt. The cultural attitude is probably changing, although we have no data from large, random and national samples as yet. It is not unusual to hear spouses exclaim: "I'd kill him (or her) if I caught him playing around" It seems that the horror of a spouse engaging in sexual intercourse with another is justification to feel that the spouse is no longer fit to live! The symbolic meaning of EMS is often interpreted as a threat to marriage. Fear is a strong emotion, and along with its closely related emotion of jealousy, fear provides a basis for not expanding erotic and emotional parameters to include others beyond the pair bond.

While there is some cultural lag, permissive changes in premarital and non-marital sexual attitudes and behavior are being reflected in postmarital patterns of marriages based on increased freedom and less possession and jealousy. Extramarital sex is a fact of North American sexual behavior. Most EMS is probably still seen as infidelity or adultery, but this book will also explore other marital concepts where sex with others is viewed as consistent with marital goals (thus, "comarital" sex, or CMS). As Jessie Bernard points out, infidelity must be redefined when the ground rules of marriage change and become more personalized; she contends we may have to choose between permanence and exclusivity in marriage. Ira Reiss (1973) observes that changes are partially due to increased emphasis on individualism, hedonism, affection, egalitarianism between the sexes, and autonomy from parents (the car, the pill, industrialization, and so on). Reiss claims that the most significant change in the fifty years from 1915-1965 is the legitimization of sexual choice; Reiss also notes that choices do not apply only to the premarital period, but to marriage and EMS as well. In other words, we can't isolate courtship choices in terms of the formal "date" and the emerging concepts of informal "getting together" without expecting that habits and desires that are learned and nurtured before marriage will affect marital and extramarital attitudes and behavior.

Essentially, we have two competing models of sexual and love expressions which begin for some in the premarital period, while for others changing concepts of marriage and the awareness of EMS or CMS come after making an initial commitment to sexually exclusive marriage. The traditional courtship model is that of dating, going steady, being pinned, engaged, and going on a honeymoon, which is supposed to build the basis for companionship, romance, and never-ending love. It has already been pointed out that such all-encompassing "total" marriages are rare (Cuber and Harroff, 1965). There is some indication that the traditional model is being affected by the emerging counter-culture and its experiments with marriage; even those who go through the formal patterns of courtship are now also more likely to live together and/or engage in premarital intercourse. *Ad hoc* marriages are often monogamous and imitate legal marriage—some live together to see if a legal marriage should be entered (trial marriage), and others simply live together and see no pressing need to legalize what already exists in terms of a marriage between two in-tune individuals. Such couples share common symbolic meanings of words, gestures, and expressions. Human existence becomes tolerable to the extent that it is lived in meaningful symbolic communication. Sex can be viewed as a language which is also enjoyable, or it can be perceived as an expression of a range of meanings—from exploitation, to sex as friendship, as love, or as fun. But is sexual freedom fun? Is it worth the trouble?

The Quest for Freedom

Most Americans probably yearn for more freedom, including sexual freedom; this quest for freedom is reflected in increasing rates of non-marital intercourse. More people enjoy sex before marriage with more people and for more reasons. And yet, mystically, Americans believe that a magic wand will turn everyone into a sexually exclusive creature with few or no desires for sex with anyone else after they say "I pronounce you . . .". It is as if a ceremony is expected to change twenty or more years of socialization.

The quest for freedom to be an individual with a positive identity is relevant in any discussion of alternative marital styles. The lack of opportunity and prevalence of conventional attitudes about EMS make it difficult to experience sexual variety. But with the second car, urbanization, improved contraception, and increased leisure time, it is easier for the *wife*, as well as the husband, to pursue emotional and sexual relationships with friends, lovers, acquaintances, or strangers. Ira Reiss sees a trend toward equalitarian marriages, as he states:

> We may expect women who have had greater freedom in their sexual orientations premaritally to express that greater freedom in marriage and to seek sexual satisfac-

tion more aggressively than in the past. We may also expect in premarital sex that women will, as I believe they are increasingly now, demand quality in extramarital sex. Thus if the husband is going to engage in extramarital affairs, then wives will increasingly feel they have a right to do the same. (pp. 25-26)

It is common to hear about marriages that broke up because of an extramarital affair where the spouse "falls in love" with another. While this stereotype is a reality for some marriages, it is not accepted in the following statement by a married man:

> There is not much I would like to change in our marriage, except I would like to have a little more freedom . . . I am attracted to other women. I like them for a pastime . . . I have never met or seen another girl I would put in my wife's place. I would like to have a little more freedom, so I could 'horse around' a little more. I would not think of falling in love with anyone else. (Burgess and Locke: p. 322)

The above statement could just as easily have been written by a middle-aged housewife (such as Angela in Bob Rimmer's latest novel, *Thursday, My Love*) in 1973 (See Chapter 21 of this book for Rimmer's thoughts) as by a married man in 1945. Changing concepts of marriage and of sexual life styles concern women as much as men.

Expanding Erotic Perimeters: Potential for Sex and Love

While Erich Fromm claims that erotic love must be exclusive, and that humans cannot love several people sexually at the same time, Bob Rimmer's concept of love, rather than being a game of subtraction as it is with Fromm, is a multiplying experience where the more you love, the more you are capable of loving. As Neubeck puts it:

> Forsaking all others has never been a realistic expectation, and, based on the assumption that there always will be others, couples can explore what the possibilities for themselves and each other should be: when, where, and how the additional individuals can be incor-

porated into the basic and nourishing unit. They must change more overtly so that their marriages will permit them to be less exclusive. (p. 198)

Alex Comfort sees sexual freedom as best expressed through group sex (see also Chapter 14 by Russell Ford). Comfort states:

... we are dishonest because we have a society that is supposed to be monogamous but in fact practices serial polygamy. Most people have been married more than once, and adultery is universally tolerated. Open marriage would simply legitimize what we already live (*Time*, January 8, 1973: 35).

Comfort is but one of several writers who are openly advocating some form of sexual freedom. In his book *Delightism* (1972), John Pflaum contends:

In a society of suffering, people cling to one another in non-productive social relationships fearing that otherwise they will be abandoned. Sufferers contract alliances intended to provide emotional defenses against isolation. These relationships are negative in origin and will persist only as long as both partners are motivated by their anxieties. Marriage and other exclusive arrangements may be better than the screaming loneliness of four walls, but they are a shadow of existence and symptomatic of a poorly designed social structure (1972: 115).

Encounter groups in the 60's and 70's may have profound effects on *renovating* traditional marriage; such groups provide fertile ground for research on human sexual and emotional potential. There are many questions which social scientists must pursue about marriages which sanction some form of co-marital or extramarital sexual freedom. What is the symbolic meaning and the effect of other relationships on marriage? As Reiss (1973) indicates, we must ask what style of marriage one has in order to discuss the effects of EMS on individual spouses and on couples. Also: To what extent is sex a communication of affection and a pleasant experience? How does sex affect friendships? Why are some people alienated from conventional marriage expectations, emerging marital styles? How do women fit into alternatives which include increased sexual and emotional freedom? How is sex dealt with in open marriages, swinging groups, communes, and group marriages? What about sexual jealousy? How are jealous feelings handled in open marriages? What is the relationship between fantasy and reality about EMS? What is the relationship between attitudes and actual sexual behavior? What distinctions can be made between marriages where the contracts were changed to accommodate sexual freedom, and marriages which were entered with some provision for sexual freedom? The questions could go on endlessly, but it remains for social scientists to study emerging sexual life-styles. Such research will be accomplished by people who care about the future of marriage. This book is an expression of concern about marriage; it is intended as a springboard to further dialogue and research about marriage and pluralistic sexuality. It is not intended to add yet one more nail in the coffin of marriage; nor is it intended to make the spurious argument that marriage and the family are on the way out as cultural institutions. There is little evidence to support such a contention. Rather, it is our intent to open up marriage so it can thrive, not as a decrepit monolith, but as a viable set of multiple possibilities in which people can act out the best imperatives offered by a truly open and democratic society. Freed of old myths, we can become more than ever freed from stultifying (and often untrue) notions of what men and women are about. If, as we contend, freedom brings more freedom and better awareness as well, the end result of rethinking the old norms of marriage cannot help but be instrumental in its renovation.

Contents of the Book: What's in It for You?

This book is not a blueprint for the future. It is an attempt to pull together relevant ideas and research on the role of sex after marriage. To this goal the book has been organized around the basic sections of "The State of Sex and Monogamy," "**Sexual Freedom For Whom?**". "**Views of Future Participants,**" and "**Marriage: Emergent Futures.**"

What we will be talking about is those long-term sexual relationships that used to be thought of in the context of marriage. To summarize the history of such relationships: Once it was assumed—by the mainstream of Western culture—that one man while others accept them? What do youth feel about marriage and and one woman (either for reasons of finance, politics, or "love") would be united and remain relatively exclusive sexually with one another. At one point the surrounding and supporting cast in this drama were all the members of the extended family; later they were only the children attached to the nuclear family. Whatever the source of intellectual and emotional encouragement, however, it was assumed that at least overtly the primary couple would limit their sexual interests to each other. There were of course minor variations on or deviations from this standard—polygamy (as in Mormonism), traveling salesmen with families in more than one city, husbands and wives with occasional (or frequent) lovers on the side... but at least lip service was paid to the standard for many years. During this period divorce was looked on askance—if it was even possible to obtain. You had to make some kind of other compensation for inadequacies in your long-term sexual relationship.

Then came a period of serial polygamy. If you considered sex of major importance in a long-term intimate relationship and sex was inadequate with one partner, you were at liberty (if you didn't mind paying the price) to try a new marriage partner. And another. And another.

At the moment we are in a still more individualized situation regarding the seeking of sexual fulfillment in a long-term intimate relationship. What will be described in the following pages are some of the ways people are currently using to reach personal fulfillment in this area. Although the majority of the chapters deal with adjustments and accommodations in an overwhelmingly upper-middle-class WASP milieu, you may take it for granted that a range from conservative to radical change exists as well in other backgrounds—ethnic, homosexual, "hippie," or whatever.

We are not advocating any of these variations as either panacea or cure for sick relationships; we believe there are relationships in which the intellectual and emotional factors are so much more important that any alteration in the sexual arrangements which might endanger these other aspects of the relationship would not be worth effecting. We merely want to explain—as Kinsey did on another issue long ago—that there are a number of people trying out different paths. If you are one of these people, you should not feel alone; if you are unhappy with your present situation, you might want to consider one of these other possibilities.

After all, as the classic tag goes, "Nothing human to me is alien."

FURTHER READING

Bach, George and Peter Wyden. *The Intimate Enemy.* New York: Morrow, 1968.

Bernard, Jessie. *The Future of Marriage.* New York: World, 1972.

Burgess, Ernest and Harvey Locke. *The Family.* New York: American Book Co., 1945.

Cuber, John and Peggy Harroff. *The Significant Americans.* New York: Appleton-Century, 1965.

Edmiston, Susan. "How to Write Your Own Marriage Contract." *Ms. Magazine*, Spring, 1972, 66–72.

Fromm, Erich. *The Art of Loving.* New York: Bantam, 1956.

Johnson, Nicholas. "The Careening of America." *The Humanist.* July/August, 1972, 10–17.

Lederer, William and Don Jackson. *The Mirages of Marriage.* New York: Norton, 1968.

Lobell, John and Mimi Lobell. *John and Mimi: A Free Marriage.* New York: St. Martin's Press, 1972.

Nye, F. Ivan. Personal Communication, January, 1972.

O'Neill, Nena and George O'Neill. *Open Marriage.* New York: M. Evans Co., Inc., 1972.

Pflaum, John. *Delightism.* Englewood Cliffs, N.J.: Prentice-Hall, 1972.

Reiss, Ira L. "Heterosexual Relationships: Inside and Outside of Marriage." (forthcoming manuscript to be published by General Learning Press).

Rimmer, Robert H. *The Harrad Experiment.* New York: Bantam, 1966.

Rimmer, Robert H. *Thursday, My Love.* New York: New American Library, 1972.

Rogers, Carl R. *Becoming Partners: Marriage and its Alternatives.* New York: Delacorte Press, 1972.

Sprey, Jetse. "The Family as a System in Conflict." *Journal of Marriage and the Family*, 1969, 31, 699–707.

Sprey, Jetse. "On the Institutionalization of Sexuality." *Journal of Marriage and the Family*, 1969, 31, 432–441.

Time Magazine. "Swinging Future" (an interview with Alex Comfort), January 9, 1973, p. 35.

Udry, J. Richard. *The Social Context of Marriage.* Philadelphia: J. B. Lippincott Co., second edition, 1971.

I

THE STATE OF SEX AND MONOGAMY

In an age in which little in our world goes unexamined and in which authority no longer holds the kind of sway we suppose it once did, it should not be surprising that monogamy, one of our most widely supported institutions, comes to be held up to close scrutiny. Although monogamy has a long history in the western world, changing conceptions of sexual identities, altered social control mechanisms involving different family forms, religious change, and looser community controls all cumulate to cast monogamy in a new light.

This section is intended to offer critical analyses of monogamy, as well as an introduction to the range of other options for sexual behavior within marriage that have been proposed or tried. As you will see, the chapters go beyond viewing all extramarital sex as adulterous and instead concentrate on spousal definitions of the legitimacy of sexual expression with friends, lovers, and other sexual partners. Spousal agreement to such sexual freedom for both husband and wife in terms of "co-marital" sexual relationships, is sanctioned in some forms of open marriage. A discussion of the realities of the changing demands for permanence and for sexual exclusivity in marriage provides a basis for thinking about some individually tailored style of marriage which suits the needs and desires of spouses, spouses-to-be, or any others who commit themselves to the difficulties and wonders of a long-term intimate, and sexual, relationship.

1

HOT AND COOL SEX: FIDELITY IN MARRIAGE
Robert T. and Anna K. Francoeur

Using the McLuhanesque terms "hot" and "cool," a husband and wife team delve into history to compare the changed meanings of sex from the sensual wholeness of expression which characterized our tribal forebears to the contemporary style of sexuality which they see as hot, genitally focalized, and highly specific in its definition and expectations. They go on to examine the potential for the retribalization of sensuality and the recapture of the cool sex experience as exemplified in some youthful circles today. Their thesis—that hot sex tends to minimize awareness of total selfhood and to imprison modern western man—is worthy of serious consideration. Their ideas for becoming more wholly human through exercise of a cool-sex, more sensual approach to life are provocative and will offer readers a new way of looking at their own realities.

Four and a half million Americans get married each year. Roughly a hundred and fifty million Americans are married today.

Yet most professional observers and laymen will agree that the traditional American marriage is in serious trouble. Countless sociologists, psychologists, theologians, and other experts have focused our attention on some fairly obvious external factors, suggesting that economic shifts, contraception, women's liberation, and social mobility are the key factors in the changed state of marriage in our society. Undoubtedly such developments have been very influential, but the real problem, we are convinced, remains mostly unexplored. It rests in the shadows of human consciousness.

This basic issue, which we try to explore here, is *a radical shift in our understanding and appreciation of ourselves and others as sexual persons.* External factors have produced a tense, still unresolved revolution in consciousness, a great shift in our sexual images. Along with our basic understanding of femininity and masculinity, the revolution wreaks havoc with our traditional appreciation of intimacy, responsibility, and fidelity in our human relations. The eye of the storm is a *new* way in which sexual persons, men and women, relate to each other.

The difficulty we face in pinning down this shift in consciousness does not mean the shift is imaginary. Every married couple in this country lives the tensions between the traditional and new sexual images and relations. Each married couple gives unique flesh to this tension, though the basic nucleus remains the same in all marriages. These tensions seem to come closest to the surface in young people looking forward to marriage and in marriages in their seventh and twentieth years.

Regardless of age, regardless of educational background, regardless of social strata and condition, most Americans breathe an atmosphere which, however unrealistically, still conditions each of us to picture married life as being conducted along very specific lines with definite expectations. *The fact of being married automatically defines a person.* It confers a definite status and set of social obligations on both husband and wife.

Expanding life expectancies, social mobility, contraception, the separation of sexual intercourse from procreation, the recognition of female sexual responses and needs, and the education and emergence of women as persons in the mainstream of life are crucial *external* factors. But their real importance is the echo and response they create in the consciousness of individual men and women. We cannot zero in on the conflicting polarity of sexual images which today threaten to tear apart every marriage in this country unless we face the issues honestly and openly.

Sex and Communications

Marshall McLuhan, the much idolized and disputed analyst of communications, loves to wreak havoc with our traditional images by twisting words that were once assumed to have clear definitions into new shapes and meanings. His message is that communications media have become ever more important than their content. A major revolution in communications media—the advent of electronics—signals an even more radical revolution in our culture and social attitudes.

In one of his earlier and more substantial works, *Understanding Media: The Extension of Man*, McLuhan explains the difference between hot and cool communications media (McLuhan, 1964:22).

> "A hot medium is one that extends one single sense in 'high definition.' High definition is the state of being well filled with data. A photograph is, visually, 'high definition.' A cartoon is 'low definition,' simply because very little visual information is provided."

The viewer is *excluded* from the photograph he looks at because the complete picture rules out any contribution or participation other than passive observation. The cartoon, on the other hand, invites participation. Its rough outline sketches provide a minimum of data and urge the viewer to fill in the image for himself. Printed book and lectures are hot media because they do not invite and encourage participation. A seminar is a cool media because it is based on involvement and participation. Television, for McLuhan, is the ultimate in cool media because it is so involving, as witnessed in the public reaction to the Kennedy funerals, or the first lunar landing.

Many critics have bristled at McLuhan's wrenched usage of simple words like hot and cool. Admittedly, this is a novel use of traditional words, provocative to some but confusing to others, especially people who love books and the clarity of the printed word. For book addicts and literate people "hot" invariably carries all the overtones of vital, stimulating, vigorous, and lively, while the traditional usage of "cool" leaves one with a picture that is passionless, uninspiring, dull, and lifeless.

In a brief but provoking article on "The Future of Sex" for Look Magazine in 1967, (Leonard, 1970), McLuhan and George B. Leonard suggested an even more controversial twist for our traditional terms hot and cool. They applied the adjectives to our sexual images and consciousness, speaking of hot and cool sex. Applied to our changing awareness of human sexuality and the retribalization of sexual and marital mores, hot and cool sex are virgin, untried, and undefined concepts.

One basic unmentioned problem is that *when McLuhan and Leonard speak of hot and cool communications, they are concerned with the media rather than with the content.* "The medium is the message." But when they move into sexual consciousness, most of their emphasis is on hot and cool consciousness—on content, rather than on media. As modes of communicating different sexual images, one can say that the well-defined images of Racquel Welch, Ursula Andress, or the Playboy/Penthouse centerfold are hot sex media while Twiggy, unisex fashions and hair styles are cool sex media because they lack definition and leave much to the imagination and speculation of the observer. But one can hardly speak of other equally concrete media of hot and cool sex. It is somewhat awkward and unuseful to say motels, drive-in theaters, affairs, and mistresses are hot sex while water beds, Woodstock festivals, and group marriages are cool sex.

Despite these limitations—and because we have not yet coined a more satisfactory label—we are not completely unhappy with the concept of hot sex. The same cannot be said for the term cool sex because of its traditionally negative connotations—really the opposite of what McLuhan and Leonard hint at in discussing the future of human sexuality. Despite all the explanations and descriptions one can offer, the term cool sex still carries with it far too many overtones of passionless, uninvolved, dull, lifeless relations between men and women. But until some inspired etymologist or linguist solves our label problem, we are left with the seminal concepts of hot and cool sex.

Six years ago, when McLuhan and Leonard first hinted at the contrast between hot and cool sexual perceptions, the concept struck us as very promising. But they have not developed the potential of this cultural perspective. Thus we would like to explore in some depth this imagery, and pursue its application to the conflicting images of male/female relations hidden in the miniature portraits we presented earlier. In other words, we would like to attempt a portrait of hot and cool sex attitudes, and then view this in the realities of two common forms of marriage today, closed and open marriages, where the meaning of intimacy, responsibility, and fidelity are set in sharp contrast. Finally we will explore a practical solution to the tension and conflict.

Hot Sex

The sexual consciousness of most Americans, and in fact, of most Europeans today, is a fascinating and disturbingly adolescent complex.

Hot sex may be a bit caustic as a label for this consciousness, but you will likely agree that it is quite appropriate after we look at many obvious facets of our traditional sexual consciousness in an abstract composite portrait. This composite may appear distorted *if* you try to see *all* our details in the behavior of one person you know well, be he friend, enemy, spouse . . . or closer home. No one person could have all the traits we give here as characteristic of the hot sex mentality. By the same token of honesty, we should be able to recognize a variety of these traits in our own awareness as well as in the behavior of others we know.

Hot sex, like hot media, has a "high delineation." The blown-up Playmate or Pet of the Month, with her outsized breasts, buttocks, and genitals in full view, offers a vivid image of the ideal hot sex female.

Hot sex today has a circus of obsessions, a whole variety of anxieties flowing from the segregation of sex and its reduction to the genitals. Hot sex is the American fascination with what appears to be an unlimited variety of "perfect" sexual techniques, positions, and combinations, all of which must be experienced. Hot sex is the worried quest for mutual orgasm at all costs, the anxious frantic search for the "perfect" partner, or rather the perfect organ. Hot sex is casual in its impersonalism: in the dark, one partner is the same as another, and often the same even in the light of day.

When human sexuality is segmented from life and highly defined in terms of genitals, it naturally has to be scheduled, arranged, planned, both in time and place: the bedroom, night, the motel, a plotted pursued affair. In this atmosphere sex holds only an explosive, volatile, tenuous place in everyday life.

Hot sex is fucking or—more accurately, when you appreciate the

Teutonic celebrational meaning of "fucking"—screwing in the most depersonalized sex-object way. In the curiously anonymous underground pornographic novels of Victorian England for instance, heroes and heroines parade their lusty adventures with no attention to the personalities involved—only an occasional mention of names, circumstances, or situations occurs but with an all-engrossing tyrannic monomania for the interlocking of genitals. Of course, such hot sex is male-dominated, guided by a double standard, and patriarchal. Playmates and pets must be totally submissive to the male whim.

In a hot sex culture there is also a figleafed obsession with nudity and with the naked female figure. Nudity, even in private or with one's spouse, is frowned on, for nudity exposes the "private parts" of the body and that means sex—genital sex.

Hot sex is entropic, self-destructive because it lives by possessing and conquering sex objects. But entropic also because of its vital pressures to perform: the destructive compulsion of the male to screw every chance he gets and the equal pressure on the female to satisfy the male ego with the blessing of a mutual orgasm.

Genital, hot sex becomes an end unto itself: sex for fun, for ego satisfaction, for ego building. In hot sex one can escape the unbearable burden of time and aging simply by multiplying experiences. A good scorecard, with ever mounting conquests, assures one of eternal youth.

Hot sex is the forbidden fruit, the thrill of cheating, the escape from the boredom and routine of everyday relations into the romantic wonderland of the affair. Even in the modern socially accepted infidelity, the swinger and spouseswapper reduce human sexuality to screwing. The swinger often evades real intimacy, real involvement. The swinger allows genital infidelity, provided one does not become "involved." The swinger does not solve his or her jealousy, which can accept a temporary safety valve swing while still viewing real intimacy as a threat and potential competition.

In a hot sex culture, marital fidelity is reduced to "what I did not do in Dubuque." Marital fidelity becomes synonymous with genital exclusivity, and intimacy can only mean sexual intimacy. For a hot sex culture such as America has had for decades, every sexually mature single person is a threat. The unmarried, the widowed, the divorced—all are *obviously* sex-starved. Intimacy of any kind with them must be resolved as soon as possible by marriage. An affair must lead to a divorce and remarriage, so all single persons are a threat to married couples.

In a hot sex culture such as ours, *couples* exist—not individual sexually mature persons who also happen to be married. Couples go everywhere together. It is often even unthinkable for a married person to go anywhere without his or her spouse, unless excused by business, housewife/motherly errands, or the safe bachelor's night out for poker, bowling, bridge, or weight-watchers.

In a hot sex culture, a wife is a female you marry to take out of circulation so she can provide you with a family: a wife belongs to her husband, her identity is drawn from him. Hence monogamy—life-long, and sexually exclusive—must obviously be maintained as *the sole way of adult life*, and everyone must be urged or even compelled (subtly and not so subtly) to marry as soon as possible. The slightest thought of an alternative to traditional monogamy is taboo. In a hot sex culture, adult sex life is based on the premise of an inviolable monolithic monogamy.

Hot sex is dualistic, agnostic. It really despises—or at best tolerates—the body, and despite all its protestations to the contrary, ultimately enshrouds the body with countless taboos that restrict touching and body contact to only the most "innocent" type. As a result, hot sex is basically sterile, antiseptic, and antisensual. Like the fabled *Love Machine* and the *Valley of the Dolls*, hot sex is cut off from the whole person as well as *isolated from nature and the cosmos*. In place of the earthly cosmic myths of primitive cultures, the hot sex mentality can substitute only the frail treacherous lure of the great orgasm hunt, the Parsiphalian quest of the perfect partner with the perfect organ and technique, the *Love Story* myth, and the belief that despite its segregation from life—in fact, *because of this segregation*—hot sex, genital sex, is IT.

In a few words, *hot sex is male-dominated, double-standard, intercourse-obsessed, and property-oriented.*

Cool Sex

Many of the common tensions surrounding sexual concepts can be traced to the inevitable conflicts our generations and culture must experience because we are in the process of transition. After centuries of gently brewing beneath the surface, a new consciousness of human sexuality is finally surfacing—not just among the young, but more vitally among those married couples in their thirties and forties.

Degenitalized in part, the relationship of man and woman can be validly expressed as a relationship of peers, between two evolving, developing, maturing, and unique sexual persons, between two unique, distinct persons. In this emerging cool sex tradition, men—and especially women—have to become conscious of themselves as individuals with a real existence outside their socially imposed stereotyped roles. Men and women must realize that in the Biblical tradition, creation is an on-going process of becoming. In many respects, as Paul Klee put it, "Becoming is superior to being." Masculinity and femininity, in a cool sex culture, lack clear definition. They are fluid, constantly changing with each individual sexual person, constantly evolving and constantly being created not as eternal archetypes, but as process incarnations, each with a unique value.

Yet for most people, even today, and more so for men than for women, the delineation of sexual intercourse has remained the dominant obsession. Even when we accept physical expression of the relationship between a woman and a man which is not limited to genital intercourse, we find our hot sex obsession with intercourse creeping into the picture.

Yet the medieval and renaissance recognition of women as persons in their own right brought an acceptance of the possibility that a woman and a man can cross-fertilize something besides egg and sperm. The emergence of woman as a peer, particularly in the American patterns of courtship over the past hundred years, has made a major contribution to the transformation of hot sex. With petting and "making out" increasingly accepted by adolescents as a way of discovering sex images, relating, and communicating, the physical spotlight on sexual intercourse continued to diffuse into all phases of life to the point where some critics accuse youth of claiming they discovered sex. In some ways, they have indeed discovered sex. At least they seem to be revitalizing some very desirable aspects of tribal cool sex.

The result of this uneven transformation is today's volatile, bewildering amalgam of hot and cool sexual attitudes. It is the conflict we all experience as we face the impossible contradictions involved in our own personal combination of hot sex attitudes from our culture and the varying degrees of accommodation we have made with the emerging cool sex mentality of our emerging global tribe.

The consciousness of cool sex requires a certain strength of self-identity. A man or woman must first of all be somewhat secure in their self-image, without relying on the blessing of society's stereotypes. In Maslow's language, they must be self-actualizing and not always turning to society or another person for approval, direction and borrowed identity. Some real degree of psychological and emotional maturity—the ability to stand alone—is essential to a cool sex mentality.

Given the low definition of masculinity in cool sex, it is no longer possible for men to judge masculinity and identity in terms of multiple conquests and (male) progeny. Nor can women continue to sum up their identity as persons in the phrases "his wife" and "their mother," or in the number of times she has produced pattering feet for the nursery.

Cool sex means considering and accepting *for others and for oneself* the possibility of real alternatives to the traditional hot sex stereotypes of breadwinner, housewife, parent, married *couple*, fair white maiden (the sexless school teacher), dark lady (seduceable secretary), and double standards. Sexual persons in a cool sex society cannot be defined in terms of roles. Every individual, each man and woman, must be free to explore and express their personality, with as little role-playing as possible and with a minimum of imperatives other than the basic rule of not exploiting others in any way, especially by using them as objects, sexual or otherwise.

Cool sexuality is expressed in integrated, holistic behavior that accepts the human body wholeheartedly and fully. It is not disturbed by nudity, or scandalized by "immodesty" as was Michol when David danced before the Ark. Cool sexual consciousness celebrates the body in the tradition of Solomon's "Song of Songs." It is involved and intimate, and simultaneously inclusive and embracing rather than exclusive, possessive, and jealous. It takes into consideration all the needs and responsibilities of *all* the persons involved in or affected by a relationship. It removes the spotlight from genital intercourse and tends to integrate a whole range of bodily intimacies, touching, nudity, and sensuality along with intercourse into the total framework of daily living.

Human relations guided by a cool sex consciousness are synergistic, rather than entropic. Cool sex does not mean the end or lack of emotion, intense feeling, concern, or warmth. What it does mean is that relations are not taken in terms of possession, or competition. A married couple will look upon their relationship in terms of (it is to be hoped) a lifelong commitment. But these pair-bonds will be set as primary relationships within the realistic context of today's life with its increasing mobility, life expectancies approaching a hundred years, contraceptives, and the liberation of women as persons in all areas of life. In a tribal culture, the nuclear family and exclusive couple in time become secure in their primary relationship and come to accept an openness and flexibility unheard of and unthinkable in a hot sex culture. This openness would accept intimate relations on all levels, including the sexual genital, within the orbit of the primary relationship. This flexible multilateral pluralism would be far more functional than the rigid couple pattern of past generations, but it would involve necessary risks. Comarital or, as we call them, *satellite relations* are based on the premise that given the complexities of today's life, the varieties of educational backgrounds and personal expectations, we can no longer expect a spouse to totally and completely satisfy all one's needs. *The comarital or satellite relation becomes possible only when one is secure in his own self-identity and in one's pair-bond relation, when one does not consider his or her partner property that cannot be shared without being lost.* The satellite relation is not the explosive affair, but a constructive complementary relation open to married and single persons, husbands and wives alike, in a context where relations are synergistic, reinforcing, and strengthening, rather than entropic and competitive.

This expansion of human relations to integrate new modes and expressions of intimacy within the couple marriage seems to recapture a consciousness that appeared in the earliest Biblical tradition but was quickly lost. The Jewish people had no word for sex, or for sexual intercourse, until they borrowed these fragmenting terms from the "more civilized" urban thinkers of Persia, Greece, and Rome. The authentic Biblical tradition speaks of the engaging, pleasuring, person-integrating relationship between a man and woman not as "making love" or as sexual (genital) intercourse, but as *yahda*, "knowing." This is no Victorian euphemism. It is indicative rather of a holistic approach to human relations uncommon in western consciousness and probably traceable to the tribal origins of Israel.

Few modern writers have been able to capture this cool sex consciousness. Many of them cannot even deal with the present tensions of ordinary people. Witness for instance the inability of John Updike, in both *Couples* and *Rabbit Redux*, to deal with questions of extramarital intimacies and relationships in anything but the totally negative threatened hot sex framework (cf. Gordon Clanton, this volume).

Only in science fiction, or the utopian essay/novels of Robert Rimmer, does one see real success in depicting cool sex attitudes (cf. Rimmer, this volume). One outstanding example is Robert Heinlein's haunting science-fiction novel *Stranger in a Strange Land*. Heinlein uses satire, humor, and fantasy to tell the story of Valentine Michael Smith, son of the first humans to land on Mars, who was raised and educated by Martians after his parents die. Valentine returns to Earth with a later expedition, only to be shocked by the hot sex mentality of earthlings. The Martian pattern of male/female relations is communal and multisensual, with no sharp cultural distinction between male and female roles. What earthlings call sexual intercourse and reduce to a matter of mere genital coupling, Valentine sees as "groking" or "growing closer," a kind of demi-erotic relating and interpersonal knowing in the original Biblical sense.

A similar verbal awareness is evident in most tribal cultures even today where a simple unsophisticated form of cool sex consciousness prevails. Most tribal cultures, for instance, have no word for illegitimacy, because all children are young persons in their own right and not the property of a particular set of parents. Often too, because of the parity of men and women in tribal cultures, there is no word for adultery. Social taboos do limit sexual behavior for the good of the community, but not because the wife or daughter is the property of some male.

Cool sex, then, is egalitarian, single-standard, sensually-diffused, and oriented towards intimacy and open relations with persons.

Marriage—Serial Monogamy

The question now is how the conflict and tensions of hot/cool sex are affecting marital patterns in our obviously changing society.

Two factors deserve comment. Our divorce and remarriage rate alone would demolish the myth that traditional life-long sexually exclusive monogamy is *the* American way of marriage. If we are honest, we would have to admit that a more common American practice is serial monogamy, with a large segment of our population having two or more spouses in their lifetime. A second fact undercuts the sexually exclusive character of our traditional monogamy myth. Marriage experts today commonly estimate that 60 percent of the married men and over a third of America's married women engage in extramarital relations sometime during their married life. Morton Hunt, author of *The Affair* (Hunt, 1969:289), is more sanguine: "Within another generation, based on present trends, four of five husbands and two of three wives whose marriages last more than several years will have at least a few extramarital involvements." Apparently, then, traditional monogamy has already yielded to serial monogamy and some sort of non-exclusive couple marriage.

We can go further in response as we did in *Eve's New Rib* and offer evidence that we are a very pluralistic society in our marital patterns. An exciting variety of male/female relationships has been gaining more open acceptance, or at least toleration, in our culture: single parents, trial marriages and premarital cohabitation, gay unions, triangle and multilateral marriages, group marriages, mate-exchanges (swinging) and a variety of communal situations. Marriage and male/female relations in America today have at least twenty basic styles, even though serial monogamy and non-exclusive couple marriages are more acceptable and prevalent.

Serial monogamy is the least radical deviation from the traditional American marriage. It changes only one factor—the life-long character of marriage—and then the modification is more often in reluctant practice than in aspirations and expectations. Otherwise, serial monogamy is very traditional. In most cases it is strongly rooted in hot sex attitudes and expectations. This fact, we believe, is the reason why the life-long character is untenable, and why a series of spouses becomes essential.

The image of marriage, both traditional and in its serial monogamy form, portrays the ideal, typical, average married couple as an inseparable romantic pair, drifting on the bright cloud of eternal youth and passing on at some imperceptible point to blissful old age as grandparents of a devoted clan. So perfectly matched is this couple that *they can expect to satisfy totally and completely all the varied complex needs and desires of their spouse*. All the high definition stereotypes of the traditional myth are maintained.

Few husbands and wives today accept the fact early in their marriages that they cannot possibly meet all their spouse's needs. Furthermore, most women in the beginning of their marriages do not consider their own needs. Why should they, for that matter? The culture women grow up in is male-dominated and guided. In the traditional myth women are taught from childhood to love, honor, and obey. Most women are conditioned to enter marriage fully convinced that they will be happy "serving" their husbands—though we seldom express it that bluntly.

In the exclusivity of hot sex and traditional marriage, two adults are expected to avoid all intimate relations with members of the opposite sex, even at the cost of considerable denial and isolation, since such relations could prove dangerous to the mythic character of the traditional marriage. The couple then is forced to live a symbiotic existence, an inseparable pair, together as much as possible, sharing everything. In this exclusive relationship the *expectation* is that two unique and individual persons will continue to grow on completely parallel tracks for fifty, sixty, or more years. To achieve this goal, the wife can of course, and often does, submerge her personal development in that of her husband and children. Even when parallel growth is attempted on an equal basis, the end result is frustration and divorce *if* the expectation is that the husband and wife can and must find all their needs met by their spouse.

Woven through this question of exclusivity is another inflammable expectation. The traditional myth, expressed in books like *The Sensuous Couple* (Chartham, 1971), argues that the sexual relationship must always retain the passion and romance of the courtship and honeymoon period. In every other area of human behavior, we accept average performances. Lovemaking, to the contrary, must always be an earth-shaking orgasmic high—everytime! And when it is not, something is assumed to be wrong with the marriage. The instinct then is to look elsewhere. Result: an affair, guilt-ridden because it must inevitably mean the end of the existing marriage, divorce, and remarriage.

The nuclear problem in serial monogamy is that it remains based on the highly defined sex roles, status, expectations, and obligations of the hot sex mentality. It produces a common type of marriage: closed, inflexible, highly structured. Given our highly mobile society where cultures and subcultures are constantly mixing and influencing each other, the rigidity and high definition of the traditional marriage is impossible to maintain for long.

In the early years of a marriage, most women today are still willing to play the traditional roles. Wives find joy in bolstering their husband's ego, doting on them, scurrying about the kitchen and new home. In later years the role-playing wears thin and the wife begins to rebel. "I'm a human being too. What about my ego, my growth as a human being, my fulfillment as an individual?" The male response is typical: "She's a ballbreaker, a nag, castrating me every chance she gets." And then, "Who needs that kind of marriage?" Divorce occurs and for the male a search for a new spouse—a sweet, very feminine woman. But is she really basically different—sweet, feminine, and docile? Or is she just a novice and willing to play the assigned role for a while?

The romantic honeymoon may last a year or two, and then the appearance of a child or two gives new focus to the relationship and distracts the couple from their changing relationship. The explosive periods for closed marriages come in two peak periods: when the last child is off to school and the wife is left home alone and when the children leave home for college or marriage and suddenly the couple is left face-to-face with nothing to say to each other because their whole world has been their offspring.

In *Future Shock* (Toffler, 1970), Alvin Toffler maintains that serial polygamy with several mates will be the dominant pattern of marriage in coming generations. We agree, reluctantly, because the average divorce and remarriage *does not come to grips with the basic problems of human relations* and our needs for intimacy and fidelity in a mobile society. It is a frustrating impossible search for a mythic ideal, for the high definition stereotyped roles and expectations of the traditional American marriage, and the hot sex mentality can exist only in the unreality of a never-never land.

Open Marriage—Flexible Monogamy

Our definition of flexible monogamy very much coincides with the description of "open marriage" offered by anthropologists George and Nena O'Neill in their best seller *Open Marriage* (O'Neill and O'Neill, 1972). Our approaches were totally independent of each other, ours working from a biological/historical/technological starting point while the O'Neills worked from the areas of anthropology and sociology. Hence the correlation is most interesting.

In a composite description of open marriage we might begin by stating that an open marriage is an honest relationship between two people who accept each other as equals, friends, and partners. It is a non-manipulative, non-exploitive relationship with equal freedom and identity for both partners. There is no need for dominance and submission on either side, no arbitrary one-sided restrictions or stifling jealous possessiveness. Neither partner is locked into a stereotyped role provided from the outside by society, relatives, or the local community. Domestic chores are shared, as are other obligations in the marriage according to real convenience and talent rather than according to some predetermined role, rule, or 50/50 agreement. Each partner has interests and friends which the other may or may not share. An open marriage therefore allows and encourages the partners to enrich their primary pair-bond relationship with a variety of relationships that complement and reinforce the marriage.

Open marriages are custom-made and highly individual. There is no single unchanging archetype, as there is for the closed marriage. And furthermore, each unique open marriage is made more unique because it is constantly growing and evolving. No couple can say they have an open marriage, because if they believe that, in complacent satisfaction the status quo of their relationship at that moment will be extended into an unchanging pattern that is only a modified form of closed marriage. At best a couple can say they are working towards an open marriage (see O'Neills' *Open Marriage* for a discussion of guidelines to achieve this goal, pp. 67-77).

Obviously much more can and should be said of the contrast between open and closed marriage patterns, but what we have said here indicates two critical concerns. One is to develop the means of evolving more easily into the social consciousness everything indicates we are headed for, a tribal culture with a cool sex mentality. The other is the more philosophical/theological question of the new meaning of fidelity, intimacy, and commitment.

Moving From Hot to Cool

Few Americans living today will ever be able to shuck off completely the hot sex atmosphere in which we were born. Yet, hopefully, more and more Americans will be able to face the problems of human relations today and accept the challenges of self-identity, maturity, and growth that inevitably accompany the tribalization of our culture on a global scale. The question then becomes clear. How can we learn to shift into the new patterns of thought, how can we learn to accept and live the new patterns of relating, when our culture is predominantly in the opposite stream?

Logically, the answer is obvious: *create a transitional tribal environment to which men and women can retreat for short periods of time, where they can learn to relate in more human and intimate ways and gain self-identity.* Then they can hopefully return to our hot sex transitional society with a new perspective.

Currently there are a number of quite varied and differently motivated experiments in cool tribal sex which all seem to share one feature in common: in the vast majority of cases they are all blind groping experiments entered into by people who are often psychologically and emotionally unprepared for the demands of their new relations and unequipped in terms of guidelines from society or past experiments. This, fortunately, is changing as society comes to recognize and tolerate more openly alternate patterns of marriage. Communications networks are developing between different groups across the country.

Fidelity, Intimacy, and Commitment

Not far beneath the surface of diffused sensuality, open sexuality, and multilateral relationships of today is the very serious ethical and theological question posed by hot and cool sex concepts. What is the real nature of fidelity? What is the relation between marital fidelity and intimacy which is so linked with personal growth?

Is the type of fidelity and commitment treasured by a monogamous couple in our hot sex culture the same kind of fidelity and commitment shared by a primary pair bond couple with a tribal cool sex mentality?

Obviously, from what we have seen so far, the answer is a resounding negative. Fidelity, according to hot sex, is crystal clear. It is exclusive and outlaws any participation or intimacy outside the marital union. Fidelity, according to cool sex, is open, inclusive, and invites participation.

Nearly two thousand years before Christ, Abraham was called by Yahweh to leave his kinsfolk and his father's house with faith that the Lord would show him a new land. This was Yahweh's covenant, that Abraham would become father of a host of nations and dwell in a promised land. Years later, when the aged patriarch was commanded by Yahweh to sacrifice his only son, his only hope of future descendants, Abraham again responded with absolute fidelity to the covenant.

Fidelity in the Biblical tradition is a very complex concept. It can be first seen as a major attribute of God: faithfulness or 'emet (Exodus 34:6). Its two Hebraic roots can be traced to $\bar{a}man$ which suggests solidity and sureness and to $b\bar{a}tah$, suggesting security and confidence. Greek roots which were later incorporated into the Biblical tradition are less certain since the Greek religion allowed practically no place for faith as such. Even so, the related Greek concepts are helpful, bringing in aspects of hope, confidence, loyalty, belief, truth, and reliability.

The fidelity of Yahweh ('emet) is frequently linked with his paternal concern and goodness (hesed, or in the Septuagent eleos). Yahweh's commitment to his chosen people required in turn fidelity from man. Fidelity then involved the whole man, every aspect of his life. It is commitment, loving concern, unconditioned loyalty. It should permeate all aspects of a person's life, beginning with his commitment to the Supreme Being and flowing through the mutual relationships binding relatives (Genesis 47:29), friends (Samuel 20:8), and allies (Genesis 21:23).

How then did this broad humane concept of fidelity as "loving concern" become restricted to sexual exclusivity in the domain of marital fidelity? Cause and effect relations are difficult, if not impossible, to trace in the history of ideas and attitudes, but we feel that something can be said in favor of one specific Biblical influence. Central to the Jewish religion, and quite in contrast to most of their neighbors, was the belief in one supreme God and the rejection of all other gods. Very early in the old covenant, the patriarchs and prophets began using one common human experience as an example, an illustration of the relationship between Yahweh and his chosen people. To explain this divine covenant and especially the fidelity of Yahweh in spite of the infidelity of his chosen people, the patriarchs and prophets spoke often of the covenant between a husband and wife.

When the prophet Osee denounced the idolatrous Israelites of his day, he drew his imagery from his own personal experiences, his tragic marriage to the unfaithful Gomer. Despite all her perfidious affairs, Osee never failed to love Gomer and seek her return to the purity and tenderness of their early love. Marital infidelity then became a useful symbol and analogy of all forms of covenant infidelity, especially idolatry. Sometime later though this imagery was inverted, and the symbol became a reality in its own right wrapped in all the sinfulness of idolatry. Instead of concentrating on the fidelity and loving concern of Osee for the unfaithful Gomer as a good symbol of Yahweh's paternal concern for his unfaithful people, we somehow began to focus all our attention on the infidelity of the chosen people and use the proscriptions against their idolatry to condemn extramarital activity.

Marriage has always had an economic basis in society. Economics is usually tightly woven into the fabric of marriage. In many simple societies marriage has been primarily an economic arrangement between two families or tribes. Love between two young people was seldom its justifying motive. In this context marital fidelity could hardly be defined in terms of selfless commitment and loving concern for the human development and fulfillment of another person. The primacy of economics in the marriage contract focused attention on the legal contract concerned with property exchange, community responsibilities, and production of progeny to continue the family line or inherit certain estates. Marriage consequently became a legal exchange of goods, the mutual exchange of the right to another's body for those acts conducive to procreation. Sexual intercourse became "the marital debt." A spontaneous person-involving act became something a wife put up with to keep her husband from sowing his seed in some other incubator—paying the marital debt. Ultimately the strength and validity of the marriage contract became totally dependent on the delivery of goods. A marriage ceremony in church was not sufficient to create an indissoluble union. Bodies had to be delivered and exchanged at least once to consummate the contract.

Sexual relations outside marriage also took on this aspect of property obsession, especially for the moralist and lawyer. Sexual intercourse for an unmarried woman was an injustice to her father or guardian who was deprived of the proper bride-price due a virgin. The unfaithful wife likewise did an injustice to her husband by depriving him of the certainty that the child she bore was his legitimate blood heir with legal right to inherit his property. For the unfaithful man there was the injustice of putting his hands on another man's exclusive property. Marital fidelity then became, in the neat definition of the Reverend Robert Capon, "what I did not do in Dubuque."

When economic considerations were primary in the marriage relationship, premarital and extramarital relations were seen and often condemned on the economic base of injustice. But they did not pose an emotional threat to the marriage. The economics of injustice could be worked out to the mutual satisfaction of the aggrieved male party and the male trespassor. But this situation began to change radically around the late 1880's in western Europe and America. Like some menopausal offspring of the courtly love tradition, a new sentimental model for familial relationships was born. One prime component of this new image was the fantastic notion that one man and one woman should mate and henceforth be responsible for satisfying all of the other's significant *emotional* needs. Prior to this time the emotional relationship of husband and wife was not very important. It might develop, and often did. But whether or not it ever appeared in a marriage, the husband was under no social constraint to relate to his wife either as lover or as friend. Marriage in fact was often seen as the last place one would expect to find an emotional loving relationship. With the advent of the sentimental-romantic model for marriage, there arose a new definition of the proper relationship between husband and wife based on the necessity of an exclusive emotional union of two parties. From this time on the extramarital affair became a real threat to every ideal marriage. The economic injustices of premarital and extramarital relations can be eliminated with contraceptives and the disappearance of the family as a self-sustaining unit of society, but there remains the romantic-sentimental myth and model.

In Biblical times, with pestilence, war, famine, and a dreadful rate of infant and maternal deaths, the average human barely survived 22 years. By the Middle Ages the average European could look forward to a life expectancy of about 33 years. A century ago the average life span was inching up over the forty-year mark. In 1900 the average American had a life expectancy of 47 years. Today the average American woman can expect to live 74.6 years, and the average American male 67.1 years. These last two figures are, of course, below the life expectancy of middle- and upper-class Americans who have easy access to the benefits of modern medicine. Yet the United States ranks 24th among the nations of the world for average male life span and ninth for women. On the eastern shore of the Black Sea the peasants of Abkhasian and the Caucasian Mountains often live well beyond a hundred years.

These statistics are important because they highlight the fact that the life-long sexually exclusive monogamous marriage evolved over a period of some two or three thousand years when the average life expectancy slowly climbed from twenty to forty years. We should also recall the frequency with which women died in childbirth, a fact which allowed most men to bury two or three wives in their lifetime and consequently be bound to sexual exclusivity with one particular woman for only a few years before death and remarriage brought a new woman on the scene. A concept of fidelity which allowed a double standard with some freedom for the male and chattel status for the woman thus posed little psychological or emotional opposition to the reduction of marital fidelity to sexual exclusivity.

Until recently most married couples judged the success of their marriage in terms of two hot sex components: 1) how faithfully does the husband meet the stereotyped role of the good breadwinner and the wife her stereotyped role as mother/housekeeper? and 2) are they both, at least the wife, sexually faithful? True, these criteria are losing their popularity and essentialness somewhat, but they still remain for many—perhaps even for most—the criteria of a good marriage.

Along with this distorted idea of what constitutes marital fidelity has come a very disastrous consequence: the inhumane restriction and limitations we must place on all interpersonal relations in a hot sex society where all single people, especially the young single girl and the "sex-starved" divorcee and widow, are viewed only as a threat to all happily married couples.

Sadly, our society with its hot sex consciousness dogmatically assumes that any and all personal relations between men and women, married or unmarried, at any age beyond puberty, will inevitably end up in bed if they get any deeper than the most superficial level. This assumption makes all personal relations highly dangerous, forbidden fruit, to be shunned even at the cost of cramping and drastically reducing our potential for growth as human persons. We grow by relating and sharing with others. Yet we try to maintain, at all costs, a society in which we relate intimately only with our spouse, and then as some sort of desexed androgynous pair with other equally desexed individuals, single and married.

Recently on a New York television interview with two charming women, one in her mid-twenties and single, the other probably in her fifties and happily married, the older woman frankly admitted that whenever any female acquaintance indicated anything more than a superficial interest in her husband, they simply never see that person again. Jokingly, the younger woman asked if she kept some poison in her cupboard for emergencies. The implication is clear: our concepts of fidelity and intimacy are horribly distorted on all levels.

In today's emerging tribal culture, conferred adulthood and sexual identity no longer works as usual. Initiation comes by experimentation, by learning, and by knowing personally. Youth must explore a variety of experiences and then choose their own adult and sexual identity. The American adolescent takes a vacation from life after puberty, withdrawing from the main stream into high school and college, where he or she can explore and experience, seeking to be faithful to himself.

Faithfulness, as Erik Erikson suggests, is essential to one's growth as an autonomous, independent, mature person. One must gain the strength to remain faithful to oneself, a power to define oneself from within and to remain constant to that self-definition whatever outside pressures one encounters, whether from the entrenched older adult establishment or from the tyrannical conformism of the peer group. One of the most devastating forms of the latter appears on college campuses when virginity for anyone over 18 is ridiculed as puritan frigidity or an unnatural hang-up.

One of the crucial factors in developing the virtue of fidelity is a growing competence and ability to integrate the personal and the sexual aspects of one's life. The whole practice of courting and "making out" can be very useful and function in this process. The American pattern of courtship helps young people develop their own sexual identity, their own sense of fidelity, by encouraging them to engage in limited, though progressively more intimate and involving relationships. In this process, the adolescent can explore the meaning of fidelity. He may learn the meaning of mutual responsibility and sharing in a growth-oriented relationship. He often learns what it means to be committed and to commit oneself. Group dating, couple dating, going steady, "pinning"—even the American engagement, which is more flexible and tentative than the European engagement—encourage an exploration of the meaning of fidelity by allowing the young person to work his way through a variety of intimate relationships and commitments, pacing himself and learning by mistakes as well as good experiences.

In a very real sense then, the Biblical concept of sexual intercourse as *yahda*, knowing, today embraces the whole range of interpersonal relationships between sexual persons. Dating, courtship, making out, sexual intercourse, all are forms of knowing which require fidelity and demand a progressively more responsible sense of intimacy and mutual responsibility for each other's continued growth as sexual persons. Loving concern (*hesed*), a solid self-identity (*'emet*), and a confidence in one's ability to handle new levels of intimacy and commitment when the right time comes (*bātah*) are the three essential characteristics of a modern concept of fidelity in the Biblical tradition. Obviously, this concept of fidelity has much to say about the possibility of an intimate, even sexual relationship complementing and reinforcing the primary bond relationship of a married couple: the possibility of a comarital or satellite relationship. It also has much to say about the "premarital" sexual experiences of young people. But its focus is on the *quality and intent* of the relationship, not on whether or not it goes beyond a certain black and white line, be this making out, French kissing, mutual orgasm by masturbation, or genital penetration.

Both fidelity and intimacy have *new meanings* in today's emerging tribal culture. This new meaning exists between a husband and wife, among married couples, between married and single persons, and among single persons, young and old.

Myths

A final closing word must be said about the mythic reality of both hot and cool sex. Both indeed exist, but both also do not exist. The hot sex traditional romantic marriage was an ideal, a myth which guided generations in their married lives. Equally so, now that we are rejecting and destroying this hot sex myth, we feel compelled to create a new myth, a new pattern, which we have called cool or tribal sex. But the cool sex consciousness we describe here is an unreal composite drawn from certain real elements in various tribal cultures of the past and present, the Marquesan Islanders, Samoans, Hindus, North American Indians, and others. Marshall McLuhan suggested once that we ride into the future looking into a rear view mirror—history. Just at the time modern technology and civilization are turning primitive cultures into fossils, modern man seems compelled to romanticize their sexual attitudes and consciousness, weaving them into a new mythic pattern for the future. It can present a new danger if we merely substitute for what we have had, the glorification of a non-existent synthesis of cool sex distilled from a variety of tribal cultures, and turn this into a mythic symbol of new patterns of relating in and around the husband/wife/family constellation.

REFERENCES

Chartham, Robert. *The Sensuous Couple*. New York: Ballantine Books, 1971.

Francoeur, Robert T. *Eve's New Rib*. New York: Harcourt, Brace, Jovanovich, 1972.

Hunt, Morton. *The Affair*. New York: World Publishing Co., 1969.

Leonard, George B. *The Man and Woman Thing*. New York: Dell, 1970. "The Future of Sex," with Marshall McLuhan, pp. 141-156.

McLuhan, Marshall. *Understanding Media: The Extensions of Man*. New York: McGraw-Hill Co., 1965.

O'Neill, Nena and George O'Neill. *Open Marriage*. New York: M. Evans, Inc., 1972.

Toffler, Alvin. *Future Shock*. New York: Random House, 1970.

2

THE MONOGAMOUS IDEAL AND SEXUAL REALITIES
Robert N. Whitehurst

Some of the ordinary assumptions which accompany our North American views of sexuality are examined in terms of the maintenance of monogamy. The Bible, pornography, youth sexuality, sex education, sexual deviancy, marriage, and monogamy are discussed from a structuralist-change view. The author's conclusions suggest that monogamy, though not dying, does not—indeed, cannot—work as an ideal in this culture. An examination of the sociological and anthropological conditions under which effective social controls create the most favorable climate for monogamy's persistence would demonstrate that North American society today has few of the qualities that would cause monogamy to flourish. We are no longer a simple, stable society governed by extended family, kin, the church, or a tightly knit community. Whitehurst suggests that it would be rational therefore to recognize some of the variant life-styles now around us in underground form and to test their validity more openly. The plea is for consideration of the alternatives allowed in a real democratic and pluralistic society.

The relationship between sex acts and marriage is in the process of changing, probably very rapidly. However, some old assumptions which do not reflect much of the reality of many people whose sex lives are not consonant with a monogamous ideal still persist. The model for understanding today's interactions is, unfortunately, an idealization and nostalgic embellishment of a past that may never even have resembled the ideal. As a step toward fuller comprehension of sex in our culture, this chapter will take up some of the commonly held assumptions that purport to help us understand sexuality and then discuss some of the reasons why monogamy cannot be a completely successful ideal today.

Assumptions about Sexuality

1. The Bible Is Against Sex

Probably the most pervasive underlying guide or model for ideas about sexuality held by both Jews and Christians—and even atheists—in North America today is the Bible. The assumptions made about Biblical edicts on the subject of sex could do with much closer scrutiny than they are usually given.

First, the Bible is not entirely either anti-sexual or pro-sexual in any of the usual meanings of these positions. If anything, it is actually both and, depending on exigetic sources used, it can be held to be either. What are generally stressed in Christian North America though, are those teachings of the Bible that are *definitely anti-sexual* in tone.[1]

There is an additional difficulty with using the Bible as the chief guide to sexual morality—aside from the fact that it can be read to support conflicting points of view with a little bit of something for everyone. A decreasing number of people see the Bible as anything more than an interesting historical document, as a literature of a romantic nomadic tribe, or at best as a general guide to behavior and ethics that are not specifically relevant to life today. Fundamentalism, perhaps like colonialism, is probably in for hard times due to lack of adherents (it remains to be seen whether certain youthful revival-type activities are more than passing fancies and fad-like behavior of the young.)[2]

2. Pornography Is Bad

In the first place, "bad" is a value judgment and therefore not measurable in objective terms. If we equate "bad" with "damaging," we can at least examine the evidence against pornography—and here the case is just not proven. The assumption is made by many that certain literature, films, and pictorializations of sex are bad and evil and will contaminate (but to what end?) the minds of youth and others; there is also a related assumption that avoidance of pornographic material somehow helps one achieve purity. This is at best a highly doubtful assumption and has been well discussed elsewhere.[3] The Scandinavian experience casts doubt on the evils of "pornography" and the data we have on the sales of such material in North America casts doubt on the serious interests of youth in this market. Anyway, if purity of mind implies refraining from thinking about sex, it is doubtful whether many of us could be called "pure of mind"—or would want to be. Prurient interests are not the sole focus of any group, any religion, or any age. Rather, all have buried inside them some of the best and some of the worst—and pornography is at best only a weak indicator of the real meaning of lives of most people and often an extremely unimportant part of it all.

3. Youth Sexuality Is Rampant

Older people, forgetting much of their pasts and remembering their sexual presents (or in many cases, their fantasy life of the present) project their own hangups and problems onto youth and assume that all youth are sexual athletes. Much of the difficulty experienced that arises between youth and parents involves subtle sexual overtones, unresolved parental difficulties, and problems of relationships that become defined as youth-sex problems. One youth, who put it aptly, claimed "Parents have dirty minds." That much distorted perception of youth sexuality occurs can be verified by casual observation of parent-youth interactions in which youth are often unfairly accused of being and doing things sexual when such things play a much smaller role than parents seem to think. This is an area much in need of good research. Unfortunately, it is an area that is likely to remain essentially untouched because of its sensitivity and difficulty in conducting such research.

4. Sex Education Is Mostly Unnecessary

Related to the above assumption is the idea that youth will act out experimentally what they learn about in the classroom. There is no way that current sex education practice can be defended as adequate or good, but this does not mean it is unimportant. Of course, in a sexually repressive society, *no* sex education would be more consistent with society's images than the vapid kind to which most youth are currently exposed.[4] Unless we become used to the idea that children are sometimes sexual, but not obsessed like adults, we cannot do anything like an adequate job of sex training or education. Only in terms of the plumbing aspects of sex can we do much—the real problem lies in learning interpersonal competence and a sense of operable values—things which we seem unable or unwilling to deal with realistically.[5] A corollary involves the notion that it is better to give (or have) "little or no information" about sex until the individual nears adulthood. This highly questionable assumption is unique in that we do not hold other spheres of learning in the same light. Society seems to presume ignorance to be the preferred state in this one area until suddenly 'maturity' makes people able to handle sexual problems—indeed a dubious bit of logic.

5. Deviants Are Sick

Persons who are non-monogamous, homosexual, or otherwise violate the code of this ethically fractured culture are often held to be sick and in need of psychiatric or other medical treatment. This concept may indeed be some kind of step forward in western man's way of explaining the source of illness and deviation, but it is probably not correct in many cases; obviously, such an attitude is not productive of life styles viable in today's world. We feel ourselves enlightened if we no longer feel that a person is inhabited by devils or evil spirits as our ancestors once did. We little realize that we are being just as mystical, although we now have a new set of vested interests—psychiatry instead of the church. We have substituted neuroses for demons and now have psychiatrists, but we still have a way to go to fully understand human behavior. Sociologists often note that it is as important to study the society that produces and labels the deviant as it is to study the deviant himself. To conclude that all who vary from the monogamous ideal are sick may be a useful approach for a society pursuing social solidarity of its citizens, but it is inconsistent in a presumably free and open democratic pluralist society, since it fails to validate the experience of a large minority. Such a judgment may not only be harmful, but it is misleading and only a sometime truth.

6. Good Marriage Means Good Sex

As an outgrowth of the 'love conquers all' philosophy, we are culturally led to believe that sex is best in a monogamous marriage where "true love" exists. Although this may often be true, it may be just as often be untrue. An analysis of the roles of 'husband' (or wife) and 'lover' in an extramarital affair might be revealing and cause some to find a real variance with stereotypes in terms of their own experience.[6]

Dr. Myers describes the variance that can occur in the relationship between good and bad marriage and good and bad sex.[7] It is obvious that the folklore supports the notion that only in marriage can a satisfying sex life be obtained. Anything that tends to lend support for another ethic would be downplayed or ignored by those whose vested interests are protected by the maintenance of conventional monogamous forms. If we knew the actual occurence of the correlations between good sex and good marriage, we might find that in actuality there is no relationship. It is obviously possible to have perfectly horrid sex either in or out of marriage, just as it is as likely that perfectly good sex can occur in either case. Our definitions of the situation being what they are in general, it is probable that some good sex occurs outside of marriage that is marred by self-definitions (culturally derived) that make it 'bad.'[8]

7. Monogamy Is Best and Is the Highest Form of Marriage

This assumption involves cultural absolutism, now more frequently held to be a naive and unpopular form of thinking about ourselves as North Americans become better educated. We now understand that there are few absolutes in the world and to assume that monogamy has been somehow sanctified by a higher power as a desired end state of man may yet require a more full examination. This notion involves ideology and not science. As fewer people yield to dogma and more begin to take on other (and broader) perspectives, the monogamy assumption—at least as an absolute for everyone—is under heavy attack. Monogamy is no doubt "best" for most people today because of the current sanctions and cultural restrictions on our knowledge. Other forms may be proved just as viable—or more so—in the future. Only openness and freedom to construct other forms will provide the context for the acquisition of this knowledge.

8. Monogamy Works

Of all the assumptions discussed above, none is more likely to be held by so many people and less likely to be true in its usually construed sense. The data on marriage, extramarital sex, and male-female relations in general in this culture tend to support the notion that we pay lip-service to the monogamous ideal but in fact do maintain a significant variety of other forms of sex life. The spate of books of recent times on the topic probably reflects market conditions; it also is a reflection of a vast disquiet in marriage as it operates today.[9] As for the reasons why monogamy does not work, we must understand some of the sociological reasons why it is naive to expect monogamy to be a fully workable solution to the problem with marriage today. The following discussion suggests that there are few facilitating factors present in our culture that would make monogamy a viable life-plan for everyone. In fact, given present trends as noted below, we might expect that monogamy will become less often the preferred mode of adaptation, at least as a life-time option for many people.

The Trouble With Monogamy

The chart that follows should help to clarify the problematic status of monogamy today. After presentation, the trends will be discussed separately.

Few people of any ideological persuasion would dispute the idea of monogamy as a beautiful mythical notion. Pragmatists, however, who insist on knowing what works and does not work are going to be less enchanted by the ideal when we attempt to make it work as we have been doing. As an idea, monogamy is beautiful to behold in its pristine philosophical purity; it is a little difficult to put the ideal into practice. In terms of the variables discussed above, the weaknesses of monogamy essentially stem from structural problems in society, and not the neurotic immaturity of its citizens. Most people respond to structures pretty much (but not entirely) as given. If there are loopholes and snags and new possibilities in the system, they will be maximized by those who feel the opportunity is there.

When community solidarity breaks down and the eyes of the townspeople no longer count as controllers of behaviour, marriage as a monolithic institution is also likely to change (since monogamy—like

Inhibiting Factors Affecting the Persistence of Monogamy as a Dominant Form

Variable:	Effect on Monogamy:
1. Weakened social control agencies	Family, community, religion now altered or ineffective as social control groupings. Sanctioning power weak.
2. Urban life-styles, anonymity, freedom variety, alternatives	Leads to experimentation, search for meaning, sense of being detached and alienated.
3. Ethic of sexual abstinence before marriage	Leads to overexaggeration of the role of sex in life, tends to force people to question vitality of their own sex lives, may further lead to dissatisfaction and experimentation.
4. Selling by sex	Makes people susceptible to media influence, associate sex with consumerism, develops obsessive concerns over sex.
5. Open opportunity for practice of variations	Broadens experimentation base, allows relatively free practice of alternate forms.
6. Affluence	Creates increased leisure, search for newness, kicks, by contrast with meaningless work leads to other experiments.
7. Equality ethic	Frees women to a new style relation with men, creating enhanced probability of new social forms.
8. Social crises	Leads to an ethic of wanting experience now, little sense of future reward, impulse gratification pattern expands.
9. Youth revolt	Leads to increased sense of irreverence toward elders and their institutions, including marriage.
10. Alienation	Leads to attempts to recapture in a repristinized setting a sense of community, fellowship with others on a broader base than the old monogamous model as norms suggest that isolation is the problem and monogamy is not the answer.
11. Rampant immorality of corporations, governments, etc.	Makes for sense of 'relative sinlessness' of those who seek alternatives to marriage and EMS.
12. Increasing premarital sex and non-marital living.	Creates legitimacy for breaking societal norms, makes for broadened sexual contacts before marriage, creates strains in narrowing sexual access after marriage—result may be dissatisfaction and seeking more sex contacts outside of marriage.

most social conventions—is held together by artifice of external controls and internal restraints). The family as an extended group as well as the nuclear family no longer has as much power or influence on behavior as it once had. It obviously relinquishes control over the individual to other agencies earlier and more completely than once was the case.

Urban anonymity provides ample experimental ground in a setting of great variety, enhanced by leisure of affluence and open opportunity for many people. Sexual salesmanship also promotes alternatives by creating dissatisfaction with self and spouse. When coupled with other factors, such as our repressive premarital abstinence ethic and the decrease in deferred gratifications, we should not expect the end result to be strong loyalty to the institution of marriage as now structured.[10] Rampant immorality of big corporations and big governments that lie and cheat to achieve goals and who bribe, deceive, and engage in a whole host of questionable enterprises cannot be thought of as a positive model for other institutions, namely the institution of marriage. There is probably much spillover of moral relativism from the outside world into personal life.[11] Carried into marriage styles, the presumed sins of extramarital sex seem truly insignificant beside some of those exposed daily in the world of the press and television. If this suggested listing is seen at all as reflecting the realities of our world, one might well ask the question 'why are so many still behaving monogamously' in the light of the levels of opportunity to do otherwise and in view of the problematic social situation in which we now live? If we knew the real answer to the question, it may be that true monogamy is simply one more myth that we continue to accept unquestioningly and that the reality is at extreme variance with the myth.

The Persistence of the Monogamous Ideal

If our previous assessment of the assumptions and the problems in contemporary monogamy are somewhere near correct, we must conclude that there is a tremendous disparity between what North Americans profess to believe and the realities they practice. Further, they must continually labor under some strain if our listing of inhibiting factors reveals anything about current social structures. There are several possibilities, all of which might be held as open hypotheses until better evidence is in: it is possible that life as we once knew it is really flying apart and that the current state of marriage is just one more indicator of our inability to get it all together. It is possible that we are so steeped in ignorance that we cannot see the forest for the trees, and that no matter what happens we will protect ourselves with myths which will persist and alter only imperceptibly with time. We may become a complex schizoid culture which can hold so many contradictions and irreconcilable opposites that we cannot comprehend or describe. The most preferable possibility is that we are becoming a true pluralistic democracy in which people can live out a variety of life styles that suit them. The dim outlines of such a happy possibility are scarcely discernible. In any event, it is fairly clear that we are faced with some kind of transitional period in which our assumptions do not match very well with the social facts about sex and marriage.

Monogamy persists in part because we have no other strongly held norms that can take its place, and it is so security-inducing (like a pill that doesn't cure the disease, but only lessens the pain) that we do not know how to get along without it. If we ever raise a generation of youth secure in themselves and detached from institutions that provide the forms of security with which we are familiar, monogamy might be replaced with another dominant form or set of forms of marriage. That time is not yet with us. In the meantime, we can look forward to even greater disruption in marriage (if our guess about monogamy proves to be correct) since the old sources of stability are not likely to return. Alternate forms will likely, at least for some time to come, reflect our old sexual norms and hangups, making it difficult to arrive at viable alternatives. If we remain as adroitly schizoid as our past tendencies would suggest we might, we may well be able to accommodate everyone into the system and learn to live in ignorance, with pluralism, or some varieties of both.

With such a myriad of expectations, emerging norms, potential modes of expression in life styles and variety of options open to youth today, there is little doubt that the future will be interesting, though confusing. Monogamy, if our analysis is correct, does not work if we use the cultural definition of the term. The fact is that it keeps on going, refuses to die (at least as an idea and an ideal) and is not likely to be replaced in the foreseeable future by anything nearly as popular. Monogamy does not work except in a minimally pragmatic sense but it does not die—in a sense we have come full circle in our discussion. We can now begin to choose our life-styles and the luxury of choice is pretty new in a world that until recently offered no such options, except for the idle rich and the privileged minorities. The downward diffusion of opportunity to vary life styles is probably one salient fact of social change in the 20th century.

Whether sex occurs in or out of marriage may be less important to the coming generation who appear less concerned with legal status than they are for moral rationales in terms of what's happening in their lives. All kinds of orientations can be brought to both marriage and non-marriage relationships.[12] Our traditional and narrow concern for sex occurring only in monogamy is being transcended by new norms and new people. The task is to make newer orientations productive of human growth, and—as the past has shown—this probably does not in the final analysis depend on a formal status. Whether we will be unable to more closely approximate this ideal as monogamy changes and our concepts broaden is an unanswered question.

Conclusion

Given the structural interpretation as described previously, it is possible to have an operable monogamous ideal in a culture in which people only experience sex with the married partner under certain rigid conditions. These conditions involve fairly stable folk-type societies, held together by religious norms and sanctions, supported by the extended family and community.[13] Murdock notes that the four functions fundamental to human social life and always fulfilled by the family in every culture are: sexual, economic, reproductive, and educational. The case can be made that in North American society, each of these is either being altered or phased out in some sense as exclusive territory for the family organization to perform. If there is any validity at all to the present volume, the area of sexual functioning in the family has been already well intruded upon, the economic function—as productive—has long since changed, and with increased female employment opportunities, a serious question about the economic functions (and interdependence) of males and females is an open issue. Much the same tenor comment can be made about families as educational functionaries. This leaves the problem of reproduction as probably the last stronghold of family effort. Given the current high illegitimacy rates, adoptive procedures opening up, ZPG concerns, and potential ability to produce children sans parents (at least without fathers), it is possible that even *this* function will be superceded.

These folk cultures also quite regularly have ritual occasions on which the norms concerning adultery are held in abeyance for a period; these folk-festivals where norms are set aside are ordinarily held to act as safety valve mechanisms to keep people monogamous at other times. These folk cultures do not sell with sex—indeed they tend not to become obsessed at all by the subject since it assumes a much more natural and normal place in their daily lives. Youth are often not restrained in premarital sexuality, and are certainly not asked to extend the period of sexual abstinence into adulthood. All these factors are different in our mass, urbanized society. We can still hold our monogamous ideal, but to make it work requires the supportive help of a number of other institutions and organizations; this we do not have. To expect most people in our society to act monogamously is to fly in the face of the structural realities and opportunities to respond otherwise. In a loose-knit culture in which the family recedes in importance, it is logical to expect higher alienation rates and more departure from conventional norms governing the sexual behavior of adults. It is possible, of course, to hold on to a definition that things remain the same, that is that monogamy really still prevails. The social functions of myth-maintenance are well known in simple societies, but in complex ones like ours, more sophisticated people are beginning to insist on applying their own critical evaluations of our folk norms, including monogamy. Although sociological awareness does not make for instant freedom, it is a step toward open dialogue and future change—perhaps even to a more integrative and fulfilling mode for less limited futures.

NOTES

1 Robert N. Whitehurst, "American Sexophobia," in *The New Sexual Revolution*, ed. by Lester A. Kirkendall and Robert N. Whitehurst. New York: Donald W. Brown Co., 1971, pp. 1-16.

2. Recent resurgence of the Jesus-types may be as much a reflection of the movement's willingness to co-opt the essence of the rock concert, and to develop a more respectable "Woodstock" experience for youth as it is an indicator of real commitment to Christianity. This is not to gainsay a continued interest in religion on the part of these individuals, but the question remains whether the original impetus was a felt need for more religion or the possibility of extending and legitimizing other youth culture activities.
3. Edward Sagarin, "On Obscenity and Pornography," in Kirkendall and Whitehurst, pp. 105-114.
4. Jessie Potter, "Sex Education: An Expert Speaks Out," *American Baby Magazine*, April, 1968.
5. These values might involve valuing oneself as a sexual person, feeling good that bodies provide pleasure, including the value of touching others as a sensual and sexual experience that is normal, fulfilling, and good. Lester A. Kirkendall and Roger W. Libby, "Interpersonal Relationships—Crux of the Sexual Renaissance," *Journal of Social Issues*, April, 1966, pp. 45-62.
6. See Ch. XV, for a discussion of these roles and their content.
7. See discussion in this volume by Lonny Myers, Chapter 22.
8. This would be a parallel experience to Jessie Bernard's observation about comparative happiness of single and married women. Also, see Jessie Bernard, "Marriage, His and Hers," Ms. magazine, pp. 46-47.
9. Among some suggested authors would be: Bernard, 1972; Francoeur, 1972; O'Neill, 1972; Hunt, 1969; Neubeck, 1969; Gordon, 1972; Otto, 1971; Skolnick, 1971; and Fullerton, 1972.
10. Widespread violation of premarital sex norms in no way can be seen as conducive to fulfillment of the rigid expectation that one will remain monogamous after marriage.
11. This is only an interesting hypothesis, since no data seem to be available to relate the spillover effect of moral relativism. If it does affect extramarital sexuality, it would no doubt be easier to make the case that sexual deviance can be positive—the pursuit of wars, shady business practices, and other deviancy of this sort more usually cannot be seen in a positive light except by strange twists of logic.
12. Robert N. Whitehurst. "Sex: In and Out of Marriage," *The Humanist*, Jan./Feb. 1970, pp. 27-28.
13. Geo. P. Murdock. *Social Structure*. New York: Macmillan, 1949, p. 10.

3

MONOGAMY: A CRITIQUE
John McMurtry

McMurtry reviews the principles underlying our monogamic-style marriages, evaluating some of the assumptions that go along with the belief that monogamy is natural and superior to other forms of long-term intimate sexual relationships. He pursues the logical problems inherent in the arguments and adds a listing of further inhibiting and destructive outcomes related to the strict practice of monogamy.

The folk myths would have it that monogamy is the most fulfilling and beautiful life pursuit. McMurtry's analysis sums up by suggesting that it has been more important as a stabilizer of the social system than as a provider of benefits for those entrapped in the institution. Finally, the reader is cautioned that old forms hang on tenaciously, and though we may now have more rational bases for the evaluation of monogamy, rational social change in this area is not likely to occur either easily or soon.

"Remove away that black'ning church
Remove away that marriage hearse
Remove away that man of blood
You'll quite remove the ancient curse."

WILLIAM BLAKE

I

Almost all of us have entered or will one day enter a specifically standardized form of monogamous marriage. This cultural requirement is so very basic to our existence that we accept it for most part as a kind of intractable given: dictated by the laws of God, Nature, Government and Good Sense all at once. Though it is perhaps unusual for a social practice to be so promiscuously underwritten, we generally find comfort rather than curiosity in this fact and seldom wonder how something could be divinely inspired, biologically determined, coerced and reasoned out all at the same time. We simply take for granted.

Those in society who are officially charged with the thinking function with regard to such matters are no less responsible for this uncritical acceptance than the man on the street. The psychoanalyst traditionally regards our form of marriage as a necessary restraint on the anarchic id and no more to be queried than civilization itself. The lawyer is as undisposed to questioning the practice as he is to criticizing the principle of private property (this is appropriate, as I shall later point out). The churchman formally perceives the relationship between man and wife to be as inviolable and insusceptible to question as the relationship between the institution he works for and the Christ. The sociologist standardly accepts the formalized bonding of heterosexual pairs as the indispensable basis of social order and perhaps a societal universal. The politician is as incapable of challenging it as he is the virtue of his own continued holding of office. And the philosopher (at least the English-speaking philosopher), as with most issues of socially controversial or sexual dimensions, ignores the question almost altogether.

Even those irreverent adulterers and unmarried couples who would seem to be challenging the institution in the most basic possible way, in practice, tend merely to mimic its basic structure in unofficial form. The coverings of sanctity, taboo and cultural habit continue to hold them with the grip of public clothes.

II

"Monogamy" means, literally, "one marriage." But it would be wrong to suppose that this phrase tells us much about our particular species of official wedlock. The greatest obstacle to the adequate understanding of our monogamy institution has been the failure to identify clearly and systematically the full complex of principles it involves. There are four such principles, each carrying enormous restrictive force and together constituting a massive social control mechanism that has never, so far as I know, been fully schematized.

To come straight to the point, the four principles in question are as follows:

1. *The partners are required to enter a formal contractual relation:* (a) whose establishment demands a specific official participant, certain conditions of the contractors (legal age, no blood ties, etc.) and a standard set of procedures; (b) whose governing terms are uniform for all and exactly prescribed by law; and (c) whose dissolution may only be legally effected by the decision of state representatives.

The ways in which this elaborate principle of contractual requirement are importantly restrictive are obvious. One may not enter into a marriage union without entering into a contract presided over by a state-investured official.[1] One may not set any of the terms of the contractual relationship by which one is bound for life. And one cannot dissolve the contract without legal action and costs, court proceedings and in many places actual legislation. (The one and only contract in all English-speaking law that is not dissoluble by the consent of the contracting parties.) The extent of control here—over the most intimate and putatively "loving" relationships in all social intercourse—is so great as to be difficult to catalogue without exciting in oneself a sense of disbelief.

Lest it be thought there is always the real option of entering a common law relationship free of such encumbrances, it should be noted that: (a) these relationships themselves are subject to state regulation, though of a less imposing sort; and (much more important) (b) there are very formidable selective pressures against common law partnerships such as employment and job discrimination, exclusion from housing and lodging facilities, special legal disablements,[2] loss of social and moral status (consider such phrases as "living in sin," "make her an honest woman," etc.), family shame and embarrassment, and so on.

2. *The number of partners involved in the marriage must be two and only two* (as opposed to three, four, five or any of the almost countless other possibilities of intimate union).

This second principle of our specific form of monogamy (the concept of "one marriage," it should be pointed out, is consistent with any number of participating partners) is perhaps the most important and restrictive of the four principles we are considering. Not only does it confine us to just *one* possibility out of an enormous range, but it confines us to that single possibility which involves the *least* number of people, two. It is difficult to conceive of a more thoroughgoing mechanism for limiting extended social union and intimacy. The fact that this monolithic restriction seems so "natural" to us (if it were truly "natural" of course, there would be no need for its rigorous cultural prescription by everything from severe criminal law[3] to ubiquitous housing regulations) simply indicates the extent to which its hold is implanted in our social structure. It is the institutional basis of what I will call the "binary frame of sexual consciousness," a frame through which all our heterosexual relationships are typically viewed ("two's company, three's a crowd") and in light of which all larger circles of intimacy seem almost inconceivable.[4]

3. *No person may participate in more than one marriage at a time or during a lifetime* (unless the previous marriage has been officially dissolved by, normally, one partner's death or successful divorce).

Violation of this principle is, of course, a criminal offence (bigamy) which is punishable by a considerable term in prison. Of various general regulations of our marriage institution it has experienced the most significant modification: not indeed in principle, but in the extent of flexibility of its "escape hatch" of divorce. The ease with which this escape hatch is opened has increased considerably in the past few years (the grounds for divorce being more permissive than previously) and it is in this regard most of all that the principles of our marriage institution have undergone formal alteration. That is, in plumbing rather than substance.

4. *No married person may engage in any sexual relationship with any person whatever other than the marriage partner.*

Although a consummated sexual act with another person alone constitutes an act of adultery, lesser forms of sexual and erotic relationships[5] may also constitute grounds for divorce (i.e., cruelty) and are generally prescribed as well by informal social convention and taboo. In other words, the fourth and final principle of our marriage institution involves not only a prohibition of sexual intercourse per se outside one's wedlock (this term deserves pause) but a prohibition of all one's erotic relations whatever outside this bond. The penalties for violation here are as various as they are severe, ranging from permanent loss of spouse, children, chattel, and income to job dismissal and social ostracism. In this way, possibly the most compelling natural force towards expanded intimate relations with others[6] is strictly confined within the narrowest possible circle for (barring delinquency) the whole of adult life. The sheer weight and totality of this restriction is surely one of the great wonders of all historical institutional control.

III

With all established institutions, apologetics for perpetuation are never wanting. Thus it is with our form of monogamous marriage.

Perhaps the most celebrated justification over the years has proceeded from a belief in a Supreme Deity who secretly utters sexual and other commands to privileged human representatives. Almost as well known a line of defence has issued from a conviction, similarly confident, that the need for some social regulation of sexuality demonstrates the need for our specific type of two-person wedlock. Although these have been important justifications in the sense of being very widely supported, they are not—having other grounds than reasons—susceptible to treatment here.

If we put aside such arguments, we are left I think with two major claims. The first is that our form of monogamous marriage promotes a profound affection between the partners which is not only of great worth in itself but invaluable as a sanctuary from the pressures of outside society. Since, however, there are no secure grounds whatever for supposing that such "profound affection" is not at least as easily achievable by any number of *other* marriage forms (i.e., forms which differ in one or more of the four principles), this justification conspicuously fails to perform the task required of it.

52—The State of Sex and Monogamy

The second major claim for the defence is that monogamy provides a specially loving context for child upbringing. However here again there are no grounds at all for concluding that it does so as, or any more, effectively than other possible forms of marriage (the only alternative type of upbringing to which it has apparently been shown to be superior is nonfamily institutional upbringing, which of course is not relevant to the present discussion). Furthermore, the fact that at least half the span of a normal monogamous marriage *involves no child-upbringing at all* is disastrously overlooked here, as is the reinforcing fact that there is no reference to or mention of the quality of child-upbringing in any of the prescriptions connected with it.

In brief, the second major justification of our particular type of wedlock scents somewhat too strongly of red herring to pursue further.

There is, it seems, little to recommend the view that monogamy specially promotes "profound affection" between the partners or a "loving context" for child-upbringing. Such claims are simply without force. On the other hand, there are several aspects to the logic and operation of the four principles of this institution which suggest that it actually *inhibits* the achievement of these desiderata. Far from uniquely abetting the latter, it militates against them. In these ways:

(1) Centralized official control of marriage (which the Church gradually achieved through the mechanism of Canon Law after the Fall of the Roman Empire[7] in one of the greatest seizures of social power in history) necessarily alienates the partners from full responsibility for and freedom in their relationship. "Profound closeness" between the partners—or least an area of it—is thereby expropriated rather than promoted, and "sanctuary" from the pressures of outside society prohibited rather than fostered.

(2) Limitation of the marriage bond to two people necessarily restricts, in perhaps the most unilateral possible way consistent with offspring survival, the number of adult sources of affection, interest, material support and instruction for the young. The "loving context for child-upbringing" is thereby dessicated rather than nourished: providing the structural conditions for such notorious and far-reaching problems as (*a*) sibling rivalry for scarce adult attention,[8] and (*b*) parental oppression through exclusive monopoly of the child's means of life.[9]

(3) Formal exclusion of all others from erotic contact with the marriage partner systematically promotes conjugal insecurity, jealousy and alienation by:

(*a*) Officially underwriting a literally totalitarian expectation of sexual confinement on the part of one's husband or wife: which expectation is, *ceteris paribus*, inevitably more subject to anxiety and disappointment than one less extreme in its demand and/or cultural-juridical backing;[10]

(*b*) Requiring so complete a sexual isolation of the marriage partners that should one violate the fidelity code the other is left alone and susceptible to a sense of fundamental deprivation and resentment;

(c) Stipulating such a strict restraint of sexual energies that there are habitual violations of the regulation: which violations *qua* violations are frequently if not always attended by (i) wilful deception and reciprocal suspicion about the occurrence or quality of the extramarital relationship, (ii) anxiety and fear on both sides of permanent estrangement from partner and family, and/or (iii) overt and covert antagonism over the prohibited act in both offender (who feels "trapped") and offended (who feels "betrayed").

The disadvantages of the four principles of monogamous marriage do not, however, end with inhibiting the very effects they are said to promote. There are further shortcomings:

(1) The restriction of marriage union to two partners necessarily prevents the strengths of larger groupings. Such advantages as the following are thereby usually ruled out.

(a) The security, range and power of larger socioeconomic units;
(b) The epistemological and emotional substance, variety and scope of more pluralist interactions;
(c) The possibility of extra-domestic freedom founded on more adult providers and upbringers as well as more broadly based circles of intimacy.

(2) The sexual containment and isolation which the four principles together require variously stimulates such social malaises as:

(a) Destructive aggression (which notoriously results from sexual frustration);
(b) Apathy, frustration and dependence within the marriage bond;
(c) Lack of spontaneity, bad faith and distance in relationships without the marriage bond;
(d) Sexual phantasizing, perversion, fetishism, prostitution and pornography in the adult population as a whole.[11]

Taking such things into consideration, it seems difficult to lend credence to the view that the four principles of our form of monogamous marriage constitute a structure beneficial either to the marriage partners themselves or to their offspring (or indeed to anyone else). One is moved to seek for some other ground of the institution, some ground that lurks beneath the reach of our conventional apprehensions.

IV

The ground of our marriage institution, the essential principle that underwrites all four restrictions, is this: *the maintenance by one man or woman of the effective right to exclude indefinitely all others from erotic access to the conjugal partner.*

The first restriction creates, elaborates on, and provides for the enforcement of this right to exclude. And the second, third and fourth restrictions together ensure that the said right to exclude is—respectively—not cooperative, not simultaneously or sequentially distributed, and not permissive of even casual exception.

In other words, the four restrictions of our form of monogamous marriage together constitute a state-regulated, indefinite and exclusive ownership by two individuals of one another's sexual powers. Marriage is simply a form of private property.[12]

That our form of monogamous marriage is when the confusing layers of sanctity, apologetic and taboo are cleared away another species of private property should not surprise us.[13] The history of the institution is so full of suggestive indicators—dowries, inheritance, property alliances, daughter sales (of which women's wedding rings are a carry-over) bride exchanges, legitimacy and illegitimacy—that it is difficult not to see some intimate connections between marital and ownership ties. We are better able still to apprehend the ownership essence of our marriage institution, when in addition we consider:

(a) That until recently almost the only way to secure official dissolution of consummated marriage was to be able to demonstrate violation of one or both partner's sexual ownership (i.e., adultery);

(b) That the imperative of premarital chastity is tantamount to a demand for retrospective sexual ownership by the eventual marriage partner;

(c) That successful sexual involvement with a married person is prosecutable as an expropriation of ownership—"alienation of affections"—which is restituted by cash payment;

(d) That the incest taboo is an iron mechanism which protects the conjugal ownership of sexual properties: both the husband's and wife's from the access of affectionate offspring and the offsprings' (who themselves are future marriage partners) from access of siblings and parents;[14]

(e) That the language of the marriage ceremony is the language of exclusive possession ("take," "to have and to hold," "forsaking all others and keeping you only unto him/her," etc.), not to mention the proprietary locutions associated with the marital relationship (e.g., "he's mine," "she belongs to him," "keep to your own husband," "wife stealer," "possessive husband," etc.).

V

Of course, it would be remarkable if marriage in our society was not a relationship akin to private property. In our socioeconomic system we relate to virtually everything of value by individual ownership: by, that is, the effective right to exclude others from the thing concerned.[15] That we do so as well with perhaps the most highly valued thing of all—the sexual partners' sexuality—is only to be expected. Indeed it would probably be an intolerable strain on our entire social structure if we did otherwise.

This line of thought deserves pursuit. The real secret of our form of monogamous marriage is not that it functionally provides for the needs of adults who love one another or the children they give birth to, but that it serves the maintenance of our present social system. It is an institution which is indispensable to the persistence of the capitalist order,[16] in the following ways:

(1) A basic principle of current social relations is that some people legally acquire the use of other people's personal powers from which they may exclude other members of society. This system operates in the workplace (owners and hirers of all types contractually acquire for their exclusive use workers' regular labour powers) and in the family (husbands and wives contractually acquire for their exclusive use their partner's sexual properties). A conflict between the structures of these primary relations—as would obtain were there a suspension of the restrictions governing our form of monogamous marriage—might well undermine the systemic coherence of present social intercourse.

(2) The fundamental relation between individuals and things which satisfy their needs is, in our present society, that each individual has or does not have the effective right to exclude other people from the thing in question.[17] A rudimentary need is that for sexual relationship(s). Therefore the object of this need must be related to the one who needs it as owner or not owner (i.e., via marriage or not-marriage, or approximations thereto) if people's present relationship to what they need is to retain—again—systemic coherence.

(3) A necessary condition for the continued existence of the present social formation is that its members feel powerful motivation to gain favorable positions in it. But such social ambition is heavily dependent on the preservation of exclusive monogamy in that:

(a) The latter confines the discharge of primordial sexual energies to a single unalterable partner and thus typically compels the said energies to seek alternative outlet, such as business or professional success;[18]
(b) The exclusive marriage necessarily reduces the sexual relationships available to any one person to absolute (nonzero) minimum, a unilateral promotion of sexual shortage which in practice renders hierarchial achievement essential as an economic and "display" means for securing scarce partners.[19]

(4) Because the exclusive marriage necessarily and dramatically reduces the possibilities of sexual-love relationships, it thereby promotes the existing economic system by:

(a) Rendering extreme economic self-interest—the motivational basis

56—*The State of Sex and Monogamy*

of the capitalistic process—less vulnerable to altruistic subversion;
(b) Disciplining society's members into the habitual repression of natural impulse required for long-term performance of repetitive and arduous work tasks;
(c) Developing a complex of suppressed sexual desires to which sales techniques may effectively apply in creating those new consumer wants which provide indispensable outlets for ever-increasing capital funds.

(5) The present form of marriage is of fundamental importance to:

(a) The continued relative powerlessness of the individual family: which, with larger numbers would constitute a correspondingly increased command of social power;
(b) The continued high demand for homes, commodities and services: which, with the considerable economies of scale that extended unions would permit, would otherwise falter;
(c) The continued strict necessity for adult males to sell their labour power and adult women to remain at home (or vice versa): which strict necessity would diminish as the economic base of the family unit extended;
(d) The continued immense pool of unsatisfied sexual desires and energies in the population at large: without which powerful interests and institutions would lose much of their conventional appeal and force;[20]
(e) The continued profitable involvement of lawyers, priests and state officials in the jurisdictions of marriage and divorce and the myriad official practices and proceedings connected thereto.[21]

VI

If our marriage institution is a linchpin of our present social structure, then a breakdown in this institution would seem to indicate a breakdown in our social structure. On the face of it, the marriage institution is breaking down—enormously increased divorce rates, nonmarital sexual relationships, wife-swapping, the Playboy philosophy, and communes. Therefore one might be led by the appearance of things to anticipate a profound alteration in the social system.

But it would be a mistake to underestimate the tenacity of an established order or to overestimate the extent of change in our marriage institution. Increased divorce rates merely indicate the widening of a traditional escape hatch. Nonmarital relationships imitate and culminate in the marital mold. Wife-swapping presupposes ownership, as the phrase suggests. The Playboy philosophy is merely the view that if one has the money one has the right to be titillated, the commercial call to more fully exploit a dynamic sector of capital investment. And communes—the most hopeful phenomenon—almost nowhere offer a *praxis* challenge to private property in sexuality. It may be changing. But history, as the old man puts it, weighs like a nightmare on the brains of the living.

NOTES

1. Any person who presides over a marriage and is not authorized by law to do so is guilty of a criminal offense and is subject to several years imprisonment (e.g., Canadian Criminal Code, Sec. 258).
2. For example, offspring are illegitimate, neither wife nor children are legal heirs, and husband has no right of access or custody should separation occur.
3. "Any kind of conjugal union with more than one person at the same time, whether or not it is by law recognized as a binding form of marriage—is guilty of an indictable offence and is liable to imprisonment for five years" (Canadian Criminal Code, Sec. 257, 1aii). Part 2 of the same section adds: "Where an accused is charged with an offence under this section, no averment or proof of the method by which the alleged relationship was entered into, agreed to or consented to is necessary in the indictment or upon the trial of the accused, nor is it necessary upon the trial to prove that the persons who are alleged to have entered into the relationship had or intended to to have sexual intercourse."
   Here and elsewhere, I draw examples from Canadian criminal law. There is no reason to suspect the Canadian code is eccentric in these instances.
4. Even the sexual revolutionary Wilhelm Reich seems constrained within the limits of this "binary frame." Thus he says (my emphasis): "Nobody has the right to prohibit his or her partner from entering a temporary or lasting sexual relationship with someone else. He has only the right *either to withdraw or to win the partner back*." (Wilhelm Reich, *The Sexual Revolution*, trans. by T. P. Wolfe New York: Farrar, Strauss and Giroux, 1970 p. 28.) The possibility of sexual partners extending their union to include the other loved party as opposed to one partner having either to "win" against this third party or to "withdraw" altogether) does not seem even to occur to Reich.
5. I will be using "sexual" and "erotic" interchangeably throughout the paper.
6. It is worth noting here that: (*a*) man has by nature the most "open" sexual instinct—year-round operativeness and variety of stimuli—of all the species (except perhaps the dolphin); and (*b*) it is a principle of human needs in general that maximum satisfaction involves regular variation in the form of the need-object.
7. "Roman Law had no power of intervening in the formation of marriages and there was no legal form of marriage. . . . Marriage was a matter of simple private agreement and divorce was a private transaction" (Havelock Ellis, *Studies in the Psychology of Sex* New York: Random House, 1963, Vol. II, Part 3, p. 429).
8. The dramatic reduction of sibling rivalry through an increased number of adults in the house is a phenomenon which is well known in contemporary domestic communes.
9. One of the few other historical social relationships I can think of in which persons hold thoroughly exclusive monopoly over other persons' means of life is slavery. Thus, as with another's slave, it is a criminal offence "to receive" or "harbour" another's child without "right of possession" (Canadian Criminal Code, Sec. 250).
10. Certain cultures, for example, permit extramarital sexuality by married persons with friends, guests, or in-laws with no reported consequences of jealousy. From such evidence, one is led to speculate that the intensity and extent of jealousy at a partner's extramarital sexual involvement is in direct proportion to the severity of the accepted cultural regulations against such involvements. In short such regulations do not prevent jealousy so much as effectively engender it.
11. It should not be forgotten that at the same time marriage excludes marital partners

from sexual contact with others, it necessarily excludes those others from sexual contact with marital partners. Walls face two ways.

12 Those aspects of marriage law which seem to fall outside the pale of sexual property holding—for example, provisions for divorce if the husband fails to provide or is convicted of a felony or is an alcoholic—may themselves be seen as simply prescriptive characterizations of the sort of sexual property which the marriage partner must remain to retain satisfactory conjugal status: a kind of permanent warranty of the "good working order" of the sexual possession.

What constitutes "the good working order" of the conjugal possession is, of course, different in the case of the husband and in the case of the wife: an *asymmetry* within the marriage institution which, I gather, women's liberation movements are anxious to eradicate.

13 I think it is instructive to think of even the nonlegal aspects of marriage, for example, its sentiments as essentially private property structured. Thus the preoccupation of those experiencing conjugal sentiments with expressing how much "my very own," "my precious," the other is: with expressing, that is, how valuable and inviolable the ownership is and will remain.

14 I think the secret to the long mysterious incest taboo may well be the fact that in all its forms it protects sexual property: not only conjugal (as indicated above) but paternal and tribal as well. This crucial line of thought, however, requires extended separate treatment.

15 Sometimes—as with political patronage, criminal possession, *de facto* privileges and so forth—a *power* to exclude others exists with no corresponding "right" (just as sometimes a right to exclude exists with no corresponding power). Properly speaking, thus, I should here use the phrase "power to exclude," which covers "effective right to exclude" as well as all nonjuridical enablements of this sort.

16 It is no doubt indispensable as well—in some form or other—to any private property order. Probably (if we take the history of Western society as our data base) the more thoroughgoing and developed the private property formation is, the more total the sexual ownership prescribed by the marriage institution.

17 Things in unlimited supply—like, presently, oxygen—are not of course related to people in this way.

18 This is, of course, a Freudian or quasi-Freudian claim. "Observation of daily life shows us," says Freud, "that most persons direct a very tangible part of their sexual motive powers to their professional or business activities" (Sigmund Freud, *Dictionary of Psychoanalysis*, ed. by Nandor Fodor and Frank Gaynor New York: Fawcett Publications, Premier Paperback, 1966, p. 139).

19 It might be argued that exclusive marriage also protects those physically less attractive persons who—in an "open" situation—might be unable to secure any sexual partnership at all. The force of this claim depends, I think, on improperly continuing to posit the very principle of exclusiveness which the "open" situation rules out (e.g., in the latter situation, *x* might be less attractive to *y* than *z* is and yet *z* not be rejected, any more than at present an intimate friend is rejected who is less talented than another intimate friend).

20 The sexual undercurrents of corporate advertisments, religious systems, racial propaganda and so on is too familiar to dwell on here.

21 It is also possible that exclusive marriage protects the adult-youth power structure in the manner outlined in Part III.

4

IS MONOGAMY OUTDATED?
Rustum and Della Roy

The authors explore the bases for expanding our awareness of marriage as an enterprise that needs opening up in terms of both training and education for marriage as well as investigation of the success of radical groups and communities. The need for institutional reforms is predicated on an examination of life in a sexualized society and the current status and demeaning nature of marriage and divorce, both of which too often isolate people from social supports and personal development.

The Roys' writing is ultimately a Radical Christian approach that calls for candor and courage to face the dilemmas of modern sexual life and its alternatives. Taking life as it is, they call for reforms that would develop a sense of community—that most important facet of life which creates a sense of belonging which they perceive is so often missing from life today. Since this lack of a sense of community—especially in the area of long-term sexual relationships—is so often a result of the ways in which marriage and divorce are handled, the case is made for radical reconstruction based on variants now practiced only in the underground. Although the Roys recognize the problems inherent in social change, they express hope that liberated humanists will work together toward more rational sex as part of a better life.

Monogamy: Where We Stand Today

The total institution of marriage in American society is gravely ill. This statement does not apply to the millions of sound marriages where two people have found companionship, love, concern, and have brought up children in love. But it is necessary in 1970 to point to the need for *institutional* reforms, even when the personal or immediate environment may not (appear to) need it. Yet many refuse to think about the area as a whole because of personal involvement—either their marriage is so successful that they think the claims of disease exaggerated, or theirs is so shaky that all advice is a threat. Is the institution then so sick? For example:

> Year after year in the United States, marriage has been discussed in public and private session with undiminished confusion and increasing pessimism. Calamity always attracts attention, and in the United States the state of marriage is a calamity.

These are the words with which W.H. Lederer and D. Jackson open their new book *The Mirages of Marriage*. Vance Packard in *The Sexual Wilderness* summarizes the most recent major survey thus: "In other words, a marriage made in the United States in the late 1960's has about a 50:50 chance of remaining even nominally intact."

Clifford Adams concludes from an Identity Research Institute study of 600 couples that while numerically at 40 per cent in this nation, and in some West Coast highly-populated counties the *real* divorce rate is running at 70 per cent, that in fact "75 per cent of marriages are a 'bust.'" And Lederer and Jackson report that 80 per cent of those interviewed had at some time seriously considered divorce. So much for the statistics. Qualitatively the picture painted by these and 100 others is even bleaker but needs no repeating here.

There is no doubt then about the diagnosis of the sickness of marriage taken as a whole. Yet no person, group, magazine, or newspaper creates an awareness of the problems; no activist band takes up the cause to *do* something about it. Some years ago, we participated in a three-year-long group study and development of a sex ethic for contemporary Americans, and we found this same phenomenon: that serious group study and group work for change in the area of sex behavior is remarkably difficult and threatening, and hence rare. Thus, we find an institution such as monogamous marriage enveloped by deterioration and decay, and unbelievably little is being done about it on either a theoretical basis or detailed pragmatic basis.

For this there is a second major reason: marriage as an institution is partly governed by warring churches, a society without a soul, a legal system designed for lawyers, and a helping system for psychiatrists who almost by their very mode of operation in the marriage field guarantee its failure. Consequently, marriage is rapidly losing its schizophrenic mind, oscillating between tyrannical repression and equally tyrannical expression.

By the term "traditional monogamy," we refer to the public's association with the word, i.e., marriage to one person at a time, the centrality of the nuclear family and the restriction of all overt sexual acts, nearly all sexually-tinged relationships and heterosexual relations of any depth to this one person before and after marriage, expectation of a lifetime contract and a vivid sense of failure if termination is necessary. John Cuber and Peggy Harroff in *The Significant Americans* have called this "the monolithic code," and it is based on precepts from the Judaic and Christian traditions. All working societies are structured around such codes or ideals, no matter how far individuals may depart from the norms and whether or not they accept the source of such "ideals."

How does change in a code or ideal come about? When the proportion of the populace living in conflict with their own interpretation of the monolithic code, and "getting away with it," reaches nearly a majority, then *new ideals must evolve* for the social system to remain in equilibrium. We are convinced that although no *discontinuous* change in the ideals of a culture is possible, "traditional monogamy" as an ideal may be altered *in a continuous fashion* in order to respond to the needs of men and women today.

Traditional monogamy was *one* interpretation of the Judaeo-Christian tradition. We are convinced that for widespread acceptability any *new* ideals must be interpretable in terms of Judaeo-Christian humanism, the basic framework of mainstream "Americanism," and the most explicit humanism so far developed. Such an interpretation is neither difficult nor likely to encounter much resistance from the many other contemporary American humanisms which have not swung far from the parent Protestant humanism. But the importance of such an interpretation for "continental" middle-class America is crucial, as the tenor and very existence of the Nixon administration bring home to those who live in the more rarified climes of East or West Coast. If a new monogamous ideal is to evolve, it must be acceptable to middle America, liberated, affluent, but waspish at heart.

Causes of the Crisis

Social institutions are the products of particular social environments, and there must be a finite time lag when an institution appropriate for one situation survives into a new era in which the situation has changed drastically. It is clear that "traditional monogamy" is caught precisely in this "overlap" of two radically different situations. It is important to identify precisely the particular problem-causing elements of change in the environment.

> The sexual revolution has made it infinitely more difficult to retain monogamy's monopoly on sex.

We live in an eroticized environment which is profoundly affecting many institutions. The change towards greater permissiveness and its effect on the sexual climate can be summed up in the aphorism, "What was a temptation for the last generation is an opportunity for this." Underneath it all are the measurable, real physical changes: the advent of prosperity, mobility, and completely controlled conception.

Parallel to physical changes are vast social changes. The eroticization of our culture oozes from its every pore, so much so that it becomes essentially absurd to expect that all physical sexual expression for a 50-year period will be confined to the marriage partner. Moreover, this eroticization escalator shows no sign of slowing down, and its effect on various institutions will be even more drastic in the future. Following are some illustrations.

The influence of the literature, the arts, the media, and the press on the climate for any institution is profound, and marriage is no exception. Caught between the jaws of consumer economics in a free-enterprise system and the allegedly objective purveyors of accurate information (or culturally representative entertainment), human sexuality has become the most salable commodity of all. Perform, if you will, the following simple tests: examine the magazine fare available to tens of millions of Americans; spend a few hours browsing through *Look*, and *Life*, and try *Playboy*, work up to something like *Cosmopolitan*. If you are serious, visit a typical downtown book shop in a big city and count the number of pictorial publications whose sole purpose is sexual titillation. Next try the paperbacks available to at least 100,000,000 Americans—in every drugstore: *Candy*, Henry Miller, *Fanny Hill*, the complaining Portnoy, valleys of dolls, and menchild in promised lands, carpetbaggers at airports, couples and groups. Does *one* speak of the beauty and wonder of uniting sex to marriage? Go see 10 movies at random. Will *The Graduate, I Am Curious,* or *La Ronde* rail against sexual license? Thus the mass media have had a profound effect on the American people's marriage ideals. They especially confuse those to whom their "traditions" speaking through emasculated school, bewildered Church, and confused home still try to affirm a traditionally monogamous system. Yet some have mistakenly denied that there is a causal relation between the media and our rapidly changing value systems. Worst of all, very few of those who urge the freedom of access to more and more sexual stimuli work to legitimize, socially and ethically, a scheme for increased sexual outlets.

> There is a vast increase in the number and variety of men-women contacts after marriage, and no guidelines are available for behavior in these new situations.

Of the sexual dilemmas which our present-day culture forces upon the "ailing" institution of traditional monogamy, premarital sexual questions now appear very minor. For all intents and purposes premarital sexual play (including the *possibility* of intercourse) has been absorbed into the social canon. We foresee in the immediate future a much more serious psychological quandary with respect to extra- or co-marital sexual relations of all levels of intensity. The conflict here is so basic and so little is being done to alleviate it, that it is only surprising that it has not loomed larger already. Traditional monogamy as practiced has meant not only one spouse and sex partner at a time but essentially only one heterosexual *relationship*, of any depth at all, at a time. We have shown above that our environment suggests through various media the desirability of nonmarital sex. Further, our culture is now abundant in opportunity: time, travel, meetings, committees, causes, and group encounters of every stripe bringing men and women together in all kinds of relationship-producing situations. Our age is characterized by not only the opportunity but by the necessity for simultaneous multiple-relationships. One of the most widely experienced examples is that chosen by Cuber and Harroff in their study of the sex lives of some "leaders" of our society. They noted the obviously close relationship of such men with their secretaries with whom they work for several hours a day. But the same opportunity now occurs to millions of middle-class housewives returning to work after children are grown. They too are establishing new heterosexual friendships and being treated as separate individuals (not to mention as sex-objects) after 10 or 15 years.

> Traditional monogamy is in trouble because it has not adjusted itself to find a less hurtful way to terminate a marriage.

From the viewpoint of any philosophy that puts a high value on response to human need and the alleviation of human suffering the mechanisms available for terminating marriage are utterly unacceptable. Traditional monogamy involves a lifetime commitment. Anything that would necessitate termination short of this must, therefore, be a major failure. "Divorce, American Style" demands so much hurt and pain and devastation of personalities that it is imperative that we attempt to temper the hurt caused to human beings. We must take as inescapable fact that about half of all the marriages now existing will, and probably should, be terminated. The question is how best this can be done to minimize total human suffering, while avoiding the pitfall that the relief of immediate pain of one or two persons is the greatest and single good. Full consideration must always be given to all the "significant others"—children, parents, friends—and to the long-range effects on society. The institution of traditional monogamy will increasingly come under attack while it is unable to provide a better means to terminate a contract than those now in use.

> Traditional monogamy does not deal humanely with its have-nots—the adult singles, the widowed, the divorced.

Statistically speaking we in America have more involuntarily single persons above age 25 or 30 than those who had no choice about a disadvantageous color for their skin. The latter have had to bear enormous legal and social affronts and suffered the subtler and possibly more debilitating psychological climate of being unacceptable in much of their natural surroundings. But this disability they share with voiceless single persons in a marriage-oriented society. Our society proclaims monogamy's virtue at every point of law and custom and practice, as much as it says white is right. Biases, from income tax to adoption requirements, subtle advertisements, and Emily Post etiquette all point to the "traditional monogamist" as the acceptable form of society. Unbelievably, this barrage goes on unopposed in the face of some tens of millions of persons outside the blessed estate. Monogamy decrees that the price of admission into the complex network of supportive relationships of society is a wedding band. Yet it turns a blind eye to the inexorable statistical fact that of those women who are single at 35 only 1/3, at 45 only 1/10, and at 50 only 1/20 will ever find that price. Is access to regular physical sexual satisfaction a basic human right on a plane with freedom or shelter or right to worship? For effective living in our world every human being needs individuals as close friends and a community of which he or she is a part. Traditionally, monogamous society has ruled, *ipso facto*, that tens of millions of its members shall have no societally approved way of obtaining sexual satisfaction. Much worse, because sexual intimacy is potentially associated with all heterosexual relationships of any depth, they must also be denied such relationships.

Here, surely, every humanist must protest. For it is *his* social ideal—that the greatest good of human existence is deep interpersonal relationships and as many of these as is compatible with depth—that is contravened by traditional monogamy's practice. Moreover, there is less provision today for single women to develop fulfilling relationships than there was a generation or two ago. The "larger-family" then incorporated these losers in the marital stakes into at least a minimal framework of acceptance and responsibility.

A Theory for Change

Any vision of a better future for society presupposes, consciously or unconsciously, a value system and basic assumptions about the nature of man. A theory of man and life must precede a theory of monogamy. Our view of the nature of man is the Judaeo-Christian one. Man was meant to live *in community*. The normative ideal for every man is that he live fully known, accepted, and loved by a community of significant others. In this environment his individual creativity and his creative individuality will be realized to the maximum extent, and he can serve society best.

Man—Community—Society

In this spectrum we have, as yet, not even mentioned marriage and intentionally so. There is a crucially important hierarchy of values, in which the individual's needs and the community's good are vastly more important than the "laws" or preferred patterns of marital behavior. Indeed, these "laws" must be tested empirically by the criterion of how well they have been found to meet the individual-community-society needs most effectively. It is important to see that the humanist is not committed, prima facie, to *any* particular pattern of men-women relationships.

Marriage, monogamous or polygamous, fits somewhere between the individual and community levels of social organization. Unfortunately, in many cultures the institution of marriage and the stress on the family has generally militated against, and sometimes destroyed, the community level of relationship.

This has not always been so—not even in America. The "larger family" of maiden aunts and uncles and grandparents, and occasional waifs and strays, has been a part of many cultures including that of the rigidly structured joint-family system in India and the plantation system of the American South. Tribal cultures abound. In the Swiss canton or settled New England town the sinews of community are strong enough to make them fall in between the extremes represented above and lying, perhaps, closer to the former. There is an inverse correlation between the complexity of a highly-developed society and the strength of community channels and bonds. It is in the technology-ruled society where we find men and women turning to the intimacy of marriage to shield them from further impersonalization when the second level of defense—the community level—has disintegrated through neglect. But monogamous marriage is altogether too frail an institution to carry that load also. A typical marriage is built frequently of brittle and weak members held together by a glue of tradition rapidly deteriorating under the onslaught of a half-dozen corroding acids—mobility, prosperity, permissiveness, completely controlled conception, and continuously escalating eroticization.

There is no question that the first and essential step in the evolution of monogamy is the recovery of the role of community in our lives. It appears to us, however strange a conclusion it seems, that precisely because our world has become so complex, depersonalization is an essential, ineradicable fact of our lives in the many public spheres. This requires then a radical restructuring of the private sphere to provide the supports we have found missing in the "traditional-monogamy" pattern. To know and accept ourselves deeply we need to be known and accepted. And most of us are many-sided polyhedra needing several people to reflect back to ourselves the different portions of our personality. With changing years and training and jobs this need grows instead of diminishing. Thus, it comes about that the humanist has a great deal to contribute to his fellows.

Our proposed modification of monogamy, then, has the re-emphasis of community as one of its primary goals. This is hardly novel, but it has been the conclusion of every group of radical Christian humanists trying to reform society for hundreds of years. And it was the New World which provided for them a unique opportunity to attempt the radical solutions. Hence, we have dotted across America the record and/or the remnants of hundreds of experiments in radical community living.

Today we believe that society's hope lies in working at both ends of the game—the basic research and the development. We need to become much more active in optimizing or improving present marriage in an imperfect society: changing laws, improving training, providing better recovery systems, etc. But alongside of that, we need to continue genuine research in radically new patterns of marriage. This can only be carried out by groups or communities. Further, we need not only those groups that seek solutions withdrawn from the day-to-day world, but those that are willing to devise potential solutions which can serve as models, for its eventual reform within the bourgeois urban culture.

Basic Research in Marriage Patterns

We cannot here do justice to a discussion of possible models for radical new patterns of marriage-in-community. Instead, we wish only to emphasize the importance of such experimentation and its neglect, in our supposedly research-oriented culture, by serious groups concerned for society. It is hardly a coincidence that the yearning for community should figure so prominently in all utopian schemes for remaking society. The contemporary resurgence is described in B.F. Skinner's *Walden Two* or Erich Fromm's *Revolution of Hope* and Robert Rimmer's *Harrad Experiment*. It is being attempted in groping unformed ways in the "hippie" or other city-living communes, and is being lived out in amazingly fruitful (yet unpublicized) models in the Bruderhof communities in the United States and Europe, and the Ecumenical Institute in Chicago. And in rereading the details of the organization of the hundreds of religious communities we find that they have an enormous amount to teach us, on many subjects from psychotherapy to patterns for sexual intercourse.

Probably the most important lesson for contemporary America, however, is that communities survive and thrive and provide a creative framework for realizing the human potential if their central purpose is outside themselves and their own existence. The second lesson is one taught by the complex technology: wherever many persons are involved, some discipline and order are absolutely essential.

Were it not for the sheer prejudice introduced by a misreading of Judeo-Christian tradition, and its bolstering by the unholy alliance of state-and-church Establishment, we may well have learned to separate potential from pitfall in various patterns of communal living. The

Mormon experience with polygamy is not without its value for us, and Bettelheim has helped shake the prejudice against nonparent child rearing drawing on data from the kibbutzim. Rimmer, perhaps, through his novels *The Rebellion of Yale Marratt* and *Proposition 31*, has reached the widest audience in his crusade for a variety of new marital patterns. He has dealt sensitively, and in depth, with the subtle questions of ongoing sexual relations with more than one partner—the threat of which is perhaps the most difficult taboo against communal life for most educated Americans. From some dozens of histories in personal and "marathon" encounter situations, we believe that Rimmer's portrayal of typical reactions is remarkably accurate. Most middle-class, educated Americans above 35 have been so schooled into both exclusivity and possessiveness that no more than perhaps 10 per cent could make the transition into any kind of structured nonexclusivity in marriage. But for the younger group, especially those now in college, the potential for attempting the highly demanding, idealistic, disciplined group living of some sort is both great, and a great challenge. It is here perhaps by setting up contemporary-style communities of concern and responsibility that young humanists can make one of their greatest contributions to society at large.

Modifying Traditional Monogamy

No company survives on its fundamental research laboratory alone, although many cannot survive long without one. Each needs also a development group that keeps making the minor changes to its existing products in order to eliminate defects in design and to meet the competition or the change in customer needs. So too with marriage. While "far-out" research *must* proceed on new patterns, we must simultaneously be concerned with the changes that can modify traditional monogamy to meet its present customer-needs much more effectively—that is to say humanely.

Our society is pluralist in many of its ideals. The first and most important change in society's view of marriage must also be the acceptance of the validity of a range of patterns of behavior. The education of our children and of society must point to ways and points at which, *depending on the situation*, it is right and proper to make this or that change. Indeed, we can doubtless describe the era we are entering as one of "situational monogamy"—that is traditional monogamy can still be upheld as the ideal in many circumstances, but, in specific situations, modifications are not only permitted but required.

Institutionalizing Premarital Sex

Premarital sexual experience is now rather widely accepted, covertly if not overtly, throughout our society. Especially when we use the word "experience" instead of "intercourse," the studies from Kinsey to Packard support a very substantial increase in necking and petting including petting to orgasm. The new rise in "keeping-house-together" arrangements in college and beyond is spreading like wildfire. We see an opportunity here for a simple evolution of the monogamous ideal within relatively easy reach. Almost all analysts believe that postponing marriage by two or three years and making it more difficult—with some required period of waiting or even waiting and instruction—would be very beneficial. Traditional marriage in its classical form enjoined a "decent" (six months to two years) engagement period partly for the same reason. One of the main drives toward early marriage is that there is no other way to obtain regular sexual gratification in a publicly acceptable manner. By one simple swish of tradition, we can incorporate all the recent suggestions for trial marriages, "baby" marriages, etc., and cover them all under the decent rug of the "engagement." Engagements with a minor difference: that in today's society they entitle a couple to live together if they desire, and sleep together—*but not to have children*. Thus, engagement would become the first step that entitles one to legal sex—publicly known sex with contraceptive devices. By no means need this become the universal norm. Pluralism of marital patterns should start here, however. Many parents and various social groups may still urge their members to restrict engagements to a noncoital or nonsexual level of intimacy; but even here they would do well to legitimize some advanced level of sexual activity and by so doing they would probably protect their marriage-institution more effectively. Our very spotty feedback from student groups would suggest that "everything-but-coitus"—which is a lot more sex than the last generation's "little-but-coitus"—has some value as a premarital maxim. The humanist must also affirm that quintessential humanness is choice against one's immediate desires. He must point to the loss by this generation of perhaps the most exquisite sexual pleasures when it comes as the culmination of long-deferred desire of the loved one. We mourn the loss of Eros in a day when Venus comes so quickly, for it is Eros, who is human, while Venus reminds us that we are *human* animals. Well may we paraphrase the Frenchman and say: "In America we tend to eat the fruit of coital sex, green."

Along with the engagement-including-sex concept could be introduced the idea of "training" for marriage. Everyone falls for the training gimmick. Driver education, often taken after three years of driving, is still useful, and is induced by the lowered insurance rates. Similarly if society required a "marriage-education" course before granting a license, another important step in improving the quality of marriage would have been achieved.

Expanding the Erotic Community in the Post-Marital Years

With the engagement-including-sex, we have broken the premarital half of monogamy's monopoly on sex. It is our judgment that for the health of the institution it will become necessary in America in the next decade to break the second half also—post marital sexual expression. (Recall that our theory demands that we seek to maximize the number of deep relationships and to develop marriages to fit in with a framework of community.) To do this we are certain that the monopolistic tendencies of relationships must be broken, and hence the question of sexual relations cannot be bypassed. We believe that in the coming generation a spectrum of sexual expression with persons other than the spouse are certain to occur for at least the large majority, and possibly most persons. If monogamy is tied inextricably with post-marital restriction of all sexual expression to the spouse, it will ultimately be monogamy which suffers. Instead, monogamy should be tied to the much more basic concepts of fidelity, honesty, and openness, which are concomitants of love of the spouse, but which do not necessarily exclude deep relationships and possibly including various degrees of sexual intimacy with others. In the studies and counseling experience of many, including ourselves, there is no evidence that all extra-marital sexual experience is destructive of the marriage. Indeed, more and more persons testify that creative co-marital relationships and sexual experience can and do exist. But most persons need guidelines to help steer them from the dangerous to the potentially creative *relationships*, and to provide help on the appropriateness of various sexual expressions for various relationships. A few practices are crucial:

> *Openness:* Contrary to folklore, frank and honest discussions at *every stage* of a developing relationship between all parties is the best guarantee against trouble. We know of husbands who have discussed with their wives possible coitus with a third person, some to conclude it would be wrong, others, unwise; others to drop earlier objections, and still others to say it was necessary and beautiful. We know of wives to say it was necessary and beautiful. We know of wives who have said a reasoned "no" to such possibilities for their husbands and kept their love and respect; and many who have said "yes" in uncertainty and have found the pain subside. Openness is not impossible.
>
> *Other-centeredness:* Concern for *all* the others—the other woman or man, the other husband or wife, the children—must be front and center in reaching decisions on any such matters.
>
> *Proportionality:* Sexual expressions should be proportional to the depth of a relationship. This leads, of course, to the conclusion that most coitus and other intimate expressions should only occur with very close friends: a conclusion questioned by many, but essential for our theory.
>
> *Gradualism:* Only a stepwise escalation of intimacy allows for the open discussion referred to above. Otherwise such openness becomes only a series of confessions.

It is important to discover the value of self-denial and restraint. It is incumbent on them to demonstrate, while accepting other patterns, their ability to maintain loving, warm relationships with both single and married persons of the opposite sex and of limiting the sexual expression therein in order, for example, to conserve psychic energy for other causes.

Providing a Relationship Network for the Single

It is principally because of the fear of sexual involvement that the single are excluded from married-society. In the new dispensation, a much more active and aggressive policy should be encouraged to incorporate single persons within the total life of a family and a community. She or he should be a part of the family, always invited—but not always coming—to dinner, theaters, and vacations. The single person should feel free enough to make demands and accept responsibility as an additional family member would. The single woman, thus loved and accepted by two or three families, may find herself perhaps not sleeping with any of the husbands but vastly more fulfilled as a woman. No couple should enter such relationships unless the marriage is secure and the sexual monopoly not crucially important: yet all concerned couples should be caused to wonder about their values if their fear of sexual involvement keeps them from ministering to such obvious need. The guidelines for decisions, of course, are the same as those above. We know of several such relationships, many but not all involving complete sexual intimacy that have been most important in the lives of the single persons. Recently, we have observed that our present society makes it very difficult for even the best of these relationships to continue for a lifetime. And we see the need for developing acceptable patterns for altering such relationships creatively after the two-to-five-year period which often brings about sufficient changes to suggest reappraisal in any case. The dependent woman often becomes confident and no longer needs the same kind of support: the independent one becomes too attached and becomes possessive enough to want exclusivity. The mechanisms we discuss under divorce should no doubt operate here as well.

Legalizing Bigamy

It may appear as a paradox, but in keeping with the theory above and the pluralist trend of society, it is almost certainly true that contemporary-style monogamy would be greatly strengthened if bigamy (perhaps polygamy-polyandry) were legalized. This would provide a *partial* solution to the problems dealt with in the last two sections; moreover, it would do it in a way that is least disturbing to the monogamous tenor of society. The entire style—contract and living arrangements of most persons—would be unaffected if one woman in 20 had two husbands in the house; or one man in 10 had two wives—sometimes in different cities and frequently in different houses. There is a substantial unthinking emotional resistance to legalizing bigamy based partly on a supposed, but incorrect, backing from Christian doctrine. There is, however, no Biblical injunction sanctifying monogamy: the Christian humanist is not only free to, but may be required to, call for other patterns. Indeed, after World War II the Finnish Church is reported to have been on the verge of legalizing bigamy, when the great disparity in women:men ratio, which stimulated the inquiry, was found to have improved beyond their expectations.

In the next decade, this ratio is expected to get as high as 7:5 in the country, and it is higher in the highest age brackets. Various gerontologists have suggested the legalization of bigamy for the aged, and the capacity for social change in our society is so weak that perhaps bigamy will have to be legalized first under Medicare! It is indeed difficult to see why bigamy should not be legalized, once the doctrinal smokescreen were to be exposed for what it is.

Making Difficulties and Divorce Less Destructive of Personalities

A reform of the total system of marriage *must* provide for a much less destructive method for terminating one. The first change required in our present ideal is to recognize that a good divorce can be better than a poor marriage. We can continue to affirm the importance of the intention of the lifelong commitment, but we must begin to stress the quality of the commitment and the actual relationship as a higher good than mere longevity. Early detection of trouble makes repair easier and surgery less likely. If we take our automobiles to be inspected twice a year to be safe on the highways, is it too much to expect that the complex machinery of a marriage could be sympathetically "inspected" periodically to keep it in the best working condition? Here the church and the university can help by showing the need for, and providing such "inspections." Conceivably a biennial or triennial marriage-marathon or weeklong retreat utilizing the newest insights of encounter groups could be made normative for all marriages. Such check-ups would in some cases catch the cancer early enough, and in others indicate the need for surgery. In any case, a failing marriage needs to be treated by a person or persons who are neutral on the value of divorce itself, committed to the goal of maximizing human potential, and not determined to preserve marriage for its own sake. We believe that a team of a marriage counselor and, where appropriate, younger clergymen or another couple who are close friends can, over a period of several months, help the husband and wife arrive at a wise decision most effectively. The use of a fixed-length trial period for either separation or continuance, after specific changes, with an agreed-upon evaluation at the end of the period has proved its real value in all the cases where we have seen it used. Our own experience has been that many of the worst situations are avoided if the couple can keep channels open to their closest friends—always working with them together. Two helpful changes need to occur here. First, it should be made much more acceptable to talk openly and seriously about marital tensions with close friends; and second, we should all learn the principle of never giving any personal information about absent *third* parties except when we think it can specifically do some positive good.

For ordinary divorce, it is difficult to see what the professional psychiatrist or lawyer-as-adviser can contribute; indeed it appears axiomatic that with traditional Freudian psychiatry there can be no compromise—it is simply incompatible with the rational approaches to helping even irrational persons. In most instances, its result is the introduction of wholly unnecessary polarization (instead of a reconciling attitude, even while separating) between two persons who were the most important in the world to each other. This we find tends to undercut the faith that such persons can ever have in any other person or cause. The price of so-called self-understanding is the mild cynicism which extinguishes the fire of the unlimited liability of love and drains the warmth and color from two lives. Neither paid psychiatrist nor loving friend can avoid the tragedy in the kind of situation when John married to Mary has become deeply attached to Alice. But this tragedy need not be compounded by bitterness, anger, and self-justification in the name of helping. We do know of couples divorcing and parting as friends: persons who *love* each other to the best of their ability and yet, after sober agonizing months of consideration, decide to separate. We know that that is the way it must happen in the future.

Conserving Ideals: Changing the Marriage Service

Because our psychological conditioning is affected, even by every minor input, we can help preserve the monogamous *ideal* by bringing in honesty at the high points in its symbol-life. This would mean, for instance, minor alteration of the traditional-marriage service, and not necessarily to "waterdown" its commitments. Thus, everyone recognizes the value of a lifelong commitment. But to what should that commitment be? To preserving a marriage when we know that half will fail and make all involved guilty over it? Why not, rather, a lifelong commitment to loving and speaking the truth in love? One can be true to this even if separation occurs. Why should not the marriage service make the closest friends—best man, maid of honor, etc., who have essentially trivial roles in the ceremony—take on a real commitment to become the loving community for the couple, covenanting to communicate regularly, stand by them always, but also to speak admonition in love whenever they see it needed. Even such a small beginning would symbolize the fact that each couple enters not only into a marriage but also into a much-needed community.

Disease Diagnosed, Prognosis: Poor

The rebellion of the young reflects only intuitively their alienation from a science-technology dominated world which they have not the discipline to understand. The need for new and revitalized institutions that would provide every kind of support to individuals could not be greater. Inexorable logic points to the centrality of community in any such attempts. Yet no American, indeed Western, sociologist or psychologist of any stature (always excepting Skinner) has paid any serious attention to their structuring. We attribute this largely to their ignorance of the primitive Christian roots of their own heritage, and see in it the great loss to contemporary humanism of the insight and *experimental data* from these bold humanist experimenters of the last century. However, it is unlikely that in the permissive society it will be possible to demand the minimum discipline required for a community to cohere. What changes can we really hope for on the basis of present observations? On the basis of emotional reactions and capacity for change in attitudes to men-women relationships, sexual patterns, or marriage, which we have observed even in the most secure and highly motivated persons, we can only be discouraged and pessimistic. Always here and there the exception stands out: concerned persons acting out love in new ways demanded by new situations. We agree with Victor Ferkiss when he says in *Technological Man*:

> There is no new man emerging to replace the economic man of industrial society or the liberal democratic man of the bourgeois political order. The new Technology has not produced a new human type provided with a technological world view adequate to give cultural meaning to the existential revolution. Bourgeois man continues dominant just as his social order persists while his political and cultural orders disintegrate.

Bourgeois man will persist and along with him, traditional monogamy. But for humanists, there is no release from the mandate to try to alter traditional monogamy to make it better serve human needs for "we are called upon to be faithful, not to succeed."

5

INFIDELITY: SOME MORAL AND SOCIAL ISSUES
Jessie Bernard

Jessie Bernard analyzes the relationship between sexual exclusivity and permanence in marriage. Her analysis suggests that there is a trend toward emphasizing exclusivity in the younger years of marriage and permanence in the later years. She examines the possibilities the socialization process holds for the development of relative independence in people—in contrast to the kind of dependence spouses develop today. The problem of dependence versus independence is then linked to a problematic future for the marital bond, especially when "infidelity" among women is more tolerated.

She also predicts a problem with the quality of relationships in future marriages. Recognizing the fact that any one person's resources are limited, there is a question whether too widely diffused an arrangement would be realistic in terms of ability to supply needs, availability of time and energy, and clear enough definitions to maintain a happy state of ongoing selfhood for the people involved. The last question raised by Bernard is in regard to how people can depend on each other for long-term support when relationships become looser and involve multiple sexual-emotional pairings. The problem of reassurance, of caring and support when multiple involvements occur, is seen as one of the thorny items that will need to be clarified in the future by research in this important area of change.

Adultery Versus Infidelity

Both exclusivity and permanence are required in marriage as institutionalized in our society. They may be incompatible with one another in the kind of world we now live in where men and women are, in Bernard Farber's words, "permanently available." Sapirstein points up the difficulties:

Monogamy began in societies which had strong religious injunctions against infidelity and used every possible device to limit the temptations. Contrast the Chinese peasant dress or the shaved head of the young Hebrew bride with the modern woman who, whether married or not, does all she can to heighten her charms (Ref. 17, p. 173).

It may be that we will have to choose between exclusivity and permanence. If we insist on permanence, exclusivity is harder to enforce; if we insist on exclusivity, permanence may be endangered. The trend, as we shall note presently, seems to be in the direction of exclusivity at the expense of permanence in the younger years but permanence at the expense of exclusivity in the later years.

Exclusivity is still buttressed and enforced by both religious and secular law; permanence, by personal promises and vows. Sexual relations with anyone other than the spouse is forbidden by the seventh commandment and also by law. Adultery, though rarely prosecuted, is a crime in most states.[1] Society itself is the injured party.[2] Exclusivity is further buttressed by way of divorce legislation: adultery is universally accepted as a ground for divorce. The spouse is now the injured party. No marital partner has to tolerate it.

Infidelity, as distinguished from adultery, is the violation of a promise or a vow. Strangely enough, there is no universal, prescribed, or standard vow required of all those entering marriage. The officiating officer seems to have considerable latitude. Some denominations in-

---

1 "American law has tended toward the proscription of all extramarital sexual relationships; but in recognition of the realities of human nature, the penalties for adultery in most states are usually mild and the laws are only infrequently enforced. In five of the states the maximum penalty is a fine. There are three states which attach no criminal penalty at all to adultery, but civil penalties may be involved in these and in many other states. . . . The broadest definition of adultery and the heaviest penalties are concentrated in the northeastern section of the United States, all ten of those states being among the 17 which may impose prison terms for a single act of extramarital coitus. In actual practice, such extramarital coitus is rarely prosecuted" (p. 429).

2 However, the law is often used for quite different ends than the protection of society. In the summer of 1968, for example, a black minister in Irasburg, Vermont, was arrested on grounds of adultery by the State Police. The Governor of the state said the State Police had "devoted their efforts to a persecution of the Rev. Mr. Johnson," and the whole episode was viewed as evidence of racism (Ref. 19). This incident illustrates the Kinsey statement that "not infrequently the prosecutions represented attempts on the part of neighbors or relatives to work off grudges that had developed over other matters. In this, as in many other areas, the law is most often utilized by persons who have ulterior motives for causing difficulties for the non-conformant individuals. Not infrequently the prosecutions represent attempts by sheriffs, prosecutors, or other law enforcement officers to work off personal or political grudges . . ." (Ref. 12, p. 429).

clude both a promise and a vow; some only one or the other.[3] Some require a promise to cleave only to one another, some do not. Some require a forsaking of all others; a few do not mention this.[4] But almost every promise and/or vow incorporates permanence. This vow or promise is for keeps, till death parts them. Permanence, in brief, is more emphasized than exclusivity in the marital promises and vows.

The precise meaning of what is promised or vowed—to love, comfort, cherish, and so on—has been elaborated by one pair of commentators. Love, they tell us, means that one will treat the spouse affectionately. Comfort means that one will impart strength, cheer, encourage, gladden, as opposed to dispiriting, distressing, discouraging, saddening, or nagging. And the promise or vow to forsake all others includes more than other men or women as objects of attraction. It may include loving one's mother more than one's spouse, or children more than husband. It includes even imaginary clinging to old flames. Just thinking "If I had only married so-and-so instead of you!" constitutes a breach of this promise. And the fantasy of other sex partners does also (Ref. 7, p. 49). On the basis of this logic, a good case could also be made for including the man who prefers his work to his wife, a situation documented at least for some tycoons and no doubt characteristic of many ambitious professional men also.

Of special interest is the interpretation by two commentators of the promise or vow to forsake all others as not demanding a too-rigid definition of exclusivity: "the right of husband or wife to the primary love of the other does not justify an insistence on exclusive possession nor condone jealousy of innocent friendships" (Ref. 5, p. 50). Satiety and boredom should be avoided; external relationships should be encouraged. To be sure, these commentators are not advocating external *sexual*

---

3 The Common Book of Prayer specifies the following promises: "Wilt thou love her, comfort her, honor her, cherish her, and keep her; and forsaking all others, cleave thee only unto her, so long as ye both shall live?" "Wilt thou love him, honor him, inspire him, cherish him and keep him; and forsaking all others, cleave thee only unto him, so long as ye both shall live?" (Ref. 4). The Protestant Episcopal promise includes: to have, to hold, to love, to cherish; the vow includes, for both partners, to have, live together, love, comfort, honor, keep and forsake all others. The Lutheran promise: to take, plight troth; the vow, to love, have, comfort, honor, keep, and forsake all others. The Presbyterian promise: to promise and covenant to be loving and faithful; the vow, to have, love, honor, live with, cherish. The Baptist promise: to take, have, hold, love, cherish; the vow, to take, love, honor, cherish, and forsake all others. The Methodist promise: to have, hold, love, cherish. The Ian Maclaren Service vow: take, love, cherish, give loyalty; the wife vows to take, love, and honor. The Community Church Service vow: to take, live together, love, honor, trust, serve, be true and loyal. The scriptural service vow: to take, love, cherish, have, hold, forsake all others, cleave to one another (Ref. 13).

4 Some include the forsaking in the promise, some in the vow, some in both, some in neither.

relationships; but it is interesting that innocent friendships—whatever that may mean—are not forbidden by the marital vows.

When we ask, therefore, what promises or vows are broken by marital infidelity, the answer is that they are promises to love, to honor, to cherish, and to comfort as well as to forsake all others and, in some cases, to cleave to one another. Strictly and narrowly interpreted, then, whenever one or both spouses ceased to love, honor, cherish, or comfort one another, they would be guilty of infidelity in the sense of reneging on a sacred promise. And, indeed, many men and women do in fact interpret infidelity in this way. But for our purposes here the common conception of infidelity, though inadequate, is accepted.

To make a distinction between adultery and infidelity does not mean that there is an inconsistency involved. Any kind of extramarital sexual relations constitutes a violation of the law and hence, by definition, adultery, a crime, an offense against the state. But they are not necessarily, nor in all cases, as we shall note presently, viewed by the spouse as an offense against him (her) or as infidelity.

Infidelity and Deprivation

If there is no deprivation of a spouse—of promised love, honor, cherishing—has a promise been violated? If a husband's relations with another woman do deprive his wife so that she suffers a real loss—emotional, sexual, or financial—there can hardly be any question that he has violated a promise; he is unfaithful to her. He is, in the popular conception, "cheating on her." Even those who accept extramarital relationships would probably not condone such deprivation of a spouse. But suppose a husband still "cleaves to his wife," that is continues to live with her, to support her, to assume all his responsibilities toward her, even to love her—perhaps more than ever[5]—so that there is no deprivation, can he still be accused of infidelity? And vice versa?

We do not know, of course, in what proportion of cases deprivation is present. On the assumption that, if infidelity causes no difficulty in a marriage, there is no deprivation present, we may find one clue in the Kinsey data, which show that so long as spouses did not know about extramarital relationships no damage was reported: "Extra-marital

---

5 There are some individuals . . . whose sexual adjustments in marriage have undoubtedly been helped by extramarital experience. . . . Some women . . . make better adjustments with their husbands. Extramarital intercourse has had the effect of convincing some males that the relationships with their wives were more satisfactory than they had realized" (Ref. 11, p. 593). "Sometimes sexual adjustments with the spouse had improved as a result of the female's extramarital experience" (Ref. 12, p. 433). These authors cite earlier studies also reporting improved marital relationships after extramarital experiences. Robert A. Harper arrives at the same conclusion (Ref. 9, pp. 384-391). One young man, discussing wife-swapping clubs, rejected the idea that infidelity was involved; the practice often enhanced the marital bonds.

relationships had least often caused difficulty when the other spouse had not known of them. . . . Some of the extramarital relationships had been carried on for long periods of years without ill effects on the marital adjustment" (Ref. 12, p. 434). Not any deprivation to the spouse but knowledge of the relationship was the damaging factor: "The extramarital coitus had not appeared to do as much damage as the knowledge that it had occurred" (Ref. 12, p. 434). Othello had taught us this long ago.[6]

But how often, one may legitimately ask, does the spouse know? Among marriages in which the wife had engaged in extramarital relations, the husband was not aware of the situation in about half (51 percent) of the cases; he knew in 40 percent; and suspected in about 9 percent (Ref. 12, p. 434). But even among the 49 percent in which the husband knew or suspected, there was no difficulty reported—and presumably, therefore, no deprivation—in about two-fifths (42 percent) of the cases (Ref. 12, p. 434).[7] If, as estimated by Kinsey and his associates, 71 percent of the marriages in which extramarital relations of wives had occurred had not developed difficulties (Ref. 12, p. 434), the inference seems justified that deprivation was not involved. The wife's extramarital relationship did not deprive the husband[8]—at least not enough to create difficulties.

Forms of Infidelity

To speak, as we have done so far, as though extramarital relationships were all of a kind, simple and unidimensional, is of course misleading. They are of many kinds and assume different forms. It would

---

[6] I swear 'tis better to be much abus'd
Than but to know't a little. . . .
What sense had I of her stolen hours of lust?
I saw 't not, thought it not, it harm'd not me.
I slept the next night well, fed well, was free and merry;
I found not Cassio's kisses on her lips.
He that is robb'd, not wanting what is stolen,
Let him not know 't, and he's not robb'd at all. . . .
I had been happy, if the general camp,
Pioneers and all, had tasted her sweet body,
So I had nothing known. O, now, for ever
Farewell the tranquil mind! farewell content!
Farewell the plumed troop, and the big wars,
That makes ambition virtue; O, farewell! . . . (Ref. 18)

[7] The proportion of cases in which there was serious difficulty when known by the husband was identical—42 percent—to the proportion of cases in which there was no difficulty at all when known (Ref. 12, p. 434).

[8] The proportion would probably be even higher in the reverse situation, that is, where it was the husband who engaged in the extramarital relations, for women were only half as likely as men to rate spouse's extramarital coitus as a major factor in divorce 27 percent and 51 percent respectively (Ref. 12, p. 438). If, however, the husband were diverting part of a modest family income to another woman, the wife might well feel that she was being deprived.

be possible to draw up a complex systematic matrix inclusive of all combinations of duration, seriousness, and intensity of relationships and discuss each cell individually. Instead, discussion here is limited to only a few forms as they have been reported in the literature.

1. Of perhaps least moral and social significance is the kind of relationship which takes the form of coquetry and flirtation—"making love without meaning it"—commonly accepted in many social circles; no seriousness is attached to it by either party or by their spouses. Sapirstein finds a functional use for it:

> The normal flirtatiousness and minor conquests which are part of every social gathering give ample opportunities for testing out the old desires. These can be shared and enjoyed together without the necessity of continually proving in the open market one's residual desirability in the romantic chase. While such a compromise is difficult in the framework of our monogamous culture . . ., it seems to be one of the few available compensations in this sensitive problem (Ref. 17, p. 173).

And this kind of relationship may be comprised in the "innocent friendship" which Easton and Robbins believe is not required to be forsaken (Ref. 7, p. 49).

This form of relationship may even include physical embrace or petting. Kinsey and his associates found that "at dinner parties, cocktail parties, in automobiles, on picnics, and at dances, a considerable amount of public petting is allowed between married adults" (Ref. 12, p. 426). At the time Kinsey and his associates were gathering their data, 16 percent of their women subjects had engaged in such extramarital petting. Kinsey was of the opinion that this kind of behavior was increasing, though he did not feel he could document such a conclusion from the data.

2. Conceivably more serious is the transient, even fly-by-night, sex-as-play form, a sometime thing that leaves little residue except as it may leave a precipitate of guilt. About 11 percent of the Kinsey female subjects (42 percent of the 26 percent who had engaged in extramarital relations) had limited their experiences to a period of one year or less. Roughly the same proportion had had only one partner. Rather than a regularly spaced pattern, it was "more usual to find several non-marital contacts occurring in the matter of a few days or in a single week when the spouse is away on a trip, or when the female is traveling and putting up at a hotel, or at a summer resort, or on an ocean voyage, or visiting at a friend's home" (Ref. 12, p. 420).

3. Quite different is what Helen Gurley Brown labels "the matinee." This is a purely playful relationship which arises between working men and women who use the lunch hour for their rendezvous at her apartment. The basic rule for such a relationship is "Never become serious." The hazards, beyond that of being found out—for, of course, it

must be secret—are that one partner or the other might become bored or fall in love and thus become serious. Either eventuality is fatal to the relationship. In fact, to forestall the likelihood that it may become serious, one of the conditions of success of the matinee is that one or both partners be happily married to others (Ref. 3, Chapter 9).

4. What might be called a quasi-matinee form of infidelity has been reported on by a team of sociologists, a form which they call the cocktail-lounge relationship (Ref. 16). Its salient characteristics, so far as they are relevant here, may be summarized as follows:

> The cocktail-lounge model is a semiserious, semicommitted relationship, semistable; that is, it is of more than transitory duration, definitely not a "pick-up" relationship in the usual sense. It tends to occur among fairly high-status individuals. Most of both men and women in the reported study had had at least some college education. The men were in business and professional occupations; most of the women were either college students (20 percent) or secretaries (33 percent). The employees of the cocktail lounge judged most (80 percent) of both the men and the women to be "stable,". . . The "natural history" of such relationships was one in which after a year or two the women marry (or remarry) and leave the system and are replaced by another cohort. The men do not drop out unless they have to leave town or, in some cases, become too old for these activities. In no case was the marriage of the man reported as disrupted (Ref. 1, pp. 69-70).

The men tended to average in their late thirties, the women in their midtwenties, the medians being 39 and 24 respectively.

5. There is, next, the long-lasting pseudo-marital form of infidelity, a relationship which Cuber has found to be very similar to conventional marriage:

> The dynamics of . . . these relationships . . . break with conventional stereotypes about them which generally run to assertions that such relationships typically follow a cycle which begins in infatuation, has a relatively short decline, ends in disillusionment, a new partner is found, and the cycle is repeated. We found examples fitting this model, to be sure, but typically the cases were otherwise. . . . In the prolonged . . . relationships there is often no more a "cycle" than there is to intrinsic marriage—the relationship is monogamous, continues "until death. . . ." Where there is a cycle in any real sense, it tends to be like the cycle in a goodly number of marriages. These relationships, like marriage, sometimes move from vitality and a strong erotic accent to a more matter-of-fact, comfortable kind of interaction. Surprisingly enough, some have settled into a kind of apathy which makes one wonder why they go on, since there are no institutional obligations involved. But perhaps senti-

ment and a quiescent kind of attachment may be stronger bonds than external social sanctions (Ref. 5).

Cuber does not judge these relationships to be any more vulnerable than sanctioned unions. They appear to have powerful intrinsic supports which psychiatrists are in a better position to evaluate than laymen. Even to a layman, however, it is apparent that there must be overriding reasons why the partners in such relationships have not married. The relationship looks very much like polyandrous marriage. Kinsey and his associates reported similar unions among their male subjects (Ref. 11, p. 593). And among the 9 percent of their women subjects who had engaged in extramarital relationships for four or more years, there must have been some of the 11 percent who had had only one partner (Ref. 12, p. 420).

6. Fantasied infidelity—relations with an imagined partner or imagined relations with a real person—is certainly far more common than acted-out infidelity, but, according to St. Matthew, no less real. "I say to you that every one who looks at a woman lustfully has already committed adultery with her in his heart" (Ref. 14). Just daydreaming. Even, presumably, looking at Playmate of the Month. Or at any miniskirted girl on the street. From this point of view it would be difficult for any man not to be judged guilty of adultery, however conformist his overt behavior might be. Or any woman, either, for that matter, who had been exposed to the seduction of an entertainment world personality. Or either husband or wife who fantasies another partner, real or imaginary, in the sex act.

This fantasy form of infidelity has been given some research attention by a team who interviewed 40 suburban couples in business-professional occupations, averaging about 30 years of age (Ref. 15). They included sexual and emotional involvements as well as merely fantasy involvement and correlated their findings with measures of marital satisfaction and of "conscience."[9] They found, expectably enough, that "the less satisfied persons seek . . . satisfaction in fantasy" more than others do, but the same was not true with respect to the conscience variable. Those with high conscience scores were as likely as those with low conscience scores to have fantasy involvement.[10]

This lack of relationship between conscience score and fantasy involvement seems to contradict Sapirstein's conclusions based on his experience with patients:

---

9 Marital satisfaction was measured on the basis of replies to 15 statements such as "My spouse loves me, confides in me, shows me affection . . ." completely, fairly much, somewhat, little, or not at all. Conscience was measured on the Psychopathic Deviate scale of the Minnesota Multiphasic Personality Inventory, a score of 61 or more indicating low conscience and a score of 60 or less, high conscience.

10 The low conscience subjects were, however, more likely than high conscience subjects to show sex involvement.

> The inability to face the extramarital urge frequently has a disruptive effect on the marriage. When these feelings are repressed into the unconscious, they almost invariably are associated with hostility to the marital partner. The man may feel that his wife is playing a potentially punishing role toward him for his thoughts of infidelity, and he may begin to resent her. . . . He may be unable to accept this hostility, and live in constant preoccupation and terror about his sexual thoughts (Ref. 17, pp. 173-174).

Perhaps the seeming conflict between Sapirstein and Neubeck is more apparent than real. The fantasy involvement may be present in almost everyone, but it may be a source of disturbance in only a few.

There seem to be no research reports on the relative frequency of the fantasy of the ideal surrogate lover we are told sometimes takes the place of the actual spouse in the coital act in order to render the experience more palatable.

7. There is a kind of noncoital, nonfantasy relationship which involves a profound sharing of the self with another, not a spouse, that is not adulterous in the legal sense though susceptible to the charge of infidelity. Such a situation was depicted in a recent London and Broadway play in which the wife is—justifiably—more fearful of the Platonic intimacy between her husband and another woman than she would have been of a coital relationship. The kind of relationship which can develop between men and women who work together as a team over a period of time sometimes assumes an emotional interdependence outweighing the marital bonds of either one without supplanting them. These may be among the innocent relationships which, according to Easton and Robbins, are not forbidden by the marital vows. It is an index of our relative concerns that little research attention has been devoted to this kind of relationship.[11]

Patterns by Sex, Age, and Class

By the age of 40, about twice as many of the Kinsey male subjects as of the female subjects had engaged in extramarital relations (50 and 26 percent respectively) (Ref. 12, p. 437).

In the Middle Ages when a man was to be away from his wife for any length of time he clamped her into a chastity belt to protect her, presumably, not only against trespassing males but also against her own carnality. Women reared in our society present—or have, until recently, presented—a somewhat different picture:

> Most males can immediately understand why most males want extramarital coitus. . . . To most males the desire for variety in sexual activity seems as reasonable as the desire for variety in the

---

11 A considerable amount of attention is devoted to "innocent" relationships in one reference (Ref. 2).

books that one reads, the music that one hears, the recreations in which one engages, and the friends with whom one associates socially. On the other hand, many females find it difficult to understand why any male who is happily married should want to have coitus with any female other than his wife (Ref. 12, p. 409).

And their specific findings corroborated this conclusion; the patterns with respect to extramarital relationships differed considerably between the sexes.

Before age 25, for example, there was no relation between years of education and active incidence of extramarital relations among women; among men, there was lower incidence among the more educated. After age 25, however, education made little difference among the men, but among women the active incidence was positively related to education, higher, that is, among the better educated (Ref. 12, p. 437). The period of greatest incidence among women was in the age bracket 36 to 40 (17 percent); among men it was highest in the late teens (35 percent) and declined consistently thereafter (Ref. 12, p. 437). In general, the incidence among men tended to be more regularly spaced; among women, as noted earlier, more sporadic.

But far the most interesting finding was one with respect to frequency of coitus per week among those who engaged in extramarital relations. In the early years it was four times greater among the men than among the women (0.4 and 0.1 respectively); in the early thirties, the frequencies were the same for both sexes (0.2). But in the early forties (41-45), it was twice as high among women as among men (0.4 and 0.2 respectively (Ref. 12, p. 437). These data suggest that, although women were less disposed to engage in extramarital coitus, when they did, it was with greater frequency.

Infidelity Tolerance

A useful concept for thinking and researching and, hence, ultimately, for counseling, might have to do with the relative tolerance of infidelity which spouses show. For such purposes we might think in terms of a gradient. For example, a spouse might: (1) reject infidelity and divorce the partner, (2) reject the infidelity but not divorce the partner, (3) accept the infidelity grudgingly, under duress, (4) accept the infidelity willingly, or (5) urge or encourage infidelity. Both ends of this continuum have been documented in the literature (Ref. 12, pp. 434-435). One's "infidelity tolerance" seems to be related to age, to sex, and to class. Women until now have tended to be more resigned to infidelity than men; about twice as many husbands (51 percent) as wives (27 percent) considered extramarital relations of their spouses as a factor in their divorces (Ref. 12, pp. 436, 438). The evidence with respect to age is not so clear-cut, but it appears that older men and women firmly anchored in a long-standing marriage tend to hesitate before breaking it up for infidelity. "In time," Kinsey notes, " love, jealousy, and morality seemed less important, and the middle-aged and older females had become more inclined to accept extramarital coitus and at least some of the husbands no longer objected if their wives engaged in such activities" (Ref. 12, p. 417). The wives of working-class men are often reared in an ethnic tradition which accepts infidelity in young men as a matter of course, as something to bear if not to grin about. In general, the cultural context in which the infidelity occurs seems to be as important as the specific situation itself, if not more so, in determining the level of "infidelity tolerance."

The Winds of Change

Despite the prevalence of the several forms of infidelity, the public for the most part still gives lip service to the standard of marital exclusivity.[12] But there are several straws in the wind which suggest that we are veering in a different direction, that attitudes, values, and behavior are changing with respect to this standard. Among these straws in the wind are: (1) the increasing emphasis on the positive aspects of extramarital relationships by researchers; (2) the greater tolerance shown at least by some theologians or ethicists; (3) the position vis-à-vis adultery in current thinking about divorce legislation; and (4) the increase in extramarital relationships among younger women.

1. One of the most interesting indications of change now taking place is the apologia which is becoming fashionable among researchers in discussing extramarital relationships. It has now become the positive, functional aspects which are increasingly emphasized rather than, as in the past, the negative and dysfunctional aspects. Kinsey and his associates noted in 1948 that the research literature to date was almost uniformly unfavorable in its judgment. "Only an occasional writer suggests that there may be values in such experience which can be utilized for human needs" (Ref. 11, p. 591). And in 1953 they pointed out that "certainly any scientific analysis must take into account the fact that there are both advantages and disadvantages to engaging in such activity" (Ref. 12, p. 491).

Gerhard Neubeck, on the basis of his research and counseling, has

---

12 On a television program broadcast January 23, 1966, 88 percent of a national sample said they believed that adultery was wrong for women and about the same number, 86 percent, that it was wrong for men as well. These proportions of the sample were not very much higher than for premarital relations: 76 percent felt them wrong for women and 72 percent for men. More than half (57 percent) considered it wrong even for engaged couples. The conditions under which the questions were administered were not described so we have no way of knowing how much of an incentive there was for overstating a conforming attitude. With respect to extramarital relations, 26 percent of the sample—more men than women—would, it was reported, consider them acceptable under certain circumstances.

also concluded that there may be a positive function for extramarital relations in many marriages.

> Marriage cannot serve to meet all of the needs of both spouses at all times. Many marriage partners define at least implicitly—certainly discretely—what area of satisfaction they will leave to outsiders, and they are not only *not* disturbed that outsiders serve in this capacity but probably relieved that they themselves are not called upon to have to address themselves to each and every need or whim of their mates. In this sense the extramarital relationship becomes supplementary to the marriage relationship (Ref. 14a, p. 15).

The current trend seems sometimes to be, in fact, not only in the direction of tolerance but even, in some cases, of advocacy. Some wives, Sapirstein notes, are relieved to find that the marriage is suffering from nothing more serious than infidelity. "If that's all that is bothering you, go ahead and get it out of your system, but please don't become emotionally involved" (Ref. 17, p. 174).

2. This positive evaluation has also found acceptance in the so-called situational school of ethics among some theological thinkers. Thus Joseph Fletcher, professor in the Episcopal Theological School of Cambridge, Massachusetts, writing in the Catholic *Commonweal*, has this to say:

> There is nothing against extramarital sex as such, in this ethic, and in *some cases* it is good.... The *Christian* criteria for sex relations are positive: sex is a matter of certain ideals of relationship. These ideals are based upon a certain faith: about God, Christ, the Church, who man is, and his destiny. Therefore, if people do not embrace that faith (and most do not), there is no reason why they should live by it. And most do not.... If true chastity means a marital monopoly, then let those who believe in it recommend it by reason and example. Nothing is gained by condemning the unbeliever. Indeed to condemn him is more unjust (immoral) than a sexual escapade (Ref. 8, p. 431).

In this emphasis on sincerity and emotional authenticity, Joseph Fletcher is articulating the creed professed and practiced by a certain segment of the younger population today. They too make a big thing about authentic emotion, about fidelity in the sense of being true to their own inner selves. They object to the games people play and to what they call adult hypocrisy. The enormous emphasis on authentic emotion, on fidelity, on sincerity tends to make the criterion for judging a relationship the way people feel rather than objective sanctions. One is reminded of George Sand's *obiter dictum* that the hours a woman spent with her lover were true and good; the nights she spent with an unloved husband were sinful and bad.

3. Another straw in the wind has to do with the trends in divorce legislation. I had occasion not long ago to review the grounds alleged for

divorce over a period of time as an index or measure of our society's legal specifications for marriage. The permitted legal grounds have not changed very rapidly, but the grounds used have tended to change from a frequent use of adultery [13] to a more frequent use of cruelty. Now we are in process of arriving at the concept of the no-fault divorce. Under this new conception, all that is necessary is for a court to find that the marriage has broken down. The only proof needed will probably be a separation for a specified period of time. Until now—by universally accepting extramarital relations as grounds for divorce—we have demanded fidelity as a legal obligation of both spouses. With the introduction of the no-fault concept of divorce, such fidelity is no longer legally defined as part of marriage. That is, a person who engages in extramarital relationships but does not wish to have a divorce cannot necessarily be divorced for this reason alone. If the spouse wishes a divorce he or she will have to separate him or herself from the other and prove in this way that the marriage has in fact broken down. The separation, not the extramarital relations, is the proof the court will need to prove that the marriage has broken down. Unless someone wishes to prosecute a man or woman for the crime of adultery, it will disappear from the scene as a legal entity for all intents and purposes.

4. There is, finally, evidence of change in the actual behavior of women over time. Kinsey and his associates reported among their subjects that by age 40, more than a fifth (22 percent) of the women born in the nineteenth century had engaged in extramarital coitus; almost a third (30 percent) of those born in the twentieth century had. At age 45, the proportions were 21 and 40 percent respectively. By age 25, only 4 percent of the nineteenth century women had engaged in such relations; twice as many (8 percent) of those born in the first decade of the twentieth century had; even more, 10 percent, of those born in the second decade had; and 12 percent of those born in the 1920's (Ref. 12, pp. 422-424).[14] It would be logical to assume that, for women born in the 1930's and 1940's, now in their twenties and thirties, the proportion who have or will have engaged in extramarital relations by age 25 is or will be not less than, let us say, about 15 percent.[15]

---

13 We know that a considerable proportion of married men and women at some time or other engage in extramarital relations (about half of the men and a quarter of the women), but adultery is rarely alleged in actual divorce. A survey of 1272 readers of the *Ladies Home Journal* in 1968 reported that 74 percent did not think a single act of adultery by either spouse should necessarily be a cause for divorce.

14 The incidence was somewhat higher among educated women after age 25 than among less educated. Increasing education over time may therefore tend to accelerate the trend if the relationship between education and extramarital relations continues.

15 The increasing salience of "wife-swapping clubs" and other forms of extramarital relationships may accelerate this trend. I am indebted to Dr. Edward J. Rydman, executive director of the American Association of Marriage Counselors, for one such example, namely, Club Rebel "formed to serve the sophisticated new generation and . . . dedicated to those who have rebelled at outdated codes and morals. . . . (Personal letter, December 30, 1968).

Wave of the Future: Permanence or Exclusivity?

In the rapidly growing form of nonmarital relationship which young people are evolving today (Ref. 1), especially on university campuses, there are no vows of permanence. Nor are there any legal sanctions to buttress exclusivity. The emphasis seems to be on fidelity based on authentic emotion. One unpublished study of such relationships by Michael Johnson at the University of Iowa reports great emphasis on exclusivity, at least for the duration of the relationship. Among the findings with respect to 28 couples are the following with respect to fidelity:

> Does living together involve some conception of fidelity? The unmarried couples were asked two questions concerning their attitudes toward "adultery": "Under what conditions do you feel it would be all right for you to sleep with someone other than your partner?" and "Under what conditions do you feel it would be all right for your partner to sleep with someone other than you?" It is interesting to note that the respondents tend to put more restrictions on themselves than do their partners. Thus 48 percent of the males as compared to 39 percent of the females say that under no conditions would it be all right for the male partner to sleep with someone else. But 59 percent of the females as opposed to 44 percent of the males say that under no conditions would it be all right for the female partner to sleep with someone else. Less than a fifth of the respondents would accept such a relationship under any conditions at all. Once again we find the females more likely to be double-standard than the males. A somewhat extraordinary discovery is that 11 percent of both males and females are double-standard in the direction of more freedom for the female. . . . As for sexual behavior, the females in our sample have more often encountered the opportunity to sleep with someone else, 78 percent having had a chance as opposed to 64 percent of the males. However, when given the chance the male is more likely to take advantage of it (Ref. 10).

The young men are theoretically more permissive with respect to women than to themselves, but less "faithful" to their partners than the young women are in the presence of temptation.

But what seems more interesting is a rough comparison with the Kinsey findings of a generation ago. If we equate the Kinsey data on the attitude that extramarital coitus justifies divorce with the Johnson data on the attitude that such relations on the part of one's partner are never justified—admittedly not a completely legitimate equating of statements from a scientific point of view, but suggestive—we arrive at Table 1. The most interesting conclusions are to the effect that more of the young people in the Johnson sample seem to adhere to the standard of exclusivity than of the subjects in the Kinsey sample. The one exception is the attitude of the men toward extramarital relations on the part of women: here the Kinsey men seem to be more conservative. But a disparity of only 7 percentage points in a comparison in which one set of subjects numbers only 28 cases is not large enough to be unequivocally credited (cell A, Table 1).

Table 1 Attitude Toward Infidelity by Conventional Spouses and by Partners in Nonmarital Unions*

	Males in		Females in	
Attitude Toward Fidelity	Conventional Unions, %	Nonmarital Unions %	Conventional Unions, %	Nonmarital Unions%
Extramarital relations by wife or partner cause for divorce, or never justified.	(A) 51	44	(B) 14	59
Extramarital relations by husband or partner cause for divorce, or never justified.	(C) 18	48	(D) 27	39

*Source: references 10 and 12.

In the other cells the disparities—especially in cell B and cell C—are large enough to be taken seriously even in so small a set of cases. The young women in the Johnson sample were far less tolerant of extramarital relations by women than the Kinsey women were, 59 percent as contrasted with only 14 percent (cell B). They were also less tolerant than the Kinsey women of extramarital relations by men (cell D). The disparity was only a matter of 12 percentage points (39 as compared with 27 percent) and may therefore only hover on the brink of statistical significance. But the disparity of 30 percentage points—48 and 18 percent—seems to me conclusive that the Johnson male subjects were more conservative with respect to extramarital relations of men than were the Kinsey subjects (cell C).

I add all this up to mean that the women in the relationships which did not promise permanence were more conservative in their attitudes toward extramarital relations both for men and for women than were the women in the Kinsey sample, and that the Johnson sample men were more conservative than the Kinsey men so far as exclusivity for men was concerned. Exclusivity seemed more important than permanence.

A *caveat* is in order. The factor of age may invalidate any reading of the accompanying table. The Kinsey data included more older subjects, and older spouses probably have more "infidelity tolerance" than younger people. Permanence far outweighs exclusivity on their scale of values, as we noted above in our discussion of infidelity tolerance. We may, therefore, be comparing young people with low "infidelity tolerance," in a naturally conservative stage of the union, with older people in a less conservative stage, with high "infidelity tolerance." In any event, in these nonpromiscuous relationships, the relative emphasis seemed to be on exclusivity rather than on permanence.[16]

Jealousy and Anxiety

From a psychiatric standpoint two facets of the problem of infidelity seem to warrant at least cursory mention: male jealousy and female security. Kinsey and his associates made a considerable point of the mammalian origin of male jealousy. "While cultural traditions may account for some of the human male's behavior, his jealousies so closely parallel those of the lower species that one is forced to conclude that his mammalian heritage may be partly responsible for his attitudes" (Ref. 11, p. 411). And Edward Westermarck, the great historian of human marriage, was of the opinion that monogamy rested on male jealousy. (Volume 1, Chapter 9). But Kingsley Davis, a sociologist, argues precisely the opposite point of view. Monogamy, by granting exclusivity to males, gives rise to jealousy. He sees jealousy as an institutional prop for monogamy. "Where exclusive possession of an individual's entire love is customary, jealousy will demand that exclusiveness. Where love is divided it will be divided according to some scheme, and jealousy will reinforce the division" (Ref. 6, p. 184).[17] I shall not go further into Davis' subtle and sophisticated analysis; this statement does not, obviously, do it justice. But I would like to suggest that jealousy as a prop for monogamous relationships seems to be in process of attrition. How many cases has any of you treated lately in which jealousy was an important element? How many plays has anyone seen which dealt with jealousy? How many movies? Television programs? Books?[18]

If male jealousy has been seen as a major support for sexual exclusivity, anxiety and insecurity have served a similar function among women with respect to permanence. As recently as just a few

---

16 There are other young people to whom neither permanence nor exclusivity is important. They believe in communal living in which everyone has access to everyone else, mutual attraction and affection being the only criteria of acceptability. It is doubtful if this pattern will find many adherents in the immediate future.

17 Davis distinguishes jealousy as a reaction to illegitimate seizure of property from jealousy as the result of deprivation of a love-object (Ref. 6, pp. 178-181). From the point of view of competitive concerns, extramarital sexual relations are more threatening than premarital to men. If a girl who has had premarital relations marries a man, he can assume that, everything considered, he was the best sexual partner. At least he had something that compensated for whatever he may have lacked. But in extramarital sexual relations he has no such reassurance. He is competing with a partner or partners who, for all he knows, may be better performers than he. And, further, a woman who has engaged in premarital sexual relations is more likely than one who has not to engage also in extramarital relations (Ref. 12, pp. 427-428).

18 Except, perhaps, in connection with homosexual or Lesbian relationships where the total matrix is so different, where outside support is so equivocal, and where, therefore, normal social processes do not operate.

years ago I was willing to say that extramarital relations had different significance for men and for women. I believed then that a woman could not be casual about such relations, that she was not likely to engage in them unless there was more than a touch-and-go depth to them, that she could not, like men, treat them incidentally. To her they implied a commitment. I am no longer convinced of this. It seems to me now that a new kind of woman is emerging—or, if you will, an old kind is reemerging [19]—on the scene. And one of the distinguishing characteristics of this woman is that she can be casual about sex, as in the past few women could. If women engaged in sexual relations outside of marriage it was because they were involved; the relation meant a great deal to them. Husbands, therefore, were justified in their alarm when they learned of them. But for many women today this is apparently no longer true. They can accept the sex-as-fun point of view without conflict. Even a regular extramarital relationship does not faze them or, in fact, necessarily interfere with their marriages.[20]

I believe that the increasing economic independence of women has played a part in this change.[21] Much of the terror which gripped women whose husbands were unfaithful to them in the past stemmed from the threat it posed to their economic security. What if the other woman won her husband away from her permanently? There is evidence in both Kinsey's statistical and Sapirstein's clinical data that, when or if she was assured that this was not likely, tolerance of infidelity increased.[22] I am, however, far from believing that economic independence tells the whole story, for there are economically indepen-

---

19 Until fairly recently it was taken for granted in many parts of the world that there would be sexual relations if almost any man and woman were alone together for any length of time.

20 An undoubtedly exaggerated illustration of this trend was presented several years ago in Paris where economically successful wives were taking on young lovers. "All of my friends have young friends nowadays. The oldest . . . is 27. . . . There are so many handsome, eager, virile, appreciative young men in Paris, why should any of us ever again put up with men who are older and more tired?" (Ref. 18) The woman quoted was a fortyish manager of a beauty salon.

21 "It's this way," Marianne said. "We are all making money nowadays. We have good jobs and we don't need what your musical comedies call sugar daddies. We can pick and choose and, after all, why not have someone who is young, easy, and amusing?" (Ref. 18a)

22 This is not to deny the anguish or the humiliation of knowing that they were less attractive sexually than the other woman. It is one of the hardest defeats in the world to take. It may be ineffable. Women learn to forgive if they have to, but rarely to forget. The wife quoted by Sapirstein who gave her consent to her husband's infidelity still did not want to know when it happened; it would be too hard to bear. "Don't let me know when you do it. I'll be hurt but I'll live through it" (Ref. 17, p. 174). The same is true of men also, of course. Acceptance of this type of defeat has been almost impossible for men to swallow. The law has been lenient if he resorted to violence, even assault and murder. But even among men change has been rapid.

dent women who are as terrified of losing men as the most economically dependent. The prostitute-pimp relationship is only the most extreme example of a situation which can occur in any setting. For psychological dependency must certainly be included in any analysis of infidelity-tolerance.

Psychological Implications

Economic independence is a fairly simple phenomenon, merely a status, not intrinsic to the person who happens to occupy it. But psychological dependency is a personality trait and hence far more complex. Sapirstein (Ref. 17), in a book that has greatly influenced my own thinking, analyzed the nature of dependency needs in marriage, showing how normal they were, in men as well as in women, and how essential their fulfillment was. The basic function married partners performed for one another was, he showed, precisely that of satisfying the normal dependency needs that everyone experiences. The countless stresses and strains and threats that life subjects us to find alleviation in the unfailing support which in a good marriage can be *depended* upon from a spouse. No matter how helpless we may feel confronted by failure and disparagement in our nonmarital roles, we know that we can *depend* on our spouses to reassure us and build us up. He was writing in terms of threats from outside of the relationship—loss of job or difficulties with the children—which required reassurance from the spouse. But infidelity is a threat within the relationship itself, threatening the spouses with loss or diminution of the very support and reassurance marriage is supposed to supply. If we cannot *depend* on our spouses for such support, we may, Sapirstein notes, turn to others (Ref. 17, p. 170).

In connection with this analysis, I would like to raise a number of questions which psychiatrists are in a better position to deal with than a sociologist.

1. Can you foresee any form of socialization which would obviate the dependency needs which Sapirstein finds so basic in people reared in our society today? If people could be reared in a way that such dependency needs did not exist, what would it do to the nature of the marital bond?

2. If infidelity tolerance in both men and women should increase, what can we expect this to do to the nature of the marital relationship itself? Will it mean marital relationships are so solid, so impregnable, so secure that neither partner feels threatened by infidelity? Or so superficial, so trivial, so expendable, with so little at stake that infidelity really does not matter? Will it mean that there is so little psychological dependency in the relationship that a threat of its loss is only a minor misfortune, not a major catastrophe?

3. The fact that in so many cases infidelity (if not known by the

spouse) seemed to cause no deprivation in the spouse raises an old question: how many people can one love or be attached to at the same time? If one is "true"—in one's own fashion—to several persons at once, what is the quality of the relationships? Does anyone really have enough resources to supply the psychological dependency needs of several persons?[23]

4. If infidelity becomes an acceptable practice, will it be possible for spouses to depend on one another for the psychological support they need? Or will it deprive them of it? Do you accept the findings on deprivation presented above? Can a person supply reassurance to a spouse if involved with someone else?

I am sure a great many other questions have occurred to you. You may even have the answers.

---

23 In Mormon polygyny there were strictly enforced institutionalized rules forbidding favoritism to any wife, which in themselves were doubtless supportive and reassuring. A man had, so to speak, to "ration" his need fulfillment efforts.

REFERENCES

1 Bernard, Jessie: Present demographic trends and structural outcomes in family life today. In: Peterson, J. A. (Ed). *Marriage and Family Counseling, Perspective and Prospect.* New York, Association Press, 1968.
2 Bernard, Jessie: *The Sex Game.* New York, Prentice-Hall, 1968.
3 Brown, Helen Gurley: *Sex and the Office.* New York, Pocket Books, 1965.
4 Common Book of Prayer. In: Leach, W. H. (Ed.): *Cokesbury Marriage Manual,* 1945, 1959.
5 Cuber, J.: Adultery: Reality versus stereotype. Unpublished paper, mimeographed.
6 Davis, K.: *Human Society.* New York, Macmillan, 1949.
7 Easton, B. S., and Robbins, H. C.: *The Bond of Honour, A Marriage Handbook.* New York, Macmillan, 1938.
8 Fletcher, J.: Love is the only measure. Commonweal 83:431, 1966.
9 Harper, R. A.: Extramarital sex relations. In: Encyclopedia of Sexual Behavior. New York, Hawthorn, 1961.
10 Johnson, M. P.: Courtship and Commitment: A Study of Cohabition on a University Campus. University of Iowa Master's Dissertation, 1969.
11 Kinsey, A. C., and associates: *Sexual Behavior in the Human Male.* Philadelphia, Saunders, 1948.
12 Kinsey, A. C., and associates: *Sexual Behavior in the Human Female.* Philadelphia, Saunders, 1953.
13 Leach, W. H. (Ed.): *Cokesbury Marriage Manual,* 1945, 1959.
14 Matthew 5:28.
14a Neubeck, G., and Schletzer, Vera M.: A study of extramarital relationships. Marriage and Family Living 24:279-281, 1962.
15 Neubeck, G.: The Dimensions of the Extra in Extramarital Relations, unpublished paper.
16 Roebuck, J., and Spray, S. L.: The cocktail lounge: A study of heterosexual relations in a public organization. American Journal of Sociology 72: 388-395, 1967.
17 Sapirstein, M. R.: *Emotional Security.* New York, Crown Press, 1948.
18 Shakespeare, W.: Othello, Act III, Scene 3.

18a Sheppard, Eugenia: Sugar daddy's on the shelf. Washington Post, Feb. 9, 1966.
19 Terry, S.: Harassing of black minister brings racism to Vermont. Washington Post, Jan. 2, 1969.
20 Westermarck, E.: *The History of Human Marriage.* New York, Allerton, 1922.

6

THE CONTEMPORARY EXPERIENCE OF ADULTERY: BOB AND CAROL AND UPDIKE AND RIMMER

Gordon Clanton

Gordon Clanton approaches the concept of adultery from a fresh perspective, suggesting that current practice can be analyzed in terms of a two-way typology which includes dimensions of approval-disapproval and clandestine adultery or consensual adultery. Although old-fashioned secretive adultery will probably always be around, Clanton urges researchers to look at ambiguous and consensual adultery as foci of changing ideas on the subject. His concern with consensual adultery leads him to a refinement of the typology, describing three subtypes of consensual adultery. In characterizing these types, Clanton draws on films and novels, making a case for these as a legitimate basis for studying ideas about marriage in our culture. His commentary about the effects of media (especially films and novels) suggests that there is a reciprocal interaction between media and "real life" which creates a readiness for the behavior being described—in this case for a specific form of adultery. Novels and films set the stage for discussion and enable intelligent people to sort out their own values and test their own experiences against the realities proposed by the media. Although the complex relationships between "nature and art" are difficult to understand from the limited research done on media impact, it is clear that media affect sexual behavior in a number of ways; increasing adultery (as defined by Clanton) especially consensual adultery, may be one of these outcomes.

I. A New Style of Adultery

Dawn[1] is an adulteress. Over the years she has had sexual intercourse with a number of men other than her husband. Her first extramarital adventure took place two years after her marriage. Since then she has been involved with a dozen or more men—a few frivolously, several in a deep emotional way, and one seriously enough to make her question her primary relationship to her husband.

Perhaps atypically, Dawn's husband (David) knew about all the extramarital involvements either as they were happening or soon thereafter. Although there have been some moments of hurt and confusion, the attitude of partners affirms Dawn's unusual life-style. They experience little regret and virtually no guilt—and they know the difference between the two. Both of them consciously seek in their relationships with one another and with others an expansion of horizons, a heightening of self-awareness and other-awareness. They are open to what the future will bring. Their lives have no fixed boundaries where friendship and sex are concerned.

Significantly, neither Dawn nor David wish things were otherwise. They appear to have no desire to limit one another's freedom to relate to others—even if such relating sometimes has a sexual component. They do not regard Dawn's extramarital relations as indicative of weakness in their marriage. Indeed, they believe that it is the security they know in their marriage which makes possible Dawn's openness to extramarital experiences.

It cannot be stressed too strongly that (apparently) none of the dissatisfaction and deception and little of the hurt that goes with adultery as it is traditionally understood mark Dawn's life. She is a good wife and mother; she is a competent professional woman. There is apparently nothing pathological or socially-destructive about the way she lives. Hers is a *new-style* adultery, adultery with the knowledge and approval of her husband, adultery without guilt or regret.

Two important questions are pressed upon us by our encounter with Dawn's story: (1) What is the word *adultery* coming to mean? (2) To what resources does one turn for helpful information and insight about the contemporary experience of adultery? This essay aims at beginning to answer these two questions.

II. The Emergent Meaning of Adultery

When a word about whose meaning there was once essential consensus comes to evoke a rather broad spectrum of mutually-exclusive meanings, the word loses its ability to communicate unambiguously. When this happens either new terms must be invented or old definitions reworked in order that meanings be clear.

Adultery is a word in the midst of such a meaning crisis. Not many years ago there was general agreement concerning its denotations and connotations. *Adultery* suggested a married person engaging in sexual intercourse with someone other than his or her legal mate. It was expected that the adulterous pair would make every effort to hide their behavior from others—especially from their spouses. A spouse, upon learning of his or her mate's extramarital adventure, was expected to disapprove, to be hurt and angry, and perhaps to seek (or at least threaten) divorce.

But in the contemporary setting this consensus is less secure. True, for many moderns the word *adultery* still evokes the responses delineated above. But the spectrum of possible understandings has broadened substantially. Some would now seek to apply the label *adultery* to certain positively-valued experiences.

But there are difficulties inherent in such usage. Consider this dictionary definition:

> *Adultery.* The sexual intercourse of two persons, either of whom is married to a third person; unchastity; unfaithfulness.[2]

Note that this definition begins with a value-free description. But then the lexicographer adds: *unchastity; unfaithfulness.* Now a value judgment has been added. Adultery *by definition* seems to involve impurity, infidelity, and lack of virtue.

Yet a growing number of married persons now include extramarital sexual experiences which occur with the knowledge and consent of the spouse as part of their life-styles. Are such extramarital experiences adultery? Yes and no. Yes in that they consist of "the sexual intercourse of two persons, either of whom is married to a third person." But *no* in that the persons involved do not view such experiences as impure (unchaste) nor do they make deception of the spouse part of the adulterous gestalt. How appropriate is the word *unfaithfulness* in describing a sexual relationship of which the spouse knows and approves? Has the husband been *unfaithful* if the wife knows what he has done and does not *interpret* his behavior as unfaithfulness? Clearly, the presumption of a link between "the sexual intercourse of two persons, either of whom is married to a third person" *and* "unchastity; unfaithfulness" is unwarranted as cases accumulate in which this link is inoperative. My own research and that of others is demonstrating that for many persons extramarital intercourse is not necessarily unchaste or unfaithful. Therefore, if the word *adultery* is still to be used, it must be stripped of its negative connotations. *Adultery* must be used neutrally to name a relationship marked by "the sexual intercourse of two persons, either of whom is married to a third person"; if further discriminations are to be made other words will have to be added.

If we wish to be true to etymology (our word *adultery* comes from the Latin *adulterare*, to pollute, to defile), it may not do to speak of "good adultery" or "loving adultery" or "creative adultery." And I have no great urge to quarrel with those who avoid the word *adultery* in reference to positively-valued behaviors. But since neologisms (such as comarital sex, multilateral relationships, and the like) create as many definitional problems as they solve and since their very novelty hampers their effectiveness, I have chosen to encourage an expansion of our understanding of the old word *adultery* so that it can be used to label some extramarital sexual experiences which are *not* unchaste or unfaithful.

The typology which follows aims at supplying a conceptual frame in which the word *adultery* might be better understood. Here I shall list and briefly describe several different kinds of behavior that might properly be called adultery and suggest how they relate to one another and overlap. Such a typology, hopefully, is not a Procrustean bed; it is not created out of nothing so that encountered bits of behavior can be trimmed or stretched to fit it. Rather, the typology arises out of inductive exploration. The actual behaviors encountered by researchers accumulate until certain generalizations and relationships emerge and *these* are summed up in a typology. The typology has no value or integrity other than that which arises because it is helpful in identifying and understanding the real behavior of real people. As such, a typology is a trial balloon, a way in which a writer says, "Here are the generalizations that seem warranted to me. What do *you* think?" In that spirit I offer the following typology.[3]

As a criterion by which to name and arrange extramarital relationships I propose we use *the extent to which the spouse knows and approves of the relationship*. If this mode of analysis is adopted, all adulterous acts and relationships can be arranged along a spectrum which runs from

> *spouse does not know* to
> *spouse knows but does not approve* to
> *spouse knows and approves.*

These three kinds of responses from the spouse of one who commits adultery become the left end, the midpoint, and the right end of a continuum and each of them constitutes an ideal type to analyze adulterous relationships.

So we might have a convenient shorthand way of talking about these types, let us give them names and spatially arrange them thus:

CLANDESTINE ADULTERY	AMBIGUOUS ADULTERY	CONSENSUAL ADULTERY

Now no extramarital relationship necessarily fits neatly into one of these three categories. Many such relationships will have elements of two of the types *or* will be best described as one of several sub-types which will be elaborated below. But, again, let us play with the convenient fictions of these three types and describe in broad strokes what each entails.

Clandestine adultery is the term I propose to describe an extramarital sexual relationship which the adulterer assumes must be kept secret from the spouse. It is expected that if the spouse knew about it, he or she would disapprove. This is the type of relationship that the indiscriminate use of the word *adultery* most frequently connotes for most people.[4]

Ambiguous adultery is marked by an extramarital relationship of which the spouse knows but does not fully approve. The adulterer reveals the involvement without knowing how the spouse will respond—but the expectation is that the response will be marked by something other than complete acceptance. Included here would be cases in which the spouse knows about an extramarital liaison but chooses not to confront the mate and demand an explanation. All adultery which is painfully tolerated as preferable to divorce would also go in this category.[5] In ambiguous adultery the spouse chooses to adapt to the mate's extramarital involvement rather than issue an ultimatum demanding its end.

Consensual adultery is the label I propose for extramarital sexual relationships of which the spouse knows and approves. Here the adultery is viewed by both spouses (at least temporarily and experimentally) as part of their life style—not as an abberation. Although some readers will have difficulty imagining a situation in which one knows and approves of a spouse's adultery, many others will recognize this as something they have done or, at least, have fantasized.[6] Here, then, we are talking about a relatively new style of adultery—adultery without deception, adultery which in the eyes of those involved is *not* marked by unchastity or unfaithfulness.

Clandestine and consensual adultery are mutually-exclusive polar opposites. In the one case the extramarital relationship is hidden from the spouse in the expectation that he or she would disapprove if he or she knew. In the other—and much less common—case, the extramarital relationship is revealed to the spouse who is expected to approve. The label *ambiguous adultery* is proposed for all those "in-between" situations in which the extramarital relationship is made known to the spouse (intentionally or unintentionally) who then responds (or is expected to respond) with something other than approval. Many well-intentioned attempts at consensual adultery are marked by this kind of confusion and pain. Of the married couples I have interviewed who claim to have made consensual adultery a functional part of their relationships, most admit that some of their experiences have been touched by jealousy, misunderstanding, and ambiguity.

Note that these types of adultery are dependent upon the way the married persons understand marriage. An adulterous relationship is categorized on the basis of how the spouse responds *and* how the adulterous party *expects* the spouse will respond.

For the near future, I submit, research and reflection should be focused on ambiguous and consensual adultery. The "old adultery" we always have with us. Clandestine adultery has been studied and editorialized about at great length. The time has come to devote our research energies to the "frontier aspects" of the contemporary experience of adultery.

But all consensual adultery is not alike. I submit that there is value in carrying the typology one step further and laying out three subtypes of consensual adultery. Here perhaps the most helpful criteria are the degree of commitment and the probability of permanence that mark the adulterous relationship. If these criteria are adopted, three subtypes of consensual adultery emerge and together form a spectrum from most commitment and permanence to least commitment and permanence as follows:

GROUP MARRIAGE	OPEN-ENDED MARRIAGE	RECREATIONAL ADULTERY

A *group marriage* is an agreement which links three or more persons in a common projection of a future together, a future marked by spatial propinquity, emotional interdependence, economic sharing, and sexual access to persons in addition to one's legal spouse or primary lover. Group marriage, in other words, is consensual adultery marked by a maximum of commitment and the highest expectation of permanence.[7]

True group marriage is rare but many persons have thought and fantasized about such a venture. Athanasiou and his associates found in their survey of *Psychology Today* readers that

> ... nine percent are in favor of group marriage and another 16% "might be interested." Fewer than half actively disapprove. This topic prompted numerous comments from readers: several said that group marriages strongly appealed to them, but as one put it, they were too "culturally conditioned" to act on the interest.[8]

Catalyst for much of the talk about group marriage is the novel *Proposition 31* by Robert H. Rimmer. Although the four principal characters in the book form a firm and permanent compact—a marriage involving four adults rather than two—most sympathetic readers do not feel drawn to emulate them. But many readers of this book and of Rimmer's other fiction *do* move toward opening their marriages to new possibilities including forms of consensual adultery marked by less commitment and less expectation of permanence than would be the case in group marriage. Group marriage, then, is currently more important as a catalytic construct which inspires openness to rethinking and experimentation than as a blueprint for the future of marriage. Discussions about group marriage might trigger responses involving two other sub-types of consensual adultery.

One common kind of response to reading, talking, and thinking about group marriage is the unorthodox understanding of marriage and marital fidelity which some observers are beginning to call *open-ended marriage*. This label describes a relationship between spouses in which it is understood that each grants the other the freedom to involve himself or herself in important emotional relationships with others with the understanding that sexual sharing may accompany such involvements. Many couples are resentful of the way in which an orthodox understanding of marriage makes it difficult for married persons to have significant and involving friendships with the opposite sex. Some who have taken the step of affirming the worth of deep extramarital friendships have taken the additional step of refusing to exclude the possibility of sexual sharing in the context of such a friendship. Thus the stage is set for a kind of consensual adultery. The resulting extramarital experiences lack the degree of commitment and the expectation of permanence (and, of course, the spatial propinquity and the economic sharing) that are marks of group marriage but such relationships are marked by significant friendship-type commitments, the sharing of affection as well as of bodies, and the relative permanence of lasting friendship. This kind of relationship is becoming more and more common and is deserving of the careful attention of social analysts and helping professionals (psychiatrists, psychologists, social workers, clergymen, and so on).

Recreational adultery is a general label for extramarital sexual experiences marked by a relatively low level of commitment and by the expectation of relative impermanence. The most widely publicized version of recreational adultery is swinging. Swinging usually involves a couple in an exchange of spouses solely for the purpose of sexual play.[9] Emotional involvements are generally discouraged. Swinging parties afford participants large numbers of potential partners. A growing literature describes this kind of sexual sharing.[10]

There are other forms of recreational adultery in which the marriage partners do not participate together. Included here would be approval of a spouse's sexual experience with a pick-up or a prostitute. What all forms of recreational adultery have in common is this: it is expected that there will be little emotional involvement in the extramarital experience. This is in sharp contrast to the kinds of relationships encouraged by an open-ended marriage.

Needless to say, some marriages in which there is a commitment to consensual adultery are open to many, perhaps to all, of the possible variations described here. There is considerable variety in the contemporary experience of adultery. The typology has been offered in the hope that the reader might find it helpful for sorting and grouping—and thus understanding—adulterous relationships of which he has knowledge whether from his own life, from the lives of others, or from fiction he has read. With this conceptual frame in mind, let us return to the second question which Dawn's story presses upon us: To what resources does one turn for helpful information and insight about the contemporary experience of adultery?

III. Helpful Resource Information on "Adultery"

Persons who engage in forms of deviant behavior can't stand alone against the world. (Note: The words *deviant, deviance,* and so on are neutral terms. They carry no implicit value judgment as to the rightness or wrongness of any act or life style.) The rebel, though his strength may be impressive, requires the context of a small community of support. Without the feeling that others share his experience and have the resources to help him understand himself, the deviant experiences unpleasant alienation and anxiety. Dawn and others like her need to know that someone empathizes with them and that there are sources of information and insight relative to the life-style they have chosen.

The truly deviant person seldom has an easy time locating his supportive community and the resources which give meaning to his life-style, but Dawn's situation was especially problematic. Her first affair took place in the 1950's. The "sexual revolution" was years away. Adultery was not so common a topic of conversation then as it is now. There was no body of literature to peruse. In fact, had it not been for the Kinsey Reports, a novice adulteress in the '50s might believe herself to be the only such person in the world! And, of course, the Kinsey studies revealed only *that* people commit adultery. There were few hints as to *why* or *how* or *with what results.* Social science had not yet begun its infatuation with human sexuality.

For the most part neither had helping professionals discovered a use for sex. Nearly all talk about "constructive adultery" still lay in the future. To be sure, a few well paid analysts in big cities could deal nonjudgmentally with extramarital sex, but most counselors, clergymen, physicians, and writers of advice columns—even most bartenders and best friends—tended to view all extramarital sex as ill-advised, improper, or downright sinful.

But Dawn discovered that there *were* sources of insight into some of her feelings and behavior. If adultery was being neglected by social scientists and counselors, it was getting considerable attention from fiction writers. So Dawn (and others like her) sought and found perspective on her life-style by reading novels, plays, and short stories of her own and earlier times.

The fiction she read reminded Dawn that she was not alone; it supplied her need for a supportive community. She knew that others had thought about extramarital sex and she understood herself better because of her encounter with their words, thoughts, and images.

Though we are not quite so deprived of support and sources of insight relative to adultery, perhaps we, like Dawn, could move toward a fuller understanding of the phenomenon, and of our fantasies and experiences of it, through the exploration of fictional treatments. Such is a prime contention of this chapter.

Writers of fiction often treat significant human phenomena long before they attract the attention of most social scientists, counselors, and the like. Unencumbered by methodological commitments, content to speak of one or two human beings without feeling the need to generalize, happy if they say something about the "human condition" but content if they do not, novelists are free to *explore* in a way that most scholars are not. The writer of fiction can link together multiple biographies with no concern to obtain a representative sample. The novelist would rather talk about one real man or woman ("real" as only a fictional character can be real) rather than expound on the most carefully constructed ideal type.

Fictional statements, if they are not always *autobiographical*, are often at least *biographical*. A well-crafted novel or short story invites the reader into some kind of identification with one or more characters in a way that the social scientist's careful profile of "the average American male" never seems to do. The reader of well-written fiction feels that the adventures have really been lived by someone—even if only in the imagination. And because they have been *lived* rather than merely observed from some value-free afar, the events, people, and feelings of good fiction supply the reader with support and resources for living his own adventures. There may be some value in seeing fiction, journalism, and hard-data social science as three different vantage points from which to observe the human adventure. Our understanding of what we are will be impoverished if we overlook any of these approaches.

Parts IV, V, and VI of this essay will presume to locate and discuss three socially-significant pieces of fiction which touch on the contemporary experience of adultery. Each is important for different reasons. Together they embrace the broad spectrum of behaviors which we lump together under the rubric *adultery* and each in its own way contributes to our understanding of the social, cultural, and ethical phenomenon of extramarital sex.

IV. John Updike's *Couples*

Couples by John Updike[11] explores the complex web of adulterous relationships that link eight New England couples in the mid-60s. The adultery portrayed is mostly of the old-style clandestine variety, but

Updike clearly believes that secrecy in such matters is inherently unstable. "An affair wants to spill, to share its glory with the world. No act is so private it does not seek applause"(124).

But Updike's characters make every effort at deception. The landscape is littered with deceived spouses, suspicions, rumors, and revelations. The couples acknowledge in the jokes they make and in the party games they play the existence of the emotional and sexual bonds which they are not free to discuss. The intramarital sparring that results is both amusing and agonizing. For example, one evening after their friends Frank and Janet Appleby have left, Marcia Smith begins to interrogate her husband Harold and this exchange results:

> 'Are you sleeping with Janet?'
> 'Why, are you sleeping with Frank?'
> 'Of course not.'
> 'In that case, I'm not sleeping with Janet.' (149)

But, of course, Marcia and Harold *are* both having affairs (with Frank and Janet, respectively). In time this becomes known among the four of them. They acknowledge their adulterous bonds and try to incorporate them into a conflict-free life-style but in this the Applesmiths (as the other couples name their foursome) are never wholly successful. Rather, Updike tells us that a "pattern of quarrel and reunion, of revulsion and surrender, was repeated three or four times that winter."(171)

Two other couples, the Saltzes and the Constantines, seem to have extramarital experiences of one another which almost fit into the consensual category but the Saltines (as the others dub these four) are on the fringes of Updike's narrative so we are not allowed to fully explore their relationship.

The central figure in *Couples* is Piet Hamema who beds down with no fewer than four other women in addition to his wife Angela. There are two emotionally-involving relationships and two less important ones. His affair with Foxy Whitman finally leads to his divorcing Angela and marrying Foxy. Piet suffers a lot. The logistics of deception and the accumulation of guilt complicate his life incredibly. As another novelist, Felix Bastian, has written:

> Sexual eccentricity has been interpreted as monstrous evil by the moralists, as a disease by the psychoanalysts, and as a matter of taste by various libertarians. What has been commonly overlooked in these, no doubt, worthwhile exegeses of the phenomenon is its everyday character as a mass of technical difficulties. [12]

Yet Piet seems never to give very serious consideration to abandoning his life-style. Adultery, despite its burdens, is too important to give up. In the words of the *Time* magazine review:

> Trapped in their cozy catacombs, the couples have made sex by turns

their toy, their glue, their trauma, their therapy, their hope, their frustration, their revenge, their narcotic, their main line of communication and their sole pitiable shield against the awareness of death. Adultery, says Updike, has become a kind of 'imaginative quest' for a successful hedonism that would enable man to enjoy an otherwise meaningless life.[13]

This notion of adultery as a location of ultimate concern, of adultery as an alternate religion, is borne out through the testimony of Updike's characters. Angela says of Freddy Thorne:

> He thinks we're a circle. A magic circle of heads to keep the night out. He told me he gets frightened if he doesn't see us over a weekend. He thinks we've made a church of each other. (12)

Other episodes and images reinforce the link between adultery and ultimate meaning. For Piet, while engaging in adulterous intercourse with Bea Guerin, "Death no longer seemed dreadful."(352) It is not without significance that Piet and his mistress Foxy are the only two of their circle of friends ("except for the Catholics") who go to church. Toward the end of the novel Piet, by then separated from his wife but not yet having moved toward a permanent bond with Foxy, watches an ancient church building burn—"struck by God's own lightning"—and then goes to bed with Carol Constantine.

Adultery, for Updike's characters, is a quest for meaning and adventure but it is a troublesome, even traumatic quest. Marriage is, by its very nature, problematic. In fact, says Updike, "Every marriage is a hedged bet." (48) But adultery is no easy way out. There is no escape from the responsibility of relationships. "The first breath of adultery is the freest; after it, constraints apeing marriage develop."(477)

Society, the couples learn, offers no rulebook for adultery. Those who transgress the boundaries of emotional and sexual monogamy must manufacture their own morality and solve their own problems. They are sailing in uncharted waters. Of the adulterous lovers, Piet and Georgene, Updike tells us: "Lacking a marriage or any contract, they had evolved between them a code of mutual consideration."(57)

But despite everyone's best efforts, the complications seem to win again and again. There are two divorces. The Applesmiths are never quite able to make their foursome work. Freddy Thorne and Carol Constantine are portrayed as pathetically compulsive about their sexuality. At one point Foxy ends her reminiscences of her affair with Piet with this resigned summary: "Adultery. It's so much *trouble*."(343)

Updike leaves it up to the reader to decide whether or not it is *worth* the trouble. Perhaps there is nothing more to say.

> Without a sacramental view of marriage, adultery becomes just a species of "visiting" or saying *Howdy*, and as a perpetually exciting theme of novels it is surely on the wane (15)

The adultery in *Couples* carries a lot of freight for the characters of the novel, but ambiguity marks their experiences of one another and adulterous life-styles prove exceedingly complicated. The reader begins to see something of the sweep and variety of extramarital sexuality, but the novel does not clearly affirm or prescribe. There is no promotion of a philosophy or a program, and few readers, I suspect, will be attracted by Updike's narrative to the life-styles portrayed.

V. Bob and Carol and Ted and Alice

A very different perspective on extramarital sex is offered in *Bob and Carol and Ted and Alice*, a film with screenplay by Paul Mazursky and Larry Tucker.[15]

Bob and Carol Sanders, affluent young marrieds who like to think even younger, attend an encounter marathon at an Esalen-like retreat center and return home to Beverly Hills feeling transformed and liberated. Their best friends, the somewhat less hip Ted and Alice Henderson, seem unable to appreciate the "new" Bob and Carol.

The Sanders' new commitment to candor does not have to wait long for a test. Bob returns from a business trip and confesses an adulterous encounter to Carol who, after being assured that Bob does not love the girl, affirms both the act and his sharing of it. In fact, Carol is so pleased that Bob is free enough to have such an experience and to tell her about it, so pleased with her own positive response, that she tells Ted and Alice the whole story. They are unable to appreciate it. Alice is devastated by the news and, by it, is confirmed in her own antisexuality. Ted, representing clandestine adultery in his attitudes and in his fantasies, thinks Bob was really dumb to tell Carol. When Bob returns (early!) from his *next* business trip, he finds Carol in bed with the friendly neighborhood tennis pro/stud. After an initial outburst of angry jealousy, Bob too is able to affirm his spouse's adultery and her candor about it.

The film's grand finale (I hesitate to call it a climax) is an *attempt* at an orgy. The two couples, pleasantly drunk, go to bed together. Interestingly, it is the women who take most of the initiative in precipitating this encounter. There is embarrassing silence and a little strained extramarital necking but they do not consummate their being together sexually. In fact, Bob and Ted, with Carol naked in the bed between them, begin to discuss the stock market. The film ends with the happy foursome still friends but not lovers. Beyond that, it is hinted that Bob and Carol will not again seek sexual experiences outside of marriage. Bob gives voice to the crucial insight:

> That's it! What the world needs now is love, not this... The trouble with my affair and the trouble with yours, Carol, is just that. There wasn't any love.[16]

The "this" which the world doesn't need is the orgy. The liberated young marrieds had worked the approval of consensual adultery into their marriage covenant but when extramarital sex with affection is tried, two things happen: (1) It does not work. (2) The earlier experiments with sex-just-for-fun are seen as failures and *that* kind of adultery is also ruled out for the future.

Although the film is essentially a slick comedy, it nevertheless offers a few usable insights into the contemporary experience of adultery. Perhaps most important: *Bob and Carol and Ted and Alice* tells a mass audience that consensual adultery exists. For millions of moviegoers this film was a first vivid testimony to the fact that it might actually be possible for extramarital intercourse, with the knowledge and approval of the spouse, to occur. *Bob and Carol and Ted and Alice* is *not* a stag film, *not* a Scandinavian import, *not* a low-budget effort aimed at intellectuals and the youth culture. It is commercial cinema featuring established and rising stars. Although its theme has not been treated in such a film before, *Bob and Carol and Ted and Alice* is not tractarian nor evangelistic. Its appearance means simply this: *American mass society is ready to be entertained rather than offended by adultery.*

Adultery, then, need no longer be bitter, painful and tragic. Adultery can now be *comic*. It can be taken much less seriously than before. The appearance of this *kind* of film about extramarital sex heralds the arrival of a new socio-sexual self-consciousness. Middle America has begun to think about the new-style adultery—adultery in which the spouse is not deceived, adultery which does not necessarily destroy marriages, adultery which (at least experimentally) is incorporated into one's life-style.

In addition to its annunciatory function—and despite its comic format—*Bob and Carol and Ted and Alice* accurately reports some of the interesting dimensions of the "new adultery." Many persons who have participated in encounter groups and related exercises of the human potential movement have in fact been moved to greater candor about their sexual feelings and more than a few have consciously tried adding extramarital sexuality to their understanding and practice of marriage. This kind of alteration of a couple's understanding of marriage is not always easy; it is often painful and conflict-ridden. Many couples who begin these explorations decide against the radical alternatives and discover a deeper commitment to the conventional pattern.

The film's portrayal of the way in which Bob and Carol work through their sharing of their extramarital experiences makes it look too easy *but* it does suggest some of the dynamics of that kind of exchange—and it raises some questions. Does Carol *really* approve of Bob's extramarital adventure or is she just trying to look liberated? Is Bob's response to Carol's experience with the tennis pro a model of mature affirmation or the product of his resolve that he will not be outesalened by his wife?

Another tinge of reality is to be seen in the prominence of the *dare* motif in the almost-orgy scene. Even among the "liberated" there are inhibitions to overcome so alcohol and strange combinations of peer pressure are needed to catalyze movement toward the radical alternative.

Many younger viewers and reviewers saw the ending of the film as a cop-out. Although movie-going America is ready to laugh along with consensual adultery, perhaps we are not yet ready really to affirm it as an option. Maybe the message is that when nice people—and, of course, Natalie Wood and Robert Culp could not play anything *but* nice people—when nice people flirt with adultery, they decide it is not the ideal course. Not only do they decide not to consummate the spouse-swap, Bob and Carol *also* seem to renounce their earlier less-involving adulteries. Note that they are not guilt-ridden or remorseful about their extramarital adventures but they do see them as less than ideal. Monogamy wins this round—but the cultural stage has been set for a major film in which the four-handed bedroom scene does *not* culminate in a discussion of the stock market.

Viewers who are put off by the "cop-out" ending should realize that the film is not *essentially* about adultery or mate-swapping except in an illustrative way. The film's main thrust, it seems to me, is this: Bob and Carol are trying to be young, to participate in the youth culture for which they were born a little too early. Their dress and grooming is modified mod. They smoke marijuana and listen to rock music. They involve themselves politically and esthetically in those things that youth endorse. And yet the final almost-orgy scene is set in Las Vegas, an entertainment center for the middle aged. The intoxicant with which they ready themselves for their liberation is alcohol, not grass. Their decision not to make it sexually is followed by Jackie deShannon singing "What the World Needs Now Is Love." The end of the film is marked not by the driving, sensuous beat of acid rock but rather by the soft sound of what juke box programs call an "adult hit." Despite their efforts, Bob and Carol do not make it into the youth culture. Not this time.

Bob and Carol and Ted and Alice depicts the new adultery not as an end in itself but as a part of the new quest for emotional openness and as a part of the age-old quest for youth and youth's prerogatives. If the film tells us that new sexual styles are not really live options for the over-30s—thus leaving the middle-aged viewer secure in his monogamy—perhaps it also tells us that modes of consciousness are emerging which, in time, will alter the way we define and live the man-woman relationship.

Bob and Carol and Ted and Alice is as humorous as *Couples* is pathetic, yet both convey a kind of ambiguity about adultery and a not-yet-knowing about its future. We are living in the transition time, in a time of not being sure, in a time in which—perhaps—we can shape and reshape values and expectations relative to human sexuality. The Updike novel and the Mazursky/Tucker screenplay both leave us wondering whether or not there is ground for hoping that we might do this wisely and well.

VI. Bob Rimmer's *Proposition 31*

Proposition 31 by Robert H. Rimmer [17] offers several perspectives on the contemporary experience of adultery; the novel has at least something to say about a number of different forms of extramarital relationships.

Horace is married to Tanya and is having an affair with Sylvia. This is a clandestine relationship. Tanya becomes romantically involved with nextdoor neighbor David. Horace finds out about this liaison and he and Tanya deal with it much as Bob and Carol dealt with one another's adulteries—except that in the Rimmer narrative the agony, while short-lived, is more real. David's wife Nancy proves less resilient; the news of the affair almost destroys her. She runs away threatening divorce and even suicide—the extreme stereotyped responses to the discovery of old-style adultery. But she is pursued by Horace who (1) seduces her and (2) convinces her that the four of them should spend some time together and talk things through. The seduction is facilitated by a convenient and very severe snowstorm which forces Horace and Nancy to share a hotel room. Rather improbable logistical accidents of this sort are common in Rimmer's fiction. The author clearly believes that even after a person has begun to liberate himself intellectually, he may yet need the right circumstances to motivate his acting upon his new impulses.

So Horace, professor of sociology and social visionary, convenes a mini-encounter group in a vacation cabin in the wilderness—complete with the books that have made him the self-actualizing person he is. This woodsy cabin scene (part II, chapters 6-9) is the essence of Rimmer. Horace reflects the author's optimism and his conviction that seemingly insurmountable problems can be solved.

> In his enthusiasm, Horace mounted the hearth and jiggled the fire into a roaring flame with a poker. "Leaving Nancy's escapade with Peter Alberti aside, and if my interest in Sylvia had never been discovered, and assuming David's brief fling with his secretary was only a reactive phenomenon, we have just one thing to contend with that makes our marital problems difficult to resolve. Tanya is pregnant and David is the father." (p. 186)

Oh, is *that* all? Rimmer clearly believes that even the thorniest dilemmas can be worked through if mature and secure adults will simply apply themselves and *believe* that they are, in large measure, masters of their fate and architects of their future. Horace continues:

> "Up to the time we discovered one another's infidelities, we were reasonably good friends. I'm not going to pretend that we loved one

another. In the past we may have had moments when we actually disliked one another as individuals or as composite married couples. . . . But, to put it in a nutshell, I think we could learn to love one another."(p. 186)

This is the key. *We could learn to love one another.* Love, for Rimmer, is learned behavior. Horace and Tanya and David and Nancy decide to try building a future together; they set about designing a group marriage. To be sure, there are difficulties and tensions, but they are all managed. There is bitterness, jealousy and misunderstanding, but none that does not melt away before rational analysis, love's warmth, and the conscious re-programming of selves.

In time the four evolve a commitment to one another which is so strong that they cannot imagine not living together permanently and when scandal strikes, all four go to work to legalize group marriage by means of an amendment to the state constitution. The novel ends with the four of them, inseparably bound together, working on that campaign, planning a house that will accommodate their combined families, and celebrating the birth of Tanya's child.

In *Proposition 31* clandestine adultery becomes ambiguous adultery which in turn becomes consensual adultery of the group marriage variety. A sub-plot involves Nancy and later Horace with a friendly neighborhood swingers' group and thus affords us a glimpse of recreational adultery. But having shown something of the whole spectrum of adulterous possibilities, Rimmer clearly opts for group marriage and through juxtaposition with other varieties makes it clear that group marriage is the highest form of variation on the marital relationship.

If both *Couples* and *Bob and Carol and Ted and Alice* ended with a question, *Proposition 31* presumes to supply the answer. And the answer it supplies is not merely for the four protagonists. It is for everyone—or, at least, it should be an *option* for everyone. So Rimmer's characters are drawn into a political battle in defense of their "better way."

Rimmer is easy to fault and many serious readers and reviewers have done so. But after one has acknowledged the novel's limitations, it is possible to move beyond criticism and salvage some usable insights.

To be sure, *Proposition 31* is "message fiction," a tract, a blueprint for utopia. Rimmer clearly wants his readers to respond with enthusiasm to the model his characters work out. There is even an annotated bibliography at the end of the volume standing ready to guide the reader in his quest for new forms of consciousness and alternate social arrangements.

Many readers of *Proposition 31* and of Rimmer's other utopian novels find the characters unreal. Whether one chooses to describe them as "too strong to be real" or as "one-dimensional," the fact remains that many readers have considerable difficulty identifying with them and are unable to locate such people in their own social worlds. In fairness, two things should be pointed out in this connection: (1) Bob Rimmer himself *is* very much like Horace and other characters in the Rimmer novels;[18] (2) Perhaps a self-confessed utopian novelist is entitled to create characters who are more *ideal* than real since by definition (*utopia* means *no where*) the goal is to describe people and institutions which are superior to any in our experience.

Rimmer believes in the power of positive thinking. Perhaps he would applaud Kurt Vonnegut's dictum: "We are what we pretend to be, so we must be very careful about what we pretend to be."[19] Rimmer personally dislikes what he calls "breast-beating fiction," fiction which devotes itself exclusively to probing what is wrong with humankind and lamenting our failures. Rimmer's fiction pretends boldly. It pretends that humans are rational, that problems have solutions, that things can get better. I find this vision refreshing even on days when I cannot believe it.

Although he proposes a radical alternative to traditional monogamy, Rimmer is rather conservative in many ways. Group sex and homosexuality are specifically ruled out.[20] The group marriage is a closed system—for people over thirty—with each member limiting himself to emotional and sexual intimacy only with the two members of the opposite sex within the group. (There is almost no mention of important emotional sharing between David and Horace.) Rimmer is clearly *not* an advocate of an anything-goes morality. He is reaching for an internally-consistent *system* of behavior, a system complete with rules and limits and responsibilities.

Despite its flaws, *Proposition 31* is an important book. It has catalyzed much rethinking and inspired many fantasies. Substantial numbers of the young and the not-so-young have subjected the taken-for-granted-ness of sexual patterns to new scrutiny because of having read Rimmer. In time someone will write a novel which treats alternatives to monogamous marriage with a little more subtlety and a little less program than Rimmer. But for now, *Proposition 31* fills a vacuum. It is the only book I know of which deals so candidly with the conscious search for a meaningful sexual future.

VII. Some Comparisons between Updike, Rimmer, and Bob and Ted and Carol and Alice

Our three fictional treatments of adultery invite innumerable comparisons and contrasts. Space limitations prevent extended discussion here but the reader may wish to explore, for example, the striking differences between Updike's and Rimmer's understandings of how a "wronged" spouse reacts when the adultery of the mate is discovered. In *Couples* Janet and Harold commit "revenge adultery" when they learn that their spouses have lovers. In *Proposition 31* Horace very self-consciously seduces Nancy, initiates the group marriage discussion, and insists that all four of them can learn to love one another. The contrast between Updike's gloomy vision and Rimmer's optimistic one is also to be seen through parallel reading of the two "showdown" scenes. When in *Couples* Ken and Foxy and Piet and Angela gather to discuss Piet and Foxy's adultery, bitterness and dismay prevail. Twin divorces loom as the only option. But in *Proposition 31*, when Horace and Tanya and David and Nancy begin to discuss *their* future in light of their adulteries, many avenues are explored and the four decide to create their own utopian framework. Which novelist is right? You must decide. But, while you are deciding, be sure also to ask: Which novelist do you *hope* is right? Which do you *wish* were right?

A mark which all three of our sources share is the relative affluence of the characters. The adulterers of Tarbox are upper-middle-class folk. The backdrops and artifacts make it clear that Bob and Carol and their friends are even more affluent than Updike's couples. And Rimmer's heroes are not only financially well off to begin with, they are able to locate benefactors who are willing to dump large quantities of *deus ex machina* money upon them and their endeavors.[21] We should begin to inquire into the class boundaries and the economic implications of the new adultery—and to ask if such deviant behavior is only the prerogative of the wealthy.

Although the Updike novel is clearly artistically superior to the film and the Rimmer book, the latter two are in many ways more socially and culturally important. *Couples* tells us again what we already knew: Clandestine adultery is complicated and painful and perhaps not worth the trouble. *Bob and Carol and Ted and Alice* announces that adultery might now be comic as well as tragic *and* that *consensual* adultery, if not the wave of the future, is at least one of the options responsible adults might experiment with. *Proposition 31* goes still further. It raises hopes—and blood pressures—in connection with a radical alternative to the dominant sexual orthodoxy. It puts us in touch with some of our own personal feelings and fantasies and leads us through an exploration of a new model. The Rimmer book brings us to the edge of our future. By unashamedly arguing for *his answer* Rimmer forces us to ask ourselves some very important *questions*. If we dwell too long on the weaknesses of *Proposition 31*, it may be because we are not ready to face those questions.

The great variety of behavior and motivation that marks extramarital relations in our time is just beginning to be appreciated. There are still big gaps which must be filled by sensitive writing and filmmaking—and, of course, it is imperative that social scientists and helping professionals develop appreciation of this variety so that they can make their analytic and therapeutic contributions.

The film and the two novels considered here teach us that while clandestine adultery is still with us, there are, emerging alongside it, new forms of extramarital experience. These new forms are complex and multi-faceted and they defy simple labeling as "good" or "bad." Ambiguous and consensual adultery are entering the corporate consciousness as socially significant forms worthy of the attention of thinking, feeling persons as they construct their own life-styles.

Couples and *Bob and Carol and Ted and Alice* and *Proposition 31* are among the resources of our time for society's on-going resocialization where sexuality and adultery are concerned. But we are *all* constantly in the business of socializing one another—formally and informally. Our further task consists of pointing out for one another helpful treatments of things that matter and responding compassionately and creatively to the probes and prods of the writers we read. This essay has tried to take some steps in that direction. More important than my typology, more important than my choice of three pieces of relevant fiction, more important than my brief reactions to them, is the contention that something new is happening in our awareness of extramarital sex *and* that novels and films can assist us in sorting out and living with our new impressions.

NOTES

1 Dawn (not her real name) is one of the persons I interviewed for a study of sexual attitudes and behavior.
2 Funk and Wagnalls *Standard Dictionary* (Chicago: Encyclopedia Britannica, 1966).
3 I have chosen, because of space limitations, to restrict myself to a treatment of adultery that is marked by sexual intercourse. It might be interesting to explore very important emotional but non-sexual relationships between people who are married—but not to each other. Also, non-marital relationships which have sexual components but which do not involve intercourse are very common and more than worthy of careful inquiry. For the purposes of the present essay, however, I shall treat only extramarital relationships marked by coitus.
4 It must be acknowledged here that there are adulterous relationships which the principals value as *good*, about which they feel no guilt, and which, perhaps, they *wish* they could share with their spouses and others *but* they do not do this because, as they understand it, the spouse(s) could not cope with the revelation. In such cases the criterion I am employing is less helpful than we might wish. It is my opinion, however, that this criterion—the extent to which the spouse knows and approves—is helpful in most cases and so I develop it even while acknowledging that it will not be the best analytic tool in every situation.
5 A survey of 1212 of its readers in the October 1968 issue of *Ladies' Home Journal* suggested that most American women are prepared to forgive their husbands at least one adulterous experience before considering divorce. 74% said that a single act of adultery by either partner should only infrequently be a cause of divorce.
6 A full bibliography of materials which treat various forms of spouse-approved adultery would be inappropriate here but for the reader who wishes to explore such phenomena further, here are some suggestions:
Alfred C. Kinsey et. al. *Sexual Behavior in the Human Female* (Philadelphia: W. B. Saunders, 1953). See especially pages 434ff. Of the 221 female respondents whose adulteries were discovered or suspected by their husbands, 42% reported that no difficulties resulted. Kinsey notes the existence of spouse-swapping and other situations in which the husband encourages his wife's extramarital intercourse.
Thomas J. B. Wilson with Everett Meyers. *Wife Swapping:* A Complete 8 Year Survey of Morals in North America (New York: Counterpoint, 1965).
Journal of Sex Research, May 1970. Several articles on "swinging" in various parts of the United States.
Robert Athanasiou et. al. "Sex." *Psychology Today*, July 1970. This survey of 20,000

readers reported that (1) 40% of the married men and 36% of the married women have committed adultery; (2) 80% of the respondents say that extramarital sex could be all right under certain circumstances; (3) The notion that adultery is all right if you do not talk about it is almost totally rejected; (4) 5% of the married respondents have participated in spouse-swapping; and (5) 41% of the married men and 22% of the married women "are interested in swapping."

Sexology magazine has published a number of articles on various forms of consensual adultery. See, for example: L. N. O'Conner, " 'Sex Swingers' Tell Why" (March 1970); Sharon S. and Thomas W. Kern, "Will Group Marriage Catch On?" (June 1970); Stephen Neiger, "Mate-swapping: How Couples Do It" (December 1970); and Stephen Neiger, "Mate-swapping: Can It Save A Marriage?" (January 1971).

Lonny Almyers and Hunter Leggitt, "A New View of Adultery." *Sexual Behavior*, February 1972

The *Berkeley Barb* and other such underground newspapers carry classified ads which testify to the existence of persons who are in the market for extramarital sex with the knowledge and even the participation of their spouses.

7. The notion of *permanence* is conceptually problematic since few of the people actually involved in group marriage are given to the use of language like "for the rest of our lives" or "till death do us part." Perhaps we could say that group marriage has a *relative permanence*. That is: Permanence is the *ideal* toward which the participants move; there is no pre-set terminal date.

8 Robert Athanasiou et. al. "Sex." *Psychology Today*, July 1970, page 43. This preaction category, the realm of thought, wish, and fantasy, has usually been overlooked by sex researchers. The *Psychology Today* study (wisely, I would argue) invites our attention to this dimension of human sexuality.

9 The terms *mate-swapping* and *wife-swapping* can refer to any of several forms of consensual adultery—group marriage, open-ended marriage, or swinging—and are not, therefore, terms that can be used with precision.

10 See especially the *Journal of Sex Research*, May 1970, for several pertinent articles. On the "rules" for swinging which couples evolve, the article by James R. and Lynn G. Smith is especially interesting. The first book-length study of swinging by a social scientist is *Group Sex* by Gilbert D. Bartell who teaches anthropology at Northern Illinois University (New York: Peter H. Wyden, Inc., 1971).

11 Page numbers cited in Part IV are from John Updike, *Couples* (Greenwich, Conn.: Fawcett Publications, 1968). For Updike's further reflections on sexuality and adultery see his exquisite short story "Eros Rampant" in *Harper's* magazine, June 1968. Also of interest in this connection is an essay on Denis de Rougement entitled "More Love in the Western World" in Updike's *Assorted Prose* (New York: Knopf, 1965). Take note of Updike's comments in the foreword of the same volume, pages ix ff.

12 Felix Bastian. *The Enclaves* (Garden City N.Y.: Doubleday, 1965), page 23.

13 This comment from *Time* was quoted in the paperback edition of *Couples*.

14 Personal correspondence from John Updike, December 1970.

15 The screenplay has been adapted into a novel by Patricia Welles (New York: Bantam, 1969). It is very disappointing. The novel reproduces the screenplay dialogue (with very few variant readings) and punctuates it with cliche-ridden descriptive passages and shallow psychologizing. This time the movie is better than the book.

16 Quoted from the novel, page 184.

17 Page numbers cited in Part VI are from Robert H. Rimmer, *Proposition 31* (New York: New American Library, 1968). Rimmer has written two other novels which offer utopian perspectives on the sexual dimensions of the human experience. *The Rebellion of Yale Marratt* (New York: Avon, 1964) treats enlightened bigamy and *The Harrad Experiment* (New York: Bantam, 1967) describes an experimental college at which male and female students are paired off as roommates. Rimmer's views are further elaborated and some reactions to them are registered in *Thursday, My Love*

(New York: New American Library, 1972) and *Adventures in Loving* (forthcoming, New American Library, 1973) as well as in the non-fiction volumes *The Harrad Letters* (New York: New American Library, 1969) and *You and I . . . Searching for Tomorrow* (New York: New American Library, 1971).

18 I base this judgment on my own extended conversations with Rimmer. Others who know him corroborate my estimate.

19 From the introduction to Kurt Vonnegut, Jr., *Mother Night* (New York: Avon, 1961), page v.

20 Group sex is sexual activity involving more than two persons at the same time. Group sex and group marriage are clearly *not* the same thing. Rimmer is opposed to group sex (see *Proposition 31*, pages 258ff). He was surprised and upset when the cover of the paperback version of *Proposition 31* announced in bold print: "The author of *The Harrad Experiment* takes group sex one shocking step further."

21 This almost miraculous intrusion of large quantities of money is a mark of all three of Rimmer's utopian novels. A wealthy home builder who is sympathetic to the group marriage idea sets up a five-million-dollar foundation and names Horace its director. Yale Marratt makes *two* fortunes, one in currency speculation and one on the stock exchange *and* is given money by an eccentric but sympathetic millionairess. Harrad College is funded by off-stage philanthropy and Sheila Cole (one of the six central characters) inherits a fortune.

7

EXTRAMARITAL AND CO-MARITAL SEX: A REVIEW OF THE LITERATURE
Roger W. Libby

The following chapter offers an extensive review of the literature on extramarital and co-marital sex. First the definitional problem of the semantics of emerging sexually liberated marriages is dealt with. Then Libby reviews and comments on the findings of studies beginning with Kinsey (excluding swinging studies, reviewed in the next chapters) and ties in non-marital and premarital trends with similar trends after marriage. Key studies after Kinsey are reported in detail and some theoretical notions are introduced to provide an overview of sex after marriage. Cross-cultural research on extramarital sex is also covered, with commentary on theoretical and methodological problems of various studies.

A major portion of this chapter covers the conflict between the ground rules of marriage styles and the sexual desires of the participants in marriage. Flirtation is discussed from the points of view of those who see it as "making love without meaning it" and those who view it as behavior that has no relevance these days. The symbolic meaning of extramarital and co-marital relationships is explored in depth, with full recognition of Jetse Sprey's theory of the increasing autonomy of sexuality from marriage, the family, and parenthood. Finally, the future of marriage is examined in the context of research and theory.

Introduction

The recent publication of novels such as *Thursday, My Love* by

Rimmer and *Couples* by Updike, books such as *The Affair* by Hunt, *Extramarital Relations* by Neubeck, and *Open Marriage* by O'Neill and O'Neill, as well as movies such as "Bob and Carol and Ted and Alice" amd Broadway plays such as "Promises, Promises" are some indication of how blatant the curiosity and obsession with extramarital sexual behaviour has become. As Neubeck (1969) emphasizes, it is quite natural that there be an eternal attraction between the sexes. While many married people confine their desires to the world of fantasy, others brave the threat of the cultural stigma of "sinner" or "cheater" in order to enter into extramarital sexual relationships. It can be assumed that there are now emerging styles of marriage based on a greater acceptance of freedom to have other sexual relationships.

Several socio-cultural trends support marriages which include sexual freedom in their "ground rules." The passing of the double standard, the changing concept of female sexual expression, wider availability of effective contraceptives, greater opportunity to carry on a discreet "affair"—thanks to urbanization, modern transportation, and the permissiveness of the mass media, all contribute to changing conceptions of "marriage." "Marriage" in this culture does not and will not always mean "monogamy," and to some couples a form of "monogamous nonpromiscuous pluralism" (Mazur, 1968) is acceptable. The trend to a more permissive courtship system is another socio-cultural trend supporting changing marital patterns. It would seem that marriage cannot stand alone in a time of social change in terms of motivations for non-marital and premarital sexual relationships, appropriate sexual expression in various kinds of relationships, and the increased openness surrounding sexual behavior in the mass media and the mass culture. Indeed, Whitehurst's (1966) hypothesis that extramarital sex may be an extension of normal behavior has relevance to marriage and the sanctioning of extramarital relationships in the present and near future.

Before proceeding with a review of the literature, let us discuss definitions for some of the words related to the subject of this chapter, as well as the need for research.

Some Nominal Definitions

Without standard definitions of concepts which describe styles of marriage it is confusing for the reader to understand the connotations of terms such as "extramarital" and "co-marital." Additionally, commonly accepted definitions of "marriage" are assumed to adequately describe "marriage" in the entire society. The assumption has been that the term "marriage" is to be equated with monogamy and exclusivity in the spousal dyad. One goal of this chapter is to dispel such rash generalizations about marriage, and to emphasize the emergence of other concepts of marriage. To accomplish this goal, we must view marriage as more than a legal or church sanctioned relationship. What does it mean when two people are said to be "married" to each other? It implies that these people intimately agree on certain ground rules and expectations (or at least profess to), and that the quality of commitment to each other is such that they are engaged in a primary and centrally important relationship. However, to be married does not necessarily mean to be possessed or to be committed to an exclusive or ownership relationship.

Similarly, to label all sex outside a marriage relationship as "extramarital" is to cloud the nature of other sexual relationships and to say nothing about the acceptance or lack of acceptance of such behavior within the ground rules of a marriage. While the most general level of description of sex outside marriage would be extramarital, a variety of sexual expression after marriage must be distinguished by the use of more precise language. Thus, the motivations and quality of an extramarital liaison may differ from the motivations and quality of a "co-marital" liaison. The Roys used the term "extramarital" to connote "situations which are not as clearly noncompetitive." They distinguished "co-marital" from "extramarital" relationships by stating that co-marital sex does not have the pejorative meanings that terms such as adultery, extramarital, or unfaithfulness tend to have. The Roys defined co-marital as:

> Any man-woman relationship, and/or sexual expression thereof, which exists alongside of and in addition to a marriage relationship. Such relationships are basically not competitive with the marital relationship; they may have a neutral or even a positive effect on it. (1968:98)

Co-marital as defined by the Roys does not necessarily mean that both spouses participate in or have the freedom to participate in outside relationships. Thus, the Roys discussed wives who "come to terms with their husbands' co-marital relationships . . ." (105), which could well indicate that the wives were inactive outside of marriage. Later they confused the issue by stating that co-marital sex is "symmetrical" for both spouses (106).

Apparently cognitive awareness of co-marital sex is not necessary for spouses in the Roys' view of co-marital sex. They mentioned that a discovery may lead to "a new and real warmth and gratitude toward the spouse—who may even be unaware of the other relationship" (110). It is unclear how open or how honest one must be with one's spouse to qualify for *Honest Sex*, or co-marital sex as defined by the Roys. Concepts such as "responsible" are not clearly spelled out. It would seem that the distinction between extramarital and co-marital is largely one of acceptance by the spouse, but this is unclear.

The Roys' breakdown of co-marital into three kinds of relationships is indicative of the broad range of possible interactions under the term "co-marital." They posit co-marital relationships from the strictly recreational level (e.g. "swinging") to a middle ground where co-marital and extramarital are nearly equated in terms of the consequences, to the smaller category where spouses engage in co-marital sex in an established and rich relationship. All three kinds of co-marital sex can be confused by using "swinging" to cover the whole range of relationships described. The Smiths emphasized that "swinging" is a much too broadly used concept to have any real utility (1970:133).

Co-marital was somewhat differently conceived by the Smiths, since they used the term to refer to:

> ... married couples who are either actually involved together in establishing relationships beyond that of the marital dyad for sexual purposes, or to couples in which there is both knowledge of and consent to such relationships regardless of whether the sexual activity includes both partners or is independent to some degree. (1970:134)

Additionally, the Smiths would agree with the Roys in that co-marital sex excludes deceitful sex or sex lacking in consent (134).

To distinguish "swinging" from "co-marital," it would seem that swinging usually involves going with a "date" (or mate) and doing it "together," while co-marital sex may only involve the *actual* participation of one spouse. If both spouses are involved in co-marital sex, they may carry on such interaction separately or together.

Some of the extramarital sex described in this chapter is impossible to categorize as either co-marital or adulterous (cheating), because these distinctions are rarely made in research (at least so far). Some prefer to call co-marital sex "consensual adultery" (see Clanton, Chapter 6 of this book), or "permissive infidelity" (Boylan, 1971). Which label is used often depends on the value judgment normally attached to the label. Thus, if the labeler disapproves of extramarital sex, negative concepts such as "unfaithfulness," "adultery," "cheating," and "stepping out" can be expected to describe all sex after marriage. Those who are more accepting of extramarital sex are likely to make distinctions between extramarital, co-marital, and adulterous behavior. For the remainder of the chapter, extramarital sex will be abbreviated as EMS and co-marital sex as CMS.

The Need for 'Relevant' Research

Although there is much talk about EMS and CMS—and a great deal of humorous and serious writing—research on the subject is sparse and lacks depth or breadth. The need for scientific data is profound. Claude

Bowman perceived the importance of doing sound research two decades ago:

> The student of social relationships wants to know what these extramarital experiences *mean* to the participants, their mates, parents, friends and society in general. One of the firmest beliefs of monogamous ideology is that such 'affairs' are sordid . . . to refer to companionship and the finer sentiments of love in regard to such relationships is to suggest, from the conventional point of view, unjustifiable euphemisms for that which is debased. . . . Yet the problem of meaning cannot be brushed aside so easily, for, to some degree, cultural definitions are self-validating. (1949:628)

Bowman's plea for research has not been answered with any in-depth study. Yet he stated his beliefs about the benefits of such research:

> If social research should begin to penetrate the moral facade, it would undoubtedly discover a variety of values in sexual intercourse where no attachments significant enough to be called love are involved. The relationship may be that of friendship or casual acquaintance, ephemeral or enduring, leading eventually to love, or hate, or indifference, or continued friendship. Through sexual experience men and women can learn a great deal about one another, not only as sexual objects but as social beings functioning in various roles. (1949:631)

In his book, *The Family in Search of a Future*, Herbert Otto related research to the need for understanding and social engineering. He stated:

> It is only with the advent of modern anthropological research and sociological theory that man has recognized his institutions, not as eternal verities, but as defined ways of being social. For the first time, he is now free to examine such institutions as marriage and the family with a certain amount of objectivity and to restructure these institutions, not in blind compliance to social pressures and economic sanctions, but in full consciousness of his needs and potentialities. . . . (1970:9)

Research is needed as an initial step toward understanding the social and sexual aspects of extramarital relationships which are sanctioned in marriage. Exploratory research must ascertain under what circumstances EMS and CMS is beneficial to individuals and/or to marriages, and when such relationships are a threat to individuals and marriages. To accomplish this, couples who agree on some form of marriage where extramarital sexual expression is sanctioned could be questioned to find out about the "ground rules" of their marriages (what situation and/or relationships are acceptable for extra-marital relationships), and the effect of their attitudes and behavior on their self-concepts, their marriages, and their extramarital relationships. Additionally, the relationships between fantasy and actual behavior and between sexual desire and behavior could be explored. An exploratory study designed to generate hypotheses for further research and to develop a typology of styles of marriage which include some provision for extramarital sexual expression (be it petting, intercourse, oral-genital sex or whatever) is much needed. Bowman's (1949) emphasis on the "meaning" of the experience is directly related to the need for such a study. Kirkendall's (1961) emphasis on understanding distinctions between relationships which foster trust, integrity, honesty, communication and respect, and relations which are exploitative is crucial to such research.

Review of the Literature

Very little research has been published about extramarital sexual relationships, especially research designed to explore the rationale for extramarital and/or co-marital relationships which are in some way approved in the marital contract.

We have no large random sample to indicate that the majority of Americans do not at some time in their married life engage in some type of extramarital sexual behavior. Similarly, no data are available to identify the proportion of marriages where some agreement for sexual freedom is existent for one or both spouses. Extreme caution must be used in generalizing from research to date.

The Kinsey Research

In his classic studies published in 1948 and 1953, Alfred Kinsey and his associates included questions about extramarital sexual behavior and attitudes. Since both studies were based on non-random samples which were biased toward northern urban populations, one must be careful when generalizing the findings to men and women throughout this country. Thus, Kinsey was presumptuous in making inferences to the "human" male and female in the titles of his books. Nevertheless, some insights can be derived from the two studies. In the 1948 volume on males Kinsey indicated that the extramarital topic accounted for more refusals to interview than any other reason (585). He also suggested that those participating in the research "... have probably covered up on this more often than any other single item" (585). He concluded that (allowing for cover-up) about 50% of married males engage in extramarital intercourse (585). Since Kinsey's average frequencies of intercourse according to age, social class, and so on can be misleading (e.g., the entire history of coital experience can take place in one week out of a year and be reported as once a week), rather than citing exact frequencies, summarizing statements will be used.

In general it was found that lower-class males have most of their

EMS at younger ages, while the opposite was true for middle- and upper-class males. As Kinsey hypothesized, this difference could relate to the higher incidence of premarital intercourse of lower-class males who have acquired the "habit" of a variety of partners, while it may take longer for middle- and upper-class males to release their inhibitions. EMS was found to be sporadic, and few long-term "affairs" were documented. EMS was most common for those from urban areas, and those who were not religiously devout (588-589). Kinsey considered sexual variety purely reasonable and normal for the male, as he concluded that ". . . the human male would be promiscuous in his choice of sexual partners throughout the whole of life if there were no social restrictions" (589). Kinsey assumed that females are less interested in a variety of partners due to a natural variation in the "conditionability" of the sexes. He attributed this to differences in nervous systems (589). However, it would seem that the twenty plus years since this conclusion (along with the Masters and Johnson, as well as socialization research) have provided some basis for making a case that cultural learning rather than any inherent differences between the sexes is the deciding factor.

Kinsey stated that EMS occurred whether or not other sexual outlets were available, or if the husband was satisfied or not at home, and that "Most of the male's extramarital activity is undoubtedly a product of his interest in a variety of experience" (590). However, when the wife was not interested in meeting the sexual needs of the husband (as in the wife's refusal of oral-genital contacts), the husband was prone to seek EMS.

Lower-class wives were often tolerant of their husband's EMS as long as they did not learn of the particulars (they *expected* some EMS). While EMS was generally less accepted in the middle-class, it was found that fewer problems existed in the upper classes because it was usually kept secret. EMS sometimes resulted in marital discord or divorce when it was found out by the wife, but ". . . it is sometimes had with the knowledge of the other spouse who may even aid and encourage the arrangement" (592). This latter citation identifies the nature of the select sample needed in future research on CMS. From Kinsey's data it would appear that most of these couples will be among the middle to upper social classes.

But what does EMS mean? The traditional double standard was noted by Kinsey, but one of his conclusions was:

> The significance of extra-marital intercourse may more often depend upon the attitudes of the spouses and of the social groups to which they belong, than upon the effect of the actual intercourse upon the participating individuals. Few difficulties develop out of extramarital intercourse when the relationships are unknown to anyone but the two persons having the intercourse. . . . Extramarital

intercourse most often causes difficulty when it involves emotional and affectional relations with the new partner who takes precedence over the spouse. (593)

Kinsey noted that some men made better sexual adjustments in marriage due to EMS, as did women who found a new partner to be exciting and educational through teaching them how to reach orgasm in their marriages (593). Kinsey did not collect data on extramarital petting behavior for men, although he did for women. It would be interesting to know the extent and motivations for those men who pet but do not have intercourse extramaritally. This writer agrees with Kinsey in that some people probably rationalize that petting is not "infidelity" like actual penile-vaginal penetration may be. Similarities between premarital and extramarital sexual moralities are probable.

In the 1953 study it was found that about 26% of the sample of married women had experienced extramarital intercourse by age 40, and that another 16-20% had engaged in petting behavior without intercourse (416, 427). Thus, although there undoubtedly was some cover-up, about 42% of the sample reported either extramarital petting or intercourse. It is reasonable to assume that the incidence of petting and intercourse is somewhat higher in the 1970's than in the pre-1953 time period when the Kinsey data were collected. But once again, Kinsey did not have a random or a representative sample of the entire nation, let alone of the "human female." As with most of the research reviewed in this chapter, the Kinsey studies made no proportional distinction between kinds of extramarital relationships (i.e., whether most or all of the extramarital sex was adulterous, or whether some of it was actually CMS).

Reiss (1960) noted that petting is related to abstinence before marriage, and that petting may be transitionary behavior, with the possibility of future cultural acceptance of intercourse. This would also seem to have some relevance to the acceptability of EMS or CMS, although future research remains to bear this out. Kinsey contended that extramarital petting was probably increasing, although he had no data to support the rate of increase (426). He indicated that "a considerable amount of public petting is allowed between married adults when coitus would be unacceptable" (426). Research should be designed to make distinctions between various levels of physical intimacy and to note how these intimacies affect individuals and/or marriages in various situations.

Females were most likely to have EMS in their mid-thirties and early forties if they become involved at all. They often preferred younger men (which may be due to the wish to feel young as well as the lure of youthful sexual drives). Females who engaged in EMS had as many or more orgasms in EMS as in their marriages (418). This is probably due to the excitement of a new partner and the likelihood of highly responsive females getting involved with EMS. As with premarital intercourse, females with more education were more likely to have EMS. About 31% of females in the college sample experienced EMS by age 40 (421). Similarly, those born before 1900 were less likely to have EMS, and high incidences were most affected by religious background (424).

Of those women who had EMS, 44% did not intend to renew the experience. Additionally, 71% of the experienced wives reported no difficulties with their marriages. This is in spite of the fact that 49% said their husbands either knew or suspected the EMS (434). In view of the finding that 29% of the females with premarital experience had experienced EMS by the time of the interviews, in comparison with 13% of those who had not had such experience, there may well be more EMS as studies continue to indicate an evolution of more premarital intercourse for females (Freeman and Freeman, 1966; Packard, 1968; Kaats and Davis, 1970; Gagnon and Simon, 1969; Bell and Chaskes, 1970; Christensen and Gregg, 1970; Hall and Wagner, 1972; Zelnik and Kantner, 1972; Eshelman, 1972). Kinsey indicated that females who had premarital intercourse were no more likely to have a variety of extramarital sexual partners than were females with no premarital experience (428). (About 80% of those women with EMS experience had one to five partners regardless of the nature of their premarital experience.)

Bell (1963) noted comparisons between sexual behavior before and after marriage:

> When we relate our discussion of extramarital sexual behaviour to premarital sexual behaviour, it becomes clear that the stated attitudes and actual behaviour are often in conflict in today's American society. More important, it indicates to the social scientist that the attitudes are not effective deterrents of non-marital coitus and are not incorporated by a number of individuals to the extent that their violation leads to any great guilt or remorse. . . . The lack of agreement between the moral sexual norms and the sexual behaviour of many individuals points up the 'schizoid' nature of sex in America. (383)

Kinsey reported several motivations for EMS for females. Females sometimes wanted to acquire social status; the desire for sexual variety was another motivation. Other reasons included: accommodate a respected friend, retaliate against spouse's EMS, assert independence from spouse or social code, and obtain emotional satisfaction and spouse encouragement (432-434). Of the latter rationale (which may change EMS to CMS) Kinsey commented:

> There is a not inconsiderable group of cases in the sample in which the husbands had encouraged their wives to engage in extra-marital

activities. . . . In some instances it represented a deliberate effort to extend the wife's opportunity to find satisfaction in sexual relations. In not a few instances the husband's attitude had originated in his desire to find an excuse for his own extra-marital activity. What is known as wife swapping usually involves this situation. (435)

Most of the husbands who sanctioned their wives' EMS did so in ". . . an honest attempt to give them the opportunity for additional sexual satisfaction" (435). Kinsey noted that while EMS sometimes led to marital difficulties and/or divorce, this was not at all inevitable. He stated:

There are strong-minded and determined individuals who can plan and control their extra-marital relationships in such a way that they avoid possible ill consequences. In such a case, however, the strong-minded spouse has to keep his or her activity from becoming known to the other spouse, unless the other spouse is willing to accept the extra-marital activity. Such persons do not constitute a majority in our present-day social organization. (433)

Post-Kinsey Research

Christensen (1962) cited two studies since Kinsey which sampled attitudes of British and French women toward EMS. Both studies were questionnaire studies. The British study was done by Eustace Chesser (1956) (N=6,000). Most of the females in his sample never desired EMS, and most of those who did desire EMS were those who were the least sexually satisfied and the least happy in marriage. Also, Chesser reported that about a third of married women believed that most men would like to engage in extramarital intercourse even if they were happily married. The second post-Kinsey study cited by Christensen was published by the French Institute of Public Opinion in 1961. Adultery was the only concept of extramarital or co-marital sex included, and it was found that nearly half of the French women believed that "nearly all men" or "many men" deceive their wives by engaging in adultery. The double standard was evident, in that adultery was considered more serious if engaged in by the wife than the husband, and half of the women thought it excusable if a man has a short and casual affair with another woman, while more serious affairs were seen as indicators of loss of love and confidence and of marital breakdown. Over a decade since the French and English studies, and two decades after Kinsey's studies, the issue of the double standard continues to surface when one discusses extramarital sex, or any sex for that matter!

While Kinsey and others emphasized the double standard, if Reiss' (1960) observations about the passing of the double standard in courtship are applicable to extramarital and marital relationships, there may be a trend to more sexual freedom (as part of the trend to social freedom) for women. As Jessie Bernard (1969) pointed out:

> ...a new kind of woman is emerging... and one of the distinguishing characteristics... is that she can be casual about sex. In the past she could not. And in the past, therefore, husbands were justified in feeling alarmed if they found out that their wives were engaged in sexual relations with another man. Because otherwise, if it hadn't been a deep relationship, she wouldn't have done so. But for the woman of today this is no longer true. They can be as casual about sexual relations in or out of marriage as men. They can accept sex at some point without conflict. Even a regular extramarital relationship does not faze them or in fact interfere with their marriage. (44)

What are the norms of expected conduct? Bernard feels that "The norm is not to be flagrant about it. It is being flagrant about it that violates the rule" (46). This may be more true of older than younger people.

It is important to emphasize that youth are likely to have somewhat different visions of what they want in "marriage" in comparison with adults. Harrop and Ruth Freeman (1966) found that 10-25% of their national sample of senior college women approved of EMS, and 5-10% approved of *and practiced* intercourse with married men. No comparable data for college men were presented. These findings must be accepted with some caution, as the authors could have been more detailed in the explanation of their methods and sample.

Whitehurst hypothesized that "... it is possible that the youthful penchant currently in vogue for honesty in interpersonal relations may lead to more, rather than less, adultery ... a new morality may be emerging which does not preclude EMS but prescribes the rules for it" (1969:137). Whitehurst (see also Chapters 2, 16, and 19 of this book) appraised the current situation as far as females are concerned:

> ... an increasing number of females are participating more freely while maintaining good marriages. It is just a fun thing to do and more and more people are finding out they can do it and still stay within the confines of the social order. In some sense, the increase in EMS is a function of the breakdown of the web of social controls, which become ineffective in this type of society. . . .

Consistent with Whitehurst's observations was the rationale for calling the April, 1966, issue of the *Journal of Social Issues* "The Sexual Renaissance in America." The web of social controls governing sexual interaction has undoubtedly broken down in other societies. The editor of the special issue, Ira Reiss, explained:

> ... it is ... true that regardless of what the past approach to sexual relations was in America, we are witnessing today a new interest, a national conversation, a more open attitude, and it is that which I am

calling the sexual renaissance. It is the rebirth of an approach to sexuality that surely was present somewhere in our ancestor's past. (1966:2)

Neubeck (1969) stressed the necessity of recognizing and understanding extramarital relations. To do this we must go beyond the frequencies offered by Kinsey and ask questions about motivations for EMS and CMS, as well as the kind of social-psychological environment in which such relationships occur. As one of the contributors to the Neubeck book, Whitehurst reported a study which did go beyond mere frequencies of intercourse. The data were based on a small (N=112) non-random sample, so caution must be exercised in making generalizations to larger populations. Whitehurst's purpose was to identify some variables which were important in understanding EMS within a sociological perspective. He contended that the monogamous base of society is maintained by boundary-maintenance through language with negative connotations. Thus, he stated that "It is no chance happening that the word 'adultery' in our society has a negative connotation but in some societies it does not" (130). He added: "We have equated adultery often with 'sick, immature, narcissistic, neurotic' and other names denoting evil" (130). Similarly, one could observe that most of our vocabulary emphasizes the negative aspects of extramarital sexuality—concepts such as "infidelity," "unfaithfulness," and "the other woman" assume that extramarital relationships are universally "bad." It would seem that these concepts would be inappropriate for describing EMS which is sanctioned in marriage (as with CMS).

Whitehurst included alienation as a major independent variable. He grouped his sample into the high and low alienated. He stated:

> That many currently feel a sense of alienation from conventional institutions and norms might not be surprising in our kind of world. Alienation, when coupled with a relatively high level of opportunity to interact with others, can be expected to create the stuff of extramarital sexual practice. (1969:134)

Harper (1967) suggested that while cultural taboos are stronger against EMS than premarital coitus, married people can generally plan opportunities which are less hurried and more discreet. Thus, Whitehurst's thesis was:

> ... the behaviour should be quite frequently expected, and if expected and explained as a socio-structural and cultural problem, it may then be construed much more nearly as normal rather than as abnormal behaviour in the kind of society we now experience (1969:136).

Whitehurst was interested in the upper-middle class because he assumed that family change most often occurs in this class. He found that 80% of the extensive extramarital involvement included high alienation men (139). Using Cuber's classification system, the low-alienation group was more likely to have "vital" or "total" marriages (139). Most of the men who abstained from EMS did so for religious or moral reasons, or out of a feeling of family responsibility. A majority of the high alienation group reported that their marital adjustment was reflected in the deviations (139). Seventy percent of the low alienation group versus only 30% of the high alienation group had indulged in "some playing around, either at parties, with office help, or others, but no serious sexual involvement" (140). Opportunity was a crucial intervening variable, as 41% of the sample stated this was a deciding factor as to whether they engaged in EMS. Whitehurst explained the relevance of opportunity to EMS:

> Opportunity appears to be dependent upon the social situation in which the male operates. . . . If reference group support is lacking . . . a male will be less likely to find opportunity unless he is a singular deviant . . . those scoring low in alienation avoid opportunities for EMS by enveloping themselves in a social structure which supports conformity (in some significant sense, this creates an impossibility for deviation extramaritally because of the web of social control with which this kind of person surrounds himself. (140)

Whitehurst was cautious in interpreting his data, but indicated that men who were high in "powerlessness" were more likely to satisfy the need for power over another in an EMS relationship (141). This may relate to the need to prove one's masculinity. Additionally, those with EMS experience were more socially isolated and were seeking intimacy (apparently) in EMS relationships. Since 67% of Whitehurst's sample had not had *any* kind of EMS, the representativeness of upper-middle class businessmen would not seem to square with the probable reality of a higher proportion of such experience (e.g., as reported by Kinsey). Whitehurst acknowledged this deficiency in his sample, and attributed it to the methodology and/or the "halo effect present in the middle class" (142). He concluded that there is a need for further clarification of the relationship between alienation, social isolation, and powerlessness, as well as opportunity for EMS (144). Since Whitehurst's sample was all male, future research will need to include a comparison between men and women.

The study which did include both sexes is *The Significant Americans* by Cuber and Harroff (1965). This study has probably provided more insights into extramarital sexual relationships which are sanctioned in marriages than any other study to date. Yet the sample was non-random and was limited to the upper-middle-class. The age range (35–55) unfortunately did not include young married couples. However, the study is rich in detail from the unstructured in-depth interviews with 437 upper-middle-class Americans. Neubeck recognized the value of the study as he included a chapter by Cuber in his recent book. In that chapter Cuber pointed out that treating all EMS as "adultery" is misleading, as no distinctions are made between the range of extramarital relationships—from the casual to the intense. He stated: "Such a category contributes nothing but a moralistic label which obscures more discriminating understanding of behaviour" (191).

Cuber and Harroff originally set up five types of marriage. They stated that "infidelity" (Cuber is guilty of using universally the negative terms he later abhors) occurred in all but the "total" marriage, but that it occurred for differing reasons. The marital type which would seem to most closely approximate marriages where extramarital relations are approved would be the "vital" marriage, although EMS is by no means sanctioned in all "vital" marriages. In some "vital" marriages EMS ". . . is not construed as disloyalty or as a threat to continuity, but rather as a kind of basic human right which the loved one ought to be permitted to have—and which the other perhaps wants also for himself" (62).

Cuber (1969) defined three types of relationships between EMS and marriage. Cuber indicated that EMS may compensate or substitute for a defective marriage, and that these marriages are often maintained without love due to the societal emphasis on the value of continuing marriage as opposed to the negative sanctions on terminating marriage (192). In such cases the extramarital relationships may be more like "marriage" than relationships meeting the legal definition of marriage. The second type of marriage which includes EMS is the discontinuous marriage. Spouses are often separated by occupational or professional roles, or by war, and agree to EMS as long as the relationships are casual and not threatening to the marriage.

Type three includes the "true Bohemians." Monogamy (as Americans are supposed to practice) is not recognized in this type of relationship, and extramarital relationships are fully sanctioned (192-193). It is likely that a significant proportion of EMS in the Cuber and Harroff study is actually CMS, although the concept was not used in 1965. This would seem particularly relevant to categories two and three.

What one expects initially from marriage tends to condition the kind of marriage which develops. Cuber and Harroff noted that "Expectations are often interlaced with ambivalence" (68). They added that it was not uncommon for men and women to doubt whether they should give up sexual variety for life to get married. An example of the frustrations and conflicts between marriage and natural desires is evident with one of Cuber's male interviewees. The man stated:

> This tying up of love, marriage, parenthood, and sex into one package is crazy for this century. They're all important, normal, healthy, and essential, really. But just because you love a woman and want her for a mother for your kids doesn't mean to me that you have to give up forever your right to sleep with another woman and enjoy her close

companionship. If we hadn't agreed on that before we got married, we'd have stayed single. But the hell of it is that it's easier to agree on it and to act on it than it is to pull it off smoothly. Deep down you also feel that love *ought* to be enough—but then it isn't. It's a mess, isn't it? (69).

Cuber and Harroff included descriptions of irregular and regular extramarital relationships of several varieties. Some were what could be called "love affairs" and others were continuous sexual relationships. An example of the latter follows:

Sure, I sleep off and on with Ross's secretary. It's not really an affair. Neither of us is exclusive about it. We just like each other that way.... Every once in a while we look at each other and sort of know it's about that time again....(154)

Cuber and Harroff placed their comments in an interpersonal framework similar to that of Kirkendall (1961). They were concerned about the quality of marriages and extramarital relationships, and how EMS relationships affect various styles of marriage as well as different people. The effects of EMS on the spousal relationship depend heavily on several factors listed by Cuber. These factors include:

... whether the adultery is carried on furtively or is known by the spouse; (b) whether the married partners agree to the propriety or expediency of such behaviour; (c) whether one or both participate; and (d) whether the condonement is genuine and based on principle or is simply the result of an ultimatum by one of the two parties (1969:193).

Cuber and Harroff pointed out that the assumption that EMS is furtive is not validated by the data, for a "considerable number of spouses have 'levelled' with their mates, who cooperate in maintaining a public pretense of monogamous marriage" (193). Additionally, Cuber and Harroff found that "triangles" are not necessarily destructive to marriage, *whether* the third person is known by the spouse or not. EMS, according to Cuber and Harroff, need not have a detrimental effect on the mental health of the participants or the spouse. This interpretation is based on Cuber and Harroff's *non-clinical* sample, while studies of counseling patients might yield far different results.

Such is the case in a study by Beltz (1969) where five couples in counseling were interviewed over five years. While Cuber stressed the subjective impressions of reality by the interviewees, Beltz emphasized behaviorist theory. All of the couples in Beltz' small sample had entered monogamous marriage, later altered their "contracts," and then sought marital counseling. Beltz made the *unwarranted* conclusion that "It does not appear possible, within our cultural setting, to maintain a marriage where extramarital sex is condoned and permitted" (188).

Cuber avoided this kind of over-generalization and concluded that the effect of EMS is particular to the situation, the kind of marriage, and the psychological stability of the spouses. An example of co-marital sex would be a woman in her late forties (with two children and a successful husband) who told Cuber and Harroff that she and her husband:

> ... live more less like single people—when something interesting comes along, for either of us, we pursue it. . . . And this doesn't mean we have separate rooms at home—or even beds. Far from it!. . . . I'd say my husband and I love each other—we just don't own each other (156).

Consistent with the co-marital concept, Cuber stated that most of his sample did not hold a double standard, so that if sexual freedom was a part of a marriage, it was true for both spouses.

As for reactive feelings to EMS, Cuber (1969) stated that "Overwhelmingly, these people expressed no *guilt* with respect to what they were doing . . ." (194). He pointed out that many EMS relationships were deep meaningful encounters without the feeling that it must last for a lifetime (as in marriage), and that EMS relationships are held together by *will* rather than by *law*. Cuber contended that long-term EMS relationships were often ". . . more psychologically fulfilling than marriage" (196). This observation would seem related to the disillusionment after twenty years of marriage noted by Pineo (1961) in his follow-up of the Burgess and Wallin study. It is quite possible that Americans expect too much from marriage, and that when these expectations are not realized, some of the emotional and sexual needs are met either extramaritally or co-maritally.

In an investigation of forty couples Neubeck and Schletzer (1962) found that low strength of conscience accompanied sexual involvement, but not fantasy or emotional involvement. Those who were among the low satisfied group sought fantasy instead of actual sexual or emotional relationships outside marriage. While the study was not extensive, some interesting hypotheses were advanced in the findings. Neubeck and Schletzer stated that "The environs of marriage are obviously too narrow for impulse-ridden individuals . . ." (151). The interviews led the researchers to suggest future research designed to answer such questions as:

> ... what is the effect of the kind and degree of involvement on the other spouse? . . . what makes for tolerance for the spouse's involvement on the other spouse? . . . after an involvement has taken place, how will the behavior and attitude of the other spouse affect future involvements? (1962:281).

Although primarily a journalist, Morton Hunt published a compilation of his empirical observations and personal insights in *The Affair*

(1969). The empirical aspect of the book was not well explained, and although two social scientists carried out the questionnaire study of 360 married people on a national basis, one is left wondering how valid or representative the study is. Hunt also interviewed 91 people in free-wheeling tape-recorded interviews. Much like Cuber and others, Hunt advanced some insightful hypotheses, but fell into the same trap of using words loosely (such as "infidelity," "unfaithfulness," and so on). He dealt more specifically with "affairs," which can be defined in several ways. Hunt cited authorities who state opinions about the value of EMS, but his conclusion is presented in his Preface. He stated:

> The evidence... clearly shows that in some circumstances an extramarital affair severely damages the marriage, the participants, and even such innocent bystanders as the children; in other circumstances it does none of these things, and is of no consequence; and in still other circumstances it benefits the individual by awakening him to his own emotional needs and capabilities... each extramarital act ought to be judged as morally evil, morally neutral, or morally good, according to the totality of the circumstances and the effects on all concerned. (xv)

Paul Gebhard was quoted by Hunt as predicting the cumulative incidence figures of extramarital intercourse in 1968 as being about 60% for males and 35–40% for females, which is "change, but not revolution" (11).

Hunt recognized that the cocktail lounge is a favorite haunt for meeting prospective sex partners, especially casual sex partners (75). This is supported by the Roebuck-Spray study (1967), which included data from 30 men and 30 women who were regular patrons of an upper-middle class cocktail lounge. Roebuck and Spray followed the activities of these sixty people over a two year period, as well as a follow-up study two years after the initial study. All who were included in the sample visited the lounge at least once a week. The employees of the lounge (bartenders and cocktail waitresses) were utilized for part of the data collection. The researchers frequented the lounge regularly and gathered additional data by participant-observation. The methodology of the study was much more rigorous than other studies reported in this chapter. However, no claim could be made for a random sample. The men had incomes above 10,000 and all of the men and the single women believed in God and attended church. Seventy percent of the men were married, while none of the women were married (40% of the women were divorced or separated, while 60% were single). It was found that 80% of the men and women in the sample were considered to be stable, and few were heavy drinkers.

A third method of data collection was interviewing all in the sample several times a year. The cocktail lounge is an ideal setting for obtaining part of a sample, as indicated by Roebuck and Spray's observations:

> The popularity of the cocktail lounge . . . stems from the fact that it is a setting in which casual sexual affairs between unattached women and higher-class men can be conducted in a context of respectability. From the standpoint of the patrons, these activities tend to be viewed more in terms of reaffirming social identities than rejecting social norms. (393)

The activities were not found to disrupt the family life of the men (395). Married men were not "driven" to the lounge from unhappy marriages. The cocktail lounge as a social organization merely provided the atmosphere for meeting needs of men and women. The single women were not interested in breaking up a home or in marrying the men with whom they had EMS. None of the women married the men they met in the lounge, and none of the men were divorced in the five-year follow-up study[1] (394). As the single women married, they stopped frequenting the lounge and were "replaced" by other single women wanting social fun and sexual interaction without the "game" of the courtship relationship. The bartenders and cocktail waitresses were often intermediaries for establishing contact with potential sexual partners. While the men believed in the double standard, they did not exploit the women and maintained friendly relationships with them. The women were not virgins. The men remained "good husbands and fathers . . . " (393). It is probable that most of the married men were "cheating" in terms of their marital contracts, but it is also quite likely that some of the men were behaving within the bounds of propriety according to their wives. The men did not feel guilty, but would feel shame if caught (393), which seems to indicate that most of the men were "cheating." Whether this is true or not is not clear from the report. The lack of married women in the cocktail lounge studied may be more a reflection of the particular lounge than of cocktail lounges or married women.

In contrast with the casual sexual relationships in the cocktail lounge, Kafka and Ryder have studied nonconventional marriages (see Chapter 18 of this book). The couples who were interviewed included a small segment of a larger NIMH sample of married couples. The sample was biased to younger couples, with husbands 20-27 and wives 18-25. This may indicate that youth are most likely to develop nonconventional marital styles. Not only were these spouses not possessive toward each other, but they encouraged the free expression of affection and stressed the present rather than the future. In contrast to cocktail

---

1   Of course divorce is only the most blatant indicator of marital failure or unhappiness.

lounge relationships, or in contrast to (recreational) "swingers" (mate-swappers), these couples placed a higher value on affectionate sex. Relationships which were more open and intimate than monogamous relationships were sought. There tended to be a blurring of work and pleasure boundaries, so that an emergent life-style was evident.

Johnson (1970) reported on the projective, fantasized and actual EMS for 100 middle-class, middle-aged couples from the suburbs of one large midwestern city. Unfortunately, he limited his indicators (or motives) for fantasized EMS to nine negative reasons based on "60 case histories involving extramarital sexual relations from the files of a Family Service Agency" (45). Thus, the only reasons for any EMS were conceived as specific deficiencies in marriage. No distinction was made between EMS and CMS. While it was found that husbands who experienced EMS had lower marital satisfaction than husbands who had not had EMS, general dissatisfaction in the marriage or over the sexual relationship was not as frequently associated with EMS for the wives (454). Thus, 30% of the experienced husbands and 60% of the experienced wives had high marital adjustment scores. When asked if most men (women) who were happily married would like to have EMS, 78% of the men and 41% of the women who had denied experiencing EMS said "yes" (452). Since 20% of the husbands and 10% of the wives stated that they had experienced EMS, the sample can be considered a conservative one, and the findings must be qualified in light of the biased sample.

Psychology Today reported the results of a sex survey of its readers (N=20,000) (Athanasiou, et. al., 1970) and while no refusal rate could be reported, the extramarital findings are probably somewhat indicative of the attitudes and behavior of a young (the majority were under 30), liberal, highly educated population. While 80% stated that EMS is acceptable in various circumstances, 21% would consider EMS permissible if spouses agree. Most (95%) reject the idea that EMS is acceptable if nothing is mentioned to the spouse. About 40% of the men and 36% of the women reported having experienced EMS, but no distinction between EMS and CMS was made. Husbands began having EMS sooner than wives, but women reported about the same frequencies as men once they began EMS (43). The Athanasiou et. al. study is probably a good example of the attitude-behavior discrepancy, in that more tend to approve than to actually engage in EMS or CMS. It is likely that the lack of opportunity to engage in EMS may be a key variable accounting for the gap between attitudes and behavior. Opportunity is limited by social constraints as well as the lack of available, willing partners and accessible locations to carry out sexual desires.

Cross-Cultural Research on EMS

Harold Christensen (1962) reported a cross-cultural comparison of the attitudes of Danes, Midwestern Americans, and Intermountain (Mormon) Americans toward "infidelity." Although Christensen's data were limited to traditional "cheating" behavior, he found that Danes of both sexes were more accepting of infidelity than were those in his two American samples. In an unpublished comparison with his 1958 samples, Christensen (1972, private letter) indicated that while the American samples did not change much in their attitudes about infidelity in ten years, the Danish sample of 1968 was considerably more accepting of extramarital intercourse than were Danes in the 1958 sample. Christensen's 1968 sample of Danes indicated that about 80% of the females and 69% of the males approved of infidelity "If he or she feels the need for sexual release (with prostitutes or others) during periods of long absence from spouse." In 1958, 36% of Danish women and 41% of Danish men approved the same statement. Additionally, in 1968 about three fourths of Danes approved of infidelity "If he or she has fallen in love with an unmarried person," while about a third of Danes approved the same statement in 1958. Similarly, while 69% of Danish women and 66% of Danish men approved of infidelity "If he or she has fallen in love with another married person" in 1968, 29% of women and 27% of men in Denmark approved the same statement in 1958. Unfortunately, Christensen did not include items with attitudinal responses to CMS. Generalization from Christensen's 1958 and 1962 samples are tenuous, in that they are based on group administered questionnaires with non-random college subjects. However, his effort to obtain cross-cultural samples is an important step toward understanding the cultural relativity of attitudes toward both premarital and extramarital sexual behavior.

Much like Christensen, Jan Trost (1970) made no distinction between adultery and CMS in his study of Swedish extramarital behavior. Trost asked a probability sample of 2,000 Swedes aged 18-60 (in 1967) the following question: "With how many persons have you had sexual intercourse during *the last 12 months*?" Trost classified all who answered that they had engaged in extramarital sex as having committed adultery, and he not surprisingly found 5% who said they had engaged in this behavior. Trost believes his data actually reflect the reality of a very low incidence of EMS in Sweden, but his data are highly biased when one considers that the study was a survey type where a stranger asked questions, and that the study was supported by a governmental committee. The 5% figure is especially limited when one considers that the question was confined to EMS in the last *12 months*. Trost's bias is clear in his report, as he states his view: "It is reasonable to assume that those being sexually satisfied within their marriages seldom commit adultery" (1970:3).

Although the full report is not yet available in America, it appears that Hans Zetterberg's data are the same data used by Trost (1970). In an article by J. Robert Moskin (1969), portions of the Zetterberg data are cited. In summary, Zetterberg found that young Swedes are having sex relations with more people and beginning their sexual lives earlier than their parents; 93% accept premarital sexual relations when engaged or going steady; 98% of the married subjects had premarital intercourse; most men have had as many as five sexual partners, while most women have had one or two partners; the double standard is more accepted by women than by men; 77% believe in limiting sex to commited relationships and believe that "promiscuity" is wrong; as Trost reported, 95% of married Swedes say they have not engaged in extramarital sex within a year; and 93% disapprove of extramarital sex. It remains for future cross-cultural research to include more sensitive methods of data collection, and to provide data on CMS as well as traditional adultery.

Marital Ground Rules vs. Sexual Desires

At least some of the marital styles which support some form of EMS will probably define EMS as a "game." Thus, Nelson Foote's (1954) thesis that sex is a legitimate form of play (where the rules are made by the players) is relevant to at least some EMS. Foote pondered how trust, relaxation, and confidence can be measured in different relationships in various erotic interactions. If sex is fun and is a game, Americans must learn to separate sex from love in some EMS relationships. Ellis contended that females ". . . who say that they can only enjoy sex when it is accompanied by affection are actually being unthinkingly conformists and unconsciously hypocritical" (1958:68). The extent to which females (as well as males) are able to interact sexually in friendships and acquaintanceships with a range of affection (as well as a range of physical intimacy) needs to be investigated.

While some EMS relationships are "games," Neubeck (1969) believes that the games concept may not be needed. He stated:

> The 'games' people 'play' strategies and counter-strategies used to gain attention, love and excitement, may no longer be needed. People may explore together what in quantity and quality the marital relationship can stand in regard to additional relations. Forsaking all others has never been a realistic expectation, and, based on the assumption that there always will be others, couples can explore what the possibilities for themselves and each other should be: when, where, and how the additional individuals can be incorporated into the basic and nourishing unit (198).

Neubeck explored the concept of "ground rules" in his book. He stressed that there are implicit and explicit rules, and the interpretation of these rules varies from person to person and couple to couple (12). It is a mistake to assume that *all* married people agree to the same ground rules, or that *all* married people stick to the same ground rules they entered marriage with. Yet, as Neubeck contended, "... ground rules are hardly ever specifically discussed before marriage, but are nevertheless *assumed* to be the same for both spouses" (13). We don't often consider ground rules until they are broken. Thus, if we agree to strict monogamous marriage (as most Americans probably do), when we find out our spouse is "cheating" we wonder where we went wrong. Yet we have no explicit ground rules to regulate fantasy about sexual relationships outside marriage. How common are fantasized "infidelities?" How does the fantasy life of an individual relate to actual marital and extramarital behavior?

Neubeck stated that we assume marriage to be an *exclusive* relationship, which is entered voluntarily and is permanent (13). Thus, to what extent does a spouse have a right to a private life and to develop other heterosexual relationships? In what situations are other relationships nurturant to marriage as well as satisfying to the self, and when are other relationships a threat to the marriage and/or the self? Neubeck recognized that while marriage is a group situation, the individual also has personal goals (15). Whitehurst (1969) referred to Bossard's belief in the "trouble" caused by an individual seeking individual development while married. Whitehurst commented: "This is a near-classic restatement of the standard sentiments of Americans about marriage" (133).

Bernard (see Chapter 5) indicated that a choice between exclusivity and permanence may be necessary. She commented:

> If we insist on exclusivity, permanence may be endangered. The trend ... seems to be in the direction of exclusivity at the expense of permanence in the younger years but permanence at the expense of exclusivity in the latter years (1970:99).

The interdependency of a marriage was cited by Neubeck, who based his statements on Kurt Lewin's field theory. One has more freedom in larger groups, which would mean that the marital dyad may be limiting by nature of the number of participants in the group. According to Lewin, marrying is a "'... symptom of desire for the least social distance'" (15). Yet, individuals differ in their needs for free space—and marriage as traditionally defined may not allow enough for needs to be met for some people. Lewin noted that too small a space leads to tension and to the seeking of less confining situations (16). Such movement can result in spousal jealousy if detected or not agreed upon. Intense jealousy is based on the "owning" of a spouse, as well as an insecurity about the lack of permanency of the marriage.

How do members of a family react when they find out their mother (wife) or father (husband) has had "boy (girl) friends"? Neubeck noted that "... as an extra-marital affair becomes known throughout the family, tolerance is needed by the other members as well as by the spouse" (8). It is important that researchers inquire into how spouses handle the issue of explaining or keeping secret their agreement to extramarital freedom in some form to their children, depending on their ages and ability to understand. Due to social pressures and lack of maturity it may be that most parents who agree on extramarital freedom (as in mate-swapping) keep these activities from their children—at least until their children are old enough to understand. Those who are seriously committed to "swinging" or to another form of CMS may or may not explain the virtues of such freedom to their children when they are in late adolescence—the issue remains open.

Neubeck stated propositions which researchers can test:

> The greater the need for freedom, the more confining the marriage environment might be, and the subsequent wish to escape from it; the greater the need for the possession of property and subsequent willingness to share property, the greater the jealousy and willingness to be faithful on one's own part (17).

The need for freedom to meet needs outside the marital relationship is related to the rather common expectation that every possible sexual, emotional and personal need will be (or should be) met by one other in the context of a marriage that lasts for an entire lifetime. Neubeck reacted to this expectation by stating: "This permanent togetherness results in quantitative and qualitative exposure that may lead to satiation, since there is only a finite number of personality aspects available" (18).

Flirtation—Danger or Fun?

It is likely that many have a desire or need to relive their dating days by at least flirting with members of the opposite sex. This playfulness and "fun" may be difficult to achieve in marriage. Neubeck stated that:

> If flirtation ... means 'making love without meaning it,' it is obviously not possible to flirt with a spouse. A spouse is not a candidate for consummation; spouses have already consummated. (19)

And yet, if one is to believe the observations of Midge Decter (which is quite difficult to do!), flirtation is an activity of the past. Decter argued:

> Flirtation ... has become, in an era which offers no sanction to chastity, an activity fraught with consequence ... there is no longer by definition such a thing as real flirtation—whose purpose is to denote a relation between a man and a woman in which each offers full tribute to the presumed erotic attractions of the other.... (1972:51)

Most people probably pretend that monogamy is the only ideal state, but secretly *wish* for and occasionally get involved with and enjoy flirtation, which sometimes leads to physical intimacy. Mazur (1968) commented on flirtation:

> The potential dangers of flirting lie not in the activity itself, but in the foolish interpretation of it by insecure and possessive partners who see it as a threat to themselves. (25)

The extent to which this is true of married people could be noted by questioning spouses about their flirting behavior and their perception of their spouse's jealousy or lack of jealousy.

Extramarital Relationships—What Do They Mean?

It is probable that the husband has more freedom to develop heterosexual friendships (as in the work environment) than the wife. Yet Neubeck cited the Babchuk and Bates study, where the researchers found that both spouses were likely to develop friendships and share confidences with members of the opposite sex (22). Is "faithfulness" only measurable in terms of physical intimacy? Can one be "faithful" to the spouse and have extramarital sexual relationships? Does this depend on the spousal agreement as to what is "faithful," or is the only baseline that of traditional monogamy?

Our culture seems obsessed with the purely physical (and emotional) aspects of extramarital and co-marital relationships. Neubeck believes that sexual needs should not be seen as different from other needs when studying marital dynamics (19). But the physical is symbolic for meeting psychological needs as well. Neubeck observed: "That marriage should serve all the needs of the spouses is built into our marital expectations, yet anyone who examines this proposition realistically is struck with its impossibility" (21). Neubeck goes on to point out that we don't live in isolation, and some needs are met outside the pair bond. The extent to which needs are met outside the pair bond remains to be documented.

Depending on the style of marriage, one's tolerance level is related to various forms of sexual expression. Tolerance level obviously is related to what the spouse perceives to be the *meaning* of the partner's EMS relationships. To use extremes—is it a casual fling or a love affair? Neubeck observed that problems of meaning result from lack of understanding, and that jealousy oftentimes results from misinterpretation of meaning. Understanding and communication are thus related to tolerance for EMS.

Neubeck's conclusion remains to be tested empirically. It was:

> ... it is now clear that marriage can work out successfully for both of the spouses even when it is not an all-inclusive relationship, when either in reality or in fantasy there are other persons who share one's life. (24)

It has been said that "variety is the spice of life." As with food, people differ in their sexual desires and tastes. But is variety of sexual partners necessarily supportive or detracting from "marriage"? Kingsley Davis contended that "The role of variety in erotic stimulation places a strain on any stable relationship, including marriage. In short, an orderly integration of the sexual drive with social life taxes to the utmost the normative machinery" (1966:331). But Davis also observed that ". . . adultery does no harm *if* the spouse approves" (334). Kephart (1966) explained that the "safety-valve theory" can be interpreted in two ways—EMS can supplement and therefore support marriage, or it can threaten marriage by "working overtime" (72). Kephart explained that the latter is true, and that the increase in premarital and extramarital sex may "have deleterious effects on the institution of marriage. . . ." (72)

The incognito erotic ranking of individuals cited by Zetterberg (1966) most likely relates to the frustrations, conflicts, and jealousies which can accompany extramarital relationships. As Zetterberg emphasized, it is not the sexual as much as the emotional involvement with a third party which violates the privacy taboo (135). But Zetterberg stated that ". . . there are many sexual relations that do not involve any emotional surrender of either party" (1966:141). Researchers need to make comparisons between extramarital and co-marital relationships of varying degrees of emotional (as well as erotic) intimacy to ascertain nuances of meaning to the extramarital and marital relationships. It should also be noted whether the incest taboo covers mutual friends of a marital couple or not, as Zetterberg suggested is true (142). Is there a difference in meaning between CMS with a mutual friend and a friend of the spouse having EMS when no relationship exists between the friend and the other spouse?

Research could well utilize Jetse Sprey's (1969) conceptual framework which sees sexuality as an emerging autonomous institution which is not tied to reproduction and child-rearing (432). The "institutionalization" of sexuality was viewed as a private, but not normless world which is still part of the social order (435). Rather than viewing EMS and CMS as "deviance" or neurotic behavior, this framework allows for an analysis of EMS and CMS relationships in the context of exchange theory. This does not mean that EMS and CMS cannot also be related to marriage, but it means that studying sexual expression in and of itself, along with its symbolic meanings, can be more objective if not universally tied to marriage. To Sprey this involves exchange "rules" within a game (Sprey is accepting Foote's "sex as play"). If the only baseline for deviance and disorganization is that of traditional reproductive morality, little objective data and explanation can be forthcoming. Sprey noted that lumping all adultery into the meaningless category of "deviance" does not aid in the study of concepts related to EMS and CMS (438). This does not mean that a structural-functional conceptual framework cannot be employed on another level to understand the effects of EMS and CMS relationships on marriage and the family. It is to be remembered that behavior can be "deviant" to traditional "ideal" norms without necessarily being indicative of disorganization. This is especially true when considering emerging marital styles. The autonomous realm of sexuality postulated by Sprey is consistent with Zetterberg's conceptualization of erotic rankings and a secret society (following Simmel). Sprey's conclusion is appropriate; it seeks to analyze EMS from more than one perspective. He stated:

> It is strongly suggested . . . that the study of sexuality—independent of its traditional linkage with procreation—can provide us with a great deal of understanding of what Marcel Mauss has called the conditions under which men, despite themselves, learn to make contracts, to give, and to repay. (1969:440)

If Nye, Carlson and Berardo's (1970) theory is correct, support for Sprey's conceptual framework is forthcoming. They contended:

> The trends in societal change are presently toward further differentiation, and since the trend toward the autonomous family is based on increased differentiation, one can predict, with some confidence, a continued trend toward autonomy for family members and a larger proportion of comparatively autonomous families. (17)

The Future of Marriage

It is difficult to say whether emerging marital styles will gain strong support in the larger culture. However, it is noteworthy that Sweden is moving toward a more relaxed view of "marriage" in its legal structure. Marriage will be viewed as a contract of convenience intended to secure parents for children.

Serial monogamy as currently practiced leaves much to be desired. Yet to expect that all should enter monogamous marriage with the romantic expectations of marital bliss in a totally exclusive relationship, is to anticipate human beings who are socialized to happily fit the same "mold." The reality is far from the expectation. Rather than happiness, many are disillusioned and caged as animals in the zoo. Cadwallader has stated:

> Contemporary marriage is a wretched institution. It spells the end of voluntary affection, of love freely given and joyously received. Beautiful romances are transmuted into dull marriages; eventually the relationship becomes constricting, corrosive, grinding and destructive. The beautiful love affair becomes a bitter contract. (1967:48)

Alternative marital structures are explored by Otto (1970), as well as in novels by Rimmer (see Chapter 21). Otto contended that the "functionality of our major institutions can be assessed by asking, 'To what extent is the institution contributing to the development, actualization, and fulfillment of human potential?' " (5) To increase the functionality of marriage Otto advised taking a pluralistic approach to marital structures. He claimed:

> This is most appropriate, for we are a pluralistic society—with pluralistic needs. In this time of change and accelerated social evolution, we should encourage innovation and experimentation in the development of new forms and social and communal living. (8)

Otto aptly concluded:

> What will destroy us is not change, but our inability to change—both as individuals and as a social system. It is only by welcoming innovation, experimentation and change that a society based on man's capacity to love man can come into being (9).

The ability to not only accept but to socially engineer change in marital styles is a task for social and political scientists (among others). This will necessitate not only a change in attitude about marriage and sex, but it will entail a change in traditional conceptions about the roles of social scientists.

To understand (let alone guide) social change, social scientists will have to commit themselves to the study of interpersonal relationships. Family sociologists will have to bury the traditional approach of ratifying the family of yesteryear, and replace the worship of monogamous marriage with an open view of emergent structures to suit a wide variety of personalities, needs, and life-styles. This means more sensitive theories and methodologies will have to be developed by social scientists who do not fear taking a journey into the "secret society." The challenge is immense, but the rewards for human beings make the effort worthwhile.

REFERENCES

Athanasiou, Robert, Shaver, Phillip and Tavris, Carol. "Sex." *Psychology Today*, Vol. 4, 1970, pp. 39-53.

Bell, Robert. *Marriage and Family Interaction.* Homewood, Illinois: Dorsey Press, 1967. (Revised edition, 1971).

Bell, Robert and Chaskes, Jay. "Premarital Sexual Experience Among Coeds, 1958 and 1968." *Journal of Marriage and the Family*, Vol. 32, 1970, pp. 81-85.

Beltz, Stephen E. "Five-Year Effects of Altered Marital Contracts (A Behavioral Analysis of Couples)." In Gerhart Neubeck, ed., *Extramarital Relations.* Englewood Cliffs, N.J.: Prentice Hall, Inc., 1969.

Bernard, Jessie. (contributor) in "Two Clinicians and a Sociologist." In Gerhart Neubeck, ed., *Extramarital Relations.* Englewood Cliffs, N.J.: Prentice-Hall, Inc., 1969.

Bernard, Jessie. "Infidelity: Some Moral and Social Issues." In Jules H. Masserman, ed., *The Psychodynamics of Work and Marriage*, 1970, and the present book (Chapter 6).

Bowman, Claude. "Cultural Ideology and Heterosexual Reality: A Preface to Sociological Research." *American Sociological Review*, Vol. 14, 1949, pp. 624-634.

Boylan, Brian Richard. *Infidelity*. Englewood Cliffs, N.J.: Prentice-Hall, 1971.

Cadwallader, Mervyn. "Marriage as a Wretched Institution." *Atlantic*, Vol. 218, 1966:62-66.

Chesser, Eustace. *The Sexual, Marital and Family Relationships of the English Woman*. Watford: Hutchinson's Medical Publications Ltd., 1956.

Christensen, Harold T. "A Cross-Cultural Comparison of Attitudes Toward Marital Infidelity." *International Journal of Comparative Sociology*, Vol. 3, 1962, pp. 124-138.

Christensen, Harold T. and Gregg, Christina F. "Changing Sex Norms in America and Scandinavia." *Journal of Marriage and the Family*, Vol. 32, 1970, pp. 616-628.

Christensen, Harold T., data cited in letter to Roger W. Libby, May 17, 1972.

Cuber, John F. and Harroff, Peggy B. *The Significant Americans*. New York: Appleton Century Crofts, 1965.

Cuber, John F. "Adultery Versus Stereotype." In Gerhart Neubeck (ed.) *Extramarital Relations*. Englewood Cliffs, N.J.: Prentice-Hall, Inc., 1969.

Davis, Kingsley. "Jealousy and Sexual Property." *Social Forces*, Vol. 14, 1936, pp. 395-405.

Decter, Midge. "Toward the New Chastity." *The Atlantic Monthly*, Vol. 230, 172, pp. 42-55.

Ellis, Albert. *Sex Without Guilt*. New York: Lyle Stuart, 1958 (and 1966).

Eshleman, J. Ross. "A Cross Cultural Analysis of Sexual Codes: Beliefs, Behavior, and the Perception of Others." Paper presented at The National Council on Family Relations, Portland, Oregon, November 2, 1972.

Foote, Nelson. "Sex as Play." *Social Problems*, Vol. I, 1954, pp. 159-163.

Freeman, Harrop A. and Freeman, Ruth S. "Senior College Women: Their Sexual Standards and Activity—Part II. Dating: Petting-Coital Practices." *National Association of Women's Deans and Counselors Journal*, Spring, 1966, pp. 136-143.

French Institute of Public Opinion. *Patterns of Sex and Love: A Study of the French Woman and Her Morals*. New York: Crown Publishers, Inc., 1961.

Gagnon, John and Simon, William. Unpublished paper, 1969.

Hall, Patricia L. and Wagner, Nathaniel. "Initial Heterosexual Experience in Sweden and the United States: A Cross-Cultural Survey." Unpublished paper, 1972.

Harper, Robert. "Extramarital Sex Relations." In Albert Ellis and Albert Abarbanel (eds.). *The Encyclopedia of Sexual Behavior*. New York: Hawthorne Books, 1961 (and 1967).

Hunt, Morton. *The Affair*. New York: World Publishing Co., 1969.

Johnson, Ralph. "Some Correlates of Extramarital Coitus." *Journal of Marriage and the Family*, Vol. 32, 1970, 449-456.

Kaats, Gilbert A. and Davis, Keith E. "The Dynamics of Sexual Behavior of College Students." *Journal of Marriage and the Family*, Vol. 32, 1970, pp. 390-400.

Kafka, John S., Ryder, Robert. "Notes on Marriages in the Counter Culture." Chapter 18 in present book.

Kephart, William M. *The Family, Society, and the Individual*. Boston: Houghton Mifflin Co., 1966 (Second Edition).

Kinsey, Alfred, Pomeroy, Wardell and Martin, Clyde. *Sexual Behavior in the Human Male*. Philadelphia: W. B. Saunders Co., 1948.

Kinsey, Alfred, Pomeroy, Wardell, Martin, Clyde and Gebhard, Paul. *Sexual Behavior in the Human Female*. New York: Pocket Books, Inc., 1965 (originally published by W. B. Saunders Co., 1953).

Kirkendall, Lester A. *Premarital Intercourse and Interpersonal Relationships*. New York: Julian Press, 1961.

Kirkendall, Lester A. and Libby, Roger W. "Interpersonal Relationships—Crux of the Sexual Renaissance." *The Journal of Social Issues*, Vol. 22, April, 1966, pp. 45–60.

Masters, William and Johnson, Virginia. *Human Sexual Response*. Boston: Little, Brown and Co., 1966.

Mazur, Ronald. *Commonsense Sex*. Boston: Beacon Press, 1968.

Moskin, J. Robert. "The New Contraceptive Society." *Look*, Feb. 4, 1969, pp. 50–53.

Neubeck, Gerhart and Schletzer, Vera. "A Study of Extramarital Relationships." Reprinted in Neubeck (1969). Originally appeared in *Journal of Marriage and the Family*, Vol. 24, 1962, pp. 279–281.

Neubeck, Gerhart (ed.). *Extramarital Relations*. Prentice-Hall, 1969.

Nye, Ivan, Carlson, John and Berardo, Felix. Unpublished paper, 1970.

O'Neill, Nena and O'Neill, George. *Open Marriage*. New York: M. Evans Co., 1972.

Otto, Herbert (ed.). *The Family in Search of a Future*. New York: Appleton-Century, 1970.

Packard, Vance. *The Sexual Wilderness*. New York: John McKay Co., 1968.

Pineo, Peter C. "Disenchantment in the Later Years of Marriage." *Marriage and Family Living*. Vol. 23, 1961, pp. 3–11.

Reiss, Ira L. *Premarital Sexual Standards in America*. New York: Free Press, 1960.

Reiss, Ira L. ed. "The Sexual Renaissance in America." *Journal of Social Issues*, Vol. 22, 1966.

Rimmer, Robert H. *Thursday, My Love*. New York: New American Library, 1972.

Roebuck, Julian and Spray, S. Lee. "The Cocktail Lounge: A Study of Heterosexual Relations in a Public Organization." *American J. of Sociology*, Vol. 72, 1967, pp. 388–395.

Roy, Della and Roy, Rustum. *Honest Sex*. New York: The New American Library, 1968.

Simon, William and Gagnon, John. "Pornography: The Social Scripts of Sexual Scripts." Paper presented at Society for the Study of Social Problems, San Francisco, Cal., 1967 (August).

Smith, James R. and Smith, Lynn. "Co-marital Sex and the Sexual Freedom Movement." *Journal of Sex Research*, Vol. 5, 1970, pp. 131–143.

Sprey, Jetse. "On the Institutionalization of Sexuality." *J. of Marriage and the Family*, Vol. 31, 1969, pp. 432–441.

Updike, John. *Couples*. New York: Fawcett, 1968.

Trost, Jan. "Adultery in Sweden." Research Report, Uppsala University, Department of Sociology, 1970, pp. 1–7.

Whitehurst, Robert. Personal communication, 1968.

Whitehurst, Robert. "Adultery as an Extension of Normal Behavior: The Case of the American Upper-Middle Class Male." Paper presented at the National Council on Family Relations, Oct., 1966 (Minneapolis, Minnesota).

Whitehurst, Robert. "Extramarital Sex: Alienation or Extension of Normal Behavior." In Gerhart Neubeck (ed.) *Extramarital Relations*. Englewood Cliffs, N.J.: Prentice-Hall, Inc., 1969.

Zetterberg, Hans. "The Secret Ranking." *J. of Marriage and the Family*, Vol. 28, 1966, pp. 134–143.

Zelnik, Melvin, and Kantner, John F. "The Probability of Premarital Intercourse." *Social Science Research*, Vol. 1, 1972, pp. 335–341.

8

SOME PERSONAL AND SOCIAL CHARACTERISTICS OF MATE-SHARING SWINGERS
Brian G. Gilmartin
and
Dave V. Kusisto

It is widely believed that the middle-class WASP is especially nonadventurous and conformist in his sexual behavior. When—as with swingers—this turns out not to be the case, we may wonder what makes these people different from other members of their cultural sub-group. For the following paper on personal and social characteristics of swingers, the authors used questionnaires and interviews to study two hundred California couples (two equal-sized groups of swingers and non-swingers). After a review of the literature on swinging, Gilmartin and Kusisto discuss their findings which significantly substantiated certain hypotheses. In effect, they found that swingers differ from controls chiefly in terms of their early family life and the present closeness to relatives outside their immediate family. Otherwise swingers resemble controls in terms of the extent of subjective personal happiness, personal "anomaly," the extent of subjective marital happiness, the amount they drink, and how bored they are with their personal lives.

There are few variables more important to the study of social control and order than that of sexuality. Even though all human beings have approximately the same sexual potentialities, there is tremendous variation in sexual expression patterns even within our own country. One aspect of sexual variation—swinging—is focused upon in this study.

It is a commonly held myth that being a white, middle-class, Anglo-Saxon Protestant requires an acceptance of the dominant cultural norms regarding sexual behavior. Concomitantly, it is widely believed that this part of the population tends to be especially nonadventurous as far as nonconformist erotic practices are concerned. It is this part of the society that gets the most education, the best jobs, and is characterized by the greatest self-discipline, particularly as far as deferring self-gratification is concerned. And it is within this very population that people are especially likely to be socially conditioned by their families into viewing deviant sexuality as mutually exclusive with self-discipline, a good education, and the like. (Deviant sexual behavior is any form of sexual behavior that doesn't abide by the behavioral expectations of any society. It should not be viewed as negative or 'bad,' but merely different from what most people do or are thought to do.)

Naturally, not everyone in this segment of the population internalizes this message, and virtually thousands every year literally disprove its empirical validity by going ahead and earning fine educations and holding good jobs while at the same time leading sexually unconventional lives. Perhaps the most interesting and theoretically meaningful of these 'respectable' although sexually deviant, adventurous groups is that of the legally married middle-class swingers. The major objective of this paper will be to shed some light on the personal and social characteristics of swingers.

For the purposes of this research paper swinging is defined as "that form of extramarital sexual behavior which involves legally married spouses together sharing coitus and other forms of erotic behavior with other legally married couples in a social context defined by all participants as a form of recreational-convivial play." We feel that this is superior to the frequently cited Symonds definition, "A willingness to swap sexual partners with a couple with whom they are not acquainted and/or to go to a swinging party and be willing for both he and his mate to have sexual intercourse with strangers." The Symonds' definition seems to be tautological in that what is being defined is contained within the definition. Moreover, many swinging couples are quite well acquainted with each other. Swinging is often referred to as "comarital sexual behavior" and as "mate sharing," so for purposes of this paper each of these terms can be regarded as synonymous. It should be noted that "comarital" is also associated with other forms of sexual expression besides swinging. For example, the "open marriage" relationship (as described by Carl Rogers in *Becoming Partners*) is comarital sexual behavior, since it shares the common element with swinging of spouse/partner knowledge and approval of sexual activity with others along with the spouse/partner.

The research reviewed here is only part of a much larger study on comarital sexual behavior which was conducted by the senior author as a Ph.D. dissertation in the Department of Sociology at the University of Iowa. A highly simplified version of the results is presented here; the reader is referred to Gilmartin for further details.

Review of the Literature

In the past few decades we have witnessed an interest in sexual behavior as a legitimate research subject. Even though numerous studies on the sociology of sexual behavior have been published, not until quite recently has there been any attention paid to comarital sex. In the specific area of swinging this is understandable since only a few scholars were even aware of American mate sharing until the latter 1960's. Though it is difficult to comprehend, conversations the senior author had with sociologists as recently as 1970 in the Los Angeles area—a melting pot of all manner of sexual diversity—revealed that some of these social scientists were not even aware that comarital sexual behavior even exists in contemporary America.

Before social scientists began investigating swinging, publications on swinging were appearing in so-called "adult" book shops. Paperback books have existed on the topic since 1965, and periodicals and magazine articles written for or about swingers (such as the semi-pornographic magazine *MR.*) have existed since 1957.

By the end of the 1960 decade sociologists were becoming attracted to the study of swinging because it is an activity which seemed to be practiced mainly by ostensibly happily married middle-class couples who are willing to challenge the widely held normative system of sexually (as opposed to psychologically) monogamous marriage. Sociologists often view themselves as practitioners of a "myth-debunking science," so if swinging could be shown to coexist with a happy, stable marital situation it would be a discovery of formidable theoretical and practical importance. Murdock (1949) and other anthropologists have already shown that a stable family system could exist for many generations under a wide variety of different structural forms. Perhaps within even a highly pluralistic society such as the United States there is more than one answer to the problem of how family systems can be structured to function smoothly; and perhaps swingers have some viable alternative answers.

In reviewing the most significant research contributions on swinging, none employed a control group (i.e. a group not influenced by the variable being studied—in this case swinging). Because the methodology of the current study did include a control group, the findings permit some tentative generalizations regarding swinging couples' differences from non-swinging couples of the same socioeconomic background. It is felt that these generalizations, tentative though they may be, provide some fairly strong suggestions as to why some middle-class people choose to become swingers. Most of the research conducted on swinging has been rampant with theoretical speculations as to the causes of this kind of deviance. This is the first study on swinging with a research design that permits going beyond mere speculation to empirically-grounded relationships.

Two of the earlier swinging studies often cited are the ones by Carolyn Symonds (1968; 1971) and George and Nena O'Neill (1970). Symonds' study was conducted in Southern California while the O'Neills' was done in New York City. Together they provide some very interesting and contrasting perspectives on swinging as practiced in different metropolitan areas. A key finding in both of these reports is that suburban swinging is governed by a markedly different set of norms than swinging in the inner city. Swinging within the city characteristically seems to involve a heavy concentration of single, never-married people while suburb swinging tends to be tightly restricted to married couples. Symonds further suggests that urban swinging tends to be much more 'utopian' than 'recreational,' and that its participants tend to be markedly more socially and politically active and liberal than those in the suburbs.

Bartell (1971) interviewed 410 swingers and engaged in participant observations in the Chicago area. Bartell did not employ a control group with which to compare swingers with non-swingers. Moreover, he was primarily concerned with the interpersonal processes entailed in becoming a swinger. In contrast to this study, his effort was not focused on the social, psychological or demographic characteristics that differentiate swingers from non-swingers. No statistical data were presented in Bartell's work, or for that matter, in most reports published on comarital sex. Even though Bartell's study has received much popular acclaim, the objectivity of the study and the broad generalizations made from a limited sample should be considered in any evaluation of the study (see Russell Ford's comments on Bartell, Chapter 14 this book).

Palson and Palson (1972) carried out a study of 136 swingers where the researchers actually participated in swinging in an in-depth 18-month study. In addition to participant observation, couples were informally interviewed in conversations which were much the same as typical discussions at swinging parties. The Palsons were primarily interested in the symbolic meanings of swinging *as defined by the participants*. In contrast to Bartell (1971), couples who desired or actually experienced emotional involvement and continuing friendships were easily identified. It may be that such experiences are far more common than is recognized in most swinging studies, in that swingers who are involved in ongoing emotional relationships are not likely to use swinger magazines to locate other swingers; it is more difficult to find swingers who have their own small group of friends. Swingers were found to naturally deal with jealousy through "individuating" behavior, where the ground rules varied to the extent that explicit or rigid rules were difficult to identify. It was important to swingers that everyone enjoy swinging. Swingers went through stages—from the initial curiosity stage to a stage of increased selectivity where uniqueness of the style of interaction developed. Marital compatibility was stressed, and most spouses were mutually supportive if any problems evolved at the parties. Although the Palsons conclude that swinging often solidifies marriages, they predict that alternative sexually-free life styles such as swinging may decrease or disappear in the future if the decline in economic prosperity can be taken as an indicator of a return to more restricted sexual behavior.

In contrast with the Palsons, James and Lynn Smith (1970) estimate that 15-25% of married couples may become involved in swinging under optimal conditions. The Smiths studied swingers who participated in sexual freedom group parties in the San Francisco area. Much like other swinging literature, they report that swingers tend to be highly educated and low on religious affiliation. Some of their findings, based on their sample of 44% married, 32% single and 25% divorced people, include: comarital sexual behavior is part of an "emergent subculture complete with jargon, symbols, communication techniques. . ." (1970:133); men usually initiate swinging, but women can handle swinging with less jealousy than men; those who stick with swinging learn to deal with sexual jealousy; jealousy between spouses is less likely with mutual spousal agreement about sexual freedom than with those who engage in conventional adultery; some people at parties observe but don't participate in sexual interaction, particularly those who are beginners at swinging; 60% had never been in therapy, and only one person sought therapy because of problems related to swinging; the conformity and strict ground rules reported by Bartell were not reported by the Smiths; and marriages can be improved by swinging and other forms of comarital sex (which dispels the myth that anyone involved in a deviant sexual life style has personal or marital problems).

Bell and Silvan (1970) interviewed twenty-five swingers. Observations were also carried out at parties. They described various kinds of swingers, such as "closet swingers" where the group is small (two or three couples), and the closed door policy is common, and open parties or orgies. In agreement with much of the swinging literature, Bell and Silvan found that most swingers view sex as recreational rather than highly emotional, and see swinging as an end in itself, instead of a means to other goals such as status achievement. Unlike the Smiths or the Palsons, Bell and Silvan conclude there are many swingers who choose the activity due to personal psychological problems. In contrast with the Palsons, Bell and Silvan conclude that swinging is likely to increase as society continues to become more liberal in sexual attitudes and behavior.

Cole and Spanier (1972) collected survey data on 579 respondents where only 1.7% of the sample in a midwestern town had engaged in swinging. Following the logic of symbolic interaction theory, the subjective definitions of swinging as viewed by the participants was a criterion for swingers' evaluation of the merits or problems of swinging, and the evaluation of marital happiness. Swingers were found to be less controlled by agents of social control (such as ones' family). Spanier and Cole (1972) found that almost seven percent of their sample would consider participation in swinging (given an opportunity to do so). Their research is limited in terms of both the sample (one small midwestern town) and the method (survey research), so as with most swinging research it is difficult to conclude much about swinging from such a study.

A recent paper on swinging in the San Diego area by Charles Varni (see Chapter 9 this book) makes a critical distinction between group and couple swinging. Couple swinging is seen to involve a more emotionally intimate and committed situation, but even group swinging is seen to involve perhaps more intimacy than was thought to be the case in earlier swinging studies.

The often contradictory findings from swinging studies is a commentary on the range of sampling methods and instruments used, as well as the personal biases of some of the researchers. A more complete understanding of these biases can be developed from a brief exposure to the research literature.

There is also a vast journalistic literature on swinging. The media have influenced the ideas of many swingers; media reports also can give one the feeling that there are many people involved in such an activity, even though the validity of the 'authentic case histories' reported in journalistic literature is highly suspect. Some of the better known journalistic discourses on swinging include Wilson and Meyers (1965), the Galants (1966; 1967), and Warren (1966).

Method

A total of one hundred swinging and one hundred control couples were obtained for the study. All of the couples were legally married and middle-class, and all were living in what may be considered suburban residential areas. Specifically, 70% of the couples were obtained from the San Fernando Valley suburbs of Los Angeles, and the remaining 30% were obtained from the East Bay suburbs of the San Francisco area. Eighty percent of the couples were obtained through various swinging clubs, and the remaining 20% were obtained through the assistance of swinging couples.

For the first time in swinging research, a control group was employed. (It should be kept in mind that a control group is a group that is stable and unchanging in relation to the variable or topic being studied, which in this case is swinging. Since the control group is not affected by the topic being studied, it offers a methodologically valid basis for comparison with the phenomenon being studied; any differences can be attributed to the phenomenon being studied.) The groups were matched on such characteristics as age, neighborhood of residence, annual income, level of attained education, and presence or absence of children. The control couples were not advised of the fact that the study was to deal with swinging; they were told that the study was a university sponsored government investigation of contemporary patterns of suburban family life. Just under 40% of the non-swinging suburbanites who were asked to serve as respondents were willing to do so. A good deal of evidence has been uncovered in recent years suggesting that volunteers for virtually any kind of study tend to be more liberal, assertive, outgoing and socially aware than those who are reluctant to volunteer. The efforts of such researchers as Maslow and Sakoda (1955) and Martin and Marcuse (1957) are especially enlightening here.

In general, the swinging couples proved a good deal more cooperative than the control group couples, as most of those who were approached indicated a willingness to be studied. Many swingers seem to enjoy talking about themselves and their life styles, particularly when they know that the person they are talking to is able to accept them as they are. Also, it may be that the more a swinger discusses his sexual ideology the more thoroughly and firmly he internalizes it and the more confident he personally comes to feel about it and about himself.

Each husband and wife in both the swinging group and the control group was asked to fill out a detailed questionnaire. Only the questionnaire data were obtained from the controls as this is all that was needed. The swinging couples, on the other hand, were also interviewed at some length. Interviews were always carried out with couples rather than with individuals.

Results

Based upon an analysis of the questionnaire and interview data the following hypotheses, except number 9, were significantly substantiated:

1. Relations with parents during the formative years were significantly less gratifying for the swingers than they were for the controls.

2. Swingers interact with relatives and kin (other than spouse and children) significantly less frequently than do the controls.

3. Swingers view relatives and kin as being of significantly less importance to their personal lives than do the controls.

4. The extent of subjective personal happiness is no different among swingers than it is among the controls.

5. Personal 'anomaly' is no greater among swingers than it is among the controls.
6. The extent of subjective marital happiness is no different among the swingers than it is among the controls.
7. Swingers are no more likely than controls to consume alcoholic beverages excessively.
8. Swingers are no more likely than controls to suffer from feelings of boredom in their personal lives.
9. Swingers are no more likely than the controls to have experienced any form of psychotherapy.

For greater elaboration on any of these findings the interested reader is referred to Gilmartin. It should be pointed out that, because of space limitations, the details of the methodology have been simplified. We shall now examine some of the ramifications of these findings.

Discussion

To begin, it should be realized that when Gilmartin undertook this study he was chiefly concerned with the issue of social control in relation to swinging. This is a new dimension in the investigation of swinging, and definitely a dimension with great potential for future swinging studies. These data clearly indicate less familial social control of swingers than non-swingers.

It is a widely accepted notion that mutually gratifying social interaction (communication) is a prerequisite for any kind of social control or influence. Most parents are strongly desirous of influencing their children in a constructive manner. Yet in their well-intentioned actions they sometimes become overbearing and excessively threatening. It is in this manner that parents sometimes unintentionally create an invisible wall between themselves and their children. Specifically, social distance within the family social system becomes an unintended, unrecognized byproduct of parents' approach to their children. Without communication there can be little social control and probably even less internalization of parental norms. It appears that the more ardently parents try to control their children, the less they are likely to succeed. The most powerful social control is that which is unfelt and which occurs as an integral part of mutually gratifying, convivial conversation and social interaction.

The data strongly suggest that swingers were far more likely than controls to have been reared in accordance with either an authoritarian or a laissez-faire kind of familial pattern. Initially these two methods of raising children appear to be quite opposite, though they do share some rather significant points in common. Both tend to be extremely insensitive to the child as a unique person with his own needs and nature.

They tend to manifest this insensitivity in different ways. The authoritarian parent views the child as a personal possession and has an inflexible set of preconceived notions as to what he would like the child to become; he or she also has an inflexible set of behavior standards which are arbitrarily imposed and enforced. Only the parent "knows" what will be good for the child and it is this which must be imposed. In contrast, the laissez-faire parent tends to be basically disinterested in the world of children. The seeming "freedom" which the children of such parents experience is basically an unintended byproduct of the parents' plain lack of interest and involvement in the daily concerns of the child. When parents are uninterested and uninvolved with their children, they remain largely aloof from them, manifesting the same insensitivity as the authoritarian parent.

Considering the relatively strained relations which swingers had with their parents throughout childhood and adolescence, it is not surprising that their informal visitation with them is now comparatively minimal. Similarly, it is not surprising that relatives tend to be perceived by swingers as having significantly less personal importance than friends.

It is interesting to note that concomitant to the finding that swingers interact significantly less with their relatives and kin than do the controls, that these findings are considerably stronger for wives than for husbands. It is quite likely that this is because women require a greater degree of functional autonomy to engage in behavior as highly deviant as mate sharing.

Swingers tend to be significantly less strongly attached to virtually all conventional agencies of social control than are non-swingers. The family is generally considered to be the most powerful of all social control agencies; it is the institution emphasized throughout this study, but the religious institution also lacks authority among swingers. For example, almost two-thirds of swingers compared to only a quarter of controls agreed with the statement that "religion is one of the greatest sources of hate, intolerance, and oppression that the world has ever known." This finding along with many others not presented here show swingers to be far less strongly committed than the controls to conventional American ideology and to virtually all social control structures.

Some writers such as the Galants have suggested that swinging activities for many have provided the development of a kind of quasi-kin group providing much of the in-group intimacy feelings conventional people find through close interaction with relatives. Some swinging studies, like Varni's, emphasize this intimacy developing among swingers, while others, like Bartell's, claim that swingers prefer not to develop any close friendship ties with the people with whom they swing, and some even prefer the impersonal anonymity afforded by large-group sex encounters with total strangers. Most of the swingers in this study, however, felt a strong bond with mate sharers everywhere. Indeed, some even maintain lists of recommended swinging couples in various parts of the country; when these couples travel they feel quite free to contact these recommended couples as they pass through the various cities.

It is not surprising that swingers interact significantly less with neighbors than do controls. It is particularly important to understand that women are around their neighbors a good deal more of the time than are men, and yet the swinging women still interact very little with neighbors when compared to control wives. Perhaps a key reason for this pattern of relative alienation from those living in the immediate neighborhood is that neighbors tend to be perceived by swingers as constituting a threat. Several of the swingers said that they frequently worried about the possibility of relatives dropping in unannounced at the wrong time! Friendly relationships with people in the same immediate neighborhood could easily expand this worry. The sight of numerous automobiles parked in front of a swinger's house might well make befriended neighbors feel either slighted or desirous of joining in.

The popular press has had much to say about swinging, particularly in relation to the last six hypotheses. It is not uncommon to find certain psychiatrists, lawyers, and theologians known to support the 'status-quo' on most matters to be hand-picked to give their opinions on swinging, and almost all assert with a high degree of confidence that it is associated with all manner of personal and social pathology. Seldom do these writers attempt to provide empirical support for their views beyond their personal interpretation of interviews that they might have had with people who sought them out for psychotherapy.

Obviously, swinging is a highly deviant activity and many consider it to be "sick" or "perverted." It is inevitable that a certain proportion of swingers will not fully believe in the moral validity of swinging. Because of this, data were collected on the "adjustment" of swingers. No meaningful difference was found between the personal happiness of swingers and controls. This finding held for wives as well as for husbands. Considering all things, the swinging couples appeared to be somewhat happier than did the controls. A tendency of swingers to "fake good" could be suspected here, but the strength and consistency of a number of other related findings suggest this is unlikely.

A large array of family research shows that the more common activities a family or marital couple share, the happier they tend to be with each other. This could offer a clue as to why swinging couples may be somewhat happier than "straights." Swinging is a "joint" activity, and a type of recreation. Unique among the various patterns of extramarital sex, swinging actually requires participation *as a couple*.

Any couple that does not appear to be happily married is not likely to be allowed entrance into a swinging group. Swinging groups seek happy and well-adjusted couples who can handle comarital sex and are not likely to cause any disharmony in the group. Besides this screening which tends to exclude unhappy couples, there is also the swinging ideology which undoubtedly has an effect all its own. One of the most common themes pervading the discussions of swinging leaders is that comarital sex embellishes and enriches marriages in all areas, and especially in the erotic sector. At the same time these leaders characteristically insist that swinging is not viable therapy for poor marriages; the very consistent message is that it can and almost always does make good marriages even better.

According to the sociological principle of the "definition of the situation," when we come to define things or ideas as real, these things or ideas tend to become real in their consequences. It seems logical that couples who have the necessary characteristics and who do not become alienated from mate sharing by a few bad experiences are highly likely to see their marriages as improving, because this is what they have expected. And the longer a couple has been swinging, the greater is the exposure to the ideology. All else being equal, frequency of exposure to the ideology should be directly related to the thoroughness of mental and emotional internalization of that ideology—and hence to the construction of an important new social reality.

The findings of the seventh hypothesis are interesting since one of the most frequently observed criticisms of swinging is that its practitioners use it as an "escape from boredom" rather than facing up to their "personal problems" in a direct and "mature" manner. The fascinating thing here is that the control group demonstrated more boredom than did the swingers. As mentioned before, the chief form of recreation for swingers is usually swinging, which is an activity the couple does together. And shared experiences for a couple seem to be more important than non-shared experiences in developing and maintaining a positive relationship. The main recreational pursuits in our society are usually participated in by just one sex. Husbands who enthusiastically practice such activities together weekend after weekend are rarely accused of being excessively bored with their lives, or of pathological escapism in order to avoid facing their psychological problems. But in reality, they may actually be escaping a good deal more than swingers. Unlike comarital sex, their recreations cannot be practiced by the conjugal dyad; in order to practice them it is usually necessary for a person to remove himself physically from home, marriage, and family for a greater amount of time and with a higher degree of frequency than is commonly necessary for comarital sex. There are no data suggesting that it is any more difficult for a person to develop a dependency or "addiction" to baseball, football, or bridge parties than it is to develop a pathological dependency on mate sharing.

The data also suggest that swingers were significantly less stable and serene than most people during their childhood, adolescence, and early adulthood, but after these periods they emerged with a degree of personal happiness and adjustment which was no different from that of "ordinary" people in the same social class. This also makes one speculate about the marital stability among swingers. As a group, swingers had been married for almost as long as controls. But while only 15% of the control husbands had been divorced, 49% of the swinging husbands had; swinging wives had also been divorced more than control wives, 34% to 14%, respectively.

The belief that sexual mate sharing causes divorce and marital and family disorganization is widely held by moralists and psychiatrists who are aware of comarital sex. Yet, despite the above findings, the present study furnishes strong evidence suggestive of an alternative interpretation. *None of the divorces occurred after a man or woman became active with either a present or a former spouse in comarital sexual behavior.* The swinging men contracted their first marriage at an unusually early age. They tended to enter first marriages with women to whom they had felt strong physical attraction, and they first married after very short courtships—well before any kind of adequately comprehensive knowledge and appreciation of the values and personal attributes of the woman could be realized. The research of numerous sociologists has shown that "love" during the early months of a relationship tends to serve as a smokescreen blinding the "lovers" to many of the most essential personal attributes of each other. This blinding smokescreen combined with the weak social control of the family and the strong psychological autonomy of pre-swinging men all function as a powerful force pressing toward early marriage.

A common outcome of these early marriages was that the men gradually began to find their partners too conventional for them. In fact, several of the swinging wives made similar points about their first husbands. Usually within the first three years of marriage the clash of developing values between the pre-swingers and their first spouses gave rise to great conflict, alienation, and unhealable cleavages.

What happened in most of these cases was that swinging for these couples actually preceded the current marriage. This is important, for it provides us with a viable explanation as to why the swinging couples were as happy, and in some respects even happier with each other than the controls even though they were, as a group, far more likely to have experienced at least one divorce in their lifetime. It would appear that when swingers choose their second spouse they tended to be quite careful about selecting someone whose major values, interests, and the like are quite similar to their own (Smith and Smith report the same finding).

Many people have difficulty in understanding how a couple could be happy and yet swing. If we are able to free ourselves from absolutist notions of reality and realize that sexual monogamy is no more instinctual for humans than is polygamy, this should not be at all difficult.

Value systems cannot be imposed on others as real because they are real for us. One of the ideals of our American way of life is sexual monogamy, and all conventional social institutions formally support it. But what sexual value system is "right" or "best" is not the issue here. To quote an old cliché, one man's meat is another man's poison—and so it is for couples.

What seems to be the crucial issue is the degree of agreement or harmony between mates as to what their values and expectations are for their relationship. If both mates have quite similar expectations as to exactly what it is they want sexually from their relationship, they have a high likelihood of success. This idea of value congruence between spouses is a common finding in family research. The more characteristics a couple have in common, the more likely that couple will achieve satisfaction. Behaviors such as comarital sex, premarital sex or marijuana use cannot in and of themselves create conflict and disharmony among people; these behaviors in and of themselves cannot cause a relationship to deteriorate, nor can they promote a diminution of positive self-regard or self-esteem. What can and does make a great deal of difference however, is 1) what the person himself thinks and feels about the behavior he has been engaging in, and 2) the degree of congruence between the internalized norms of the spouses.

One of the more meaningful findings of the current study concerned the control group's involvement in extramarital sexual activity; it was not found to be an uncommon phenomenon at all. In fact, 31% of the husbands and 8% of the wives claimed that they had engaged in EMS at some time in their present marriages. What may be an even greater surprise is that the vast majority of both husbands and wives in these relationships viewed their marriages as being either 'happy' or 'very happy.' There was no indication of any kind that the controls in these marriages were any less happy than those controls whose marriages had remained fully free from any form of extramarital coitus. It should also be noted that deception had been involved in almost all of the control group marriages which involved extramarital sex.

Mention should be made of hypothesis 9, which was not substantiated by the data. It is the opinion of the senior author that since swingers led a stormier youth than controls, this may be one reason why more of them were at some time involved in psychotherapy. However, at the time of the study *fewer swingers than controls were seeing a psychiatrist or clinical psychologist.*

It is not possible to give any composite and encompassing statement on the effect of swinging on the conjugal relationship and on family life. Bartell (1971) suggested that swinging is likely to be very good for some couples and very bad for others; but he did not elaborate. We conclude that swinging cannot in and of itself precipitate negative consequences for any couple or person. *The consequences of swinging depend on the social and cultural context within which it occurs.* If the internalized norms and values of a person are either in harmony or in potential harmony with the ideology of swinging, then that person could not be "turned off" by this form of nonconformity. If the spouse of that person shares nearly the same outlook on life, and if their relationship is a good one, then it is highly unlikely that any active involvement of both in mate sharing would undermine the quality of their marriage. But for the couple who is not already happy with each other, it is highly unlikely that they will become any happier through swinging. If anything, they may ensure the deterioration of their relationship. Similarly, if the values of a husband and wife regarding sexual mate sharing are markedly incongruent, the swinging experience will probably do considerable harm to the marriage.

Some Further Analyses and Speculations

A sizeable minority of the American population has a strong need for sexual variety beyond a sexually monogamous situation. This gives rise to the question of why comarital sexual behavior is not a great deal more widespread than is reported. Comarital sex offers a very rational sexual alternative for those couples who aspire to achieve sexual enjoyment with more than one person. The possibilities for sexual variety are nearly limitless in a comarital situation.

A partial explanation of this may be that most people have a fear of being in on the vanguard of anything new; swinging is not any exception. In order for swingers to change their life styles from the 1950s, some sort of stimulus would have to appear on the scene, such as the journalistic articles that have been produced. The media helped create the *illusion* of the prevalence of swinging, and also provided a credible and easy-to-follow guideline for entrance and active involvement in swinging. Even though the kind of personality likely to be attracted to swinging might be less afraid of being in on the avant-garde, swinging is a sufficiently nonconformist recreational style that a considerable amount of thought is probably needed prior to participation.

In short, very few people are likely to have the courage to turn their fantasies into reality. It requires far too much work, patience, perseverance, and dedication to a particular deviant ideal for most people to take swinging seriously. There has long been a precedent for conventional adultery, for visiting prostitutes, call girls, pick-ups, as well as for carrying on affairs with others. Given the widespread availability of "illegitimate" sex through these conventional means, why would anyone want to take risks on something that was not tried and true—particularly when both the wife's awareness and her willingness to go along and involve herself would necessarily have to be solicited? For even though swinging offers perhaps one of the more rational sexual outlets for a married couple, it does require work to swing.

The more conventional forms of extramarital sex continue to be the norm for those involved in extramarital sex. This is not to say that swinging will not eventually become the norm for those desirous of sexual variety. As swinging gets more exposure, and as those involved continue to work out guidelines that best satisfy their needs, swinging is likely to become more accessible to the general public. It is relatively easy to become involved in sexual mate sharing. The most difficult aspect for a couple aspiring to comarital sexual involvement seems to be that of working out mutually acceptable ground rules to comfortably permit the incorporation of swinging into their marriage.

If the findings of this study are corroborated by future research, sociologists will have some of the necessary tools for predicting which people will swing. This predictive ability is the ultimate goal in the social sciences. For example, from this study we see that from childhood swingers are significantly less emotionally dependent upon their parents and kin than others. They also tend to interact with parents and kin less often. They tend to develop strong needs for heterosexual social interaction significantly earlier in life than do the controls.

It is interesting how well some of the concepts of previous sociological sex research fit into the findings of this study. For example, consider the following proposition from Ira Reiss (1967):

> The degree of acceptable premarital sexual permissiveness in a courtship group varies directly with the degree of autonomy of the courtship group and with the degree of acceptable premarital sexual permissiveness in the social and cultural setting outside the group.

This is concomitant to our findings that swingers appeared to be especially autonomous (relative to those of the controls) from the influence of their respective kin family networks (family systems). With this in mind, our proposition reads:

> The degree of acceptable extramarital sexual permissiveness in a marriage group varies directly with the degree of autonomy of that marriage group and with the degree of acceptable extramarital sexual permissiveness in the social and cultural setting outside the group.

Furthermore, for most of the swingers the peer group seemed to be by far the most salient element of the social and cultural setting outside of the respective marriages. Because the atmosphere in many of the swingers' families of orientation had not been very warm or emotionally gratifying, the swingers of this study learned early to very largely depend on the peer group for recognition, respect, and various other satisfactions. While the controls depended primarily on the family and to a lesser extent on the peer group for these satisfactions, the swingers seemed to depend primarily on the peer group.

Reiss' (1967) second position appears also to be of particular relevance to our data. It states that:

> The stronger the amount of general liberality in a group, the greater the likelihood that social forces will maintain high levels of sexual permissiveness.

Reiss' data on premarital sexual attitudes tend to support this proposition quite well, as do our data on comarital sexual behavior. Specifically, a generally liberal group can be seen as one that stresses individual rights and autonomy and that underplays the importance of conformity and tradition. It follows that such an orientation favors the autonomy of marriage and courtship institutions, and a high degree of permissiveness. As our data indicate, swingers were a great deal more liberal and permissive than controls on virtually every dimension that was checked.

From the work of Harold Christensen (1970), further insights can be obtained that are relevant to the present study. His work made it clear that few if any of the various consequences to which "nonconforming" sexual behavior had been alleged to give rise are actually caused by sexual behavior itself. In essence, the real cause of negative (and quite often of positive) consequences tends to be the pattern of internalized norms and expectations of the participants in the behavior. In simple terms, Christensen's "principle of value relevance" means that the values people hold are relevant to their behavior and to the outcomes or effects of this behavior.

His theory is especially important in enabling us to arrive at a valid understanding of the causes of comarital sexual behavior. In America a considerable amount of autonomy from the kinship system and other conventional agencies of social control seems necessary to enable people to explore deviant alternatives such as comarital sex; this is what these data suggest. However, Christensen's work has revealed that such autonomy is probably related to the exploration of deviant sexual alternatives only in those social settings where full and complete sexual monogamy is espoused. In societies where the kinship and religious institutions do not condition their young to believe that all forms of extramarital sexuality among married persons are wrong, we would not expect to find such behaviors as comarital sex associated with estrangement or autonomy from the kinship system or from the conventional religious structures. In order for social distance from parents, relatives, or kin to be associated with involvement in any specific behavior in any particular society, that behavior must first be defined by the dominant norms of that society as deviant and undesirable.

It has been a recurrent theme throughout this paper that swingers break away from parental controls earlier than non-swingers, and that swingers become involved to a greater degree with peers. For example, dating, going steady, and erotic behavior start earlier for swingers than for controls. In essence, it would seem that swingers tend to learn early that many of life's greatest pleasures and adventures could be experienced through heterosexual involvements. It therefore cannot be considered particularly surprising that swingers were attracted to deviant life styles.

The socialization process for swingers is quite interesting, particularly since it usually involves an effort by the husband to involve the wife in swinging. It usually is the wife who is at first reluctant to try swinging, and then only after some successful and satisfactory encounters does she come to define swinging as pleasurable. However, various studies on sexual mate sharing indicate that once the female begins to enjoy swinging she is more satisfied with this form of sexual expression than is the male. This could be due to the perhaps limitless sexual potential of the female (see Pepper Schwartz, Chapter 12 this book).

Quite commonly when a husband wishes to interest his wife in comarital sex he will leave some swinging literature and perhaps some pornography on the coffee table before he leaves for work in the morning. The wife will notice this and characteristically react with strong negative emotional feelings. This can be called the "revulsion" stage. Depending upon how strong her feelings of revulsion are, out of curiosity she is likely to glance over the material. This revulsion stage can be relatively short-lived, or it can be permanent, depending upon the strength of the woman's internalized norms. In any case, this stage is likely to be fraught with a considerable amount of open weeping in her husband's presence and loud emotional argumentation.

Assuming the woman's background is not too conservative and that the husband manages to offer primarily intellectual arguments pertinent to the swinging ideology about why they should at least try swinging, she is likely to gradually move toward the "resistance" stage. During this stage she begins to learn that some very respectable people like herself swing. The husband may even invite a couple that swings for a chat. He will perhaps keep his wife in the dark about the sexual behavior of the couple for the first couple of hours. Since the wife will usually have established some rapport with the other wife, by the time the conversation turns to swinging she typically finds it impossible to react in a very negative or insulting manner.

The argumentation between husband and wife during this stage tends to lack the emotional fervor which prevailed during the "revulsion" stage. The wife reacts primarily with intellectual arguments of her own as to why she should not swing. The husband counters each one of these with the appropriate points from the swinging ideology which, by that time, he will know fairly well.

The resistance stage can last for several months. If the husband is successful, the wife is likely to move to the "resignation" stage. During this stage the wife resigns herself to try out a swinging party. At this stage the most crucial consideration is whether or not the first introduction to swinging is pleasant. Those couples adequately familiar with the swinging ideology will usually be able to avoid serious problems. On the other hand, naive couples occasionally make serious mistakes during their first one or two swinging encounters. They may arrange to meet a couple—sight unseen—at a motel; or they may invite a couple to their home without having previously investigated them. Many of the people interviewed for this study mentioned having had some extremely unpleasant experiences because of having violated the principle that one must never commit oneself to a swinging encounter without first having interacted with the couple at a bar or a restaurant or in the company of mutual friends. It seems likely, however, that for many women such highly unpleasant experiences could send the wife back from resignation to revulsion, and at the same time greatly reduce the husband's desire to press the issue further. Because of the highly glamorized case histories prevalent in the swinging literature many men harbor very unrealistic expectations with regard to the experiences swinging will afford them.

After resignation the next stage through which many women go is "acceptance." This stage usually comes about after a few favorable swinging experiences. Quite characteristically, it does not last very long. After a few more swinging parties most women progress to the "enthusiasm" stage. They find that in addition to no longer feeling any guilt they actually begin to relish comarital sex to an even greater extent than their husbands.

As Reiss has suggested, since women come from a more conservative social milieu they tend to be more sensitive to liberating social forces once they have been exposed to them. Their greater ultimate enthusiasm for swinging may in part reflect this greater sensitivity. This speculation is supported by our finding that swinging wives tend to support the normative regulations of the swinging ideology to a significantly greater extent than their husbands do. It is as though they find it necessary to substitute one firm normative structure for another—while men seem to be comfortable under a looser type of normative organization.

In conclusion, sexual mate sharing by itself cannot either help or harm a marital relationship. What is of vital importance is how the couple views their behavior. If both partners can be both mentally and emotionally satisfied in a swinging situation, then this type of sexual expression will not do any harm to their relationship. If both partners see swinging as an essential part of their relationship, then swinging is "right" for them. In summary, comarital sex should be viewed as an alternative unconventional marital life style in the contemporary United States; it can be seen as constituting one of several alternatives to ordering the sexual drive of adult members of society. If the participants all share similar definitions and expectations for their mutual behavior, there is no reason why their behavior should not co-exist with more traditional marriage forms.

REFERENCES

Bartell, Gilbert D. *Group Sex*. New York: Signet, 1971.

Bell, Robert R. and Lillian Silvan. " 'Swinging'—The sexual exchange of marriage partners." Paper presented at the Society for the Scientific Study of Social Problems, August 31, 1970, Washington, D.C.

Christensen, Harold and Christina Gregg. "Changing sex norms in America and Scandinavia." *Journal of Marriage and the Family*, 1970, 32, 616-627.

Cole, Charles L. and Graham B. Spanier. "Becoming a mate swapper: Some thoughts on how the process works." Paper presented at the Midwest Sociological Society, April 21, 1972, Kansas City, Missouri.

Galant, M. and K. *Sex Rebels*. San Diego: Publisher's Export Company, 1966a.

Galant, M. and K. *The Lesbian in Group Love*. Cleveland: Century Books, 1966b.

Galant, M. and K. *Mate Swapping Syndrome*. Los Angeles: Triumph Fact Books, 1967a.

Galant, M. and K. *The Swinging Bisexuals*. Cleveland: Century Books, 1967b.

Galant, M. and K. *Wife Swapping in Business*. Cleveland: Century Books, 1967c.

Galant, M. and K. *Wife Swapping: The People*. San Diego: Publisher's Export Company, 1967d.

Gilmartin, B. G. "Relationship of traits measured by the California Psychological Inventory to premarital sexual standards and behaviors." Unpublished Masters Thesis. Salt Lake City: University of Utah, 1964.

Gilmartin, Brian G. Ph.D. dissertation, in process, University of Iowa, Iowa City, Adviser, Hallowell Pope.

Martin, R. M. and F. L. Marcuse. "Characteristics of volunteers and nonvolunteers for hypnosis." *Journal of Clinical and Experimental Hypnosis*, 1957, 5, 176-179.

Maslow, A. H. and J. Sakoda. "Volunteer-error in the Kinsey study." In Jerome Himelhoch and Sylvia Fava (eds.), *Sexual Behavior in American Society*. New York: Norton, 1955.

Murdock, G. P. *Social Structure*. New York: Macmillan, 1949. O'Neill, G. and Nena O'Neill. "Patterns in group sexual activity." *Journal of Sex Research*, 1970, 6, 101-112.

Palson, Charles and Rebecca Palson. "Swinging in wedlock." *Society*, 1972, 9, 28-37.

Reiss, Ira L. *The Social Context of Premarital Sexual Permissiveness*. New York: Holt, Rinehart and Winston, 1967.

Rogers, Carl. *Becoming Partners: Marriage and Its Alternatives*. New York: Delacorte Press, 1972.

Smith, James and Lynn Smith. "Co-marital sex and the sexual freedom movement." *Journal of Sex Research*, 1970, 6, 131-142.

Spanier, Graham and Charles Cole. "Mate swapping: Participation, knowledge, and values in a midwestern community." Paper presented at the Midwest Sociological Society, April 21, 1972, Kansas City, Missouri.

Symonds, Carolyn. "Pilot study of the peripheral behavior of sexual mate swappers." Unpublished Masters Thesis. Riverside, Cal.: University of California, 1968.

Symonds, Carolyn. "Sexual mate swapping and the swingers." *Marriage Counseling Quarterly*, 1971, 6, 1–12.

Varni, Charles. "An Exploratory Study of Spouse-Swapping." (See his Chapter 9 in this book.)

Warren, J. T. *Age of the Wife Swappers.* New York: Lancer Books, 1966.

Wilson, T. J. B. and E. Myers. *Wife Swapping: A Complete 8 Year Survey of Morals in North America.* New York: Volitant Press, 1965.

9

CONTEXTS OF CONVERSION: THE CASE OF SWINGING
Charles A. Varni

Here Varni analyzes the social contexts of conversion to swinging in terms of processes and beliefs. He notes modes of involvement and suggests a typology which goes beyond the investigative interests of previous researchers. Selection methods and effects of swinging are shown to be interrelated with previous as well as emergent definitions of the swinging scene as seen by pairs in the process of engagement and disengagement. Swingers are defined as hard-core, egotistical, recreational, interpersonal, or communal. The belief system of each type of swinger is examined in the context of swinging for the pair. The chapter closes with a comparison between the guilt-producing affair and the potentials for positive integration of a relationship in some swinging situations. Varni claims that many people are engaging in something like the swinging process while not giving their behavior that label. According to Varni, greater honesty about EMS is needed in order to examine the social context more intelligently.

Introduction

Change in beliefs, attitudes, values and behavior is characteristic of human existence in twentieth century mass society. Much of this change is prompted by our environment as we adapt to an everchanging (and ever more menacing) technology while others have their genesis in a new value or attitude we take as our own and seek to live by. This paper will concern itself with changes of the latter type in which a person seeks a change in his or her belief system such that behaviors and/or ideas which were once unacceptable become acceptable. Social psychologists refer to this phenomenon as "conversion" and usually reserve it for the more profound—usual polar—types of change experienced by an individual, for example, the change of religious beliefs from Catholic to Jewish or the change of political beliefs from Fascist to Communist. Rather than developing a general theory of conversion, in this paper I wish to direct my attention to one particular conversion—and the actual beliefs and behaviors which result from the change.

In short, then, this paper will address itself to swinging—the phenomenon of married couples exchanging spouses for the expressed purpose of sexual interaction, most usually intercourse—and to the process of conversion involved in becoming a swinger.

Research Methods

In undertaking this study it was my desire to understand the world of swinging as swingers themselves understood it, and thus I chose to utilize a particular form and degree of participant observation known as a covert researcher role.[1] The choice of this research method does not at all mean that my data were "limited" to the commonsense understandings which swingers possessed of their own behavior, but rather that analysis of the phenomenon would be grounded in the experience of swingers themselves.

In order to gain entrance into the world of swinging my wife and I presented ourselves as a couple favorably disposed to the idea of swinging who wanted to meet with swingers in order to get a better idea of what it was all about. To make contact with swingers I placed advertisements in a local "underground" newspaper (which is one method used by swingers to meet one another). The first ad read, "Young sociologist and wife desire to learn about swinging. Phone 282-," and the second, "Couple, attractive, 26 and 25, who have yet to swing, desire to meet swinging couple. P.O. Box -." There was little difference in the type or amount of response (other than phone calls from non-swingers) to the two advertisements.

Through these initial contacts meetings were arranged with sixteen swinging married couples, usually in their homes. Because it is in the face-to-face meeting between researcher and subject in which data are collected that the issue of validity is paramount, I would like to briefly describe selected background expectations and taken-for-granted understandings which characterized our meetings with swingers.

First, there was an assumed mutual interest in swinging. I assumed this of the couple because they responded to the advertisement and they assumed it of me because I placed it. Couples assumed my interest to be personal, that is, my wife and I represented potential swinging partners. Second, there existed an assumed dichotomy of knowledge about swinging in which my wife and I were the receivers of information and the other couple the givers. This "student-teacher" relationship characterized all of the interactive situations. Third, I strove to create a feeling of mutual trust in which the couple would feel comfortable being open and honest about their feelings and attitudes. To facilitate this mutual trust, I utilized two complementary methods. First, I tried to demonstrate that I was being open and honest about my own feelings and attitudes which, besides providing a role model when necessary, helped create the impression that I was a person who could be trusted. Second, I was generally accepting and non-judgmental of the person's actions, beliefs and attitudes. My role was that of the interested and understanding listener. I had no "hidden" questionnaire and I tried to facilitate the couple expressing those aspects of swinging they felt to be most important or relevant.

The recording of data took place immediately upon leaving a meeting. My wife and I dictated everything we could recall that was said or expressed. I later transcribed, organized, and added to these recordings.

With regards to the degree of participant observation, neither my wife nor myself engaged in any sexual interaction with any of the couples we met. We maintained, throughout the study, the role of novice swingers. I cannot, therefore, characterize my relationship with the swingers as an intimate one. However, given the limits of my researcher/swinger role and the interactive situation, I feel a sufficient amount of intimacy was attained. Total time spent with each couple averaged about three hours.

Findings

Social Characteristics of Swingers

All of the swingers we met were white and the great majority can be characterized as being middle- to upper-middle class in socioeconomic status. Occupations of the men included district sales manager, Private in the Marine Corps, restaurant manager, engineer, office supply salesman, computer salesman, retired Navy chief, commercial artist, realtor, lawyer, mathematician, company president, and student. Some were unemployed. Their ages ranged from 19 to 60 with the majority being less than 33 years old. Length of marriage ranged from three months to thirty years, the majority falling between two and six years. Although the frequency varied, almost all couples reported swinging no more than twice a month. All but three of the couples had children and all lived in the greater San Diego metropolitan area.

Definition of a Swinger

There are two essential conditions which, when taken together, define what it is to be a swinger. First, the married individuals engage in extramarital sex with full knowledge and consent of one another.

There is no ignorance, lying, or cheating involved. Second, the couple engages in extramarital sex as a couple—both in terms of time and, to some degree, in terms of space. The fact that they "do it together" is emphasized by all swingers and constitutes the necessary definitional condition. Because they engage in extramarital sex with the full knowledge of their spouses and because they do it together, swingers do not think of themselves as adulterers. In contrast, they see themselves as having transcended the perceived pettiness, hypocrisy, immaturity, and dishonesty of adulterous affairs engaged in by the majority of married couples. This definition of what it is to be a swinger, while providing legitimation and reinforcement to a swinging life-style, at the same time disavows any deviant label and, with some success, turns it around and applies it to those non-swinging marrieds who engage in extramarital sex.

Becoming a Swinger

I earlier characterized the conversion process as one in which beliefs and/or behaviors which were once unacceptable are redefined in such a way as to now be acceptable. A major problem for any person undergoing the change in morality implicit in conversion is that of having to "break away" from the social control bind of the previous belief system. That is, any system of beliefs carries with it a certain conception of what is right and wrong and it is always wrong to advocate a way of being which is in opposition to the belief system. Social control mechanisms are developed which seek to prevent or, at the least, discourage persons from giving up the belief system. These mechanisms may range from physical punishment to loss of material possessions to loss of self-respect. For example, in converting from Catholicism to Judaism a person must first cope with the social control mechanisms of the Catholic church which seek to prevent persons from leaving the church, this threat taking the form of being forever damned in the eyes of God. It can be seen that the really essential part of conversion is that of neutralizing the social control (i.e., moral) binds of the belief system one is giving up. As we shall see below, becoming a swinger involves a change in the social meanings of sexual behavior and swingers must "deal with" the social meanings of sex of the "old" belief system.

What is the belief system or social meanings of sexual behavior which swingers converted from? It is one commonly held by many persons in our culture, namely the "double standard." The double standard of sexual behavior means that sex without love and extramarital sex are wrong for a woman while sex without love and, to a lesser degree, extramarital sex are acceptable for a man. The swingers I met had generally subscribed to this meaning of sexual behavior. For example, eleven of the sixteen women reported being virgins when they met their husbands and most stated they used to have "puritanical" attitudes towards sex. The men reported having "some" sexual experience prior to marriage and a few reported extramarital experiences.

The problem for the man in "dealing with" the proscriptions against swinging was that of accepting the idea of sexual freedom (within the confines of a swinging relationship) for the wife. The "usual" response of men who want sex outside of marriage is to engage in extramarital sex, not swinging. Why would a man reject the double standard and accept the idea of swinging? There are two typical reasons which are given by two different types of men. The first type I call the user. This type uses his wife to gain entrance into swinging. He does not appear to be very concerned with her feelings or desires. He has little ego involvement with her and his rejection of the double standard is on Machiavellian grounds. The second type I call the encourager. This type rejects the double standard on more idealistic grounds, mainly egalitarianism. He feels swinging will be a positive experience for both him and his wife. The togetherness and openly and honestly expressed sexuality which he perceives as being part of swinging appeal to him. I characterized five men as users and eleven as encouragers.

In all but one case, the man initially brought up the idea of swinging and invariably met with a negative reaction by the wife. The most typical reaction of the woman was a feeling that something must be wrong with her or with the marriage coupled with a strong sense of revulsion for the whole idea. At this point the husband began a "convincing (or coercing) process" which usually sought to allay the wife's fears. Most began with reassurances that the marriage was not falling apart and then continued over a period of days, weeks, or months to point out the advantages of swinging. Of the different methods of persuasion used, one of the more innovative was a primitive form of conditioning. As his wife was experiencing orgasm George would speak of the virtues of swinging and the possibility of experiencing this state of bliss with another man. Another read his wife popular articles on swinging, being careful to omit any negative references.

The main problem for women in "dealing with" the proscriptions against swinging was their equating sexual encounters and love. Most women had great difficulty in separating the two, considering that it would be almost impossible to engage in successful sex without involving some degree of love. Coupled with this problem was the fear that perhaps their husbands no longer cared for them and that their desire to swing marked the beginning of the end of the relationship. Few women allowed themselves to entertain positive thoughts about swinging although a few reported curiosity at what it would be like to be with another man. Despite the husbands' convincing process, every woman approached her first swinging experience with varying degrees of anxiety, apprehension, and misgiving. The men were also anxious and apprehensive but less so than the women. With the exception of two, every woman stated she agreed to try swinging once in order to please her husband.

The main effect of the first swinging experience was to greatly reduce the level of anxiety, especially the woman's, and thus provide a climate in which the experience could be evaluated in a more "objective" light. If anything, the experience was anticlimactic in relation to the woman's expectations. The typical response was that it was not such a big deal after all. Many women had guardedly positive remarks to make such as, "Well, it wasn't as bad as I thought it would be," or "I might try it again."

The factors which appeared to be important in a woman's becoming favorably disposed to swinging are (1) her perception of her marriage relationship and (2) her own subjective experience. If she feels that her marriage relationship has not been damaged, she is relieved; if it looks as if it may have been improved, she is pleased. If her subjective experience was not negative, she is relieved; if it was at all positive, she is pleased. Most women appear to attach more importance to the first factor, especially in the early stages of becoming a swinger. Later on, when assured that the relationship is not threatened, her subjective experiences take on greater priority. The same two factors determine the man's response but the degree of importance attached to either factor is more variable. For some men (the users) their own subjective experience may be more important than any possible effects on the relationship, and for others (the encouragers) just the opposite may be true. However, all men have a vested interest in their wives obtaining a positive experience since their continued swinging is dependent on her participation.

The new meaning which sexual activities comes to possess for many persons after their first swinging experience may be accounted for by a "meaning void." Novice swingers who approach the swinging situation with definite expectations (even if they are unspecified) and have these expectations radically unfulfilled, will be thrust into a situation which is existentially experienced as being meaningless or having ambiguous meaning. New meanings are "created" to fill this void. These meanings are developed by the individual as he interprets his experience with relation to earlier expectations and to those meanings which are supplied by other participants in the situation.

If nothing traumatic happens in the first swinging experience, the couple will likely try it again. The second encounter (other things being equal) is usually more enjoyable since the couple has a more realistic expectation about what will take place and, with lower levels of anxiety, they are more able to relax and enjoy themselves. This second experience, if it proves to be non-threatening and especially if it is enjoyable, is usually the clincher in that it validates the non-uniqueness of the first experience.

If a couple decides they will not continue swinging, swingers report, it is almost always because of unmanageable jealousy on the part of either the husband or the wife, sometimes both. Swingers agreed that the prerequisites for successful swinging are: (1) the couple has a viable (strong) marriage relationship based on love; (2) each of the partners has no serious "hang-ups"; and (3) that there be no jealousy.

Forms of Swinging

On the basis of group size preference, swingers can be divided into two groups, those who prefer to swing with only one couple at a time (I call these "one couple" swingers), and those who prefer to swing in party situations involving three or more couples (I call these "party swingers"). Of the couples I met, seven were strictly one couple swingers and never attended parties. The other nine couples were party swingers although they also swung in one couple situations.

The stability of membership in the swinging group ranges from: (1) the very stable group which is characterized as close-knit, cohesive, with little membership turnover; (2) the fairly stable group which is a relatively large group of swingers who are known to one another, are loosely organized (sometimes in cliques), and have a somewhat fluid membership; and (3) the unstable group which consists of couples who come together for one night only.

The very stable group exists as the ideal for many swingers. It consists of anywhere from five to ten couples who find a high degree of need satisfaction from one another. They are a very close-knit group and are very compatible with one another—ideologically, intellectually, emotionally, and sexually. Many swingers expressed a desire to form a very stable group and were on the lookout for couples they would want to join. Some thought of the group as being quite utopian, along the lines of the free love "nests" developed by Valentine Michael Smith in Robert Heinlein's novel, *Stranger in a Strange Land* or the group marriage idea presented by Robert Rimmer in *Proposition 31*. Both of these books, especially Heinlein's, were mentioned by swingers as utopian ideals which they agreed with in principle.

The one very stable group I had contact with was made up of eleven reportedly happily married couples who met together two to four times a month. The meetings took place in either a private home or weekend resort motel. The group was very private and the members very secretive about their identities for fear that their occupations and community standing would suffer if their swinging activities were discovered. The group was formed in order to overcome the problem of jealousy which members had experienced in their earlier swinging. There were definite rules of membership, the most important being that

(1) all members must be sexually acceptable to one another (heterosexually) and (2) there was no swinging allowed outside of the group. They did not allow any drug use, homosexual participants, or unmarried couples. New members were first screened and had to be found acceptable to all group members. Initial acceptability was largely determined by physical attractiveness and the lack of any significant "personal defects." Deviant individuals were openly confronted with their rule-breaking by other members and if they did not change, they were excluded from the group. The members saw themselves as a very close-knit group and their relationships with one another were both sexual and social. Usually a different couple hosted each meeting and they determined how couples were to be paired off during that session. The first pairing of the evening was always heterosexual and the individuals were obligated to have some sexual interaction with their partner which resulted in orgasm. This impersonal pairing was reported to guard against the development of jealousy. After the first pairing individuals were free to make whatever alliances they wished. All of the women had experienced homosexual liaisons within the group as had two of the men. Most of the members found it stimulating to observe one another and usually the sexual behavior was highly visible.

The fairly stable group was, by far, the most commonly encountered. The mix of anywhere from ten to thirty couples who make up the group is loosely organized with members being directly or indirectly known to each other. When a couple has a party they will invite from this "pool" a number of couples. Also invited may be some "new" (not necessarily novice) couples acquainted with the host or a guest. Thus a party may consist of couples who are well acquainted, somewhat acquainted, and not acquainted at all.

The party situation itself resembles any other weekend evening social gathering in a private home with couples either sitting in one room or freely circulating. Most persons have drinks and the conversation revolves around common areas of discourse such as jobs, children, what the individuals have been doing since they last saw each other, and generally superficial topics. The host will many times help facilitate the transition from social to sexual behavior by calling attention to the fact that it is time to get started or by dimming the lights. Other transition devices, known as "ice-breakers," are sometimes used (such as sexually-oriented parlor games or erotic movies). The role of the ice-breaker is often crucial and a few swingers reported they had sat around for hours at parties where everyone was afraid to make the first move.

The selection process whereby individuals make their temporary alliances is similar to that of a large group of people making dates with one another. As is common in our culture, the man is usually the overt aggressor in the partner selection process. It is his responsibility to make first contact. The woman is not passive in this dating game and through the use of eye contact, smiles, and other conversations of gesture, communicates her availability or attraction. The man's invitation to swing is usually preceded by some light, "get to know one another" conversation. The man's invitation to swing is significant in that he has presented himself to the woman and now asks her judgment of him as someone she would like to have intercourse with. Even though swingers have greatly "normalized" sexual behavior, this invitation to sex is still more significant and involves substantially more aspects of the man's self than does an invitation to coffee. To be rejected as a sexual partner could be damaging to a person's self-concept or, in the least, result in hurt feelings. Swingers seek to minimize these risks in the following manner. When a woman rejects an invitation, the rejection is made in such a way that no negative valuation of the man is evident. The woman usually places the cause of rejection on herself by utilizing excuses such as "I don't really feel like it right now," "I'm a little tired at the moment," or "I just finished with another man." Taken at face value, the meaning of the rejection is that the man approached at the wrong moment and might be successful at another time; but, in actuality, it constitutes a rejection of him as a sexual partner. The meaning of the rejection is shared by the individuals and is verified by the fact that rarely will a man make a second attempt to swing with the woman unless she has given him "obvious" reason to ask again.

The general acceptance of the giving and receiving of rejection among swingers is facilitated by two commonly held norms. First, that no one should do anything they do not want to. This norm supports the woman in her rejection of the man. Second, that no one should be coerced to do anything they do not want to. This norm exerts pressure on the man who may be so inclined. Also, acceptance of rejection by the man is made easier because (1) his sense of self is not overtly threatened by the form of the rejection and (2) he can always find a woman who will swing with him.

The visibility of sexual behavior in the fairly stable groups varied from high to no visibility. For example, Jack and Jill were members of a group in which all sexual behavior took place behind closed doors. After a couple arranged to swing with one another they would retire to the bedroom fully clothed, do their thing, and then get completely redressed and return to the living room to repeat the whole process later on. Another couple, George and Marty, were social nudists and they remained nude at swinging parties they attended but all of their sex took place behind closed doors. There is quite an overlap between social nudism and swinging although the extent of overlap is not known. Swingers estimate that anywhere from 10 to 30 percent of their numbers are nudists. Social nudists usually remain nude at parties regardless of the other couples' states of dress or undress, but they do not necessarily engage in visible sex. Bernard and Barbara, both in their late fifties, were members of a group in which some of the couples engaged in highly visible sexual behavior and others did not. In the group Bob and Betty belonged to almost everyone enjoyed highly visible sex and most of it took place in one room.

The unstable group consists of a number of couples who meet at a "swing club" and participate in a "one-night stand." A swing club is to swingers what a "gay" bar is to homosexuals. It provides a place where swingers and would-be swingers can meet one another and form temporary sexual alliances. At the time of this study there were no swing clubs in San Diego although a few existed in Los Angeles, the most popular being "The Swing" located in the San Fernando Valley.

The types of parties which originate from these clubs vary in size and visibility of sexual behavior. For example, George and Marty would usually end up at small parties involving three to five couples. They did encounter problems in the form of couples who were not really sure that they wanted to swing and persons who became too intoxicated. Abe and Ann attended swing club originated parties which were given by very wealthy persons, for example, one party involved upwards of eighty persons and lasted for two days. There were special rooms designated for drug users and homosexuals and all sexual behavior was highly visible.

One other type of swing club which exists in the Los Angeles area is the "key club." These clubs, rather than being an open, public gathering place such as a cocktail lounge, have membership fees, entrance requirements, dues, and a private clubhouse. For example, one club had a $80 membership fee and dues of $20 a month. These fees entitled members to use the club house, an old mansion, Thursday through Sunday nights for swinging activities. The club also sponsored parties and outings and supplied members with the phone numbers of other members who lived in their geographical area.

Very few of the swingers I met cared for the unstable group situation and only two couples were at all actively involved in it. The unstable group provides persons with a fairly impersonal and anonymous environment in which they can engage in sexual behavior and this appears to be its main attraction. Originating from a public club, it also provides an accessible means for novice swingers to meet other swingers.

Party swingers perceived certain advantages to this type of swinging. First, at a party there were a relatively large number of potential partners to choose from, a distinct advantage over one couple situations. Second, sociability and the chance to meet different types of persons was emphasized by party swingers. Third, two couples said they enjoyed the greater impersonality afforded by the party situation as they had previously experienced trouble and uncomfortableness in extricating themselves from one couple situations in which they did not want to swing and felt this was easier to do in the party situation. Fourth, sexual stimulation and enjoyment, for both men and women, was felt to be another advantage. Both sexes reported multiple orgasms. Some women cited their advantage over men of being able to continue intercourse while men had to wait for another erection. Along this same line, half of the women said they greatly enjoyed the feeling of being desired and wanted by a number of men.

The other basic form of swinging is the one couple type. One couple swingers do not attend parties and this fact distinguishes them from swingers who swing in both party and one couple situations. One couple swingers usually seek an interpersonal rapport with their swinging partners and, either through experience or intuition, have come to the conclusion that a party situation is not conducive to fulfilling this desire. The party is seen as an impersonal experience. One couple swingers want more of a friendship-type relationship with their swinging partners. They want to engage in non-swinging social and recreational activities with them.

One couple swingers differ in the spatial distribution of their sexual behavior; three couples preferred to be in the same room, three preferred to be in separate rooms, and one had no preference. Same room swingers like the feeling of doing it together and enjoy watching one another. Different room swingers emphasized the individuality of the experience and were against same room swinging. When these two types met, the same room swingers deferred to the wishes of different room swingers.

Methods of Meeting and Selection Factors

There are three methods used by swingers to make contact with one another. A common one is advertising in a local newspaper, usually of the "underground" variety. The ads are worded similarly to the ones I placed and are accompanied by a post office box number. In responding to an ad, swingers will usually give a brief description of themselves, any special sexual desires, and their phone number, or they may ask the originating couple to respond in a like manner. In either case, a phone call is usually placed. The first meeting between two swinging couples is most always defined as being strictly social in nature and there is no expectation to swing on the part of either couple. The role of the purely social meeting is to allow the couples to meet face-to-face so they may evaluate one another as potential swinging partners.

There are many reasons, some being more universal than others, why couples reject one another as swinging partners. This rejection may take place any time during the meeting process described above. For example, most swingers will not cross "racial" lines. They will usually not swing with unmarried couples, reportedly from fear of contracting venereal disease. Interpersonal compatability, in various degrees, is desired by many swingers; lack of it will be cause for rejection. Also, differentials in age are important to "younger" swingers who will not usually swing with those defined as "too old," although the converse was not true for "older" swingers. All persons felt to be unclean about their bodies and "weirdos" are rejected.

The closest thing to a universal factor of acceptance among swingers is physical "attractiveness." An "attractive" couple, on their appearance alone, would be accepted as swinging partners by most couples. However, an "unattractive" couple would not experience universal rejection for "unattractiveness" is much more particularistic in nature—one man's weed being another man's flower. Attractiveness constitutes a sufficient but not necessary condition of acceptance among swingers.

It appears that the selection factors which operate in swinging to bring people together and drive them apart are little, if any, different than those operating in the larger culture. Some swingers are highly selective, swinging with only one out of every ten couples they meet and others, with less stringent requirements, swing with eight out of ten couples they meet.

A second method used by swingers to meet one another is personal referral. A couple may feel that their swinging partners would like another couple they know and thus ask permission to give the other couple their partner's number so a meeting can be arranged. These "matchmaker" arranged meetings will usually not have the strictly social expectation since there is an assumption that the couples will be compatible.

A third method consists of direct contact between swingers. This contact rarely takes place in everyday life but rather in known spots where swingers congregate, such as private or public swing clubs.

Effects of Swinging

The most often reported effect of swinging (by eight couples) was an increased feeling of warmth, closeness, and love between the husband and wife. This feeling was most intense when they returned to each others' arms after swinging with another couple(s). It was as if the swinging experience was proof and validation of their love. They could ignore one of the traditional and (supposedly) essential boundary determining criteria of marriage, that of sexual fidelity, and find greater strength, security, and trust in their relationship. Another reported positive effect was a more fully developed knowledge and competence in sexual technique. Three couples reported a more enriched and active social life as a benefit of swinging. A number of couples felt that swinging had facilitated their becoming more open and honest with one another in all areas of their relationship. Four women reported not being completely happy with swinging. Two of the women had originally agreed to swing on the condition that their husbands no longer "sneak around" behind their backs. These women felt more in control and less threatened by the swinging situation. The other two said they had never really enjoyed swinging but continued in order to please their husbands.

Swingers engage in a wide variety of sexual behavior, most of it heterosexual, some of it homosexual. Heterosexual behavior consists mainly of varied positions of vaginal intercourse and oral-genital sex. Many swingers were introduced to the varied forms of sexual activity in swinging, especially those of an oral-genital nature. Homosexual behavior, consisting mainly of cunnilingus between two women, is not uncommon. Three of the women had had homosexual experiences in swinging situations. Homosexuality involving men is rare.

Becoming a swinger is most always accompanied by a change in the meaning of sex. First of all, the meaning of what is appropriate sexual behavior, in what situation, and with whom is changed. It is more broadly defined to accommodate a wider range and choice of behavior. For example, the woman who, in the presence of her husband, engages in mutual oral-genital sex with a relative stranger whom she does not love, appears to have "taken on" a different meaning of sexual behavior. The meaning of the idea of exclusivity of sex between the marriage partners as symbolizing devotion, trust, security, or love to one another has been transformed to just the opposite, that is, non-exclusivity comes to symbolize many of these same things. The meaning of sexual behavior as a thing in itself is also transformed from one of relative non-acceptance to one of relative acceptance. Sexual behavior loses its mystery, secretiveness, "something done in the dark" aspect and takes on more the character of a taken-for-granted, normal activity.

Typology of Swingers

The term "swinging" encompasses a wide range of behavior. The following typology was developed with the idea of sensitizing persons to the varied forms of behavior included within this range. Its sole function is to communicate a "feeling" and appreciation for the world of swingers. Although presented in a crudely continuous fashion, it in no way purports to be ideal, pure, nor exhaustive.

The major criterion around which the typology is organized is the degree of emotional involvement a swinger desires with his or her partner(s). Generally speaking, movement along the "continuum" from "hard-core" to "communal" involves going from unstable to very stable group or couple affiliation, from user to encourager husbands, and from having non-swinging to swinging friends. Also, the meaning of sexual behavior (and thus, by definition, of swinging) differs among the types. It should be pointed out that this is a typology of individuals, not couples (although at times I treat it as if it were). While it is usually the case that both members of the dyad come to have the "same" desires with regard to swinging relationships, it is not always so.

Hard-core swingers are ones who want no emotional involvement with their partners and, with little selectivity, swing with as many couples as possible. Other types of swingers feel them to be cold, unfeeling, and deviant. Often the woman who is married to a hard-core swinger is coerced into swinging. Hard-core swingers participate in unstable party and one couple situations.

Egotistical swingers seek little emotional involvement with their partners and are usually fairly selective. They want purely sexual/sensual experiences and seek to gratify their own sexual needs and desires, which may involve feeling attractive, virile, sexy, and desired by other persons. Swinging is viewed as a separate and distinct part of their lives and they have very few, if any, social relationships—much less friendships—with their swinging partners. They enjoy both party and one couple situations. The husband uses his wife and she may never become a very devoted swinger.

Recreational swingers emphasize the social aspects associated with swinging. They are members of fairly stable groups, enjoy both party and one couple situations, and engage in non-swinging activities with one another. Swinging is viewed as an entertaining, social, "get your kicks," hedonistic activity in which significant emotional involvement with the partner is neither needed nor desired. Recreational swingers have both swinging and non-swinging friends. Wives are both partially used and encouraged by their husbands and usually become dedicated swingers.

Interpersonal swingers desire and emphasize close emotional relationships with their partners. They are seeking intimate and viable friendships with couples with whom they can share themselves emotionally (which includes sex) in an open and honest manner. Usually the husband has encouraged his wife and they both see swinging as having a more or less "natural" congruence with their total lifestyle. They are likely to be quite selective about whom they swing with, prefer one couple situations almost exclusively, and many of their friends will be swingers.

Communal swingers are very similar to interpersonals except that they advocate some form of group marriage, an idea rejected by most all swingers.

Of the thirty-two swingers I met, none were hard-core, five were egotistical, eleven were recreational, eleven were interpersonal, one was communal, and four I could not categorize.

Concluding Remarks

I would like to conclude this paper with a few observations and comments on the place of swinging in contemporary American society, especially its place in the so-called sexual revolution.

When I first talked to my parents about the subject of my thesis research my mother commented something to the effect, "Oh that's been going on for a long time, Charles, only we called it an affair." It should be obvious from my research that swinging in no way resembles the common, garden variety affair. The affair breeds deceit, while swinging encourages openness and honesty; the affair involves one spouse, swinging involves both; the affair often results in guilt, swinging often results in closeness. Swingers have their extramarital sex together and openly and this makes it a truly revolutionary form of social action in the context of America in the 70's, revolutionary in the sense of being a radically new form and type of sexual expression. It is not new historically, but certainly in this epoch.

In projecting the future historical significance of swinging one must ask—significant for what? If swinging results in widespread characterological change in those who participate (and thus brings about social structural change), then I would say it has significant consequences. That is, do swingers also undergo a conversion in other basic beliefs about human relationships or do they maintain a more narrow path of change devoted mainly to sexual relationships? Do they seek openness and honesty in other relationships? Do they advocate moral freedom for all persons?

By and large, my data show that a typological and, to some degree, generational gap exists among swingers in that the older, recreational type seeks to be liberated only in terms of what counts as an appropriate sex partner and shies away from the emotional involvements. They want sex but fear relationships. On the other hand, younger, interpersonal swingers seek the close and warm ties which characterize emotionally open relationships. So, to answer the questions posed above I would have to say that interpersonal swinging may have significant historical consequences for it is part of a new way of being while recreational swinging is only another extension of modern day alienated existence.

The significance of interpersonal swinging is that it represents only the tip of a vast iceberg—the iceberg (should I say warmberg?) of open, honest, actualizing, non-possessive and non-oppressive human relationships which have become the ideal for millions of young people. Remember that my study deals with *swingers*, persons who label themselves as such and answer advertisements in newspapers. If swingers were the only Americans experimenting with open and honest relationships involving co-marital or extramarital sex, their significance would be nil, but they are not. For millions of young people sex outside of marriage (or ongoing two person relationships) is becoming an accepted ideal, if not a practice. And it is not promiscuous sex, as commonly conceived, but rather sex as *part* of a more fully open and honest friendship. For many persons the idea of going through thirty to forty years of their lives with only one sexual partner is becoming more absurd everyday. And because these same persons choose to live their lives in an open and honest manner, the affair is an unattractive alternative. They are developing relationships based on more humanistic (dare I say realistic?) grounds of non-oppression and self-actualization rather than sexual fidelity. In short, and paradoxically, the significance of swinging is that so many people are doing it who don't call themselves swingers.

NOTES

1   This chapter is a revised and expanded version of an article which originally appeared in the *Pacific Sociological Review* ("An Exploratory Study of Spouse Swapping," *Pacific Sociological Review*, Vol. 15, No. 4, 1972). Jane L. Varni was an invaluable fellow researcher on this project. For a more complete account of the development of my research role, see my "An Exploratory Study of Wife Swapping," (unpublished Master's Thesis) California State University, San Diego, 1970. It should be noted that as a "participant observer" I did not observe persons swinging but rather observed their reports of the acts and subjective meanings of swinging.

10

SEXUAL ASPECTS OF GROUP MARRIAGE
Larry L. and Joan M. Constantine

The authors use both psychological and anthropological viewpoints to discuss motives for entering group marriages. They describe the various patternings of sex life in marital groups they have examined and find that personal growth reasons often are a primary consideration in joining a group. Although sexual reasons for joining a group marriage are important, they conclude that jealousy over sex poses less of a problem in the dynamics of group marriage than does the fact that a complex and difficult range of interpersonal problems must be worked out in a non-supportive cultural environment. Although group marriage is unlikely to cure marital problems already existing, in many instances the group can and does give significant support for growth of its participants. As in normal marriages, in group marriage sex often tends to become the arena in which other problems are fought out—the visible sign that something is wrong. Sex as a problem was not significant in the breakup of groups, although groups did tend to break up after relatively short periods. The authors conclude that there are many important lessons to be learned from group marriage research that have implications for other marriages, particularly open marriages of the future.

From three years of multidisciplinary research (1973), we have found contemporary group marriage to encompass a variety of complex, multidimensional relationships. These marriages included anywhere from three to six conjugal partners, each of whom considered himself or herself to be married to at least two partners.[1] The average group consisted of four adult partners and three children (usually the children of the couples' pre-existing conventional marriages). Without exception, the group marriages we have studied have involved far more than sexual exchanges; yet, in the final analysis concurrent sexual partnerships with more than one partner is one of the chief characteristics of group marriage. This chapter will focus on the sexual element of group marriage, using concepts as well as data.

Often reporters, writers, and sometimes family scientists want most of all to know the details of the group marriage's sex life, although sex is but one of many elements of the relationships in a group marriage. So common is the insistence on sexual details that participants frequently react with a defensive posture which down-plays the importance of sex in the relationship.[2]

From presentations to college and professional audiences we have learned that the group marriage concept is surprisingly threatening to many people. The readers of *Life* magazine (Flaherty: 1972) were more than twice as likely to approve of premarital cohabitation than to approve of group marriage, but four times as likely to accept group living without sex. Nine out of ten disapproved of group marriage. However, it is apparent that more educated and professional groups are more approving or interested in group marriage, as more than a fourth of the 20,000 respondents in the *Psychology Today* survey (Athenasiou, 1970) were interested in or in favor of group marriage.

The issue *is* sex, but not sex *per se*. Rather, the issue is sex in a group, which means the maintenance and acknowledgment of more than one sexually intimate relationship at a time.

An Explanatory Model

If 90% of the public are threatened by group marriage, then the few who find the idea personally attractive and the even smaller proportion who actually create such relationships are of singular interest. Our research focused particularly on the motivations for participation in group marriage. As we extended our formal understanding of the reasons why some people strive to develop these relationships, we also added to our informal understanding of why many more people run the other way. In the end, the answers seemed in many respects to be covered by a single conceptualization of human sexuality.

Group marriage evokes strong positive and negative reactions because it is tied into very basic and nearly universal human desires—desires as operant in the antagonists as in the advocates.

In the course of our research we formulated an elementary model of human sexuality—a model based on diverse anthropological, ethological, and psychological evidence. Sexual attraction between individuals is of course largely a function of cultural conditioning and individual socialization as screened through some measure of innate propensities. The desire for actual sexual encounter is mediated by social factors (such as status and opportunity). Within all these variables two factors act to amplify or generate sexual attraction—novelty and intimacy. We postulated a human tendency both to seek new and different partners and to sexualize relationships of established proximity, propinquity, and interpersonal intimacy.

It is our contention that an impartial review of the cross-cultural evidence must lead to the conclusion that humans are probably polysexual by nature (that is, tending toward a preference for sexual relations with a variety of partners, without necessarily separating them in time). Some data strongly suggest that polysexuality is an *inherent* propensity. For example, even in the most restrictive and punitive monogamous societies, both men and women are found to engage in non-marital sex, resisting cultural counter-conditioning, and risking even grave consequences. It seems equally evident that the desire for sex in the context of on-going intimacy is both strong and widespread, if not universal.

In the end then, group marriage occurs or presents a profound threat because nearly everyone has the desire for sexual intimacy with those they are interpersonally intimate—including a best friend's spouse, the good neighbors across the street, and members of the immediate family. It is acknowledged in diverse disciplines from anthropology to psychology that incestuous desires are nearly universal. We believe this applies not only in quasi-family environments such as communes and extended family groups, but in the nuclear family as well. The ubiquity of incest taboos attests to the commonness of the underlying link between sexual desires and intimacy. The strength and generality of the incest taboo makes strong reactions against group marriage more understandable; most people will be close to a number of people but will have few individuals (likely only one) with whom they can be openly sexual.

But societies more often taboo than approve open multiple relationships. One explanation lies in the ways in which the emotional energy vested in human polysexuality becomes channeled. Multiple relationships are more complex than simple paired relationships. Where multiple relationships are sanctioned, those conflicts in time and space which arise will be visible and open, becoming part of the social process of the group which validates them. On the other hand, the group which prohibits multiple sexual relations transforms the consequences from social effects into internal conflicts within individuals; sexual attractions and the desire for actualization will be present nonetheless. Societies tend to condone or promote those behaviors which appear to have fewer undesirable social consequences. Thus, taboos on multiple sexual relations are more likely than approval; the negative consequences of the taboos are intrapsychic, and less socially obvious (or perhaps more deferred) than are the consequences of open multiple sexuality.

If common propensities are indeed involved, we do not expect that those who participate in group marriage will differ fundamentally from the great masses of people who reject it.

The Participants

The people who formed group marriages were found to come from a wide range of backgrounds spanning from lower to upper social classes. They were somewhat better educated and somewhat younger than the national average. Their religious up-bringings varied, but an unexpectedly high percentage claimed an ethical-humanist background and an even higher percentage accept that label now. In most cases their childhoods were unexceptional. Most were married and entered the group relationship with their spouses. Those marriages were for the most part happy. On a standard measure of marital adjustment,[3] participants' scores were average, but significantly more clustered than the normative population. The lifestyles included group marriages within agrarian communes, urban groups, group marriages nestled in the suburbs, and a few small towns; most were urban or suburban in setting. Politically, participants leaned somewhat toward the apolitical left, but there were also conservatives and revolutionaries among them.

The prior sexual experience of participants does not distinguish them. Almost all had had premarital intercourse. They had experimented with a variety of sexual practices. Consistent with the Kinsey averages, somewhat over half had been involved extramaritally *before* the group marriage experience. Quite a few of these earlier extramarital experiences had been open and shared with spouses, which is probably unusual. About half had experimented with mate-swapping, believing it to be based on more than sexual exchange. Most were disappointed and dropped out of swinging.

Frequently the group marriage commitment began with very early cross-marital sexual involvement and in a number of cases participants felt that sex had occured too soon in the group marriage.

Motivation and Personality

Sex is among the real reasons for people entering group marriage. Eighty-eight percent said that a variety of sexual partners was among their reasons, but sex was not the most important motivation. Only 18% said it was an important motivation; among the other more important motivations, *personal growth* is most relevant. Indeed, an interest in genuinely intimate interpersonal relations and the personality growth potential in interpersonal processes is characteristic of group marriage participants.

We also undertook a study of the personality characteristics of participants as an indicator of possible deeper motivation for group marriage participation. If a desire for multiple intimacy is simply human, then we would expect the few who actualize it to be more in touch with their human needs and desires. Since the unstated taboo on multiple intimacy seems to be quite strong, we would expect those who "violate" it to show less need to conform or defer to such social pressures. It is plausible that both their sexual needs and their needs for variety are above average. In that sex is only one modality or means of expressing the multiple intimacy of a group marriage, we would suspect that participants would have a capacity for intimacy in a broad sense.

To explore these hypotheses we employed two widely used standard psychological instruments, The Edwards Personal Preference Schedule (EPPS), purporting to measure the levels of fifteen normal personality needs, and The Personal Orientation Inventory (POI) consisting of two scales and ten subscales which are elements of self-actualization or high-level emotional functioning; the POI is a measure of psychological health. From the scales on which participants differ significantly from established norms, we can construct a composite picture of personality structure as motivation.[4]

In simplest form we hypothesized certain basic *needs* which the individual must be *aware* of and must be capable of carrying over into *behavior*. Three elements are required: needs, awareness, and the ability to actualize in behavior. The three basic needs or drives derive from the model given above: sex, change or variety, and intimacy. The EPPS scores of participants did reveal a significantly high need for change (and a complementary low need for order) plus high needs for heterosexuality and for intraception. The need for intraception includes the need to know and understand other people, which is related to intimacy needs. The POI results also showed exceptionally high capacities for intimacy and a high awareness of their own needs and feelings. As for actualizing the satisfaction of these needs against social counterforces, participants were inner-directed (rather than other-directed), high in the need for autonomy, flexible in application of their values (high existentiality), spontaneous and freely expressive of their needs and feelings, very low in the need for deference to others and to norms, and low in any need for feeling guilty.

The elevated scores on eleven of the twelve POI scales suggests that participants are normally healthy psychologically. For this group, emotional problems can be ruled out as motivations for entering group marriage.

Sexual Life in a Group Marriage

What *is* the sex life of a participant in a group marriage like? The multiple sexual involvement and the process of building new intimacy can initially be all-consuming. While this first flush of a new relationship inevitably recedes, participants report that both their frequency of sexual relations and their enjoyment of them remained at a higher level than before they entered the group relationship. An element of this continued enthusiasm is undoubtedly the fact that sexual pairings were changed often within the group. Early in the history of most groups, this change of partners was fixed by a schedule of rotation, typically allotting three to four days with each partner. In theory rotation equalizes sexual opportunity, forestalls jealousy and possible incidental rejection, and saves the energy and anxiety that might otherwise be invested in a repeated decision-making process. In practice only the last has held true, and most groups have moved gradually toward more flexible and informal means of pairing as their interpersonal skills grow.

Along the way, many strategies for pairing have been tried, with even an occasional resort to a deck of cards. One group created a scheme whereby women controlled the sleeping arrangements one month and men had the choices the next. Bedroom arrangements vary, from each person having a bed and personal room to all participants in a single bed (as in some triads). Since the mode is four people (two men and two women), the most prevalent setup is one bedroom and one bed per two people. Space is a factor; there may only be three bedrooms for six adults, and it is much easier to fit three in a bed than five or six.

Infrequently, all or a group of the partners in a group marriage might hop into bed together. Their experiences with group sexual encounters do not form a single pattern. Rarely does a group attempt to share sex communally as a steady diet; more commonly, group sex is an occasional result of particularly strong group feelings. Characteristically, participants have reported their group sexual experiences to be profoundly moving, though occasionally tinged with competition or anxiety. With one or two exceptions, sexual contact between members of the same sex have only occurred in this group context. This last finding is especially significant in that participants as a group considered same sex physical expression of affection to be natural and desirable. There was a phenomenological difference in the way participants perceived and organized the experience of *ambisexual* encounter in a group and *homosexual* encounter in a pair. Since they held consistently liberal attitudes on homosexuality and seemed to accept this component in themselves, we conclude that the phenomenological distinction between ambisexual experiences is meaningful and significant.

Sexual Problems and Sexual Jealousy

A minority of the attempted group marriages were motivated by sexual and relationship problems in the existing conventional marriages of the participating couples. The troubled couples often believed that multiple intimacy would help solve their problems, but usually the problems were exacerbated. At the very least, multiple intimacy is a setting in which the submerged elements of relationships—the hidden contracts and unexamined patterns of all marriages—are likely to surface in ways that invite and may even demand creative resolution. The highly-motivated couple generally uses the situation and the emerging material as part of a process of further building their relationship. When known or significant difficulties lead people into group marriage, they are unlikely to make a success of the group relationship or solve their problems.

In a couple of instances, the motivating problem for one of the couples was their inability to time their climaxes well enough to satisfy the wife. These couples hoped that relationships with more sexually-sophisticated couples would teach them how to achieve mutual sexual satisfaction. Both husband and wife found they could achieve sexual satisfaction with their new partners, but were unable to carry this into their existing marriage, in part because each interpreted their new success as evidence that the problem lay with their original partner. Group marriage now appears to be equally inappropriate as blanket security to cover an insecure partnership, as a committee solution to communications problems, or as a sexually highlighted solution to economic difficulties.

Group marriage participants, like all marriage partners, can have problems even where the relationships are basically sound. Some of these have been manifestly sexual. They have experienced isolated bouts with temporary impotence, vaginal pain, premature ejaculation, monellial infections (which can keep manifesting itself among the female partners until the doctor catches on and treats all the partners at once), and even an occasional simple lack of passion. But to date, we have found no specifically sexual problem which seems unusually (in comparison to monogamous marriages) prevalent in group marriages, except in that sex is the arena in which relationship issues are so commonly presented.

Quite often, sexual encounters provide the trigger or releasing mechanism for jealous behavior. In society at large, the absence of jealous reactions would be suspect in a situation where a partner becomes sexually intimate with another person. Of course, sex is not the only trigger for jealous behavior, but sex does appear to most people to be unusually important in this context. What makes sex important is that people believe it to be important, taking it as signifying crucial elements of relationships—especially deep (perhaps total) involvement and exclusive commitment.

Through jealous behavior, people signal their fear that they might lose something they value. Many elements of a relationship may be valued: for example, companionship, intellectual stimulation, support, and sex. Anxiety results from situations that appear to someone to carry the potential for ultimate loss of such valued aspects of a relationship. But anxiety is only the primary feeling and is often transformed into anger, rage, despondency, and other feelings which give rise to the behavior we all know as jealousy.

For a person for whom sexual involvement is the symbol for the entire relationship or a sign of a commitment which can only apply to one partner, sexual "infidelity" portends not merely the loss of one opportunity for sexual encounter, nor even simply the changing of the sexual element of a relationship, but the loss of the whole relationship which is what sex symbolizes to that person. Given the traditional symbolic meaning ascribed to sex, jealousy is the expected outcome of multiple sexual intimacy.

Group marriage participants also experience problems with jealousy; 80% considered jealousy to be a problem, although jealousy was *rarely* regarded as serious, becoming significantly less of a problem as individuals and groups matured. Many learned creative ways to deal with jealousy, accepting jealous behavior as signalling the need for exploration of what might be at stake in their relationships at that time. For them, the symbolic meaning of sex is not traditional. They see sex primarily as communication, as one of many means of expressing themselves with each other, and as a natural concommitant to intimacy rather than as a token of fidelity or an exclusive privilege. For all these reasons—maturation, interpersonal skills, and a non-traditional interpretation of sex—jealousy has generally been more manageable for group marriage participants.

The Open Pair

Human sexuality has been linked with the formation of durable paired relationships or "pair bonds."[5] It has not been unequivocally established that humans form pair bonds in the same sense that many other animals do. Even the existence of human pair bonds does not preclude the possibility that lasting and meaningful bonds with other partners can also be formed. In the group marriages studied, the preexisting pair relationships in which participants were involved at the outset of their group marriages continued to be distinguishable both by outside observers and by participants even in the oldest groups (about five years). That is, the prior marriages continued to be special or carry primacy in some sense long after the establishment of multiple intimacy. In nearly all cases, these "pair bonds" survived group dissolution; only a few couples separated in the process or as a result of group break-up.

The pair bonds of group marriage participants are unusual in that they are not exclusive; they are open to both alternate sexual and interpersonal intimacy. The same is true of the group bonds, for most of the groups were found to permit and validate further intimacy beyond the group marriage. Thus the group marriage itself was often an *open marriage* in which partners could, if they desired, form and maintain significant relationships with people outside the group, without the group necessarily regarding this as disruptive or a violation of faith. We believe this will be the prevailing pattern for group marriages, since the motivating factors in forming the group do not disappear after formation.

Of the possible bonds in a group marriage, the bonds between same-sex members appear to be especially salient in determining group success. Comfort with simple physical expressions of affection, though not necessarily overtly sexual expression, may contribute substantially to the quality of same-sex bonds. For example, two men who can express anger, distrust or frustration, but cannot communicate simple affection are likely to have difficulties sharing a household. In general, women have formed good same-sex relationships more readily than have men, in part due to greater opportunity and because women have usually been less severely socialized against same-sex affection than have men. As an extension of this, more women than men in group marriages have resolved their ambisexuality which is also true in other emerging sexual patterns.[6]

Meanings

Most group marriages studied had broken up by the conclusion of the research. Sex was rarely a significant problem while the groups remained intact, and the longer a group lasted, the less likely they were to report sex-related problems. Nor did sexual issues figure importantly into the breakup of groups. Others have reported findings supporting the view that sex is not really a problem in group marriage as many might expect it to be.[7] Indeed, sex may be one of the positive elements in an otherwise difficult relationship.

We believe that the implications for more conventional marriages are the most important outcomes of our research.

The needs for sexual experience, variety, and intimacy which motivate group marriage are present in everyone, even if to lesser degrees.

There also appears to be a fundamental link between interpersonal involvement and a human propensity to sexualize relationships. With greater individual and collective awareness of these drives or tendencies there is likely to be even more extensive experimentation with a variety of marriage and family life styles permitting multiple intimacy. In view of the current trend toward a pluralistic society which is more tolerant of alternate life styles, translation of awareness into behavior should prove for many people to be even easier in the future. Thus many of the special problems of today's group marriages may soon be quite general and unspecial. Coping with relationship complexity and the allotment of time and energy are part of close multiple friendships even where sex is not involved.

The reduction of jealousy and development of productive ways of dealing with jealous behavior could be of great value, even for couples having conventional, closed relationships, with neither open multiple sexual involvement nor much in the way of interpersonal closeness outside marriage.

It now seems clear from research that a group of people can become deeply mutually involved in each other's lives and even extend their intimacy to include sex, and yet remain friends. Open, multiple sexual pairings can be handled by individuals and the group in which they occur, as can the jealous behavior that may accompany the early stages of such relationships. While this may not appear startling for those who have experienced such relationships, the potential impact of such a "discovery" could be profound.

NOTES

1 Three-person marriages are not group marriages by traditional definitions. The correct term for the relationships studied is "multilateral marriage," but this is a technical issue beyond the scope of this chapter. See Larry and Joan Constantine, "Group and Multilateral Marriage: Definitional Notes, Glossary, and Annotated Bibliography." *Family Process* 1971, 10.
2 See, for example, Ruthie Stein, "Not Just an Ordinary Family." *San Francisco Chronicle*, August 28, 1970, p. 19.
3 An adaptation of the Burgess-Cottrell Marital Adjustment Form. See E. W. Burgess and P. Wallin, *Engagement and Marriage*. New York: Lippincott, 1953, and Burgess and Cottrell, *Predicting Success or Failure in Marriage*. Englewood Cliffs, N.J.: Prentice-Hall, 1939.
4 The complete report is found in *Group Marriage*, 1973.
5 For a detailed discussion of the role of sex in bond formation, see Francois Duyckaert's *The Sexual Bond*. New York: Delacorte Press, 1970, and James Ramey, "Emerging Patterns of Behavior in Marriage: Deviations or Innovations." *Journal of Sex Research*, February, 1972.
6 Gilbert Bartell, *Group Sex*. New York: Peter H. Wyden, 1971.
7 Reese D. Kilgo, "Can Group Marriage Work?" *Sexual Behavior*, 1972, 6, 2.

REFERENCES

Athenasiou, Robert, et. al. "Sex," *Psychology Today*, 1970, 14.

Constantine, Larry and Joan Constantine. "Sexual aspects of multilateral relations," *Journal of Sex Research*, 1971, 7, 204-226.

Constantine, Larry and Joan Constantine. *Group Marriage: A Study of Contemporary Multilateral Marriages*. New York: Macmillan, 1973.

Flaherty, Tom. "In defense of traditional marriage," *Life*, November, 1972, 1959-62.

11
APOLLONIANS AND DIONYSIANS: SOME IMPRESSIONS OF SEX IN THE COUNTER-CULTURE
Mervyn Millar

In this chapter a member of Bennet Berger's research group discusses some of his impressions gained through several years of studying specific communal groups in the San Francisco Bay area. He characterizes the approaches taken by particular groups—and by various individuals within those groups—as either dionysian (hedonistic or free-form) or apollonian (relatively conventional and ritual-oriented) in their basic approach to life and to sex. He further divides the groups he studied in terms of the tightness and looseness of their social structures (creedal communes such as Yoga centers being considered tightly structured) and relates those dimensions to attitudes about sex. In summary, he points out that almost as wide a range of sexual practices exists among members of communes as does among any subgroups or classes in straight society.

Traditionally in this civilization sex has always been an area of experience highly charged with anxiety and secrecy. The body is covered, only certain aspects of the sexual self revealed to others, and sexual experience shared in the dark with only a husband or wife. A prime element in the counter-culture thinking is an attempt to accept the body—and sexuality—as "natural." This perspective holds that sex should simply be accepted and enjoyed for what it is, a natural function. It shouldn't be regarded as something extra-special that has to be sought out. Nor should it be regarded as something that has to be hidden from others. In examining the behavior of certain people who consider themselves to be members of the counter-culture, to see what they reveal to each other, what is hidden, what is considered a personal possession, and what the person would share with others in the area of sexual experience, I have developed what might be called an "impressionistic" study.[1] I haven't been able to administer questionnaires on sexual attitudes and behavior to a random sample of counter-culture members with results generalizable to some total population, but I have become aware of a number of patterns in the process of doing other research among counter-culture members.

At this point, it seems very difficult to determine who are the members of the alleged counter-culture. Depending on one's distance from the phenomenon the uniformity of the counter-culture appears to change. From the vantage point of the "straight" world "freaks" and "heads" are easily identifiable. But from the midst of the "head" scene it is the variety that strikes one more than the similarity. No doubt it has always been difficult to circumscribe the parameters of the bohemian sub-culture, or any expressive movement that stresses individualism. But at least until the collapse of the Haight-Ashbury scene it was possible to conceive the counter-culture as a unified phenomenon. The number of individuals involved in past bohemian expressions have been small enough so that they could be seen concentrated in certain run down parts of the city. Many thought the labels "beatnik" and later "hippie" were adequate to distinguish members of these groups. But now we are left with an amorphous term like "counter-culture" and the specific categories such as "politico," "beatnik," "hippie," or "head" no longer seem adequate to cover all varieties of those espousing ideas that seem counter to the established order. With increased numbers, drawn from different sectors of the larger society, and with the passage of time and specialized developments, the contradictions or variety of approaches found within the counter-culture have become more noticeable. So now there are many different individuals and groups who consider themselves members of the counter-culture, and who indeed share many ideas, values, and modes of behavior, yet who also differ greatly from each other.

In Berkeley and other Bay Area environs I have "hung out" with people in various communal situations, and have visited at least 6 large groups that consider themselves as a "commune." I also have some information from colleagues engaged in the same study, who observed a variety of groups briefly and one or two intensely. But most of this article is based on my experience with and thinking about two particular communes. Both of these groups are urban communes that have several houses in close proximity to each other close to academic centers in the Bay Area. They have between 50 and 100 adult members, with larger membership in the summer and less in the winter. One group has a charismatic leader, with the group based around his teachings. The other group has several dominant members who informally influence the group direction. One group has a super-personalistic perspective, has faith in supreme beings that direct all activities here on earth. The other group has a more social conception of causation; they tend to be more politically oriented. One group runs a health food restaurant as an economic source. The other group deals drugs, and searches for odd jobs. Both groups maintain open recruitment, resources permitting. And the "religious" group seems to be composed of people from the lower middle-class. The other group has a more working-class orientation. The style of these two groups differs greatly and I think this has influenced me to emphasize the difference between the dionysian and apollonian elements in the counter-culture.

Dionysian and Apollonian

The hedonist and the ascetic are two ancient roles in counter-cultures throughout history, stretching back on the one hand to shamen and primitive revelry with images of mixing strange potions and dancing naked drunkenness reeling about the campfirelit night. Or, on the other hand, images of chanting and cosmic lights of meditation in Himalayan caves. I could try to paint a picture of each of these styles in all their differing dimensions, pointing out contrasts in room furnishings, dress, or foods, for example; but here I only want to consider their differing sexual attitudes and behavior.

I will frame my interpretations of life in communal groups in terms of these two ideal types, but the reader must realize that these are the extremes of a continuum of sexual expression. Any one individual might be looked at in terms of the continuum and considered more dionysian than apollonian in comparison to someone else. Any particular individual may be thought of as loose in one way, yet tight in another. But the terms serve a function in giving the flavor of a general life-style.

Whatever their other differences, most members of the counter-culture are concerned with re-defining the self. They want to break out of the self imposed on them by parents, schools, employers, doctors, and so on. This "rational" self seems too narrow and constricted. It is oriented toward maintaining a "sane," courteous front to others. It is based on the idea of "having to stay alive." There is the sense that the self has to maintain itself in the face of others. There is a concern of increasing assets, of competing for the scarce resources, and a feeling that everyone else is trying to cut the self down, to score points. The self is centered in thought and calculation. Present gratifications are sacrificed in favor of long-term future development. Impulses are suppressed for building civilization. The hip perspective on "straight" society is closely akin to the Freudian view, where an over moralistic super-ego, and a reality manipulating ego, prevent the expression of the id. Freud's theory was based on an intellectual tradition that seems to derive from the counter-culture. But unlike Freud, the hip view is more in tune with Reich's view that the id should be expressed. The feeling is that if the ego is broken through and the aggression released that the erotic will be freely expressed, and without repression there will be no more blocked energy converted into aggression.

The hip view sees man as basically good. The desire is to break through this rational self, to break down the barriers of the ego. The person must die to this narrow self in order to be re-born in a greater self. Growth will entail the suffering of exploration. The attempt is to dwell in the depth of the present moment. To remain in consciousness seeing through the illusion of the self and the arbitrary rules enforced by other social members. Sex may be one way of reaching this state. From the Freudian view the hip ideal is to reach the "oceanic state," to regress to a point before the development of the ego. But sex may be only one way to get out of the self and intensify sensation. "We have to get out of our minds to come to our senses," says Allen Watts, a guru highly respected by many heads. Another way to come to your senses is to detach the consciousness from the physical body, to see the body as separate from consciousness and part of a lower material plane. If the person were able to stay in this state of consciousness then sex would be only one form of deep sensation. In fact, from this mystic state every movement, each sound, each sensation would be sensed as an erotic experience.

For many hedonists sex is enough in itself, sex for the sensation. But some hedonists like to see sex as making them better more liberated beings. This is the pronounced form found with people into humanistic psychology, encounter groups, and the like. The attempt is to open the self to sensuality, to become loose. In Reich's terminology encounter types are self-consciously trying to loosen the character armour, to relax, to just "let it happen," to "flow with it," and to trust others. I might point out here that some hedonists aren't so concerned with loosening the boundaries and barriers of the self, they may just be concerned with achieving their own sense of pleasure, and may not be seeking union with others. Even those hedonists who are seeking such fusion will be unlikely to approach it with the kind of organization shown by some encounter group types. Most hedonists are less self-conscious about sex, and favor spontaneity. Indeed the use of sex as a means of achieving growth in the encounter group scene seems almost instrumental. And in the section on communes I will point out that the organization of sexual exchange fits with a tighter social organization.

For some hedonists there is a sense in which sex should be a childlike expression. They feel that the child is natural and spontaneous, he acts as he feels without the restraints of society. They would like to be able to act without cerebration, but directly and innocently. As in Freudian theory the child is seen as inherently erotic. The child tunes in naturally to the oceanic state, and is constantly sensing in an erotic way. Freud termed the infant's sense of the erotic *polymorphous perverse*, because the child could sense the erotic in any part of his body. But as we mature our erotic sensations become continually more focused in the genital areas. Hedonists attempt to return to this state of undifferentiated sexuality. There is an image of being totally erotic, sensitive to touch in any part of the body.

Another part of this perspective that seems to emerge from the early beginnings of the counter-culture—again an idea that Freud picked up—is the basic bisexuality of humans. Each being has both male and female hormones, therefore a male and female nature, animus and anima, active and passive. But this belief has different consequences for hedonists than ascetics, or for dionysians and apollonians. The dionysians seem to feel that ideally the person should be able to take his or her pleasure where they can. They would look on any kind of sexual activity as "natural." Indeed there is an image of the ideal being as expressing both the male and female. This image of the counter-culture is put together nicely by Norman O. Brown in *Life Against Death*. Some segments of the counter-culture look on those who won't engage in homosexual activity as being uptight and unable to accept a basic part of their nature. They seem to regard their ability to hug and kiss a member of the same sex in public as a mark of their avant garde status. This stance has become especially fashionable among some females with the emergence of Women's Liberation. While few hedonists have reached this degree of "liberation," this image has become an increasingly popular one in the counter-culture.

One of the counter-culture tenets is that men and women in the straight world have been locked into traditional roles. Women have been stuck serving men, being considered passive and non-sexual beings, while men have been considered the dominant, and sexual seekers. Women have had to emphasize the non-aggressive and emotional, while men have had to suppress the soft and sensitive to succeed in the competitive world. Some feel that Woman's Liberation is the very heart of revolution, for when women have been liberated there will be no more dominance and aggression that is caused by the *macho* syndrome. And some dionysians welcome women's liberation because it seems to open the possibility of increased sexual expression.

Some dionysians seek out sex, may even build their identity around a sexual orientation. But the aim of the dionysian seems to be to allow sex to become just another part of a full life. The feeling is that too much has been made out of sex by the "straight" society. Because of the rules against sexual expression a natural function is repressed. But still it needs expression; the sexual forces find release in strange and indirect ways. Because the need for sex can't be directly satisfied it becomes an obsession of the culture. So there are sexual displays everywhere. Sex is used to keep the individual dissatisfied and under mild tension so that more goods can be consumed. Sex then becomes part of the capitalist world, something else that the individual competes for and strives to get. And those at the top have more chances to score. Sex is seen in quantitative terms, as in the number of others one has seduced. The "head" scene holds out the idea that when it is allowed full expression sex will no longer be such an obsession but just a natural part of life.

Many communards feel that the interest of the "straight" society in their sexual habits is part of this morbid curiosity about the repressed and sinful. They feel that "straights" project their repressed desires for orgies and such to communards and then seek to punish them for it. Some heads feel that the whole generation gap and the attempted repression of them by "straight" society is based on sexual jealousy. The "straights" feel that they are missing out on all kinds of wild scenes and unspeakable pleasures. They imagine that they are past such opportunities and seek to prevent their sons and daughters from enjoying what they were afraid of. Heads see the singles bars, cocktail lounge pickups, massage parlors, porno book stores, and prostitution as part of the whole repression syndrome wedded to capitalism. In this sense there is really less interest in sexuality in the counter-culture than there is in straight society.

Indeed some religious groups in the counter-culture have a much "straighter" attitude toward sex than the average middle-class citizen. Members of most of these groups orient around the separation of spirit and matter—concentrating on the sense of consciousness as an ever-present possibility for us to realize, perceiving the world from a consciousness that seems eternal, while the body and the objects of the phenomenal world seem transitory. The physical is seen from consciousness, soul, or spirit, as a mere veil that prevents the consciousness from fully perceiving itself. The body is seen as being of a much heavier vibration, a slower moving vibration of the basic particles. So the body is perceived as lower than the soul, for spirit has a higher, more rapid vibratory level. These groups conceive of there being a basic energy or spirit, a One-ness, from which the phenomenal world is fashioned, in all its apparent diversity. But within this One-ness are levels of consciousness or spirit. Often these groups practice a way of being by connecting with the consciousness as an expanding and eternal presence—they wish to perceive through the body but not to become identified with it.

Sex is looked on as a prime matrix for bringing the consciousness down into the body. When consciousness becomes focused on the sexual then it functions at a lower vibration. The ability to remain in a sense of spiritual bliss becomes agitated. The sense of being able to love everyone and everything in a spiritual way becomes narrowed down to the flesh of a particular person. These members of the counter-culture see a unity of spirit and body, but they see the spirit has a finer, more harmonious, more blissful state, than the states of the body. From what some members of such groups say it seems as if they regard the seminal fluid as charged with some kind of extra energy, so that just the release of fluids is considered to deplete the energy available for higher consciousness.

While the dionysian is able to engage in sexual trips for the sensation itself, the apollonian feels that sex should be engaged in for the furtherance of some end. A few groups actually give the feeling that the only time they really feel justified in taking part in such physical activity is when there is the chance that the female can become pregnant. (Just why they want to bring higher consciousness into the world in the form of a human body receives varied explanation.) One religious group feels that the couple should have sex only when the female is fertile. Most members of these groups are opposed to birth control of any form, especially pills. These things are seen as "un-natural." Most members of one group that held this belief seem to use the rhythm method. And they also practiced a form of birth control by "mind over matter." When members of this group talked about sex it was often in connection with pregnancy and children; often cautioning that sex can lead to pregnancy, and stressing that the couple should be ready to accept the responsibility of a child before they engage in such behavior.

Members of this same group also spoke of sex as being something that the organism needed to express. They spoke of the body in a "scientific" way, as a kind of machine. They felt that the body has these certain sexual energies and drives that have to be released. If they aren't released then some strange build-up will occur, and the rest of the system might be poisoned with the trapped sexual energies. So sexual activity was looked upon objectively as something that needed to be released. Members of the group spoke of sex outside of procreation as serving a "healthful" function. And some members of the group spoke of trying to develop a sense of soft and light sexuality. They emphasized how intercourse was no longer such a physical thing for them, now it was more of a combined spiritual experience. While they are making love they leave their bodies and travel through past lifetimes on their time track, through other astral and etheric spheres, and visit other planets in the galaxy.

For the dionysian any kind of sexual behavior could be seen as "natural," but the apollonians in the counter-culture also have a conception of the "natural"; however, theirs is much more in tune with traditional and much narrower religious conceptions. Usually in this conception of the "natural" there is only one right way to do it. This particular way of doing things is usually "found" by the people, and/or it is sent to them by some kind of higher force. The dionysian usually has no code that informs his or her behavior; they develop a strictly situational code—in terms of "What is good, is what makes me feel good." But the ascetic groups have a code handed down from an ancient tradition, or channeled through a charismatic leader.

While both hedonists and more ascetic types feel that males and females are basically bi-sexual, they differ in what they feel is "natural" for men and women to do. Hedonists feel that the "natural" is created. Out of the un-differentiated erotic, certain body parts, certain acts are defined as "natural" and certain "un-natural." The view of the hedonists is closer to the sociological perspective of the "construction of reality." But the more "religious" groups conceive that there are certain pre-set "natural" ways, independent of man. So they usually feel that homosexuality is "un-natural." They feel that men and women naturally complement each other. Those groups that do not celebrate a monkish way of total celibacy feel that a man and woman are incomplete until they join in a relationship with a member of the opposite sex.

And while hedonists feel that men and women should loosen up the particular roles and take on some ways of the opposite sex, the religious groups usually try to maintain the traditional separation between the sexes. Many of these groups feel that men and women are equal partners in service of the group or its goals. But usually in these groups the men are the leaders. And often they may maintain, either explicitly or implicitly, the view that the males are more oriented toward the abstract search for spiritual union. The females are to follow the light of males who lead the way. Another part of this view is that women are more connected with the Cosmic Creativity at a more subconscious level. These groups usually feel that women achieve satisfaction by bringing a new being into the world, but men have to seek fulfillment outside themselves. This view of women sees the relationship of the sexes as similar to the yin-yang: Two inseparable forces, with woman seen as dark, yielding, enveloping, and the male seen as light, intrusive and active. These groups feel this "natural complementarity" should be maintained, that women should continue to take care of the house and children, while the men maintain the more instrumental roles and also the prime religiously expressive roles.

So the hedonists are oriented toward the body. They want a loose conception of the "natural." They feel that we need to release the blocked sexual energy within our beings. They wish to increase the variety and number of sexual partners. And they stress a more diffuse eroticism versus the specific conception of genitality and sexual acts of the more religious groups. While the hedonists seem to feel that self growth through eroticism, or sex for itself, is the major goal, the religious groups feel that energy should be sublimated to higher goals. They take part in sex sparingly. And when they have sex they tend to interpret it as a spiritual experience. Generally, though, they consider sexual behavior a lower form of involvement to meditation, or they look on it as an obvious physical orientation that should lead to union with a higher force. And they tend to maintain a more traditional attitude toward homosexuality and male and female roles.

Sexual Styles and Sharing

Of course these observations are generalized from groups that contained legally married couples, couples with a long-standing relationship, and individuals who paired off with a different partner every week or even every day. How do these partners view other sexual activities within their communal circle? I will try to more closely define the idea of a loose or tight sexual style by trying to relate these styles with sexual sharing in a tight or loose living arrangement.

First, though, I would like to outline the way most members of communal groups arrive at communal life. For most of them, the arrangement begins during their later teens or early twenties. Youth is considered in our society as a temporary period between families—the one that raises the individual and the one the individual raises. The youth comes of age in the "family of orientation." During this period of life there is generally a sanctioned moratorium on full commitment to social responsibilities. It is a time of experimentation, when the youth is searching for a place in society and a mate to establish a "family of procreation." During this interim the youth relates mostly with a same sex peer group. For these groups there is a stress on living for the moment and seeking pleasures. These are the alleged "happiest years of your life"—carefree youth, without the responsibilities of a family to succor and support but also without the stability, meaning, and future orientation given by such an important and pervasive social form. With the increased efficiency of industrialization, and an increasingly complex society, more youths are able to enjoy this carefree fling for a longer period of time.

Many youths travel from across the country to those communities where others like themselves are already seeking pleasure and answers. They band together in extensive and intimate networks. Often they live together to save money on rent and food. Not yet secure in the hierarchy of occupational niches, they depend on each other for support—depending on who has money at the time. They get by on odd jobs, menial labor, or various illegal activities, such as dealing drugs. Many meet members of the opposite sex and settle into couple relationships that differ little from most marriages in the larger society, except that they may be even more fragile relationships. Many couples may just center on each other, and after some time when their peers have been scattered through travel, liaisons of their own, or seeking jobs, find themselves alone together. Other couples attempt to remain in an intimate network of other couples and single friends of both sexes. And, of course, many hip couples must also maintain communal situations out of necessity.

On a continuum of social organization we would have the more unstructured "non-creedal" groups (anarchistic groups that leave sexual behavior up to the individual) at one end, and the more structured "creedal" groups (in which behavior is prescribed for the individual) at the other. So at one end we have groups that demand the individual's total commitment; and at the other end, groups that allow the individual more latitude in shaping his behavior. It would be the groups at either end of the continuum of organization that would deviate most from the conventional sexual patterns, rather than just the groups at the least organized level. To see this we will also have to list these groups on the continuum of sexual expressiveness from dionysian at one extreme to apollonian at the other. So we could look at these groups along two continuum: social cohesion and sexual expressiveness, using tight and loose as the extremes on both:

Sexual Expression[2]

Social Cohesion of the Group	Tight (Apollonian)	Loose (Dionysian)
Tight	Hare Krishna	Manson Family
Loose	Lama Foundation	Morning Star Ranch

By cohesion we mean how close the individual feels to the other members of the group, how committed the individual is to the group and its goals, and how much of his property and possessions the person is willing to share. And by tight social cohesion we mean that the individual is willing to commit himself totally to the group, that he is willing to share all that he has. Generally there is more stress on cohesion in "creedal" groups. By loose cohesion we mean it is left to the individual to share what he wants with other members of the group. Generally the "non-creedal" groups are more loose. But some of these groups may actually show great cohesion based on long acquaintance-ship. But even groups that have a high level of cohesion may not share sex with the rest of the group. That, in part, depends on the group's sexual orientation.

By sexual expression we are referring to both the individual's attitude toward sex, whether sex is looked on as a lower form of behavior, or is seen as a means of growth. So it would also refer to the individual's orientation to sensuality. The loose person in this case would be attempting to perceive any part of the body as sexual, any type of touch or caress anywhere as erotic, while the tight orientation would be inclined to consider only conventional genital areas as sexual. And this view would also limit the kinds of erotic coupling engaged in by group members; the most tight would only take part in sexual intercourse in the missionary position.

But the tight-loose differentiation can also be used to refer to the choice of sexual partner. In the tight orientation the person would only have sex with one's legal mate. At the loose extreme the person would have sex with anybody, members of the same or opposite sex, in couples or any-number-can-play groupings. Sexual behavior would be highly promiscuous. Now there are differences within this continuum, in that an individual, or group, may be loose in one aspect but not in another. So a person may be attempting to become more open, warm, and loving by having conventional sexual relations with several members of the opposite sex. Or another person may be attempting to develop increased sensitivity, striving for the ideal of the polymorphous perverse, or total eroticism—yet only seek this enhancement with their legal mate.

Among these groups we find varied combinations of cohesion and sexual expression. Rosabeth Kanter found that the most durable 19th century communes had a charismatic leader and also regulated the individual's sexual behavior. She writes, "Stable communities, then, set policies on the issue of exclusive intimacy or institute practices designed to cope with potential dyadic withdrawal. Successful nineteenth-century groups often discouraged couples in one of two extreme and experientially opposite ways—either through free love, including group marriage, in which every member was expected to have intimate sexual relations with all others, or through celibacy, in which no member could have sexual relations with any other." (Rosabeth Kanter, *Commitment and Community*, Cambridge: Harvard Univ. Press, 1972, p. 87) In terms of our continuums these groups would fit high on cohesion, or have tight social organization. And the groups that prescribe celibacy would be placed as tight on the level of expressiveness, while the groups that instituted group marriage would be termed loose.

In most of the tightly organized groups in the counter-culture, celibacy rather than group marriage is the rule. Most of these groups tend to be apollonian, or tight sexually. Most of them are religious (or, in some respect, creedal) groups. They tend to "sublimate" all possible sexual energy to further the group's goals, and/or to achieve the spiritual state the group regards as ideal. Sexual activity is often looked on as a lesser form of pleasure to carrying out spiritual exercises. These groups usually contain both single members and couples, but all the members will conduct themselves in the celibate style. While married members will live together, usually sharing a single room, still their first commitment will be to the group, or its way, rather than to their partner. For some of these groups dedication to the marriage partner is a prime means of maintaining commitment to the group. But these groups generally play down the importance of sex, and also attempt to limit members becoming too attached to particular other members. Rather than investing one's energies in particular relationships, the members will be urged to invest their energies in the group as a whole. This orientation cuts down sexual jealousies. Without the tension of erotic bodies, and the possibility of sexual encounters, the members can relate to the others as brothers and sisters in *agape*.

There are also some groups that have little sense of cohesion yet are more in the ascetic or tight direction sexually. It seems that this is usually the style for mystics. They tend to want to get into themselves, to contact a higher force through attaining a certain concentrated state. Most mystics in the counter-culture see the guru as more of a hermit, a loner, and seeker. Although most Oriental type communes are very closely ordered by a set of traditional rules, and/or by a strong willed guru who is to be completely obeyed, there are some groups that seem to be more a collection of individuals each on their own trip, seeking their own cosmic consciousness. These groups are usually smaller. And there is no sexual sharing. But here the asceticism doesn't really enhance a sense of solidarity. Though it would still hold down jealousies, at least of a more conventional sort, it would be an inadvertent consequence, not a rule to ease communal living.

Some groups seem to have both a loose organization and a good deal of sexual expression. These groups are loose on both dimensions. These groups are very much in the hedonist direction. They like to "hang out" and have a good time. They may take a lot of drugs—smoking weed through the day, snorting coke, and taking LSD on a regular basis. In most of these groups the people may be "into sex," in the sense that they would see the ideal of total eroticism, but there usually isn't much sharing of sexual relationships. Most couples are monogamous, but in some groups there may be a good deal of switching around. Of course, sharing here doesn't mean in some kind of organized way. There is rarely "swapping" of partners, although there might be an occasional spontaneous bit of group sex. But there may be "pairing off" of people already coupled, with lots of talk about who is desiring whom, and how the partner feels about it. There may even be some secret liaisons, and others that the group attempts to ignore. These groups usually don't have an agreed upon policy of sexual expression. Rather they are following what feels good at the time, though there may be a felt sentiment for sharing sex. Since hedonists usually place themselves ahead of the group, there would be little willingness to set up a policy, or try to organize their sex "trips." Such structure as a group marriage would call for seems oppressively "straight" to hedonists; they are much more inclined to spontaneity, and would see some sort of sexual schedule as confining. In these groups the individual's sexual behavior is pretty much his own "trip."

Sexual jealousies and conflicts can flare up in a situation where there is a good deal of sexual expression and little sense of cohesion, and many of these groups break up quickly after forming. But another common pattern seems to be for couples to break up shortly after coming into the group, find new partners and settle down to a monogamous situation again. If such groups are able to survive the initial experimentation among their members, they may move increasingly to an ascetic and organized direction. They may become less sexually oriented, and become more organized with a greater sense of cohesion. Some of these groups may become interested in a traditional religious scene. If they don't develop into a "creedal" commune, they may not become so tight as the other communes. For in these groups usually the couple relationship and individual families remain strong and separate units. The commune is formed around the couples, rather than the couples being totally absorbed by the group. Members of these groups are more committed to the sexual relationship than they are to the group as a whole.

The last category on our dimensions are those groups that are loose sexually and also have a close sense of group cohesion. Such groups are rare. Presumably a traditional group such as Oneida would be placed in this category. They would be termed "loose" because they attempted to maintain group marriage. Every individual in the group was considered one unit, none were to be attached to another member in a couple. Each person was to remain accessible to approach by any other member in the group. The person had to renounce any too-intimate relationship with one other person. This presumably allowed the individual to remain free from a possessive relationship and also maintain open-ness to the rest of the group. From what I've read the Oneidans certainly seemed to enjoy sex, but it would be hard to think of them as really "loose," or as dionysians. They seemed much too committed to a goal beyond themselves, and they seemed to interpret sexuality in too mystic a fashion for us to see them as "mere hedonists."

I haven't heard of any really large commune trying a group marriage with similar form as the Oneida community. The group marriage experiments have all been carried out by small groups of three, four, or five couples. And these people do not seem to have a broad ranging vision of social change. They don't seem oriented to changing the larger society, but more focused on finding some kind of sexual satisfaction. I get the impression that "complex marriage" was only one aspect of a fairly radical social experiment by the Oneida people, it wasn't a prime reason for their getting together. It seems as if people who currently enter into small group marriage experiments in the counter-culture are suffering, or feeling confined in their present relationships and the group provides a chance for them to find fulfillment. Often these groups have been made up of older middle-class couples, who, after maintaining adult roles in the larger society, decided to drop out to find a more meaningful way of life. If these people express an affinity to a particular tradition, it is to humanistic psychology.

Some of these groups start out by getting together and seeking sex with others in the group. But it seems as if these groups usually get around to setting up some kind of schedule. This insures that everyone knows who the others will be with on a particular night. This, again, prevents two people from becoming too attached to each other. And it insures that each member in the group has someone for each night, unless there is an uneven ratio of males to females. These groups usually don't accept single members. They may continue to spend the night pairing off, and/or they may get together for group sex. These groups try to maintain a tight sense of cohesion. Although they are not as oriented to strong leaders as the other groups that could be considered tight, still they try to set up a more organized living structure than the other hedonists we've mentioned. For these groups explicitly intend to share sexually. They come into a communal situation, and want to develop cohesion, in a very intentional way. But, while showing some tendencies toward tight organization, they do not feel that the individual should be subordinated to the group.

There are some groups in which sexual sharing can lead to a breakdown of cohesion. But when the group has instituted some structure within which sharing can take place, whether it is a group sex or nightly pairing off form, then loose sexual expression, or sharing, can bring about an increased sense of cohesion. So in the terms we have been using, loose sexual expression can lead to tight social cohesion. Or we can see sexual sharing as an expression of cohesion. But sexual sharing does not necessarily mean the people are "loose" sexually. We have seen evidence that some groups exist where the members have a very hedonistic and loose sexual orientation, yet maintain a tight group.

These groups haven't intentionally formed to develop a new social order, nor to become sexually liberated. They are usually "noncreedal," although they may develop a more formal creed over the course of time. But usually they don't set up structures so that they can have group sex, or exchange partners. The sense of cohesion in these groups isn't expressed in more scheduling, rather these groups are more oriented to spontaneity, and synchronicity. Their sense of togetherness often develops through repeated drug experiences. These groups usually develop toward the ideal of direct communication of consciousness through ESP. They want to develop a group mind, and a group marriage in the sense of *Stranger in a Strange Land*. Their vision of a total communal eroticism may be guided by a charismatic leader. And, if they get into group sex, their sexual orientation is much more spontaneous and loose than the other groups we have considered.

The Manson Family is certainly the most famous communal group that might fit the category of tight cohesion and loose sexual behavior. Several members of communes feel that Manson was framed by the government to make all communes look bad. They feel that many people got the impression that all communes have group orgies while high on acid from the incredible press blow-up the Manson case received. But Carl Rogers writes:

> It is curious that the group fulfills two of the characteristics found by Kantor (1970) to make for permanence in the last-century communes. There was a charismatic leader—no one can doubt that—with

an ideology, no matter how warped or twisted. Also sexual behavior was regulated by the leader, with members having little or no choice. In this case the girls—with or without their acquiescence—were available for sexual intercourse with Manson or any of the men in the group. (Carl R. Rogers, *Becoming Partners: Marriage and its Alternatives*, New York: Delacorte Press, 1972, p. 153)

And according to some sources apparently there were some homosexual desires and behavior among the females and males in the group. Such bisexual tendencies are more readily accepted by females than males, because of the stress on masculinity and competition in this society. But with the decreased stress on masculinity, and the dropping out of the competitive economy, such homosexual relations between males could be more common. Usually such tendencies are focused on more among middle-class encounter-group types. In groups that maintain an image of the *macho* homosexual tendencies are usually repressed. But in some groups where the males have a delinquent orientation and have spent time in jail, homosexual contacts may occur. These groups usually don't evolve a "position" on sexual matters. But over time they may become increasingly "creedal" as they adopt justifications for their behavior from other members of the counter culture.

To summarize: I have compared communal groups on their sexual expression and group cohesion. Groups with loose cohesion have a low level of sharing. Groups with a tight sense of cohesion usually have a "creed" that members are expected to accept. Though there are some groups where the members are very close to each other and haven't evolved a formally accepted framework for the enterprise. Usually "creedal" groups have a sexual code that applies to all members of the group. The loose communes leave sexual behavior up to the individual. Some groups in the counter-culture are loose sexually. This may mean that they are "into sex"; they are hedonists and may be oriented, at least in image, if not behavior, to bisexuality and total eroticism and group sex. Usually groups that have a sense of tight cohesion are also tight in their sexual expression; they tend to be highly monogamous and ascetic. Few groups have been able to maintain close cohesion and loose sexual behavior. Hedonists are usually adverse to organization, even of pleasureful endeavors; and jealousies usually become rife when there is sexual sharing without group control. Hedonists are more oriented to sexual sharing on an informal basis; and this means, in most cases, loose social organization. There are many groups, perhaps most, where the organization is loose, based around couple relationships, and there is little, if any informal sexual sharing. And, indeed, these people feel no inclination to expand their sexual contacts.

These criteria for comparing groups could be extended to a comparison of individuals. Talking about groups as a whole implies that most of them have a unified conception and code of sexual behavior. But some groups have a good deal of variety among their members in terms of sexual style. Some groups may contain both sub-groups that are monogamous and rather ascetic and others that are more interested in expanding sexual contacts and hedonistic. Usually as the larger group develops, the social organization will tighten up—or they may break up. Of course, as the group becomes more cohesive, variety is cut out.

Thus, the counter-culture furnishes examples of the same range of behavior as exists in the "straight" world (if you include all of its socio-economic classes). It's just that in the counter-culture it *looks* different. But maybe, like long hair, traditionalist society will begin to feel more comfortable with these "new" ways and even—eventually—adopt them as their own.

NOTES

1 This study was aided by Grant No. MN-16579-03 from the National Institute of Mental Health, Department of Health, Education, and Welfare.
2 I feel I should point out that the groups I have placed in these categories were not the groups I have studied directly. I picked well-known examples from the commune literature that illustrate my perspective. The categories themselves were culled from my own field work, but following standard sociological procedure, they must remain anonymous. The groups used as examples seem similar along these dimensions to the ones I studied—at least so far as I'm able to ascertain from reading about them. Descriptions of all these groups seem to occur in a host of journalistic books on communes. See, for instance: Richard Fairfield *COMMUNES U.S.A.*, Penguin Books, Inc., Baltimore, 1972; Richard Atcheson, *THE BEARDED LADY*, John Day Company, New York, 1971; Robert Houriet, *GETTING BACK TOGETHER*, Coward, McCann and Geoghegan, Inc., New York, 1971.

II

SEXUAL FREEDOM FOR WHOM?

Whenever freedom of any kind is discussed, the question arises: yes, but for whom and to what extent—are there to be no limits? As far as we are concerned, sexual freedom entails sensitivity and responsibility and is not to be equated with sexual license, "promiscuity," or con-games. Our ideal is to give each individual the freedom to choose, in full knowledge and with care and good judgment, what is right for him/her—whether the choice be a varietist ideology or a monogamous union.

As it stands now, none of us are really sexually free. Early in the socialization process, humans commonly receive indoctrination about gender identity, sex mores, and marriage. Just as most parts of our western society have set rigid standards about what constitutes maleness and femaleness and about what is permissible in terms of sexual behavior, so they have offered no viable options to monogamous marriage. The web of social control has kept people from sexual freedom by not teaching them how to make a choice of a sexual life-style based on sound information and experimentation rather than blind acceptance of traditional standards.

We live in a sexually schizoid culture. On the one hand we pay lip service to personal freedom and the opportunity to develop a sense of self through choosing and relating as one feels and wishes. On the other hand, though, the negative connotations of hedonism and the "pleasures of the body" keep us from being very adventuresome or inventive in an important area of our lives. For some centuries we have treated the mind and body as separate and we still look to St. Paul and Plato for support in proclaiming the superiority of mind over body.

The prohibitions against freedom of body do not begin with adulthood. Pre-adolescence is a period when we learn many of our inhibitions. Touching genitals, for example, is strongly proscribed by many American parents; sexual pleasure is seen as "bad." Guilt induced through parental frowns, slaps, and other gestures returns in later life to remind us that sexual or sensual pleasure is disapproved of. The attitude which denies that infants are capable of eroticism, which holds that we don't become sexual beings until the magic stage of puberty, would also need to be altered if we are to have true sexual freedom.

In an unpublished manuscript on pornography, Paul Brians delineates some of the bases of sexual freedom currently present in our culture. He refers especially to the Human Potential Movement (with Maslow, Perls, Rogers, and Otto as its standard-bearers) as one of the bases for sexual freedom. The Women's Liberation and Gay Liberation movements support the Human Potential Movement and are as well advocates of freely arrived at sexual choice. Another basis for sexual freedom *should* be found in revolutionary political movements where the extension of a sense of community encourages sharing rather than competition, but this last has not yet caught on in America to any large extent.

In the following chapters you will discover some ways in which people want to be—and are trying to become—sexually free.

12

FEMALE SEXUALITY AND MONOGAMY
Pepper Schwartz

In discussing female sexuality as related to monogamy, Schwartz points out the many and complex ways in which the double-standard continues to keep females in a sexually subordinated position. She develops a case for the consideration of female sexuality as much more akin to that of some males who are liberated, sensitive, and relatively free. The problem of lack of opportunity to disengage oneself as a female from older sexual ethics raises interesting questions about the implications a new attitude would have for men as well as for women.

When (if) sexual independence is gained for women, what indeed is likely to be the outcome? Of course many difficulties will have to be faced by the woman who attempts to act out a sexually liberated role, even though there are potential rewards in terms of an enhanced sense of self. Still Schwartz admonishes women to stop "taking what they get" from men and begin to examine critically the context of the give-and-take in their sex lives. This insightful analysis also includes an examination of the major myths surrounding our conceptions of female sexuality. Insofar as women and men together reevaluate their sexual relationships, all stand to gain from the perceptive and critical views developed in this paper.

Current research on female sexual capability (Masters and Johnson, 1966) and recent ponderings on the possible effects of a "sexual revolution" (Davis, 1970; Smith and Smith, 1971) make it incumbent on sociologists, and certainly on feminists, to comment on the effects these changes will have on life styles and interpersonal relationships. In this instance the author, who considers herself bound by both mandates, wishes to examine the interaction of the reconceptualization of "female sexuality" (new information and new options) and the restructuring of marital dyads—particularly the organization of marital sexuality and the appropriateness of confining one's adult sexual experience to one "life partner."

While the sexual revolution has supposedly made sexual experimentation and alternate marital styles possible (Whitehurst, 1972; Wells and Christie, 1970), it seems clear that traditional values of monogamous marriage prevail for the vast majority of people in Western society. Some leeway is possible and extramarital sex may be tolerated (Neubeck, 1962) or adapted to the structure of the relationship (Cuber and Harroff, 1965) but at least at the level of ideology (if not practice) the monogamous nuclear family model is still safely ensconced in the mainstream of American life. This, of course, is not to deny that some behavior patterns have distinctly changed and attitudes toward them have been modified.

Premarital sexuality among the young has significantly liberalized, and negative sanctions for this behavior are increasingly rare (Davis, 1970). But it is also true that liberalized behavior patterns are misleading if we think of them as signalling great changes of consciousness. For example, it is still true that premarital sex, except for the small minority, is only sanctioned when it falls under permissiveness with affection (Reiss, 1971) or "sex with meaning" (Lever and Schwartz, 1971). "Sex as play," or recreational sex is only seen as reasonable behavior for both sexes by a small group of men—and a very small group of women (Lever and Schwartz, 1971, and Vreeland, 1972). At least 50% of all men and 26% of all women engage in extra-marital sexual relations (Kinsey, 1953; Bell and Peltz, 1972), but few families are honest about what is going on and few try and integrate it into the consciously evolved philosophy of the marital relationship. The double standard, to make this point another way, still exists in exactly the same form it used to, only with slightly more liberal dimensions. A woman can now sleep with a man before marriage, but while her boy friend may sleep with twenty women, more than three or four for her might be described as pathological. The male may take pride in his numerous affairs and regard them as proof of his desirability and talent—but his female counterpart has no legitimate way to use her own experience as self-affirming. Somehow the word "stud"—or the adjectival phrase sexually "*accomplished*"—sounds awkward, misplaced, or at best exotic for a woman. Such an attribute is not seen as making her a more polished, desirable being. If a woman has had 100 lovers or if she believes in a co-marital sexual life style (free and openly acknowledged sexual access to others outside the marital dyad), it scares off about 98% of the men who might otherwise want a "committed relationship" with her. Such behavior is almost never seen as enhancing or creative or necessary for the formation of an independent individual who knows what she wants because she has had enough experience to have a firm sense of what is appropriate or inappropriate for her needs and personality. Advocating a good deal of sexual experience for women is not seen as a responsible hypothesis—even if individuals are willing to agree intellectually that women should be allowed the same freedoms as men (and not all people agree on that premise). However, it is precisely this theme that the present paper deems important: *the need and/or the advisability of a different interpretation of female sexual behavior.*

Perspectives on an Historical Inheritance

Of course it is difficult to propose a new model of female sexuality when certain myths about female sexuality continue to exist despite information to the contrary. The "professional" literature (psychological, sociological, medical, and the like) still defines female sexuality in terms of its adjustment to marital—and thus jointly agreed upon behavior rather than discussions of what is uniquely female (Gordon and Shankweiler, 1971, Laws, 1971). Sexuality, as it is constructed in marriage, and less often, as it is constructed during courtship, is seen as normative and "normal"; the breadth of female capacity suggested by Masters and Johnson's research is disregarded. Women for the most part accept the idea that their sexual experience will be taught to them and defined for them by men. If their own needs seem to be incongruent with what they expect (i.e., they are still unsatisfied after one act of intercourse), they generally *will* themselves to conform to what they *can* expect. Failure to be satisfied, or desire for a different pattern of interaction, is most often taken as personal failure or failure of the couple. The question of what the woman needs—or the appropriateness of the arena of interaction (i.e. marriage)—is not often seriously questioned.

It is not surprising that the questioning is narrow in focus, for what happens in bed is generally reflective of the greater social system of the interactants. As Kate Millet says: "coitus can scarcely be said to take place in a vacuum...it serves as a charged microcosm of the variety of attitudes and values to which the culture subscribes" (Millet, 1970:23). Thus we only have to look at interpretations of female sexuality at various points in history to note how amazingly congruent the definitions of female sexual "possibility" are with the actual structure of female interaction in the family and state. A couple of examples chosen from a myriad of possibilities may serve to illustrate. For example, Hawks and Wooley (see Sherfy, 1971) point out that from 1200 to 800 B.C., before the transfer of property to blood relatives and before the male's role in reproduction was completely understood, women were considered sexually insatiable and allowed considerable sexual freedom with a variety of partners. On the other hand, when transfer of property to the eldest male became a cornerstone of English common law, female sexual freedom was considered dangerous and fear of mixing up lineage and the transfer of property caused the image of women to be re-interpreted and her sexual proclivities to be curbed. Suddenly woman was seen as having distinctly repressible needs and laws were passed to punish anyone who might transgress the new morality.

Closer to home, when the "feminine mystique" of the 1950s exhorted women to be better homemakers and mothers and stay out of the labor market (Freidan, 1963), it also began to create ways to make home more exciting and enticing. Sex was used as a "lure to marriage" (Laws, 1971) and sexual "cookbooks" (sometimes called manuals) were written exhorting a woman to be exciting for her husband after his long day at the office. Speaking in the tones appropriate for extolling the sanctity of the home, female sexuality was seen as another marketable item that a woman should develop to give to her husband as a reward for providing a wonderful home—and for the purpose of inducing him to stay in it. Sex was respectable again for women—but only in the specific and "blessed" state of the monogamous marital dyad. The husband was seen as the "needy" partner and the orchestrator of sexual moves. The woman was to be the instrument that brought out his true artistry (Gordon and Shankweiler, 1971). Her own needs were glossed over. If she was a good and mature wife, which meant, at least during this time, being able to have vaginal orgasms—and even better, simultaneous orgasms (hers vaginal)—she would be happy and satisfied. Those women who had sex in other contexts or, as in the language of *True Romances* articles, had "urges" that they acted upon in the "heat of passion," were doomed to disreputability, illegitimate children, and ultimate degradation. They would be denied anything more than a short, and probably unfulfilling, night of sin.

Lest we feel that the 1950s is now ancient history, one must add that present day sexual mystiques follow this model surprisingly closely. While female sexuality has acquired some legitimacy outside of the marital framework (Bell and Chaskes, 1970), there is still no sexual "model" equivalent to the male's. Men are still seen as needing some 'random' sexual experience and women who approximate the same activity are considered "problematic" if not clinically ill. The "*Cosmopolitan girl*" or the "sensuous woman" have a certain leeway, but it is questionable how much. At what age does the unmarried highly experienced playgirl begin to get disreputable? Is it at an older or younger stage than her male counterpart? Is the unmarried woman somehow seen as more pitiable than the unmarried man—even though we know that the unmarried man has much more trouble surviving than the unmarried woman (Bernard, 1972)? And what about the woman who is unfaithful to her husband? Isn't she viewed as a bit more bizarre than the man who exhibits the same behavior? It would seem that the woman is still tied to the ideology of the sanctity of home and family—and sexual repression (Limpus, 1970). Despite the titillating options hinted at by *Cosmopolitan* and similar magazines, the same message is before us: sexual fulfillment is through one man and through one institution—the monogamous marriage. Even among those who will consider living together as an option (Lyness, Lipetz and Davis, 1972), the monogamous model remains. A female's needs are still "willed" to be fulfilled through the relationship with one man, regardless of how that may match up with a woman's sexual desire or drive. Women are used to modifying that desire to fit their more important needs: food, shelter, protection, and security; most have ceased to be analytical about their sexual situation. Even when the situation arises that makes them independent of such considerations (personal wealth, a successful career, a bevy of admirers, and so on) they are so used to having other exigencies define their sexual and marital structure that they do not reevaluate their life style. They believe the myths they have heard about their emotional and sexual needs.

A Reconsideration of Some Well Accepted but Questionable Hypotheses

What are these myths that are so powerful in defining female sexuality and so irrevocably place them in the context of restricted sexual experience and monogamous marriage? Let us look at three that seem most central and have had the greatest impact.

Myth 1: It is assumed that women need a committed (love) relationship for sexual satisfaction.

Myth 2: It is assumed that female sexual satisfaction can best be produced in a monogamous marriage. It is assumed that one man and one woman will eventually work out a sexual system that is mutually satisfying for a lifetime. Such a relationship might need work (therefore the marriage manuals on how to please your spouse), but it is definitely possible for two people to provide all of each other's sexual needs.

Myth 3: It is assumed that the marital dyad cannot tolerate any additional sexual access by third parties. A female interacting sexually outside the dyad will destroy the dyad.

I will deal with each myth separately.

Myth 1: Only commitment and love produce female sexual satisfaction.

The conceptualization of a woman *inherently* needing a great deal of emotional input in order to function sexually (as opposed to the male who can enjoy sex merely to satisfy his "animalistic" urges) is not supported by available evidence. While it is true that Kinsey and others (Kinsey, 1953, Masters and Johnson, 1966) found women were *used to* and *trained to* need emotional support to allow their sexual selves to surface, it is not true that women are incapable of acting otherwise. Given the appropriate socialization women can enjoy sex for sex's sake just as well as men can. There are biological indications and plenty of sociological evidence to say that love and sex are separable for women.

On the biological question, a recent study (Waxenberg, 1969) has demonstrated that when a woman's ovaries are removed and the source of androgen cut off, the erotic component is damaged, but the affectional response remains. This implies that *physiologically* love and sex are indeed separable for a woman and that it is the experiential world—not the biological inheritance—that determines how she combines the two.

In reviewing other research on the interaction of hormones and behavior, there is further evidence that sex drive may vary according to the ratio of androgen to estrogen in the body. A high androgen to estrogen ratio indicates a more aggressive sexual nature—a low ratio indicates readiness for a more passive response (Money, 1965). While this raises the possibility that hormone levels may have something to do with sexual appetite, it also might lead us to believe that this sexual appetite might be identified with "androgen" types or "estrogen" types—and not according to sex. In any case, before we could get too enthused about this new definition of "capability" we would have to take into account studies of transsexuals that show *regardless* of the genetic inheritance, the sense of sexual self—even about something as basic as one's gender—is more dependent on the individual's psycho-sexual development than on biological inheritance or even the outward appearances of sex roles (Money, 1968). It is the sexual "script" that one experiences that shapes that person's sex drive and teaches him or her what kind of sexual being he or she is (Simon and Gagnon, 1970).

If we accept the idea that we have no biological evidence of a woman's lesser sexual needs, or of a gene-linked need for sex with love, we still must ask why the social reality exists. That is, *why* do most women subscribe to the "love and sex" and the "lesser need" theory of their own sexuality? We can approach this in three ways: her socialization, her access to information, and the structural directives of the society in which she lives.

Socialization

An overwhelming theme of a woman's life is that she is responsible for her sexual activity. She is the one who gets pregnant, bears any social stigma, and gets devalued by giving favors too casually. In order to cope with these considerations, and in order to be a "successful" woman, she learns a very important lesson: she must always be the partner *in control.* Control becomes an important value.

Of course by becoming successful as a "controller," the girl or woman also becomes somewhat alienated. She begins, as Simone de Beauvoir (1953) notes, to see herself as an object, a fascinating object, an object that can be used cleverly and to advantage, but nevertheless, less than a real person acting freely. A teenage girl, if she is to keep her social standing in her community, had better keep her wits about her. So, if she is necking in a car, there are three people in the back seat—herself, the boy she is necking with, and herself watching herself. In a classic sense, she must be somehow removed from the action.

The girl must be intensely aware of her market value. This tells her how much she can get away with, how much pleasure she can give (or receive), and how much credibility she will develop among her peer group (i.e., what she can deny and what can be believed). "Reputation" is of no minor value. It ranks women both with men and with other women. Knowing this, the girl learns to control her emotions under the most sensual and desirable interactions.

Even as she grows out of the more demanding social network of adolescence, the female cannot forget the lessons of her teenage years. While for those whose education is not over, college will be much different—there will be more liberal men and her female friends will be more supportive and less willing to judge her (Lever and Schwartz, 1971)—there will still be enough exceptions to that rule to make life harrowing. If she chooses to take her college or young adult years as a chance to be totally free, she will find that stigma and her resultant decreased market value will still occur. If she is one of a few strong, "eccentric" women she may be able to win her own kind of respect from those who regard her as bizarre, but still not "sick." However, for most such women, the price of gaining sexual freedom is losing the respect of others.

Finally when a woman gets older, perhaps married or engaged or even dating older men who have given up their stricter standards of morality, she will probably receive cues that at last she can be sexually free and responsive without incurring negative interpretations of her behavior. But unfortunately, she finds that she still has trouble "letting go." She has trained herself too well to be the free sexual being the new morality allows her to be. Internalized restrictions carry on, even against the person's conscious state. It is not difficult to see how this kind of sexual script makes a woman reject sexuality outside of a committed (love) relationship as a violation of the norms which protect her and determine her worth as a sexual being. To protect herself, she begins to be unable to function in any situation that makes her at all insecure or in doubt of the other's motives. She no longer finds herself attracted to people until her role is defined as worthy and dignified. And she devalues women who act in any other way.

On the other hand, if we look at those women who deviate from this set of prescriptions, we know that all women do not require either "respect" or security to function sexually. If these women are professional sexual objects (such as prostitutes), we have evidence that their ability to respond is impaired. They grow cynical and very often reject men altogether. But we know little about their less "business-like" sisters: the women who are sexually free, able to hold their own in their community, able to justify their acts, and able to attract (albeit a smaller number of the male population) people who can accept them and respect their idiosyncratic life style. We know little of the socialization of these women—the Isadora Duncans, the free spirits of their generations. How they developed a different sense of sexual self is as yet unanalyzed by sociologists. Further research would be indicated to see how such women, many successful in careers and in marriage, manage to deal with the control-and-discipline ethic and still lead a "male" kind of sexual life style.

Access to Information

It is not only socialization and peer group experiences that make a woman feel that love and sex must go together. A woman has no other visible and viable model for female sexual response. Texts on family, courtship, and mental health all say that the natural expression of sexuality for a woman lies in her ability to cathect a single male. "Sex as play," sex as experimentation and a way of learning about oneself in a friendly, but "not serious" manner, is never prescribed and rarely even tolerated among the "experts." Some professionals, notably feminists, have begun to write about new ways of organizing relationships—but this material is only beginning to be available to the average woman. What might the effect be, for example, if these new ideas, backed up by "authorities" were given space in all the texts and manuals that women read? Laws (1970) hypothesizes that men help define their identity from a variety of sexual experiences and that similar behavior by females might be valuable for the construction of an independent assessment of self and a strong sexual identity.[1] If this

---

1   Editors' note: It may be that in the event women were granted similar opportunities, men would come to lose much of their felt control and superiority. It is an open question if men really want sexually free women in any more than some superficial sense; they like women who respond sexually when they call the signals, but the truly sexually *equal* female may be much too threatening and an intolerable burden for most men—given current kinds of male insecurities. Thus, sexual unfreedom for females may be a price that is willingly paid for male superiority; if freedom breeds freedom as suggested, men may not want to opt for an equality-in-relationship but may prefer to keep the old-fashioned zero-sum game going wherein what one sex loses, the other gains. We do not as yet have true equality in sexual interaction.

were given sociological credence and if it were researched, offered in professional discussions of courtship, and seriously considered by counselors and advisors, more women might opt for a different pattern of learning about their sexuality. Women accept the fact that one matures by learning about one's self through interaction with others and that one cannot be a socially adept individual if one has not had a variety of social experiences. What might be the effect of offering this simple analysis of interpersonal relations and extending it to the sexual arena? There seems to be some indication that if such a model received serious consideration by professionals it would also receive consideration and validation from a variety of women who are struggling to decipher their sexual code and identity.

Structural Directives

This culture assumes that the family is the integrative mechanism that ties the individual to the greater society (Goode, 1964). Thus, it is to be expected that sexual patterns are oriented to helping stabilize the family as the basic societal unit. To this end, it is inconvenient to have a population of sexually free women whose emotional attachments, 'illegitimate' progeny, ideology, or independence of livelihood, may help undermine the family's status. If women did not attach sex to marriage, did not need to get married, and the family was therefore a less identifiable unit of society, the society would be less immediately controllable and organizable. Thus, unwilling to cope with changing the value of "Kinder, Kuche, and Kirche," the society values all characteristics that tie the individual to the home. In this sense, it has proved efficacious to make the female dependent on long term relationships for her sexual release. Marriage—as the only healthy place for sexual expression—is validated by governmental (read Nixon's pronouncements, among others), institutional, and professional spokesmen. The family is to be woman's great contribution to society, her anchoring point in life and her focus of identity. Whatever freedoms she may achieve in the job market or elsewhere are not to infringe upon or change her dedication to her children and her monogamous marriage. Otherwise woman's liberation will have "gone too far." Reform such as child care can be understood, but new freedoms, such as sex outside marriage, are seen as destructive and the work of "radicals." If the family cannot be preserved as it is, then the woman's movement is dangerous.

Since the structure of the family generally determines what is "unchangeable" and "natural," it is no wonder that feminists see the family as the major barrier to rethinking sexual roles, sexual identity and power relationships (Millet, 1970, Firestone, 1971, Greer, 1971, etc.), while anti-feminists, (Mailer, 1971, Dector, 1972) raise an outcry at anything that threatens to re-evaluate either its sexual or sex-role organization. As an introduction to this controversy, we know there is some evidence that women do not have to have, do not necessarily want, and can function quite well without emotional or marital commitment in sexual relations for long periods of time—and sometimes indefinitely. The literature on "swingers" shows that women can enjoy sex much as men do, with little or no attachment, just for the "fun" of it, (Bartell, 1970) or with varying degrees of affection depending on which partner they are with (Palson and Palson, 1972). Women, in "rap groups," will tell about getting sexually "hungry" and having fantasies of having sex at their own leisure without the demands of a deep relationship (Schwartz, 1972). Women who have had committed or emotional relationships often state they are capable of experiencing periods of time in their life where minimum involvement with a sexual partner is desirable (such as right after getting out of a draining relationship or when one's career is demanding much time and energy). Admittedly, these women are most often able to be independent on other grounds—they can support themselves, they are generally highly educated, and they often have deviant socialization patterns (such as a mother who encouraged their sexual freedom). Nevertheless, the fact that they are exceptions does not negate the fact that the thoughts they have and the life styles they practice are possible for other women who may want these kinds of options but need support to justify them for themselves. While the sample is small, and deviates from the norm, there is no reason for us to think it is "sick." Let us examine Myth 2, keeping these data in mind.

Myth 2: The best sexual relationships occur in the marital framework.

This value statement contradicts all that we are learning about female sexual capability. While we do not have much research on the subjective meaning of female sexual experience (i.e., a woman's own interpretation of "vaginally" versus "clitorally" stimulated orgasm, or how she enjoys sex with her lover as opposed to her husband), we do have enough data to evaluate women's objective sexual performances. For example, we know that women are capable of multiple orgasms so that while most women (Bell, 1972) have only one or possibly two orgasms in a single sexual encounter, they are capable of having many more. In one case, Masters and Johnson showed that a woman could masturbate up to and over 50 times to orgasm at one "sitting." The average woman's *capacity* was much greater than presupposed: what she did all depended on her desire, her general physical condition—and of course the ability of her partner to satisfy her if the orgasms were to be achieved through intercourse.

The discovery of female capability, that women can come to orgasm many more times than the male, and that each orgasm after the first becomes more and more intense at least clinically, if not always subjectively (Masters and Johnson, 1966) should have great meaning for women. While every woman will most likely not want to have orgasm 50 times at each experience, she may wonder what kind of orgasmic release she *would* like to experience. If she has trouble reaching orgasm, she might wonder if it would be easier for her after the first few attempts, or after prolonged coitus. If she reaches orgasm easily, she might wonder if the third or fourth orgasm puts all of the other experiences to shame. The important thing to note is that most women read this kind of material and wonder what effect the experience might have on them—but very few of them *know*.

One reason few women know the extent of their own sexual capability is that they depend on one man to perform with them and have only a few experiences to round out their sexual repertoire. Because they have wanted to have sexual interactions that did not devalue them as people, most women have not had intercourse with many or several men in one day (or the chance to find one of those men who can keep going all night and day). They may not be able to distinguish between a man who is "sexually talented" (sensitive, patient, imaginative, and loving during the encounter) from one who isn't.

The majority of women take what they get, blame many or most of the inadequacies of the relationship on themselves, and haven't the vaguest idea about how to demand more for themselves or give more to the other person. Generally, whatever the male brings into the sexual relationship determines its boundaries. If he brings a lot, the woman gets a lot of sexual activity; if he does not, the relationship usually remains at that level. But even the most talented lover cannot provide a partner with the kind of variety of interpersonal experience, or chance to explore one's sexuality as can a variety of people. And to some extent, a long term sexual relationship—as in a marriage—must get stale and unimaginative at points. Marriage manuals would exhort couples to be "creative," to give in to each other's desires and generally lie a little if it makes the other person happy to think their partner is enjoying himself or herself. None of the experts suggests the easier and more obvious answer: do it elsewhere with someone who enjoys it. Why demand everything from one person? It is unfair and troubling to have to be all things at all times. *No one* can do it so why should any of us— man or woman—feel that we *have* to?

Of course, this kind of philosophy is impossible in marriage as it is now constructed. First of all it implies that the best sexual adjustment cannot be contained within marriage (Laws, 1972) and second, it suggests that even those people who want a committed relationship can bend that relationship so that it allows other sexual partners. This is an upsetting and destructive idea to most women—and men—who immediately begin to fear being compared, or being seen as inferior, or losing their husband, wife or lover. What *would* it mean if we accepted the idea that no one person could sexually fulfill any one other or that we need *different* kinds of experience and that comparisons of "better" or "worse" are sometimes irrelevant? There are a number of possible ramifications. First, it seems likely that a new kind of sexual self would emerge—one created by self-definition instead of definition by others. This would mean individuals would know their own needs, know when they were satisfied or unsatisfied, and negotiate a sexual pattern that would be responsive to a number of partners. Secondly, it might also remove fears of unfavorable comparison, by showing that sexual experiences vary and each experience can be valued for its own kind of contribution.

It might also mean the women would discover the extent and degree of their own sex drive instead of having it defined by "available resources." It might also mean that the demands that make partners afraid that they will be unable to satisfy each other would be less encompassing.

Of course, this is a conjecture, depending on several kinds of conditional hypotheses. Right now, it is enough to say that at least at a physical level we can conclude that marriage may not be the best outlet for the physical possibilities of female sexuality. The emotional considerations may be more subtle to discern. The critical question is—can a relationship be sustained under such conditions? Can a woman or man share such intimacies and still have a satisfactory life together? Can the family be sexually modified or must sexual liberation completely destroy the committed dyadic relationship? This leads to Myth Three.

Myth 3: Can the marital framework sustain "outside" exploration of female sexual response without destruction of the marital dyad?

Or the same issue can be looked at another way: Is a woman's utilization of her complete sexual capacity inimical to monogamous marriage and if so, is it anomalous with any kind of dyadic construction? The proposed answer is yes; it is probably antithetical to monogamy—but probably not to other kinds of marital or dyadic organization. However, it will necessitate radical adjustment, and the family structure will be more vulnerable and less necessary than at present.

While some women's sex drives—even when fully awakened—may be easily satisfied and many women will have long periods when their sexual appetite is dulled, it is hypothesized that sexually liberated women will generally desire more sexual activity than one monogamous, long-term relationship can provide. Since their sexual needs will transcend what the marriage can provide, the link between sex and marriage will be altered.[2] Women will be much more hesitant to get

---

[2] Editors' note: Of course, there is a sexual logistics problem inherent in this model of future marriage—such as the question of where are the available men to come from, given the freeing-up of female sexuality? It is probable that even if such a state were to occur, there would be few enough females indulging in the new sexual freedom, so there might still be a plentiful supply of willing male partners. In some future, however, the problem of balance of available sex partners may prove to be a thorny one.

married since they will face much more than just a general restriction of freedom; they will face the possible loss of sexual satisfaction. If they cannot negotiate a different kind of marriage, (i.e., non-monogamous) they may choose to defer legal or even interpersonal commitment until their needs for security, children, etc., change their priorities. They may desire to put off marriage until their thirties, while men, having sexual needs that are more easily satisfied and desiring the traditional advantages of having a wife (cook, mother, housekeeper, and the like) may press for earlier marriages. However, if other expected reforms accompany this change in female consciousness (such as equality in the job market, access to prestige positions in society, child care, and so forth), both men and women may see advantages in either staying single or having more open relationships. Clearly, the structure of the pursuer and the pursued would change.

Definitions of relationship and affection would change, probably enough to allow non-monogamous, affectional relationships. Sexual intercourse would not be seen as the ultimate expression of affection and closeness. There might be a possibility that some women will start looking at men as conquests and sex-objects much as men have often regarded females, especially when they have had non-committed sexual relationships. Women will suddenly have new standards with which to judge sexual performance, and technique and talent will now be evaluated in relative terms. The possibilities are numerous and though they may lead in different directions, it seems inevitable that there will be a profound impact on marriage.

Thus, the scene would be set so that a new construction—a nonmonogamous construction of the marital dyad—would seem reasonable and appropriate. Since the sexual act would have new meaning and probably be seen as less "all-defining" to its participants, non-marital sexuality would be a less disruptive act than in families operating under traditional normative expectations. In fact, it might be much more difficult to conduct the totally monogamous marriage since sexual restriction might result in frustration and the creation of a hostile and tense marital environment. When expectations change, it is hard to rely on old and unresponsive institutions.

Nonetheless, we already know that marriages, even operating as deviant structures in a monogamous system, can tolerate non-marital sex and still maintain their continuity. Traditionally, only men have been allowed the liberty of relating sexually to persons outside the marriage and they often have rationalized their actions by saying that they "can handle it" while their wives would become "too emotionally involved." Under a more egalitarian model, we know that non-marital sex can exist when adequate rules, ideology, and trust have been established to protect the original couple. The literature on co-marital sex may gloss over many of its problems—the control of jealousy, loss of romanticism, and possibility of romantic attachment to the outsider—but it also shows that a variety of sexual partners in an open and egalitarian framework does not signal the end of the marital dyad. The exploration of female sexuality may exert strains on the couple, and certain retrenching and dissolution will occur, but marriage or emotional attachments are not impossible. There is no reason to believe that even though people may practice sexual intercourse outside marriage that this makes them any less desirous of a long term, stable, loving and committed relationship. If anything, the mercurial nature of affairs and the elation which comes from arousal states (Walster, 1971) infuses all on-going interactions, and makes one continuing relationship even more attractive to the interactants.

The Importance of an Ideology

It is useful to note at this point, that the liberation of female sexuality and its concomitant effect on family structure is not envisioned as a mere phase in a "sexual freedom" movement. Rather, female sexual freedom and reorientation of marital patterns is seen here as part of a significant chain of events well within the matrix envisioned by feminists as liberating all people from the oppression of definitions that do not relate to the human organism's *potential for being*. If such sexual changes were to take place in the exploitive framework of win-lose competition, the effects of such change would be similar to women winning the vote and then using it to vote as their husbands directed. Liberation without ideology—in this case without a feminist-humanist ideology—is merely hedonism that will only flourish when historical conditions and economic exigencies are lush enough to afford the individual such "frivolities." If the exploration of woman's sexual being is not seen as one of a human's sovereign rights and the right to determine an appropriate marital style is not seen as part of the struggle for self-determination, then we are reduced to the cork-popping, "live for today" imagery of the flapper and the "moment in time" historical hollowness of the 30's. What is suggested here is a much more important personal and sociological question. We are concerned here with the redefinition and reorganization of sexual intimacy and family life. Thus, what is being advocated is nothing less than a radical re-evaluation of family structure and female self-knowledge and identity. As more and more women insist upon the integrity of their bodies and their psychosexual well-being, the impact on all of us will be truly revolutionary.

REFERENCES

Beauvoir, Simone de. *The Second Sex*. New York: Knopf, 1953.

Bartell, Gilbert D. "Group sex among the Mid-Americans." *Journal of Sex Research*, 1970, 113-130.

Bell, Robert, and Jay Chaskes. "Pre-marital sexual experience among coeds, 1958 and 1968." *Journal of Marriage and the Family*, 1970, 32, 81-85.

Bell, Robert, and Dorothyann Peltz. "Extra-marital sex." unpublished manuscript, 1972.

Bernard, Jessie. "Marriage: Hers and His." MS. 1, 6, December, 1972, 46-49.

Clavan, Sylvia. "Changing female sexual behavior and future family structure." *Pacific Sociological Review*, 15, 3, July, 1972, 295-308.

Cuber, John F., and Peggy Harroff. *The Significant Americans*, New York: Appleton-Century, 1965.

Davis, Keith and Gilbert Kaats. "The dynamics of sexual behavior of college students," *Journal of Marriage and the Family*, 1970, 32, 390-397.

Decter, Midge. "Toward the new chastity." *The Atlantic Monthly*, 230, 1972.

Firestone, Shulamith. *The Dialect of Sex*, New York: William Morrow, 1970.

Friedan, Betty. *The Feminine Mystique*, New York: Norton, 1963.

Goode, William J. *The Family*. New Jersey: Prentice-Hall, 1964.

Gordon Michael, and Penelope J. Shankweiler. "Different equals less: Female sexuality in recent marriage manuals." *Journal of Marriage and the Family*, 33, 3, August, 1971.

Greer, Germaine. *The Female Eunuch*. New York: McGraw-Hill, 1970-71.

Kinsey, Alfred, Wardell Pomeroy, and Clyde Martin. *Sexual Behavior in the Human Male*. Philadelphia: W. B. Saunders Co., 1948.

Kinsey, Alfred, Wardell Pomeroy, Clyde Martin, and Paul Gebhard. *Sexual Behavior in the Human Female*. New York: Pocket Books, Inc., 1965.

Laws, Judith Long. "Toward a Model of Female Sexuality." *Midway*, 1970.

Laws, Judith Long. "A feminist review of the marital adjustment literature: The rape of the locke." *Journal of Marriage and the Family*, 33, 3., 1971, 483-517.

Lever, Janet, and Pepper Schwartz. *Women at Yale*, New York: Bobbs-Merrill, 1971.

Limpus, Laurel. "Sexual repression and the family." In *Liberation of Women*. Boston: New England Free Press, Spring, 1969.

Lyness, Judith C., Milton E. Lipetz, and Keith E. Davis. "Living together: An alternative to marriage." *Journal of Marriage and the Family*, 34, 2, May, 1972, 305-312.

Mailer, Norman. "The prisoner of sex." *Harpers*, 242, March, 1971.

Masters, William, and Virginia Johnson. *Human Sexual Response*. Boston: Little, Brown, 1966.

Millet, Kate. *Sexual Politics*. New York: Doubleday, 1969.

Money, John. *Sex Errors of the Body*. Baltimore: Johns Hopkins Press, 1968.

Money, John, and Anice Erhardt. "Progestin-induced hermaphroditism: IQ and psychosexual identity in a study of 10 girls." *Journal of Sex Research*, 3, 1, 1967, 83-100.

Money, John, Anice Erhardt, and Ralph Epstein. "Fetal androgens and female gender identity in the early treated adrenogenital syndrome." *The Johns Hopkins Medical Journal*, March, 1968, 122.

Money, John, Anice Erhardt, and Daniel N. Masica. "Fetal feminization induced by androgen insensitivity in the testicular feminizing syndrome: Effect on marriage and maternalism." *The Johns Hopkins Medical Journal*, September, 1968, 123.

Neubeck, Gerhard (ed.). *Extramarital Relations*. New Jersey: Prentice-Hall, 1969.

Palson, Charles, and Rebecca Palson. "Swinging in wedlock." *Society*, 1972, 9:4, 28-37.

Reiss, Ira L. *The Social Context of Pre-Marital and Sexual Permissiveness.* New York: Holt, Rinehardt, and Winston, 1967.

Rossi, Alice. "Maternalism, sexuality, and the new feminism." New York: 1971, unpublished paper presented at the 61st annual meeting of the American Psychopathological Association.

Schwartz, Pepper. "The sexually liberated woman." Unpublished paper, 1971.

Sherfy, Mary Jane. "A theory of female sexuality." *Journal of American Psychoanalytic Association,* 1966.

Simon, William, and John Gagnon. "Psychosexual development." In *The Sexual Scene.* New Brunswick, N.J.: Trans-Action Books, 1970.

Smith, James R., and Lynn Smith. "Co-Marital sex and the sexual freedom movement." *Journal of Sex Research,* 1970, 6:2, 131-142.

Walster, Elaine. "Adrenaline makes the heart grow fonder." *Psychology Today,* 1971, 5:1.

Wells, T., and Christie, L. "Living together: An alternative to marriage." *The Futurist,* 50-57, 1970, 50-52.

Warenberg, Sheldon. "Psychotherapeutic and dynamic implications of recent research on female sexual functions." In George Goldman and Donald S. Milman (eds.), *Modern Woman: Her Psychology and Sexuality.* Springfield: Illinois, Charles C. Thomas, 1969, 3-24.

Whitehurst, Robert. "Changing ground rules and emergent life styles." *Family Life Educator,* Sheridan College, Oct. 1972. Oakville, Ontario. (Also this volume)

Vreeland, Rebecca. "Sex at Harvard." *Sexual Behavior,* 2, 2, February, 1972.

13

THE DOUBLE STANDARD AND PEOPLE'S LIBERATION
Ronald Mazur

The many ways in which people become polarized in their interactions are discussed and related to male dominance. Men, being in the position to make their definitions stick in our culture, have in the past created definitions which protected the preserves of their own vested interests. Thinking in artificial dichotomies such as husbands versus wives, heterosexuals versus homosexuals and so on has led us into the impasses we see about us everywhere. Mazur exposes the double-standard base of these dichotomies and challenges the reader to consider some trends in the counter-culture that are in opposition to double-standardism. His concerns reach across boundaries of sexual exclusivity, bisexuality, and the development of a pleasure ethic of sex as a play activity. The requisite conditions enabling us to go beyond the double-standard are delineated, Mazur noting in conclusion that all else in the sexual revolution will proceed apace once women have been liberated from the constricting past.

The term "double standard" is commonly applied to a specific area of the human condition: namely, the sexual; and even more specifically, to premarital sexual behavior and standards. Sociological analysis keeps the public preoccupied with the number of people, or the percentage of a prescribed population, which may be engaged in a given category (behavior, opinion, change, or relationship). The focus on quantitative factors is central to the lively (and sometimes ridiculous) controversy among the professionals as to whether the contemporary sexual scene should be classified as revolutionary, evolutionary, or status quo-maintaining. Our obsession with charting incidences of sexual behavior and counting orgasms is a kind of cultural voyeurism. Since we are not about to expose ourselves in honest behavior we would rather peek into other people's lives and live vicariously. We can also have fun by condemning or shaming others who challenge our particular version of decency. And finally, after we count enough heads and watch cautiously until the creative becomes commonplace, we can then safely leap into our cipher in the mass and enjoy a new experience. In the expression of our sexual desires, hopes, and needs, most of us are moral cowards.

The double standard as such is not necessarily cowardly. On the contrary, it is a *standard* which many men and women willingly accept if not choose. But what we fail to realize is that there is in fact a multiplicity of sexual standards operative in America. The major issue is not the quantitative weight of any one standard over another, but the quality of interpersonal relationships to be realized within any one of the standards. In our society, which is struggling to provide greater freedom for a broad variety of sexual standards and lifestyles (sexual pluralism), it is any person's privilege and right to live by the double standard. What must be rejected, however, is the tyranny of the standard when it is imposed upon those who repudiate it for their own lives and who see its destructiveness on those young men and women who are kept ignorant of other options for contemporary man-woman relationships.

Although there are indications that the double standard is on the decline, it is by no means dead and it continues to provide, for better or for worse, countless young people with both the ground rules for sexual behavior and the framework for masculine and feminine roles. Speaking of present-day premarital sexual standards, sociologist Ira Reiss [1] believes that there are four major types: Abstinence for both sexes; the Double Standard defined as "the Western world's oldest standard, which allows males to have greater access to coitus than females"; Permissiveness with Affection, an increasingly popular acceptance of intercourse for both sexes when a warm and stable relationship prevails; and Permissiveness without Affection which allows both sexes equal sexual experience even in relationships which require only mutual consent without emotional strings attached. Regardless of how influential other standards may become, and no matter how many creative variations may be developed, it is likely that the double standard will continue to shape relationships for a large number of people into the foreseeable future. For in addition to providing sex-role models and defining the privileges and penalties for the behavior of both sexes, the double standard is tacitly condoned by both Judaism and Christianity; social institutions provide for its perpetuation; the education establishment promotes it; and a host of myths reinforce it. The double standard rests on the assumption that sex pleasure is not for everyone and that men need it more and know best how to enjoy it while protecting their women from its hazards. Such protection is, of course, "necessary" to uphold the moral order, to make women happy, and to preserve the family. These are the deeply held convictions of many men and women who see the double standard as a small price to pay for the sake of such worthy goals.

Again, the problem essentially is not that there are people who hold to the double standard; it is that our society incorporates and sanctions it and persecutes in various ways those who conscientiously hold other standards and seek to live alternative or nonconventional lifestyles. It is also important to recognize that the double standard of sexual morality permeates vital areas of intimate relationships other than just the premarital. Consequently, the person who repudiates double standardism finds that a social web of conformity creates sticky problems in several areas of interpersonal encounter.

Single Men Versus Single Women.

As has been noted, premarital sexual behavior draws a great deal of attention and concern in our society. It is almost as if men and women are embarrassed to seem interested in sexual pleasure once they are married. Much safer is it to use the children as the focal point for adult interest in sex. True, there are obvious legitimate concerns such as pregnancy, venereal disease, and social ostracism. We also make a tremendous emotional and financial investment in our children and dread the "ruination" of their lives through sexual folly. But the hazards of premarital sex go beyond these fears and even beyond the traditional risks of the double standard penalties.

The ground rules of the double standard are shifting in a gradual but devastating way with the female being trapped in a double bind: if she is sexually inexperienced she is "out of it"; if she takes her sexual freedom seriously, she is "trash," or, at best, not "the kind of a woman that I'd want to be the mother of my children." The usual penalties imposed upon the female under the double standard result in higher incidences of guilt on the occasion of the first intimacy; lower incidences of masturbation; and the indictment of "promiscuous" applied almost exclusively to them while corresponding male behavior is considered "adventure," "experience," "conquest," and "virile." Where the shifting double standard now really begins to destroy male-female communication and compatible mutual game playing is *after* the period of engagement. Whereas previously the relationship of engagement signalized permission for sexual exploration and experimentation, it is now becoming a deed which the male uses to claim exclusive rights to the female who, in turn, is required to end her intimate relationships with all other male friends and lovers in order to devote herself solely to the "winner" of her body. It is becoming more common for young men not to be at all bothered by or about the premarital sexual experience of their girlfriends, but they are still playing a game of conquest and possession. With great cool, gentleness, and *joie de vivre*, the psuedo-liberated single male relates sympathetically to the single female who is struggling for autonomous identity and sexual freedom. This promising communion between the sexes is, however, shortlived, for as soon as that emancipated young woman consents to a primary one-to-one commitment, the double standard heart of the male beats mightily and he suffocates the flame of love with possessiveness and jealousy. This is not to say that only males are possessive and jealous, but in the premarital stage they are becoming more devious about it, victims of their own con game. With justifiable bitterness, Shulamith Firestone, in *Dialectic of Sex*, excoriates the deceptions of male-designed sexual freedom which does nothing more than provide the men with a greater supply of free lays: "The rhetoric of the sexual revolution, if it brought no improvement for women, proved to have great value for men. By convincing women that the usual female games and demands were despicable, unfair, prudish, old-fashioned, puritanical, and self-destructive, a new reservoir of available females was created to expand the tight supply of goods available for traditional sexual exploitation, disarming women of even the little protection they had so painfully acquired . . . (but) even the hippest want an 'old lady' who is relatively unused."[2]

The above kind of delayed double standard double-cross is not yet common in our culture and is more likely to occur in urban colleges than among other young adult populations in this country. Indeed, young adults in certain geographical regions and social classes would still consider the old-fashioned prerogative of sex-with-engagement (Permissiveness with Affection) as being daring and radical. There is also another population of young men and women, small but growing in number, who are sexually liberated and doing a new thing together as they develop an equalitarian standard of sexual morality. But it is disheartening to see how adaptable the destructive aspects of the premarital double standard can be: the value of virginity is being rejected, only to be replaced by the delayed arbitrary judgment and possessiveness of the male, and young adults of both sexes still face the bleak prospect of continued mutual manipulation.

Parents Versus Children.

Another form of the sexual double standard which can be destructive is embodied in the myth which declares that sex is only for adults. There is assumed to be a magical moment of maturity beyond which sex is mentionable and before which it is simply not acknowledged as an essential human experience. Though parents by and large favor some form of sex education in public and religious schools, their naivete is nevertheless incredible. Too little is offered much too late: it is as if parents refuse to recognize their children as sexual and sensual beings. Children, of course, tend to reciprocate the insult and find it hard to believe that their parents, and adults in general, can participate in and enjoy sexual intimacy. It is sad when children lack adult models who express emotional warmth and playful physical closeness, who admit to a lively interest in sex. Too many parents not only conceal their earthiness, but even worry about their children or make them feel ashamed when they exhibit or acknowledge an interest in sex. Parents tend to feel uncomfortable talking to their children about sex unless they can tell jokes on the one hand, or, on the other, speak in ethereal, poetic, or religious terms.

Fortunately, some progress has been made in sex education in the last generation or two. It is now undoubtedly rare for parents to conduct a bedcheck to make sure the child is sleeping on his back with arms outside the blankets lest the unspeakable vice be committed in the unguarded moments of sleep. Masturbation is generally understood and accepted as a natural process of self-discovery and self-enjoyment, and children today are spared the shame and hangups which not too long ago were the horrendous heritage of most men and women. Curiously, however, parents and educators consider the lack of condemnation of masturbation sufficient to the educational needs of young people. This is still a negative approach to the subject, for a more honest and helpful service to children would be to make sure that all girls and boys, by the end of the seventh grade at least, were made aware of the positive and beneficial aspects of masturbation: benefits such as relaxation of physical and psychic tension, comfortableness with sensuality, self-knowledge and self-acceptance, and empathy with the sexual need of the other sex.[3] Even at the present time, this is still too much to ask of most parents because it is so difficult for adults to accept and feel comfortable with the sexual needs and development of children. It is amazing how much can be blocked out of adult memories! If parents themselves did not initiate a double standard which creates a make-believe world of nonsexual children, they would experience less anxiety about their children's behavior and would be privileged with greater sharing from young people who, regardless of new attitudes toward sex, are still searching for honest and creative relationships.

To be sure, the problems of sex education and permissible sexual behavior for young people are complex and involve more than the parental double standard. But a start must be made somewhere with realistic and forthright education for human sexuality—education which adults need as much as children. How this will be accomplished on a wide social scale is yet unclear and even a controversial issue. One interesting proposal, by Harriet F. Pilpel, general counsel for Planned Parenthood-World Population, is that the sex education needs and civil rights of children should be protected by law and be taken as seriously as the rights of parents and society. She suggests that ombudsmen be appointed to speak for children and is convinced that "adequately serving children's needs also serves the best interests of their parents and community" (SIECUS Newsletter, October 1970). Perhaps we wouldn't need some official to speak on behalf of children if parents and educators had the courage and sensitivity to help them appreciate without fear their own being—genitals included.

Husbands Versus Wives.

In light of the fact that the overwhelming majority of men and women marry, it may seem preposterous for serious scholars of family life to wonder if marriage has a future. Yet, a long-time observer of man-woman relationships, sociologist Jessie Bernard, states frankly that marriage is a poor status for women and she offers the startling proposal that celibacy be considered as an honorable alternate status for women.[4] And in almost every major popular family magazine today, there are articles detailing the troubled condition of the institution of marriage. One of the major forces relentlessly demanding a re-evaluation and reformulation of the marital relationship is the Women's Liberation Movement—a resurgence of the feminist movement which won the voting franchise and then seemingly dissipated by 1930. The new Movement, though diffuse and eclectic, has a cohesive and radical cutting edge which will not be blunted in its effectiveness until human relationships and society are reshaped to allow all women full self-realization as persons.

Because of the work of the Women's Liberation Movement, the double standardism of male chauvinists and their co-opted female victims has been mercilessly exposed. The scholars and leaders of the Movement have amassed a devastating indictment of the male's total cultural and personal ego trip—a trip made on the free-to-all-men ticket of the double standard. It is interesting to note that discussion of the double standard by psychologists, sociologists, and other professionals has mostly been confined to premarital behavior and rarely analyzed in any depth. The *Encyclopedia of Sexual Behavior*, for example, includes no article on the subject and cites only three minor references to the double standard in the index.[5] It is remarkable how sensitive most aware adults are to the issues of the double standard considering the fact that it is only within the last several years that women in any significant number began again a revolt against their inane condition. As recently as 1964, in her comprehensive analysis of the status of women, Alice S. Rossi could say, regrettably, "There is no overt anti-feminism in our society in 1964, not because sex equality has been achieved, but because there is practically no feminist spark left among American women."[6] Betty Friedan's *The Feminine Mystique* (1963) had not yet made its impact, but it didn't take long for the awakening of the American woman. It is disturbing that six turbulent years after sociologist Rossi's understated challenge, two male sociologists would claim that "the role of women has changed very little, and today they are even more committed to the home and children than they were in the 1930's during the last gasp of feminism."[7] Feminism did not, however, die in the 1930's. It merely smoldered until the secret spark was bellowed into a roaring and hot movement by Friedan and her colleagues. After handling hot steel during the war years of the 1940's, women again were faced with a better reality. Men determine the purposes and structure of social institutions, define sex roles, judge sexual behavior, set the conditions for economic independence, commit all physical and human resources to national priorities which they determine, and on top of it all evaluate the sanity of women. It is no wonder that almost all men know in their hearts at least one prayer: "I thank thee, Lord (ol' Buddy), that I was not born a woman!"

One of the critical questions the Movement poses relates to the impact it will have upon husband-wife relationships. No definitive answer is yet possible, but a reasonable guess is that the Movement will cause more trouble than peace, at least for a transitional period. The number of divorces and unhappy marriages is evidence that husband-wife warfare is rampant, and consciousness-raising sessions aren't going to make women any happier with their predicaments. Ultimately, the Movement will contribute to the humanization of both sexes, but for the time being it must risk the opening of festering hates and resentments in marital relations. Men have been the exclusive objects of devotion by mothers who knew no better, and adult males unconsciously expect to occupy the place of the deity in the lives of their wives. There are even a sufficient number of wives who exalt this juvenile expectation to the status of "true love." Men and women who accept the double-standard marriage can share a common value framework and make each other content within that context. But even this is becoming more difficult to accomplish, for the traditional uneasy truce which suffers adulterous cheating on the part of the husband is about to break down because women are weary of the hypocrisy and are more willing to face the consequences of painful marital confrontation. Husbands do continue to have the upper hand, for all the world loves a lover (male), and the wife who is so crass as to object is a "bitch," while the wife who is independent enough to have her own male friends and night out is a "whore." Women who are relatively happy with the way things are will bitterly resent the Movement for raising issues they would rather not confront. Not all women seek the same kind of liberation, and it will be important for the Movement not to alienate needlessly those women who choose to maintain the status quo for their lives and their marriages.

The leaders of Women's Liberation are prepared for a male countermovement and are consolidating for survival. Their expectations of male reprisals may not be unfounded, and if their analysis of the extent of female subjugation is correct, it can be anticipated that the radical aspects of the Movement will be totally ignored if not suppressed. There is, however, another small but determined movement in our society which repudiates the double standard of sexual morality and is a strong supporter of the liberation of women in all areas of society; this is the Movement for Alternative Lifestyles.

The Movement for Alternative Lifestyles is more amorphous and eclectic than the Women's Liberation Movement and it doesn't even merit capital letters and a grand name. But it's for real and it's changing the lives of people and will eventually make permanent changes in American social institutions. This movement includes such experiments in sexual freedom and interpersonal relations as: *noncontractual cohabitation*, so-called trial marriages, a version of which is finding an accepted place in co-ed dormitories on various campuses; *group marriage*, in which three or more persons create a marital covenant with every other member of the group; *communes*, in which married couples and/or single persons share living resources and also accept mutual responsibilities for community but without necessarily permitting group sex or partner sharing; and *swinging*, so-called spouse swapping, which promotes the kind of group sex which couples participate in together but with a minimum of emotional commitment to the other couples. Styles can, of course, be combined into several variations. Another less well known option or alternative in marital patterns is the *open-ended marriage*, with which this book is concerned.

Fundamental to all of the new options, however, is the conviction that women have an equal right to sexual experimentation, satisfaction, and freedom. And where single-standard restrictions are valued, voluntarily accepted, and self-disciplined, the male also has an equal responsibility to maintain the same values and behavior as his partner. Ultimately, it is a profound yet joyful quality of sexual intimacy and interpersonal sharing which husbands and wives are seeking for themselves, each other, and for their friends through new lifestyles.

Heterosexuals Versus Homosexuals.

In no other aspect of sexual behavior is the double standard more vicious than in the conflict between heterosexuals and homosexuals. This conflict is commonly presented in terms of normalcy versus deviancy, but this framework itself is a propaganda success of heterosexuals. What is universal or normal in human sexual behavior is for two persons to need each other for mutual sensual enjoyment. Nothing in human nature requires that two persons engaged in such pleasure be of different sexes. Human beings are human beings, and however they may please, comfort, support, inspire, or love each other is of human value. Though it is unusual in our culture for persons to direct sexual passion, with or without love, to members of the same sex, such behavior and relationships can contribute to the mental and physical well-being of both persons involved. Wherever and however two people touch across their loneliness to satisfy their needs, a human event takes place. Heterosexuals set for themselves exceedingly high expectations and standards of sexual fulfillment, but they deny homosexuals the same rights and opportunities. Because of customary religious condemnation, cultural conditioning, the threat of the unusual, and personal hangups, we prefer to assign homosexuality to the realm of the perverse and the pathological. It is ironic that the prejudice against homosexuals should provide common ground for some clergymen and psychiatrists who otherwise would have little to say to each other. The Victorian moralizing of a few psychiatrists makes them sound like preachers and anti-homosexuality crusaders. Even the modern "apostle of sane sex," Dr. David Reuben, writes on the subject of homosexuality with a pseudo-scientific moralism, thereby justifying those who were afraid to ask in the first place.[8] Though his opinions are expressed with sarcastic humor rather than melodramatic Victorian self-righteousness, Dr. Reuben presents a grossly distorted view of same sex behavior. His outrageous generalizations about the character and motivation of homosexuals are based on his selection of case studies, second-hand reports, and medical gossip, all of which involve bizarre behavior or psychopathology to begin with, and he completely omits any discussion of homosexuals who are emotionally healthy and creative. The entire presentation is without compassion or empathy, shallow in understanding, and a cruel caricature of homosexuals. It is to be hoped that this Krafft-Ebing type of catalogue of sexual horrors will no longer frighten or shame people into conformist behavior.

One of the experiments in sexual freedom which will eventually bridge the tensions and distinctions between homosexuals and heterosexuals is the phenomenon of group sex as a form of play. The John Birch Society and the Christian Crusade evangelicals were perceptive when they shifted their coordinated and massive attack against sex education in the schools to a campaign against sensitivity training in the schools. When significant numbers of people become involved with the widespread encounter/sensitivity training movement, unpredictable changes are bound to occur in people and society. If men and women shed inhibitions, risk openness and intimacy through touching, and discover the pleasures of shameless sensuality, then all of the familiar protocols of sexual behavior soon become questioned and challenged. In effect, people become less afraid to exhibit and receive physical affection. That such a cultural development can be considered dangerous to established morality and American civilization is a commentary on the impoverishment and fragility of our venerable values—or at least on the way in which those values are being interpreted. The ultraconservatives are at least more prophetic in their alarm than are the liberals who, in their analytical supercool, quibble about the precise degree of social change. The encounter/sensitivity movement, in spite of its potential dangers to any unwary individual who cannot cope with its personalized impact, is creating a new class of sensually adventurous persons; men and women who rejoice in their flesh-and-bloodness; who delight in mutual exchanges of being-with-you-in-the-flesh-pleasure; who affirm their sensual condition without shame. Sexual playfulness for such persons is a more creative and zestful way of living than the self-stultification which so many people face as their fate. Instead of the overbearing ogling of males or the come-on twittering of frustrated females, a more honest delight in mutual sensual exploration is possible. The essence of the sexual revolution is not revealed in the statistics of who-does-what-to-whom-how-many-times; it is in the new attitude of sex as play and the willingness of people to act accordingly. It is probable that only a very small percent of those who have had "growth group" experience will experiment with group sex. Of that number there will be those who decide that this type of activity is not their thing. Others, however, will discover that they have a capacity for sensual enjoyment with members of the same sex as well as with those of the different sex. It can be a discovery which is mind expanding and spirit freeing—a dazzling escape from emotional captivity which leads to sweet freedom in a new world. Suddenly, the sexual population is no longer divided into only two types, heterosexuals and homosexuals, with their respective stereotyped roles. To become a *bisexual* is to discover the joy of relating with sensual affection to those of one's own sex, and astonishingly, those people who were once impersonal competitors are now potentially personal friends; it is to discover the other half of humanity of which the self is part. And by experiencing one's own homosexual potential, homosexuals no longer seem queer, for now we can empathize with their feelings without threat to our own masculinity or femininity. The variety of sexual patterns increases and enriches all. Instead of only two styles in opposition to each other, we have a range of behaviors:

    exclusive heterosexuality
    bisexuality with dominant heterosexuality
    bisexuality with dominant homosexuality
    exclusive homosexuality

These categories could undoubtedly be refined. Are there, for example, people who are bisexual with equal preferences? Is it possible for a given individual to move through two or all of these categories at different phases of his life? As usual, the language of sex becomes a problem, and descriptive phrases can sound awkward. Even definitions are not uniform. The term "bisexual," for instance, can refer to a hermaphrodite, a person born with both male and female organs. Its use here, of course, refers to a person who experiences sexual intimacy with others of each sex.

Beyond the Double Standard.

The double standard of morality has lost its pre-eminent status in contemporary human relationships, but it will long exist to some degree in some form or other. Perhaps no other standard will take its place, for the present challenge is not so much to replace it with one ideal substitute, but to create a social climate which fosters pluralism in sex standards and allows for experimentation in lifestyle. The varieties of sexual expression and the meanings each individual attaches to his experience are incalculable. Tension between standards will not be eradicated and people will continue to feel conflict with each other, but the tension can be creative and the conflicts can be growth opportunities if we could learn to value differences and to appreciate each other's humanity. Even sexual freedom can rigidify and become oppressive if the people who consider themselves liberated become pridefully intolerant of the values, preferences, and conditions of others. The British psychologist Derek Wright raised a valid issue in a *Life* magazine editorial (November 6, 1970) when he wrote on "the new tyranny of sexual liberation." In that provocative article he warns: "We begin to grade our sexual partners, as they us, though we do not talk about it. And standards are rising. Too often for the sex experts, the merely possible is instantly the optimal, and tomorrow, for the rest of us, the normal. How we pity or scorn the impotent and the frigid! While, absurdly, some people use sex to exorcise their insecurities, others who find it difficult, distasteful or merely dull conclude that they are odd, outcast and, most desolating of all, inadequate. It is so easy to build a prison around a man by convincing him he is a prisoner." Even among the supposedly sexually enlightened the grading often takes place. It is dismaying how persons who are sensitive, informed, and experienced will nevertheless have stereotyped expectations of the sexual responses of a partner. If technical performance (for example, strength of erection of clitoris, nipples, or penis; timing and intensity of orgasm or ejaculation; level of excitement and response to certain stimuli; endurance in certain positions, etc.) does not conform to textbook standards or does not measure up to prior encounters of memorable climax, then disappointment, doubt, or analytical probing ruin the pleasure of the experience. The sheer delight in being naked together and appreciating the specialness of the moment, the joy of intimacy, the sharing of sensuality can be entirely missed by those who are preoccupied with the end result of the Big O. Yes, there is tremendous value in being knowledgeable about the usual sexual responses of men and women; it is important to anticipate the needs and desires of your partner and to bring him/her to complete satisfaction when possible and desired. But this type of expertise need not be the focus of the experience—it can be the background which enriches the pleasure and value of two (or more) persons creating a beautiful time of affirmation and affection. The combinations and varieties of level of lust, genital intensity, orgasmic patterns, physiological endowments, mood on the occasion, etc., are endless, and every act of intimacy is unique, never to be precisely duplicated. Enjoyable sex requires relaxed humor and the ability to appreciate the wonder of the moment on whatever level it can honestly be felt.

To go beyond the double standard, then, it is required of us that we be autonomous, to stand on our own values, to resist enslavement by any sex ideology, and to focus on whole persons as well as on genitals. Of society, it is required that the conditions for, and rights of, sexual freedom be established and upheld in order that all standards and lifestyles may be practiced as long as they do no violence to individuals or interfere with the civil rights of others. This task is overwhelming but possible of accomplishment if enough people will work to shape a social order which holds human well-being and community as high national priorities. The quality of personal lives cannot be enriched within a dehumanizing social environment; society cannot be radically reformed without men and women who are willing to act with courage. Professor Arnold Birenbaum of Wheaton College (Mass.) captures the interdependence of self and society in relation to sexuality with the observation that "The failure to achieve an independent sexual life, as part of an independent personality, is the result of the absence of any society-wide effort to bring about the removal of the fragmenting character of modern society. To create the autonomous personality, we must put an end to conditions which produce self-estrangement. The effort itself must involve the self in all its complexity, otherwise the sexual revolution only serves to continue the sense of helplessness, bewilderment, loneliness, and self-estrangement. It cannot be done for us but only by us."[9] In other words, the issues of sexual values, relationships, and behavior cannot be isolated from the political, economic, racial, and other critical issues of our time. The search for happy sex is ultimately self-destructive if it is not related to the context of total human sexuality and the search for the meaning of life. The social action of homosexuals and lesbians, for example, is redeeming for them as human beings and redeeming for society, which is humanized in the process of response and change. Their sexuality is affirmed ("I am a whole male/female person!") and the restoration of dignity gives them greater meaning in life ("I will not hide in shame, I can contribute to society!"). The humane and reconciling approach and the constructive recommendations of the final report on homosexuality of the National Institute of Mental Health (October 1969) is a hopeful example of the fact that sexual prejudice and myths can be overcome and social policy transformed, once enlightened women and men apply themselves to the task. Of course, the implementation of that report remains to be accomplished.

In any case, before we can achieve a national condition of liberated people—men, women, and children—the hard issues raised by the Women's Liberation Movement will have to be faced and resolved honestly and directly. There is no getting around it. The Movement is serious and will not fade away, and all people will benefit from its reformation of human communion and community.

NOTES

1. Ira L. Reiss, "Premarital Sexual Standards" in *Sexuality and Man*, edited by SIECUS, p. 40 (Charles Scribners and Sons, 1970)
2. Shulamith Firestone, *The Dialectic of Sex*, pp. 160-161 (William Morrow and Co., 1970)
3. See Ronald Mazur, *Commonsense Sex*, pp. 31-34 (Beacon Press, 1968)
4. Jessie Bernard, "Women, Marriage, and the Future," *The Futurist*, pp. 41-43 (April, 1970)
5. Albert Ellis and Albert Abarbanal, eds., *The Encyclopedia of Sexual Behavior* (Hawthorn Books, 1961)
6. Alice S. Rossi, "Equality Between the Sexes: An Immodest Proposal," *Daedalus*, p. 608 (Spring, 1964)
7. John H. Gagnon and William Simon, "Prospects for Change in American Sexual Patterns," *Medical Aspects of Human Sexuality*, p. 113 (January, 1970)
8. David Reuben, *Everything You Always Wanted to Know About Sex But Were Afraid to Ask*, pp. 129-151 (David McKay Co., 1969)
9. Arnold Birenbaum, "Revolution Without The Revolution: Sex in Contemporary America," *The Journal of Sex Research*, p. 266 (November, 1970)

14

GROUP SEX AND SEXUALLY FREE MARRIAGES
Russell Ford

In this chapter, Ford raises the issue of sexual freedom and defines it in terms of internal freedom. He rightly notes that we are all variously raised "unfree" because of the sanctions, including that important one of guilt, that limit our powers of even choosing to choose. Ford demonstrates that our social environment is still unliberating, no matter what ostensible options have been discussed. He talks about group sex as a harbinger of change, a force for liberalization, noting that there are a number of rationales that can support the entry into experimentation today.

The expanded number considered as loved-ones, increased sharing, and the joys of the triad are discussed at highly personal levels. Ford's concluding comment should provoke further thought—if not action: "Consider the possibilities."

Let us begin with some definitions. Group sex is not particularly hard to define, so let us reserve discussion of it for later. Sexually free marriage—indeed, sexual freedom itself—is a much more elusive concept. As a result of the intellectual backlash against the various liberation movements of the 60's, it is fashionable in some circles to deny that any very substantive reality lurks behind the word "freedom," or to link it so intimately to a counter-balancing "responsibility" that it loses all meaning. Yet I insist that "sexual freedom" is neither an empty concept nor a self-contradiction.

On the most simplistic level, of course, sexual freedom would seem to mean the freedom to do whatever you want sexually. In this sense, the main obstacles to sexual freedom are physical limitations (no man can experience what it feels like to have his clitoris licked, for instance), informal social pressures (your date has to be assured that you "love" her before she will go to bed with you), and restrictive legislation (group marriages are not legally recognized, and may in fact be illegal). Nothing much can be done on the physical level, of course. The struggle for sexual freedom would seem to imply re-education of the narrow-minded agitation against restrictive laws. When all such laws are stricken from the books and when social pressures to conform have died away, then a certain measure of sexual freedom will have been attained. But this probably does not sum up what most of us mean when we use the expression "sexual freedom."

To be sexually free implies not only freedom from external restraints, but freedom from internal inhibitions. And here things become much more complex.

Theoretically the truly sexually free person is free to choose any pathway of sexual expression, from perpetual orgies to celibacy. This is, in a sense, true. But let us take the extreme case—celibacy. Was St. Augustine free when he chose celibacy as his life-style? It is true that at the time the church did not demand celibacy of its priests. Yet the Manichean doctrines which Augustine studied clearly reinforced the idea that celibacy was a great virtue. So did the writings of Paul. And Augustine was wracked with guilt over his illicit affairs. When he gave up his fiancee upon his conversion to Christianity, it was an act of conscious sacrifice patterned on many examples before him. For Augustine celibacy was a logical choice—because of his upbringing and his environment. In a way, he was not *free* to see marriage as a fully Christian alternative for himself.

I have taken Augustine as an example because his personal attitude toward sexuality had an overpowering effect on subsequent developments in western civilization. Plato, Paul, Jerome, Augustine—these are the men mainly responsible for the ascetic ideal in the West. Can we honestly say that when we follow in their footsteps we are choosing freely? Are we not rather acquiescing to an old pattern with enormous authority and emotional weight behind it? Few people choose to have no sex purely because they do not feel sexual. Most such choices are the result of an *anti*-sexual education.

Similarly, those who say they freely choose to be monogamous may be fooling themselves. We are all becoming familiar with the housewife, stung by what she thinks are the ideas of women's liberation, who insists that she *likes* housework and that she has freely chosen it as her way of life. Yet, if all occupations were open to women and girls were not educated to expect housewifery as their lot in life, might not many of these same women have chosen differently? Monogamy, too, is a role for which we are educated; society rewards those who play by the rules and punishes those who break them.

Because of the overwhelming influence of education and environment on our decisions, sexual freedom is necessarily a relative matter.

But if we allow ourselves to sink into an absolutely deterministic outlook on life, the very idea of freedom becomes nonsensical. You are what you are, and you feel the way you feel. There is no such thing as liberation.

But here we are falling into a philosophical trap. Sexual freedom is not really an ideology; it is a *feeling*. The best we can hope for is to *feel* free.

Here at last is something we can deal with. I do not ski, and I do not make love with men. Skiing does not repel me—I'm simply not interested. But I am frightened of homosexuality. I have freely chosen not to ski. I doubt seriously that my choice to not engage in homosexuality is free. That does not mean that in order to free myself I must override my feelings of aversion and fear and try homosexuality. If I did so it would be because I was driven by a compulsion to prove something—which would be unfree behavior. But I recognize that if I could get over my aversion to homosexuality I would be a freer person. Possibly once I got over this aversion, I would discover that homosexuality did nothing for me. Having tried it and found it unrewarding, I could freely choose to not engage in it further. I think then I would feel free.

For a married (or unmarried) couple, things become more complicated. If one partner feels that having an affair is the right thing for him/her, but the other partner is filled with uncontrollable jealousy and rage at the very thought, the first partner is not free. To be free as part of a couple is much more difficult than to be free as an individual, because by joining themselves together as a unit, two people have made themselves to some degree responsible for each other's feelings. But the way in which sexual freedom is determined is much the same for a couple as for an individual.

If you, as a couple, choose not to go to an orgy because you are afraid it will stir up feelings of possessiveness and jealousy, then you are not free. If you feel no fear of an orgy, and you are fully informed about its nature, and you have the opportunity to go to one, and if you then choose not to go because the idea simply doesn't appeal to you—or you'd rather do something else—then you are measurably more free.

Sexual conservatives will argue that in this "permissive" age, promiscuity is encouraged, and self-restraint is the brave choice of the minority. This is patently nonsense. The churches, the schools, the newspapers: all the major organs of our society continue to preach premarital chastity and monogamy. The very notion of "permissiveness" carries with it the idea that this wicked behavior is being *permitted* rather than encouraged. A permissive society is not one in which most people are free to do what they want; it is a society in which *some* people are allowed to behave in ways of which *most* people disapprove. Imagine a presidential candidate who came out for sexual freedom, even one who went no further than advocating the legalization of the bedroom activities of the majority of voters. Could he be elected?

No, our environment is still distinctly sexually unliberating. The predominance of erotic material in advertising is an index of our repression and sexual hunger, not of our liberation.

It seems undeniable to me that for the vast majority of people sexual freedom would mean more sex, with more people, in a greater variety of ways. And this includes group sex. Most avoidance of group sex is now based on ignorance and general anti-sexual attitudes. Eliminate these restraining factors, and many more people would engage in it. And as information on the subject becomes more widely available and as more people become fully accepting of their sexuality, that is exactly what is happening.

But as is inevitably the case with any emerging social phenomenon, the recent growth of group sex in certain segments of our society has given rise to a multitude of misconceptions, fears and alarmed reactions. Until very recently, the notion of group sex was inextricably linked in many people's minds with the decadence and fall of ancient Rome. Who has not heard of "Roman orgies"? Yet even this near-universal image has a very flimsy basis in fact. Authorities who ought to know better quote Juvenal's description of the supposedly orgiastic rites of the *Bona Dea*, to which only women were admitted. Yet, it is obvious that the account in his Sixth Satire, which is a classic of misogyny, is simply the product of an overwrought imagination, stimulated to paranoia by exclusion from these rites.

A few of the more outlandish emperors did hold rather wild parties, but only a relative handful ever engaged in public sex, and this on rare occasions—so rare that they have come down to us in the history books as remarkable events. Tacitus and Suetonius did not chronicle such events as normal, but as highly exceptional. Using their accounts to create an image of ancient Rome as a whole would be like assembling an account of the contemporary United States from the headlines in the *National Inquirer*.

Ancient Athens at the very height of its political and cultural power was infinitely more open and liberated sexually than Rome ever was. If there are parallels to be drawn between Rome and our own nation, the most remarkable similarity is in the hypocritical puritanism of both nations in sexual matters.

Thus when modern scandal-mongers accuse the U.S. of being a contemporary Rome, they are not far off the mark, though in a way they do not intend. Like the Romans, we are the masters of an empire which has made us enormously rich, but which we tell ourselves we have assembled for the good of mankind—in the interest of world peace and prosperity. Like them, we pass harsh laws pretending to enforce the strictest monogamy and then break them freely. Also like them, we have been unable to successfully integrate sexuality into the ideals of our culture. Our religion, our morality and our politics are basically anti-sexual.

But in the midst of this generally anti-sexual culture, there are forces for change at work. One of these forces is the growth of group sex.

Group Sex

Now for our second definition: Group sex is simultaneous sexual activity between three or more people in proximity to each other. All participants need not be directly involved with each other, but the style of "closed swinging" in which couples exchange partners for private sex would be excluded. The sexual activity of some participants may be limited to mere watching at times. Group sex is not necessarily the same thing as a group grope. It may, and often does, consist of several couples making love in the same room, without physical interaction between couples.

Many of the people who engage in group sex regularly call themselves "swingers," though not all swingers are orgiasts, and not all swinging is at parties. Nevertheless, most swingers are orgiasts, and the term "swinger" is used in this chapter as a handy label for participants in group sex. It should be noted that many swingers object to the term "orgy," though others, like myself, use it freely. And to get one final definitional problem out of the way, swingers *never* use the term "wife-swapping," so popular among the general public. The exchange is mutual. "Co-marital sex" is one widely accepted scientific term.

What follows is based partly on my reading of the books and articles listed in the annotated reading list appended to this chapter. There are several scientific studies of swinging of greater or less reliability, and many popular accounts of group sex by and for participants. My list contains the best of them, with special emphasis on their relevance to group sex.

Several of the authors of even the scientific studies seem to be secret swingers, but they do not reveal that fact in their publications. I respect their right to conceal their activities and appreciate the consequences uptight America visits on the sexually liberated even today; but I prefer to openly state that I and my wife have been and continue to be participants in group sex, including several full-scale orgies and a number of intense three- and four-way relationships. I regret that I have to use a pseudonym to protect myself, but I would rather be honest about my activities and inclinations and lie about my identity than vice versa. My comments are obviously influenced by my personal experience in group sex, which has been positive and rewarding.

When Gilbert Bartell's *Group Sex* was published, I was at first elated to find a serious study of swinging available in book form to the general public; but my elation changed to disappointment as the reviews revealed that many readers were receiving a badly distorted view of group sex as a result of the special nature of Bartell's sample.

Obviously a rather hip young professor, he found the suburbanites he studied amusing and even somewhat repulsive; and he allowed his reactions to color his findings. Other studies counterbalance his bias, but they are relatively unknown to the public at large. I can only present a few brief comments here on popular misconceptions of group sex and refer the interested reader to my reading list.

"Wife-swappers" were no sooner reported in the press than they were pronounced "sick" by establishment psychiatrists who had never met them. Dear Abby and other pundits of popular wisdom continue to look upon swinging as some sort of loathsome disease. This notion seemed at first to be borne out by Brian G. Gilmartin's study (see Chapter 8 in this book) which found that swingers had received psychiatric counseling much more frequently than non-swingers. This finding was supported by Lynn G. Smith's study of the Sexual Freedom League.

There are a couple of possible explanations for this phenomenon, however. Gilmartin notes that swingers are deviants in our society, likely to have undergone stress in divorcing themselves from cultural norms. Yet it is interesting to note that in the vast majority of cases the psychiatric counseling occurred *before* the individual's entrance into swinging. Swinging evidently does not cause unusual emotional distress. Further, swingers have very low rates of hospitalization for psychiatric reasons. Perhaps swingers are apt to be the kind of self-aware persons who would more actively seek counseling than the average citizen, who won't go near a "shrink" unless he can be convinced he's crazy. No study has shown any greater unhappiness, instability or preponderance of any other harmful trait among swingers than among the rest of the population. They seem to be no nuttier than anybody else, only better counseled.

One of the most persistent claims made by swingers which has been incredulously received by non-swingers has been that group sex has actually improved their marriages. Although this question needs further study, and it is apparent that swinging has occasionally led to divorce, the preponderance of the evidence is that many marriages actually are improved by the activity. Brecher's survey contains many interesting comments on this matter.

If we think of ourselves as a monogamous people, then this assertion may indeed be surprising; but we should be more realistic. The majority of American marriages contain at least one adulterer. The majority of this adultery is "cheating"—hidden, guilty affairs carried on in secret. Swingers cooperate in seeking and engaging in extramarital sex, and for many of them the result is a less destructive, even beneficial outlet for sexual desires which don't fit in the monogamous pattern.

Perhaps the most common flaw in popular accounts of group sex is the idea that all such experiences must be essentially alike. This is a great error. Orgiasts are young and old, atheist and religious, reactionary and revolutionary, straight and hip, dopers and drinkers and total abstainers, married and single—some are even virgins! About the only things they are not is sexually chaste or monogamous. Kindred spirits (the name of one swinger publication, incidentally) are drawn together, and there are student groups, communal groups, military base groups, celebrity groups, and the couple down the street that invites their best friends over for an evening of sex a couple of times a month. Thus a single orgy, or even a detailed study of orgies within a particular social subgroup, cannot possibly give an accurate impression of what group sex is in all its variety. I would like to briefly describe some of the possibilities.

Let's start with an image which is very wide-spread in the minds of non-swingers, and very rare in reality. A group of middle-aged husbands and wives gather together and play some game which results in the wives being traded off, going home with someone else's husband, and balling him. This image was not too far removed from reality a decade or so ago; but only a tiny handful of traditional older swingers still tolerate such highly organized mate-swapping in which one has no free choice of partner.

Bartell did find instances of highly authoritarian group sex party hosts, but most swingers disliked and avoided them. John H. Pflaum suggests that an authoritarian leader in therapeutic orgies may help to relieve the participants of a sense of responsibility and allow them to do things they will enjoy but which they would not normally do spontaneously. Authoritarian group experiences like the ones he describes have been tried by some people within the Sexual Freedom League with a certain degree of success. It is often remarked that at parties where the host is too nondirective, the activity may never get off the ground. The most common kind of leadership is exerted when the hosts disrobe as a signal for the beginning of the swinging part of a party.

Yet the latter kind of authoritarianism is obviously far removed from the formal rigidity of the old-fashioned mate-swapping parties. The goal is to ease people into a situation where they will feel free to act spontaneously on their desires, whereas the older parties were dominated from beginning to end by structure. Costumes may have been prescribed, partners assigned, and even the specific sex acts and their duration laid down as part of the rules for the evening. This sort of thing is extremely rare at present.

Perhaps the most common sort of group sex is much more intimate: two couples swinging together, or a couple swinging with a third person. They may get together through advertisements in one of the many swingers' publications or underground papers. The majority of swingers avoid such correspondence with strangers, however. They may learn that friends are swingers and become involved through them. Very often couples seeking group sex simply seduce their best friends, extending the friendship into the sexual area. In other cases, one of the marriage partners has been having an affair, and there is a decision made to bring the third party into the marriage relationship on a sharing basis.

From these varied beginnings, many kinds of experiences can result. There are highly organized swinging groups in every sizeable city. Parties are held at which the guests may know each other only slightly. Some swingers make it a rule never to swing more than once with any one couple, to prevent emotional entanglements. Through continual correspondence and referrals from previous partners, they ensure themselves a never-ending stream of new couples. Such experiences are likely to be rather impersonal, purely physical affairs. Great care must be taken not to offend these literally naked strangers, and an ethic has been developed among party-goers which avoids gratuitously insulting those one declines to ball with.

Making it with friends and lovers is a very different kind of experience. Since most women seem to be able to develop ambisexual feelings quite readily, it is not at all uncommon for a husband and wife to mutually enjoy a triad with a woman. This can extend to a very intense three-way emotional involvement, as has been the case in a few instances involving my wife and myself. Such triads have been found by investigators to be the most prevalent form of successful group marriage.

Women come to ambisexuality easily. Estimates of the rate vary from 92% (Bartell) to 60% (O'Neill) to 25% (Smith). Males are much more conditioned against homosexuality in our culture (though the Smith study of the Sexual Freedom League found as many males as females engaging in such behavior, perhaps an indication of a trend among younger hip swingers). Thus triads with two males are less common, and when they occur, the males seldom make love with each other, concentrating on pleasuring the female.

Some swingers rigorously exclude love from their swinging experiences; but like many others, we feel free to expand the circle of our love continuously to include people who play an important role in our lives. Yet we do not feel it necessary to be in love with all our sex partners.

Groups like the Sexual Freedom League hold parties which draw on dues-paying members and function as an important activity of the organization. On the other hand, a group of friends sitting around together feeling good may find that they have spontaneously evolved into a group sex experience. This probably happens less often than people wish it would, but more than one encounter group has been known to slip into this sort of thing as a natural by-product of the feelings of warmth and closeness developed by deep-level interaction. The Sexual Freedom League has taken advantage of this fact by creating encounter groups specifically aimed at readying participants for sexual freedom, and many parties use "sensitivity" exercises to get things going. I myself have found that a technique in which the group massages and undresses each individual in turn provides an excellent means for making the transition from a non-sexual party to a good orgy.

Some communes (but only a minority) make group sex a part of their regular routine. The Weatherman communes, for instance, practiced a systematic form of sexual exchange aimed at thwarting "pair-bonding" and hopefully cementing the emotions of the group members in ways which would reinforce their political purposes. A television documentary on the religious group, The Children of God, claimed that some members of the leadership regularly engaged in group sex, though this was denied by the leaders themselves. Still other groups of young people who just happen to live together to save money sometimes find themselves experimenting with group sex just as a fun thing to do. The possible variations are virtually endless.

The Benefits from Group Sex Orgies

But why bother? What good is group sex? Even if the participants don't seem to be notably damaged and not all swingers are like the middle-brow conformists depicted by Bartell, why should a sensitive person concerned with sexual freedom take orgies seriously? There are many reasons.

First, if it is a good one and the couple can feel comfortable in it, an orgy can be a lot of fun. The term "recreational swinger" has taken on some unfortunate connotations, but recreational sex need not be a distasteful experience for a loving, sensitive person. After all, not all sex can be procreative, deeply mystical, passionately loving, or character-transforming. Much of it is just plain enjoyable. Swimming in a mountain lake, listening to good music, preparing and eating fine food, having enjoyable sex—all of these are recreational activities which can be richly rewarding without necessarily being peak experiences. Most people will feel the earth move under them very few times during their lives. All the rest need not be a waste. Good sex is good for what it is. Those who are always straining for the peaks ofeen find they become frigid or impotent through too much trying.

Some people find it impossible to think of sex in such terms. It is too intense, too personal, too exalted. Fine, if they feel that way, they should avoid recreational sex. But as always, we must ask whether their attitude is not mostly the result of previous repression. In my own case, I have not found that experiences with casual recreational sex have detracted in the slightest from my ability to experience extremely intense, quasi-mystical sexual encounters. I suspect we will ultimately find that a variety of sexual experience will prove to be one of the marks of a fully healthy human being.

Privacy is a major hangup with many people. It is even something precious to them, an important value. It is true that I find it annoying to have distracting onlookers observing my sexual experiences if they are not a part of them; and I am prepared to accept the objections of those who say they don't want to watch me doing it in the road in front of their house (although I do resent having to clothe myself whenever prudes are around)—but to me an insistence on privacy as a prerequisite for each and every sexual act smacks of shame. I agree essentially with the ancient Cynic philosophers who reasoned that if sex itself is not shameful there is no reason it should not be done in public. If a thing is good between two people, it may be even better shared. Here is a good test of your motives for demanding privacy: you insist on having just the two of you present when you make love—would you feel comfortable masturbating while your partner watched? If he/she enjoyed it? Examine your reasons for your answer.

It is often said that all swingers must be exhibitionists and voyeurs. This is true in a sense, but only in the sense in which we all indulge in exhibitionism when we wear sexually attractive clothes and display voyeuristic tendencies by enjoying the sight of stimulating photographs or persons. Strictly defined, these tendencies are only deviations when the afflicted person can find sexual satisfaction through no other means. Any sexually normal person finds delight in contemplating his/her lover's body and in being contemplated. Many profess to find the sexual organs themselves and sexual intercourse an ugly sight. All I can say is that I do not find them so, and neither do many other people; and those who are most outspoken in this regard appear often to be markedly antisexual in general.

Watching one beautiful person is nice. Watching two beautiful people is nicer. Watching two beautiful people make love is nicer still.

One of the great benefits produced by group sex which almost every participant experiences, is the enormous feeling of freedom which accompanies it. We all have residual guilt and shame feelings about sex, and seeing it out in the open is a tremendously liberating experience for many people. Even a nude party, such as may occur without specific sexual activity, usually makes the participants feel good, open, warm feelings. So-called "nude therapy" depends on this fact. It motivates the skinny-dipping at rock concerts and the popularity of sauna parties.

Almost everyone has fantasies about group sex. Orgies are probably among the most common suppressed dreams of the average person. Then we learn it is possible to live out these fantasies: to watch others making love and be watched, to make love with two people at once, to form a "daisy chain." One also learns that real life is not the same as fantasy. Not all the people may be attractive. One may be rejected or reject someone else. Nervousness may prevent erection or orgasm. The intense group experience in which everyone dissolves together in oceanic ecstasy is rare. Yet a fantasy which must be lived through and dealt with in real life is ultimately much more rewarding than one which remains festering in the imagination. In my own mind, living through an orgy is much more mature than fantasizing one.

Even an impersonal orgy may be rewarding. There are times and moods in which a person wants and needs only pure sex—without the rich web of a more complex relationship to interfere with its purity. People at some orgies are there to be just that for each other. Call it "using each other" if you will, but only in the sense that people use each other in any cooperative effort for their common good. I too find cold, uninvolved "trophy-hunting" swingers who cannot connect sex and love repulsive, but it is sad to see people limit their sensual experience by insisting that they must love each and every partner. Most people find sex in a love relationship the best kind of sex, but fewer are satisfied with loving sex alone. Sometimes plain old sex sex is what is called for, and orgies provide it without misunderstanding or exploitativeness.

On the other hand, many people live closely together for years, sharing their good and bad times, aiding and comforting each other, sharing many aspects of their lives—but excluding sex. Sex can be a very friendly thing to do with someone.

Bartell stresses the use of group sex as a means of avoiding marital jealousy. Most marital partners crave some variety, but they are afraid to be "unfaithful" because they don't want their partner to feel jealous. Many people find that jealousy is not necessarily a function of sexual exclusivity. There are many ways of being jealous. Many people do not mind if their spouse has sex with someone else as long as they are aware of it only indirectly. Others are not jealous if the "unfaithfulness" takes place in their presence. Others do not object to extramarital sex, but to extramarital love. Group sex, in which all the participants are together, mutually pleasuring each other, avoids many of the strains which create jealousy.

I feel myself that as much as I enjoy group sex, there are times when my wife and I desire and enjoy separate affairs. I feel threatened only if I fear the other two may split off and form a couple in *opposition* to me. If the other persons are simply included in our circle of affection, then it adds to our marriage.

Finally, a group can give the individual support in exploring pathways a couple might hesitate to try. A man desiring anal intercourse, but whose wife does not enjoy it, may find a willing partner at a party. Many women find themselves trying and enjoying homosexuality for the first time at a party. Even ambisexuality in men is becoming less rare among the younger hip swingers. Pflaum suggests that same-sex couples may find it easier to experiment with ambisexuality if they are held and caressed by members of the opposite sex at the same time, and there are accounts of just such events at parties.

In our society, sexual expression is usually tied up in innumerable restrictions and prohibitions. Courtship, seduction, legal barriers, even marriage—all these stand in the way of free, spontaneous sexual expression, which is one of the most deeply felt desires of people in our culture. In a group sex situation, despite the fact that there are distinct pressures against such options as total abstention or rape, the range of possibilities for truly free, spontaneous sex are enormously widened.

Thus group sex represents not only an opportunity for sexually free couples to exercise their freedom, but it can be a tool for bringing about that freedom within an expanding marriage. Although not everyone will find orgies to their taste, they are definitely no longer something to be relegated to the realm of fantasy. Any adventurous couple can find people for group sex experiences if they are willing to exert a little effort.

"Consider the possibilities." Indeed.

REFERENCES

Popular Accounts by and for Swingers

Ford, Russell. "Our Experiences with Group Sex," in *Adventures in Loving*, ed. Robert Rimmer. New American Library, 1973.

Kronhausen, Phyllis and Eberhard. *Freedom to Love*. Grove Press, 1970. Based on the film by the same title. The book contains a panel discussion on swinging and group sex by a group of swingers. Unfortunately this excellent little volume is currently out of print.

Poland, Jefferson and Sam Sloan (eds.). *Sex Marchers*. Elysium Incorporated, 1968. The history of the Sexual Freedom League, edited by its founder.

Poland, Jefferson and Valerie Alison (eds.). *The Records of the San Francisco Sexual Freedom League*. Olympia Press, 1971. Interviews with women members of the SFL.

Screw: The Sex Review. Pertinent articles appear in nos. 54, 57, 63, 67, 68, 89, 103, 120 (my article on troilism), 151, 155 and 157. Back issues are available at one dollar each from Milky Way Productions, Box 432, Old Chelsea Station, New York, New York 10011. The best of these articles will appear in *The Screw Sex Manual*, edited by myself.

Sexual Freedom. The official organ of the Sexual Freedom League. Pertinent articles appear in issues 8 and 9. Back issues available from S. F. Book Service, P. O. Box 1403, San Francisco,

Webster, John. *Sex Is for Giving: The Swing to Extramarital Fun*. Elysium Incorporated, 1968. An enthusiastic account of the swinging life, including group sex, by a participant. Webster's observations coincide remarkably well with the findings of the more scientific investigators of the subject.

Scientific Studies of Swinging and Group Sex

Bartell, Gilbert D. *Group Sex*. Peter H. Wyden, 1971. The first serious study to be published in book form. Welcomed in the popular press at least partly because it reinforces the popular image of conformist middle-class mate-swappers. Despite Bartell's awareness of other swinging styles, he occasionally overgeneralizes from his very restricted sample and has misled many readers into thinking the Chicago suburban scene is typical. The title is misleading; the book is not about group sex as such, but about swinging.

Bell, Robert R. and Lillian Silvan. " 'Swinging'—The Sexual Exchange of Marriage Partners." Paper presented to the Society for the Study of Social Problems, Washington, D.C. August 1970. Survey of current research. Recognizes the possibility of loving swingers.

Brecher, Edward M. *The Sex Researchers*. Little, Brown, 1969. Chapter 9, "When Sexual Inhibitions Are Cast Off." Another, earlier survey, but drawing directly on research materials rather than published articles. Stresses the great variety to be found among swingers.

Constantine, Larry L. and Jean M. "Sexual Aspects of Group Marriage," Chapter 10 of this book. Part of the Constantines' ongoing study of group marriage.

Denfield, Duane. "Toward a Typology of Swinging: The Trophy Hunters." Paper presented at the Groves Conference on Marriage and Family, San Juan, Puerto Rico, May 8, 1971. Contains a good survey of other studies, stressing the variety among swingers. Denfield notes that the trophy-hunters so decried by "utopians" have probably been studied out of proportion because of their accessibility. Swingers who do not advertise or join large groups are difficult to contact.

Gilmartin, Brian G. and David Kusisto. "Some Social and Personal Characteristics of Mate-Sharing Swingers," Chapter 8 in this book. Gilmartin's study matches swingers against similar non-swingers. The point has often been made how straight and ordinary swingers are; but Gilmartin found them to be more rebellious, politically more liberal, and more compassionate toward oppressed people than non-swingers. It would appear from this that sample bias has been rampant in many of these studies.

O'Neill, George C. and Nena. "Patterns in Group Sexual Activity," in *The Journal of Sex Research*, Vol. 6, No. 2, May 1970, pp. 101-112. Reports research done during work on their new book *Open Marriage*, but the book does not contain any of their findings on swinging. Brecher points out some of the contrasts between the New York scene studied by the O'Neills and Bartell's suburban Chicago scene.

Palson, Charles and Rebecca. "Swinging in Wedlock," in *Society* (February 1972), pp.28-- 37. They found affection to be important in the sample they studied.

Smith, Lynn G. *A Preliminary Exploration of Sexual Freedom Groups*. Unpublished thesis, University of California at Berkeley, 1968. A study of members of the San Francisco Sexual Freedom League. Like Gilmartin and Symonds, Smith takes a much more positive attitude toward group sex, contrasting strikingly with Bartell. Her findings will be included in the Smiths' *Co-Marital Sex*.

Spanier, Graham B. and Charles L. Cole. "Mate Swapping: Participation, Knowledge, and Values In a Midwestern Community." Paper presented at the annual meeting of the Midwest Sociological Society, Kansas City, Missouri, April 21, 1972. The first random-sample study of swinging. Contains the best survey of other research. Contains nothing specifically on group sex; but outstanding for its methodological soundness.

Symonds, Carolyn. *Pilot Study of the Peripheral Behavior of Sexual Mate Swappers*. Unpublished thesis, University of California, Riverside, 1968. An important study done in Los Angeles. Symonds makes a distinction between "recreational" swingers and "utopian" swingers which has been widely adopted, but which is too narrow. Her utopians were probably the founders of the Sandstone community described in issue no. 105 of *Rolling Stone*. Lumping all swingers who do not resemble them together as "recreational" is quite misleading.

Varni, Charles A. "Contexts of Conversion: The Case of Swinging." Chapter 9 in this book. Varni suggests a much broader range of possibilities than Symonds' neat dichotomy between utopian and recreational swingers.

Manifesto.

Pflaum, John H. *Delightism*. Prentice-Hall, 1972. An extraordinary book by a research psychologist and therapist describing an approach the author calls "orgy therapy," in which group sexual experiences are used to open persons up and increase their capacity to relate deeply to themselves and each other. Connects group sex to the human potential movement. Pflaum goes far beyond many swingers—advocating, for instance, the inclusion of children and animals in his therapeutic orgies. Contains some fine orgy recipes. Mind-blowing.

15

LESBIAN/WOMAN
Del Martin and Phyllis Lyon

In this excerpt from their book, Del Martin and Phyllis Lyon explain some of the problems faced by homosexuals who want to establish a long-term intimate relationship. How do Lesbian lovers meet, how do they feel about themselves and each other, how can their relationship withstand the limited tolerance—or outright condemnation—they receive from society at large? According to the authors "Recognition of the latent homosexuality in heterosexuals and conversely, the latent heterosexuality in each homosexual is essential, if we as a people are ever to resolve our sexual hangups."

We have found some interesting anomalies in the butch-femme pattern over the years. One which crops up rather consistently is women—usually divorced and, we suspect, not Lesbian at all—who pair up with butch Lesbians. In these partnerships the entire male-female dichotomy is acted out to the nth degree. The femmes insist that their butches wear only male clothing and that they appear and act as nearly like the stereotyped male as possible. Marty, who succeeded more in looking like a young boy than a man, although she was in her thirties, told us: "I wouldn't mind wearing women's clothes. It would make life much simpler. But Ruth won't hear of it. She threw all my dresses and things out."

Most of these femmes have been divorced more than once. It appears that they have been so badly treated by men that they can't bear the thought of remarrying. Yet their only knowledge of a relationship is that of man to woman, so they fashion their own "man" out of the woman they can relate to. It does not make for a happy situation for either party, and usually the twosome doesn't last very long. . . .

The minority of Lesbians who still cling to the traditional male-female or husband-wife pattern in their partnerships are more than likely old-timers, gay bar habituees or working-class women. The old order changeth, however, and as the women's liberation movement gains strength against this pattern in heterosexual marriages, the number of Lesbians involved in butch-femme roles diminishes. There can, however, be some strange situations, even in a world where women's consciousness is being raised. We recently heard of a leader in the women's movement in Los Angeles who speaks out strongly against male domination and chauvinism. Yet in her relations with another woman, she plays the traditional male chauvinist butch role—not because she wants it that way, but because her friend insists.

Lynda, speaking as the new "woman-identified" woman of Gay Women's Liberation at the 1971 Council on Religion and the Homosexual symposium, was challenged by someone in the audience because of her apparently masculine attire. But Lynda explained, "This short haircut, because it is mine, is a woman's hair style. These so-called men's boots, because I am wearing them, are women's boots. This pipe, because I am smoking it, is a woman's pipe. Whatever women wear is women's wear. It is a matter of individual choice—and comfort."

Individual choice, too, is granted (if sometimes grudgingly) by Lesbian feminists to their sisters who still cling to their butch-femme roles. When a number of "enlightened" Lesbians, during the 1971 Gay Women's West Coast Conference in Los Angeles, loudly and openly ridiculed a traditional-style wedding taking place between two women at the Metropolitan Community Church, other truly enlightened sisters were enraged. To add their opprobrium to that which these women were already experiencing from society was, to them, unwarranted and unconscionable. Coming from them it was even more oppressive than the societal oppression they had gathered together to protest. Differences though there be in philosophy, politics or life style, the right of individual choice and of human dignity is basic to the sisterhood. What is rejected, however, is the transference of male chauvinism in adopting traditional sex roles. Most Lesbians, whatever their life style, are striving today for more egalitarian relationships.

We have watched the decline of the butch-femme concept of relationship for sixteen years. It has been a gradual decline, and, as we mentioned, the stereotype has not yet vanished. As a life style it has many disadvantages, as does the same concept—person as property—when applied to the heterosexual union. One of these disadvantages is the jealousy which invariably creeps in. Jealousy of one's partner, especially obsessive jealousy, indicates an uncertainty of the relationship and bears witness to the fact that the two partners feel somehow possessed, like chattel, by one another. Observation would indicate that more jealousy is engendered in a butch-femme relationship than in a woman-to-woman partnership, probably because of this underlying possessiveness. If you are sure of your partner's love, if your partner is a person and not a thing, then jealousy either doesn't exist or is extremely minimal. The high incidence of jealousy imputed to the Lesbian by many of the so-called experts on the subject simply doesn't exist.

Certainly we had a problem with jealousy early in our togetherness. While Del was babysitting with her daughter, Phyllis was still dating Jim. Now Jim was a holdover from Phyllis's "straight" days and had been the only person she had known, of her own age, when she had returned to San Francisco from Seattle prior to her commitment to Del. She had never been remotely romantically interested in Jim, though he was in her, but she hated to "hurt his feelings" by making the break. And at that time she surely didn't have the nerve to tell him she was a Lesbian.

For obvious reasons this whole situation didn't sit well with Del. It just didn't seem right, and she wasn't convinced there was "nothing" between them. Phyllis did break the friendship off, but not before some dramatic scenes between us. But Phyllis laid down the law. One of the reasons she had broken up with the man she had been engaged to had been his unreasonable jealousy. She wasn't going to go through that again. So she flatly told Del she would not tolerate any jealousy. And it worked. By and large, we have not been troubled with jealousy over the years. We know where we stand with each other.

While there is a certain amount of jealousy among Lesbian couples, as between heterosexual couples, the Saghir-Robins study indicates that jealousy comes in last as a reason for relationships breaking up. Further, many women who break up their relationship as lovers remain fast friends. This wouldn't be possible if the split had come over jealousy rather than a change in, or loss of, emotional attachment, the reason given for most "divorces."

Illustrative of the changing attitudes among Lesbians are Helen and Ann, young, socially aware, hip and long haired. Helen, twenty-five, has been married and Ann, twenty-one, holds deep religious commitments. Both are active in DOB and the women's movement. They have lived together for a year now, sharing love and work. Coming down the street holding hands, dressed in jeans and old army shirts, their long blonde hair hanging free, they certainly don't fit any of the stereotyped images of the Lesbian. There is no butch or femme in their world. But there once was.

"When I first got involved in gay life," Ann says, "I decided it was best to be butch. So I found a girl and we settled down. She did all the womanly things and really fussed around the house, making curtains and ruffly things. She looked to me to make all the decisions—she acted as if she didn't have a mind at all. It was a drag. So, I did what any self respecting male would do: I went out and found another girl."

It didn't take Ann long, however, to find out that equality in a relationship was important. And, says she, "There's certainly no problem being bored with Helen—she's got a mind of her own for sure."

Much change has taken place in the way all women (straight or gay) in this country think about sex roles and personal relationships. There appear to be three strong influences: (1) a questioning of religious dogma, exposing myths and re-examining the taboos, thereby developing a new code of sexual and social ethics; (2) research on human sexuality, opening up avenues to more widespread sex education, and discovery of "the pill"; and (3) the various liberation movements which all decry the use of labels to separate people and which raise the question of what it really means to be human.

Masters and Johnson, in their classic *Human Sexual Inadequacy*, found that religious orthodoxy was the single biggest contributor to sexual dysfunction, a fact those of us who have worked with homosexuals have known for years. The guilt heaped on those women, straight or gay, who have been brought up in Roman Catholic or fundamentalist religions particularly, can be unbearable. It is the cause not just of sexual inadequacy, but of alcoholism, drug addiction, misery and suicide. While Protestant denominations in this country are beginning to rethink traditional attitudes, their statements are still too cautious and tentative—and too late for many.

Though many churchmen have come a long way in understanding the humanity of homosexuals, many are still caught up in medieval concepts. Just recently a young woman called Phyllis to ask about scriptural references which didn't damn the homosexual. She indicated that she had gone to a Methodist church in San Francisco seeking understanding and help in solving her dilemma. "I'm married," she said, "but I believe it is a great mistake for me. I asked the minister why it was wrong for me to live with the woman I love in a union that seems so very natural. I asked why it would be right to stay with my husband in a union that is unnatural for me and to which I could never give my all. The minister's reply was that only if I stayed with my husband would I be 'welcome' at his church."

The homophile thrust for freedom and equality has forced some clergymen at least to recognize that love and sex between two persons of the same sex can be, and are, equal to and as valid as that between two persons of the opposite sex. Such a realization leads inevitably to a re-evaluation of the sacred institution of marriage. If the church recognizes love between two homosexuals, it cannot very well continue to condemn love between two heterosexuals who have not bothered to "sanctify" their love through wedding vows. Theologians are presently wrestling with these problems.

Change is also coming about in terms of women's sexual awareness and activity. Because of better birth control methods, especially the pill, women are for the first time relatively free of the fear of pregnancy. They are less tyrannized by their biology and thus begin to question their traditional roles. The women's liberation movement serves as a catalyst, challenging all women to question both their sexual and social roles. As a result, many more young women are experimenting sexually than ever before. In fact, if there is truly a sexual revolution in progress, it is among women, not men. A recent survey of the sexual activity of college men and women made by the Institute for Sex Research indicates that, when compared to earlier figures (approximately twenty years ago), the number of men engaging in premarital sexual intercourse has remained static, but the number of women so engaging has doubled. This, then, does at least establish basis for the hope that woman, whatever her sexual orientation, is moving toward more acceptance of herself as a sexual being.

The advent of the "flower children" in 1967 brought with it a marvelous idea: to take each person for what she or he is as a person, not for skin color, sexual orientation, status or any other artificial quality. Out of this idea of love came a great deal of sexual experimentation among people of the same and opposite sexes. If you grooved on someone, a logical extension of that feeling was sex—and it didn't matter what the sex of the grooved-upon was. Thus the idea of bisexuality, always with us, became much better known.

This concept of bisexuality was extended into the women's movement. As women in their small consciousness-raising groups began to come to terms with themselves and sought an equal partnership with men, they found that their husbands and/or lovers were not so willing to give up their roles of supposed supremacy. Their men, not having gone through the same consciousness-raising process and not understanding how they, too, are oppressed by their own stultifying "male" roles, were still clinging to the status quo, still steeped in male chauvinism. As a consequence, and because these women could not and would not turn back to the old ways, many of them vowed not to have anything more to do with men until such time as they could come together as equals. Having become more sexually aware and having made this decision, these women were then faced with finding alternatives to heterosexual coitus for their sexual satisfaction. Their options were: celibacy, masturbation, or Lesbianism. A good many, preferring and needing a close personal relationship, have deliberately chosen the latter. The experience of both the hippies and woman-identified women would indicate that the "nature" of mankind, which has heretofore been obscured by biological and biblical scripting, may indeed be bisexual.

Those naturalists who have condemned homosexuals not only point to Adam and Eve, but to lower animals as proof that our true nature is to be heterosexual. However, biologists have observed homosexual contacts in widely varied species of mammals, and anthropologists have found homosexual practices in almost all cultures. Biologists have observed homosexual activity in rats, mice, hamsters, guinea pigs, rabbits, porcupines, marten, cattle, antelope, dogs, cats, goats, horses, lions, sheep, monkeys, chimpanzees and pigs.

Drs. Clelland S. Ford, anthropologist, and Frank Beach, psychologist, in their book *Patterns of Sexual Behavior*, claim that human homosexuality is the product of our fundamental mammalian heritage of general sexual responsiveness. Cross-cultural and cross-species comparisons suggest to them that a biological tendency for inversion of sexual behavior is inherent in most, if not all, mammals, including the human species. They, of course, added that homosexuality, while prevalent, is not the predominant sexual activity observed in these societies and animals.

Freud, we pointed out earlier, postulated that a homosexual component can be found in the sexual development of every human being and that there remains in everyone the residual manifestation of bisexuality. Wilhelm Stekel, a coworker with Freud, stated flatly in his book *Bisexual Love*, "All persons originally are bisexual in their predisposition. There are no exceptions." It was his contention that the struggle between the two components of a person created neuroses and anxieties. At the age of puberty, however, the heterosexual represses his homosexuality, sublimating it in the more acceptable proprieties of friendship, nationalism, social endeavors and gatherings. The homosexual, on the other hand, somehow pushes the "wrong" button and represses his or her heterosexuality instead. But in either case, since no one manages to overcome his tendencies toward the other type of sexual behavior completely, both homosexuals and heterosexuals carry within themselves a predisposition to a neurosis. But here is where the heterosexual bias steps in. Somehow it turns out, according to Stekel, that homosexuals *are* neurotic because of their unexpressed heterosexual potential; heterosexuals, however, merely have the potential for neuroses because of their unexpressed homosexual component.

In more recent times Dr. Albert Ellis, sexologist and executive director of the Institute for Rational Living in New York City, has stated that those persons who are either exclusively heterosexual or exclusively homosexual are neurotic. The Kinsey studies verify that American men and women are not necessarily as exclusive in their private sexual behavior as they may pretend publicly.

It has seemed to us, as we have met and talked about homosexuality and human sexuality with thousands of persons, that indeed we all have the potential to respond erotically to both sexes. That we do not use this potential is due to the church-imposed morality under which we all suffer. A child is born a sexual being, neither hetero nor homo. As Dr. C. A. Tripp, psychologist, pointed out in 1965 during a symposium at the University of California School of Medicine, most human sexual behavior is *learned*. It is only in the lower animals that it is totally instinctive. The higher on the evolutionary scale you are, the less instinctive are your sexual reactions. So our life experiences "teach" us our sexuality, which may turn out to be hetero, homo or bi. The Kinsey staff, in *Sexual Behavior in the Human Female*, pondered the fact that given the physiology of human sexual response plus our mammalian background of behavior, "it is not so difficult to explain why a human animal does a particular thing sexually. It is more difficult to explain why each and every individual is not involved in every type of sexual activity."

The evidence indicates we may be purely sexual at birth, but that our society channels us primarily into accepted modes of behavior or, sometimes, those not so acceptable. We may have the capacity for bisexual response, but social mores from both sides of the fence tell us no.

At least three-fourths of the Lesbians we have known have had heterosexual intercourse more than once, either in a marriage situation, while dating, as an experiment out of curiosity, or as a test of sexual identity. For the majority of these women the experience was good, erotically: that is, orgasm was achieved and there was a pleasurable feeling. But there was not the emotional involvement which was present in a Lesbian sexual relationship. And that is what makes the difference. As Masters and Johnson so well argued, an orgasm is an orgasm, no matter how it is achieved. The body goes through the same physiological pattern, whether orgasm comes through a loved one or the edge of a vibrating washing machine. The "quality" of the orgasm differs—not within the body, but within the head. There is, after all, a great deal of difference psychologically between your lover and your washing machine.

What has happened with the advent of a more permissive partner-changing and sex-switching sexuality is that a number of Lesbians have gotten pregnant, accidentally. A heterosexual woman on the prowl will usually take the pill, or use some other method. A Lesbian caught up in the concept of loving persons as persons is very likely to be totally unprepared for a roll in the hay with a sperm-spouting male. This happened to a friend of ours who, having nothing special going with a woman, ended up in bed with a young man she had met and enjoyed. It was a classic tale—one shot and she was pregnant. In this case all has turned out well. The young woman is mature and intelligent. She has subsequently set up housekeeping with an equally intelligent and mature woman. She decided to keep the baby and the two of them appear to be doing a better job of child-rearing than many heterosexual parents. This, however, was a unique situation. It could have happened to someone not so mature who didn't want children (or wasn't ready to take on such responsibility) and who would have faced the trauma of all unwed mothers: do I keep the baby, have it adopted, get an abortion—or kill myself?

Over the years we have known a number of persons who considered themselves bisexual. Their complaint, almost universally, was that no one understood the bisexual, that she or he was much more discriminated against than a homosexual, since the straight community usually considered the bisexual to be homosexual while the gay community figured the bisexual to be simply a homosexual who, for one reason or another, hadn't yet been able to admit this fact. The bisexual, then, who has not repressed her or his ability to respond erotically to either sex and who might very well be expressing the true "nature" of the human species, is spurned in both the heterosexual and homosexual communities. Perhaps if these two warring camps declared a truce and discontinued the practice of repressing one or the other of their same-sex and opposite-sex response components, we might have a chance of finding out what the nature of sex is all about.

With the givens of Freud and Stekel—that we all have both heterosexual and homosexual inclinations, either of which, if repressed, leaves us with a predisposition to a neurosis—then insistence on a heterosexual identity as the only acceptable one obviously is detrimental to every one of us psychologically. Because we have bowed to the Judeo-Christian tradition, we have been bound to the unhealthy antisexual (not just antihomosexual) attitude that pervades our culture. We have never allowed people to respond to one another openly and reciprocally without rigid role definition. If we were allowed "to do what comes naturally," we might possibly come to understand the ambisexual nature of the human animal. If the idea of sex could be cleansed and the guilt we have felt about it could be purged from our minds, we would be rid of our sexual frustrations and hangups. We could expand our consciousness beyond our present preoccupation with the who-what-why-where-and-how of the mechanics of genital contact and fascination with the measurements of physical attributes (breasts, penises and orgasms). Allowed the freedom to be human, we might find that a new sexuality would emerge, encompassing not only the sensual, but also the trans-physical qualities of love, empathy and concern for one another's personhood, regardless of gender.

★ ★ ★

There are also "loners" that come in twosomes. Some couples do not choose to mix with or identify with the homophile community in any way. The fear of exposure is of course the major reason for isolation. But there is another reason why such a couple prefers to travel exclusively in heterosexual society. One or the other, or both, may be fearful of the competition that other gay women may present. If a partner doesn't know other people and has no contact with them, she is less apt to wander. Such a couple will isolate itself from the gay world either in mutual agreement or at the demand of one partner or the other.

After twenty years of such lone togetherness Zelda and Marney came to the DOB office. Marney had seen a copy of *The Ladder*, and her secret longings for the companionship and social outlet of a group could no longer be suppressed. But she was obviously too eager, too enthused over her new acquaintances, and too involved in DOB activities to suit Zelda. They didn't stick around, though they did invite us over to their home for dinner a time or two. Then we heard they'd moved—left the Bay Area completely.

Some such couples extend themselves only to heterosexual couples. Others more commonly find their friends among gay men. Wanda told us that the only close gay friends she and Sally had were men because they were more available, more supportive, and you could relax with them more easily. "With them there are no sexual connotations. But if you were a previous friend to some one partner of a Lesbian couple, there is always a barrier—you are forever a threat to their relationship."

But some couples are loners not so much by choice as by circumstance. Merle and Jean are farmers. Because of the novelty or eccentricity (depending on your point of view) of two women tending chores without a man around, it's taken them a while to become accepted in the small rural community where they are located. Their "gay" life is limited to their own relationship, reading material, sporadic correspondence and infrequent visits from friends they had known before they "retired." Occasionally they run into pairs of women in town whom they may wonder about, but if they become acquainted at all (which is seldom, because of the demands and constant attention to their crops and farm animals), nothing is said. It takes too long to build up to such "confessions." There isn't enough time.

By and large, most Lesbians opt for a one-to-one, long-term relationship as an ideal. The most common question put to a couple is, "How long have you two been together?" Whether or not these pairings last, as in heterosexual marriage, depends upon the degree of their maturity, their level of sexual adjustment, how well their personalities mesh, how much they have in common and how well they manage their outside commitments.

Society's refusal to recognize their "marriages" has been a source of friction and anguish for many Lesbians—and for many reasons. Because she becomes aware of her homosexuality and acts upon this self knowledge does not mean, as people often suppose, that the Lesbian automatically rejects all of the values she has been taught. For every Lesbian has been born of a heterosexual union, has been brought up and conditioned in a heterosexual family and environment, and is steeped in a predominantly—almost exclusively—heterosexual culture. And the Lesbian, being a woman, has been steered throughout her early life toward an expectation of falling in love and getting married—though her mentors did not have in mind her doing so with another woman.

★ ★ ★

It is a mistake, of course, to assume that Lesbians, any more than heterosexuals, "walk off into the sunset and live happily ever after," a conclusion that movies are fond of prescribing for heterosexual couples. Lesbians have their marital problems too, but unfortunately until most recently (and it is still all too uncommon) there has been no marriage counseling available for their taboo relationships. Society tries to pull them apart rather than help to keep them together. Dr. G. DiBella, who is affiliated with Metropolitan Hospital in New York City, has been doing research with gay couples who have been together at least ten years in order to develop a marital counseling program for homosexual couples. Occasionally we have also run across marriage counselors in San Francisco who have worked with gay people. This is an area, or occupation, where there is a definite need.

While it is true that the two of us started out in 1953 on a "till death do us part" and "faithful forever" basis, formalizing our relationship has never appealed to us. We consider love and sex our own private affair and much prefer "living in sin." We have no hangup with God. Our troubles stem from Man, for whom we have no need in our togetherness and from whom we do not require magic words or mystic ritual to solemnize our love or make it binding.

Besides, we have witnessed all too often what happens when a common-law husband and wife have been pressured into marriage. Somehow the love and concern they once felt for each other give way to possessiveness and the demand for certain rights institutionally bestowed upon them, and the couple winds up in the divorce court. What keeps us together is not a piece of paper or words. What keeps us together is feelings—of love, commitment and mutual respect.

We certainly champion those women who, because they feel a genuine, deep, personal need for public and religious recognition of their union, are willing to fight for their equal rights. And we must admit that if their efforts to legalize homosexual marriage should materialize in our lifetime, we just might give the idea some serious consideration. The economic exploitation of homosexuals who are always considered to be "single" persons, no matter what their true marital status may be, and who are taxed on this basis at the highest possible rate, has always been particularly galling to us. As a minority people we have always had to pay a disproportionate share of the tax burden, but without the benefits accorded to heterosexuals.

For some, marriage means a religious sacrament and commitment. For others it may also take on a legal significance in terms of community property, the filing of joint income tax returns and inheritance rights. Recognition of a Lesbian union might also serve to validate the couple who wished to take on the legal responsibility of adopting homeless, unwanted children. It would also simplify insurance problems, making the couple eligible for family policies, for family rates on airlines travel and for that matter, for "couple" entry to entertainment functions, too.

★ ★ ★ ★

Aside from the external obstacles to a Lesbian's choice of life style, there are always the eternal psychological ones. Perhaps the most prominent internal pressure is the hangup with the Christian concept of monogamy and fidelity. Jeanine, for instance, ended her friendship with Tomi abruptly when she came to the realization that Tomi had "seduced, or at least tried to seduce, every girl friend I ever had. We'd been friends for almost twenty years! And somehow it just never penetrated. After the episode with Relta last week, though, I began to think back. Sue just laughed at Tomi. Gerry told her to go to hell. Although Flora was intrigued and flattered, Tomi didn't really make it with her either. She did with Lorrie, though," Jeanine recounted. "What kind of a friendship would you call that? Sick—that's what it is!"

Most Lesbians lead quiet unassuming lives and expect fidelity from their partners. There are some, like the heterosexual swingers, who may opt for extracurricular activities. And sometimes one partner will stray, with or without the knowledge or consent of the other.

Interestingly enough, as some Lesbians are striving for recognized marriage, others, particularly the younger ones, are seeking less traditional modes of relationship. As the years rolled by and we had piled up a respectable "together" record, we found that some of our friends were looking to us as an ideal or model couple. "If you two ever break up, I'll jump off the bridge" or "I'll give up gay life" were some of the comments. However, the scene is changing today. They're not saying that anymore.

Now some of our younger Lesbian friends are willing to allow us this one-to-one relationship if that is our bag, but they don't want to be restricted to this old hat kind of life. As with youth elsewhere they are protesting the validity of the nuclear family. We therefore find younger Lesbians (and some not so young) who feel perfectly free in playing the field, in entering into an affair with another woman without the thought that it will, or must, last forever. Communes are forming among Lesbians; non-monogamous relationships are being experimented with: sexual freedom indeed seems possible in certain circumstances. In all these experiments, the desire is for the freedom to choose alternate life styles.

Carl Wittman, in *Refugees from Amerika: A Gay Manifesto*, published by the Council on Religion and the Homosexual, explains it this way: "We have to define for ourselves a new pluralistic, rolefree social structure. It must contain both the freedom and the physical space for people to live alone, live together for a while, live together for a long time, either as couples or in large numbers; and the ability to flow easily from one of these states to another as our needs change."

Along with the concept of communal living another arrangement has developed: a contract between the two women involved, a one- or two-year lease, so to speak, which can be renewed or dropped at expiration date depending upon the success of the mutual venture. This alternate life style, which developed out of the encounter group and liberation movements, requires that the parties involved in the partnership be honest with each other, state clearly what they want out of the relationship and what they are willing to give, and evaluate their successes and failures, much as a profit and loss statement, at regular intervals. These Lesbians don't want to stay together out of misplaced loyalty or because of historical longevity; they want to be sure that the challenges continue, that they don't grow stale, that they continue to grow and develop personally and together.

★ ★ ★

Whenever DOB has received some publicity in the media, the biggest response has come from heterosexually married women. Some complain about their sex life and wonder if a Lesbian relationship might bring them satisfaction. Some only recently discovered, after marriage, that they had a strong Lesbian component in their makeup. Others, who had deliberately given up the gay life for the security of heterosexual marriage, find they cannot ignore their Lesbian nature. They aren't necessarily looking for sexual or romantic contacts, but for understanding, for a chance to express the feelings which they have tried so long and so hard to contain. Others are torn between a Lesbian affair they need and want, and their prior commitment to their husbands and children. But all have one thing in common: there is no one, no public service agency, no priest or therapist they feel they can turn to without being held in jeopardy.

The need for adequate and nonjudgmental counseling is paramount. Recognition of the latent homosexuality in heterosexuals and conversely, the latent heterosexuality in each homosexual is essential, if we as a people are ever to resolve our sexual hangups. The need for realistic sex education, not just the biblical or reproductive variety, is vital. The National Sex Forum in San Francisco has recently developed an educational program for those in the helping professions (medical doctors, psychiatrists, psychologists, social workers, teachers, clergy, et al.) so that they may provide such counseling in the future. The Forum, which takes an aesthetic view of human sexuality, emphasizing both the value of sexuality and of proficiency rather than constraint, makes the following assumptions: (1) the most significant factor in sex education is that sex can be talked about casually and nonjudgmentally; (2) individuals should be allowed meaningful exposure to a realistic objectification of the range of behavior into which their own experience and those of other humans fall; and (3) the person who teaches, counsels, or gives advice (regardless of professional qualifications) should have a low burden of sexual guilt feelings so as to be of service to others rather than serving his or her own needs. Unfortunately, the assumptions of the National Sex Forum are not yet widely accepted, and in the meantime, the Lesbian suffers.

★ ★ ★

Though customs and language may differ from country to country, Lesbians are pretty much the same around the world. Even in nations where laws proscribing homosexual activity have long since been repealed, the stigma attached to being a Lesbian still remains. The Lesbian thus leads her life at many levels, with varying degrees of openness. She meets her partners more easily in gay bars, at homophile organizations, by correspondence and world travel. She also meets others by chance acquaintance on the job (as we did), in the waiting room of the doctor's office, in the classroom, at the veterinarian's, at the laundromat, at the supermarket or in the women's movement. Such chance acquaintances may require playing a "cat and mouse" game for a while to determine that what one suspects about the other is really true. What happens after that, what life style the Lesbian adopts, is determined by how much she is inhibited by cultural conditioning, religious persuasion, family ties, and economic dependence on the status quo. All of these factors have a direct bearing upon the Lesbian's personal relationships. The life style she adopts is generally not so much a matter of choice as the means she employs for her own self protection. But as more and more Lesbians become self determined rather than society driven, new and more open life styles for Lesbians will necessarily emerge.

III

VIEWS OF FUTURE PARTICIPANTS

The first two chapters in this section by Whitehurst, and by White and Wells, are based on original research on how the unmarried view marriages of the future and sexual life-styles which they see potential for, or lack interest in. The third chapter is based on youthful participants in early marriage; Kafka and Ryder present their findings from original research documenting the realities of counter-culture marriages—with the variety of ground rules, joys, and problems experienced by the participants in variations of traditional marriage.

The comparison of attitudes of future participants in marriage in the first two chapters and then the comparison with the actual experiences and attitudes of early participants in the third chapter should provide some insights into the transition stage from those who are not far removed from being married to those who have recently taken the big step into some alternative sexual life-style—all of which takes place with little normative guidelines or cultural support. While Kafka and Ryder indicated a rather small proportion of counter-culture marriages which were identified by chance in their national random sample of marriage, it must be recognized that the proportion may be higher than such a study has revealed, and that the proportion of youthful marriages and near-future marriages which incorporate some form of extramarital or co-marital sexual freedom is probably increasing as premarital and nonmarital sexual behavior continues to become more acceptable and practiced with a variety of partners and, for a range of reasons—from those of pure hedonistic pleasure to love or friendship. It should also be noted that attitudes about marriage (as in White and Wells) and marital options are necessarily affected by the openness or lack of openness of the mass media in exposing alternatives.

16

YOUTH VIEWS MARRIAGE: SOME COMPARISONS OF TWO GENERATION ATTITUDES OF UNIVERSITY STUDENTS
Robert N. Whitehurst

This chapter analyzes two essential questions to help understand the direction of youthful intent regarding marriage. University students were surveyed to find what they felt was wrong with marriages of their parents' generation and this was compared with their views of hopes and aspirations for their own marriages. Whitehurst's conclusions suggest that youth desire much change in marriage when they compare their impending marriages to those of their parents, but that their vision is essentially limited to such changes as avoidance of materialistic styles, avoidance of early marriage, and increasing communications. Unexpectedly large proportions of the sample felt that multiple love relations were possible for them, however, and experimentation with new life-styles was not unusual.

Since campus housing arrangements are in process of change, an analysis of the impact of more frequent collective living styles is undertaken. The author's conclusions suggest that many youth in universities will continue collective housing and life-styles after leaving campuses as they find much learning and satisfaction in them. The potential for more rapid, total, or revolutionary change in marriage, however, cannot be implied from these data. Although high proportions of the sample believed in the viability of simultaneous multiple love relations, there is doubt as to what this will mean in relationships contracted by young people going into marriage.

This chapter deals with attitudes of university students as they look at the marriages they know something about in their parent's generation as contrasted with their own marital expectations. The thesis is that there are some changes in the offing, that these may be of importance, and it is useful to ask people considering marriage what's wrong with marriages of their parent's generation, and then compare these responses with what they say they will do to improve their own relationships as they embark on marriages or other male-female relations. The data from 300 cases of introductory social science classes allow some exploratory-nonrandom hypotheses to be drawn about the possibilities for changes in the near future.[1] Although it is likely that no sweeping or revolutionary changes will soon occur, it is probable that changes that do evolve will have an impact on many marriages, and that the older monolithic, conventional system of marriage will be faced with important changes and adaptations by more people.

In general it is consistent with other information about changes in youth attitudes toward established ways of doing things to suggest that there will be less emphasis on institutionalized styles of life, more on personal and existential meanings and less blatant materialism and related emphases in relationships, all accompanied by somewhat changing economic outlooks and concerns about the future.[2] In the following paragraphs, a discussion of what's wrong with parental (i.e., the previous generation's) marriages—as seen by youth—will be followed by some themes and patterns which appear as alternatives to the problems of the kind of marriages prevalent in the previous generation. Before summarizing, some of the discriminating variables in the student sample will be discussed in terms of factors relevant to understanding marital change.

What's Wrong With Parental Marriages

Of the total respondents to the survey questionnaire (N=300), nearly 84% gave some kind of answer to the two open-ended questions at the end of the structured portion of the survey. The first question asked students to describe what's wrong with marriages in the generation of their parents. Three dominant themes recurred: Nothing is wrong (22% of those answering); marriage is too materialistic; and there is too little communication. About 12% complained that marriage was too tradition-bound, 7% said it was dull, and fewer said there is too little freedom, females are subordinated, and people who marry have too little in common.

It is fairly obvious that these middle-class students did find some things they felt were negative in marriages in their parents' generation. It is just as obvious that as many felt that "nothing" was wrong as any other response. We might interpret this to mean that very large numbers of people have no plans (at least in their first college year) to depart from the model provided by the preceding generation. This is indeed the only viable explanation that is consistent with other findings on this topic. Despite discussions about pot, free sex and swinging on college campuses, most youth are still essentially conventional. This does not mean that they are "pure" in the sense of the Protestant ethic, but rather that they are indeed following the role models of their predecessors—continuing the double-standard and preparing for conventional family roles, including "normal" extramarital ventures. This is in spite of increased strength of norms on campuses about honesty, growth and openness in sexual and other relations. My tentative conclusion is that things will not change for most people, given at least minor variations on current themes moderated by new technology, *slightly* better sex education for the next generation (and that still won't be much), and perhaps more sexual freedom for a *few* more—but little promise of much that is really new or innovative.

But what about those who did find more real faults in their parents' system of marriage? One can only speculate about the effects of heavy resistance to parental materialism. One result could be (when coupled with increased leisure), a future of increased involvement in home rituals if more craft items are produced, fewer items purchased; perhaps life in general could be enriched and simplified, while family life becomes more meaningful. Such a satisfactory outcome may be too much to expect though, as most fathers and husbands seem to use increased leisure time for sports, male pastimes, or increased work involvement. A generation of new-style involved-at-home fathers is not yet in the offing. A functionalist view of the sentiments expressed by the anti-materialists in our sample might suggest that this norm may facilitate adjustment to the future. If it turns out to be a world in which less productive work per person is adaptive, then the new sentiment may well become a universal norm rather than a passing fad of university students. It remains to be seen, however, whether the strong anti-materialist sentiments supported by youthful peers may not be altered when the practical exigencies of married life occur and in this day-to-day coping they may find other definitions of reality will be needed.

As for problems of communication in marriage, it is somewhat similar to the old saw about education being the answer to nearly all social problems. In one sense seeing communication as the key is correct, but merely emphasizing the importance of "communicating" is a simple-minded approach if taken too narrowly or seriously. Few ask the question about the functionality of non-communication in marriage. If values in a relationship are very dissonant, communication can only make things worse unless there is some realistic basis for resolution of newly opened areas (or reopening already touchy sore spots). Most data, experience, and observations have led me to believe that a little communication can be a good thing, but expecting it to serve as the nexus of marriage problem-solution is naive and may well lead to little but a further rise in divorce rates. Lack of communication can as easily be seen as a solution as a problem. An example might include the case of an average wife who becomes intrigued with joining a women's liberation group. If she has an average husband (even one whose lip-service loyalty is on her side) she is much more likely to get flak and create difficulties than to find peace by trying to communicate each detail of her newly-emerging consciousness and anger to her husband. However, if the conflict persists long enough, (assuming both are no more neurotic than average), they may ultimately "get it together" as a couple. There is of course at least an even chance that matters would never get as far as this happy outcome since men tend to maintain the greater balance of power and women fear recriminations, loss of status, and the prospects of facing life alone too much to endanger their uneasy security at home. Communication, in short, cannot be relied on often in an average marriage to really resolve problems. Often problems are walled off, situations circumscribed by silent contracts to not discuss the thorny issues because everyone knows there will be conflict. The really competent pair who can do it by themselves is a rarity, in spite of books to the contrary.[3] The pair who really want to "get it together" and seek outside help and find someone competent to give them realistic assistance is also a rarity. In short, really adequately communicating pairs in this society are scarce; this does not change the social fact that people see lack of communication as a problem and wish it would not be so in their own marriages. Wishing does not make it so, and this structuralists' view is that it cannot become so without basic restructuring of the socialization experiences of both men and women.

The task is to make men more sensitive and aware of what is taking place, to make them more flexible and empathic in communication, able to hang into a relationship when emotionally challenged instead of acting as an emotional coward as most of us do—fearing the wrath of the little woman who understands how a six-foot man can be afraid of her! Women, in turn will need more broadly-based kinds of acquaintance with the world of maleness coupled with better training to handle and accept the reality of a daily unglamorous routinized relationship, complete with diapers and toilets, vomit and dirty sinks with dishes, and the dullness of motherhood as well as other common realities. As an example of the disparity of views held by the sexes, the following will show something of the differences that may be related to present high levels of non-communication.

Females in the sample were about 2 times more likely than males to cite marital communication as a problem in the older generation. In the same ratio, women were more likely than men to consider marriage as dull and were 3 times more likely to register the feeling that marriage was unfair because it subordinated women. It should also be noted that no men in the sample wanted to strive for greater equality in their marriages. Of those who said marriage is not for them, the respondents were more likely to be females as males (39% males, 62% females). Whether these are rumblings stirred by brewing liberationist sentiments or whether these same differences are not new is a bit hard to say for sure. We do know that women have always registered different feelings and expectations about marriage, but the complaints may be relatively new.

Consistent with other information on conventionality, social controls, and marriage, none of the respondents who were from ethnic backgrounds (self-identified) or considered themselves as "very religious" said that females were subordinated by men in marriage.

Although responses from the strongly religious and ethnics were predictably very conventional, about 12% of those finding things wrong with parental generation marriages claimed they were too tradition-bound. Without further probing it is difficult to interpret just what they meant by this. A general feeling is that older marriages tend to get in a rut and become just too predictable. Let us turn to an evaluation of what youth hope to do in their own marriages that would correct the problems they saw in older marriages around them—how they hope to capture the intimacy and romance they believe should exist.

Making A Good Marriage

Of those answering the open-ended item dealing with things to do to make one's own life or marriage better to avoid the pitfalls now seen in older marriages, an overwhelming majority (73%) claimed they would stay single longer. The missing empirical referent here is a specific definition of what constitutes 'longer.' We do not know how much longer people consider useful. A general impression suggests that most people feel it would be better to wait until they are twenty-five or thirty years old before they marry. One possible interpretation of this datum is that since (if) sex of the premarital variety seems no longer to be a large hangup, people will indeed not become propelled as often into hasty sex-driven marriage relationships. With the instant impact of the morning-after pill and greater availability of abortion (to negate any potential pregnancy), there is a decreased likelihood of future shotgun weddings. All this supports change; whether the responses in this sample are already reflecting some of these changes or not is as yet unknowable.

There is also a factor which may need some explaining in terms of the frequency of registering sentiments as to how to make one's marriage better. After the above mentioned 73% of those responding to "stay single longer," the next categories had no more than 7% of respondents making any further suggestions. Among the most important of these recurring themes (7% each) were the expressed desire to live for the day (not to worry about the future), to work out more open marriages, and to engage in better family planning. Existential themes stressing spontaneous decisions, spur of the moment arrangements, and keeping an open mind were all mentioned. This is no doubt a reaction to youth's feeling that their elders live in an overstructured, rigid, over-controlled, and over-predictable world. The "hang-loose" ethic has made its mark on most phases of the youth culture, although there are limits to its application. Again, it may be that life in the university atmosphere more easily lends itself to this kind of life-style. If a student misses classes for a day, the consequences are not equivalent to those faced by a father with a mortgage and outstanding bills who misses a day's work. The hang-loose approach may be a response to a world held to be non-manipulatable, ready to be snuffed out at any time by wars, bombs, or pollution—if not by individual death from automobiles or violence in other forms. Insofar as these threats are seen as (or remain) real, the adaptation is relevant. However, carrying the hang-loose ethic into all aspects of life from college on undoubtedly will have interesting corollaries both for the individual and for our society's future.

A minority of those surveyed appear to be affected by talk of open marriages and actively feel that they should be working toward making this a more viable choice. Of those seeing more open marriages as desirable, women were four times as likely to support this goal as men. This lends some small support to the thesis developed by Jessie Bernard in her recent work on marriage and women.[4] Women were also about three times as likely as men to claim they would solve their future marital problems by more careful mate selection. There were again striking variations in the frequency of awareness of certain problems and solutions between the sexes. Better family planning may mean little more than avoidance of premarital pregnancy and/or too-early pregnancy and having fewer children than most families that serve as current role models. Recent announcements by *Statistics Canada* to the effect that Canada has reached ZPG may reflect this reality of the ideal of smaller families in a crowded world. Current choices about family planning also seem to be influenced by the notion that young parents have less freedom of movement, a truncated social life, and more economic problems than do couples with a wife left free to work in the early years of marriage.

Marriage Attitudes

A series of questions tapped feelings about current topics and some changes occurring in marriage and sexual relationships. The data are at times unclear and apparently contradictory in places and need further clarification in future research. The following items were scaled on Likert-type scales and will be discussed here as percentages either agreeing (two categories of choices) or disagreeing (two categories—strongly disagree or disagree).

Twelve percent of the total sample agreed that monogamy is dying. This appears to include an unknown proportion who feel this way but regret its presumed impending death, as well as those who are happy about it. Of those who agree, twice as many singles responded this way as marrieds. It might be construed as a personal inconsistency to believe in the death of monogamy and to be married—although this does not necessarily follow. Faith in marriage would appear to more or less follow commitment to the institution, but again, not necessarily. Fifty-two percent said they did not plan conventional marriages similar to their parents, but as already reported, few of the open-ended responses indicate revolutionary alternatives. Of these, 88% were singles. The easiest interpretation of this datum is that once married, the vision of attaining a radically different marriage from that of one's parents may be examined in the light of reality—in essence, being married may introduce a sobering element of reality about the possibilities of restructuring one's own life more creatively and romantically. This might be merely a fantasy-luxury of the not-yet married. If this luxury were not allowed (to believe that one's own marriage would not be conventional and would be unlike the parental marriage), it might be that fewer people would marry.

Possibly the most striking single piece of information about which there was consensus was the item dealing with the notion that a good marriage is possible to develop. An overwhelming 96% of the respondents felt that they were capable of doing it. Perhaps this should not be surprising in a culture that provides so few alternate avenues for adult identity expression outside marriage. It might be the ultimate personal affront to be forced to recognize that one is not really capable of having a successful marriage. The possibility of a successful marriage is nearly universally accepted as an idea—that is, everyone felt *they* could do it; it is interesting that prior data tended to emphasize sentiments that quite often people married who were not personally mature or otherwise not ready for it.[5] Few of our respondents seemed to carry such a felt burden as a self incapable of contracting a good marriage. It may seem a bit incongruous that 19% of our sample claimed that they would not contract a legal, conventional marriage similar to their parents. It appears to be self-reassuring to believe that at least one *could* do it and be successful if such a choice were made.

Of the total, 18% said they would seriously consider a group living situation for themselves, although there were more singles than marrieds who were positive toward group living. That 13% of the marrieds said they would live in a group setting might be seen as a larger than expected proportion.

A striking 58% agreed that it is possible to love (including sexually) more than one person at a time. Maybe not surprisingly, more marrieds than singles subscribed to this belief. If beliefs are increasingly followed by consistent actions, we can predict a continued trend toward more extramarital involvements in the near future. To try to make this datum consistent with some other more conventional attitudes, it may be necessary to note that pure motives, attitudes, and feelings are indeed rare and that people do hold beliefs tentatively that are not consistent with each other. It is fairly clear that stronger pressures to adapt new thinking about monogamy are afoot. Having agreed with the premise does not mean that all these people will have affairs, group marriages, or multiple sexual contacts. Holding the belief does, however, materially enhance the possibility of further considering the behavior for themselves—given the relatively free social context of a pluralistic society. As the end of the 20th Century draws ever nearer, it appears that the certainties of life once experienced by North Americans no longer operate at the same level of surety.

One of the consequences of this decreased certainty in life may be increasing ease of relativization of those things once called "sin." In twelve years of university teaching, I am struck by the frankness of people from all spheres to admit the ease with which they do things which they themselves once categorized as wrong, sinful, or evil. This can be seen in part as a response to adult realities; we learn to work the system and avoid compulsive conforming habits when they have little or no relevance in the bureaucracies which rule our lives. It is also in part a growing sense of disease within a system which is being redefined as less morally right and therefore less morally relevant. Sexual interaction has not escaped the notice of those involved in this onsweep of moral relativizing.

Conclusions

In this sample of university students there are several indications of change affecting the potential futures of man-woman relationships in and out of marriage. In rank order of most frequent to least frequently occurring responses, these items and their evaluations follow: A large majority of the students (96%) felt that they were capable of contracting a good marriage, even though some of them claimed they did not intend to do so. This appears to be a necessary kind of self-definition in this culture—that is, to not be able to sustain the notion that one could become married successfully may be too painful for all but the most hearty and deviant to face. Nearly 60% of the sample claimed they were capable of loving (including sexually) more than one person at a time. The meaning and interpretation of this is a bit unclear. The proportion is much higher than expected, especially in a conservative area where many ethnics and Roman Catholic people reside. It may be no more than a momentary consensus when campus life is making its normative mood felt; it may, however, be much deeper and longer-lasting than can be seen at the moment. If so, this kind of normative change will be felt in succeeding behavior of large numbers of people in their own marriages. Over half of the sample claimed they would follow marital and sexual life-styles at variance from those of their parents. The range of perceived potential here runs all the way from developing anti-materialist attitudes to group marriages and communal life styles. It is clear at any rate that there is awareness of some need to change, but how much, how fast, and the implications of the directions of change are not too clear.

Of the total sample, 19% said they would be willing to try group living arrangements. This proportion is higher than expected, and may in part be attributed to a local tendency for males and females to structure off-campus co-op housing on their own. This is no doubt an already-advanced social-sexual arrangement on many campuses and will grow in the near future. The popularity of dormitory, single-sex housing is declining. Campus norms tend to downgrade in some cases those who persist with traditional housing arrangements. Whether this means more sexual activity among university youth is likewise not known. An informal paper suggests that there are specific conditions under which informal "incest taboos" arise in quasi-families of unrelated people in campus housing.[6] The informal incest taboos are fairly regularly broken; we know little about these mechanisms except that the norms do arise and there are certain ways of circumventing them.

A persistent question arises as a result of co-op off-campus housing which is desegregated. Will there be lingering effects (positive motivation to continue this life-style) once the individuals leave the campuses? At least some of the local students living in co-op housing find it a very rewarding life-style and find a sense of community coupled with real decreases in alienation. This may be seen as an indication of willingness to continue collective living experiments.

About 12% of the sample felt that monogamy is dying as a way of life. This may or may not be an important indicator of potential change and could reflect recent media activity in this sphere as well as critical thought as to the future of monogamy. Some of those who registered this feeling were obviously not happy about the prospective demise of monogamy and this may simply reflect a doom and gloom attitude of the traditionalist preacher who needs something to rail against. Uninformed lay people may often view high divorce rates as a simple effect that must be caused by the death of monogamy, which is obviously an oversimple and incorrect reading of the state of marriage.

Among the discriminating variables that are associated with divergent views of marriage or of monogamy and its future, ethnic, religious, and sex variables merit some interpretation. Ethnicity and religiosity together are still probably the most powerful predictors of conventionality. A very small minority of those who considered themselves as either religious or ethnically identified or both, held attitudes favorable to group living, multiple love partners, or otherwise indicated attitudes toward alternatives to monogamy.* Religion or ethnicity may provide positive emotional support for good marriages in some cases, and it is clear that insofar as these forces operate forcefully in terms of the real threat of negative sanctions, they will continue in their effect. If changes in disidentification with ethnicity and religion continue as most of the literature suggests, there will be fewer people willing to settle for the confining life-style of conventional monogamous marriage.

The most important differentiating variable for this (as for most samples) was sex. Women have come to view their own hopes, destinies, and fears in recent years in much more clearly articulated ways so that they become more differentiated from the views of men. Their concerns are clearly indicated in the data, which show that equality, openness of marriage, better planning of families, more careful mate selection, and concern over inadequate communication is much more often a concern of women than men. Until and unless men and women come to share views as to what are problems and solutions, the disparity of these non-converging worlds will continue to create hardships for both.[7]

In summary, one further comment is in order from the vantage point of sociology and social controls regarding change. Although the data herein may be construed to indicate very real changes on the part of some university people at a particular point in their life-cycles, we do not know how much real effect these changes will have in coming years. Rather significant proportions indicated a willingness to try life-styles at variance with those practiced by their elders. On the one hand, there is a context of social change that creates openness of opportunity in unparallelled ways. People of radical persuasion often tend to omit one variable in their hopeful expectations of rapid social change—the intrusion of real negative sanctions that tend to delay the pursuit of real change. Although it is true that many young people find a positive sense of reward, pioneership, and cameraderie in the pursuit of new life styles, these are by and large a hardy bunch who do not represent anything like the majority. Most of us in this society will still find the threats of being shunned, ostracized, and in other ways threatened (mostly economically) too high a price to pay for engaging in a deviant life-style. People in general find the path of least resistance less strewn with hazards to the pocketbook. Job and community security are just too important for most to risk by openly living in an alternative marriage pattern. Until we can open up the system to a truly democratic-optional life-style set of possibilities that removes the negative sanctions for living other than monogamous lives, we can expect only minor social changes. Most will still continue to opt for clandestine affairs.

---

* See Gilmartin and Kusisto (Chapter 8, this volume) for support for this idea as applied to swinging behavior.

Even though the costs here may be high, they are not as high as those exacted by an openly defiant alternative life-style. In this sense, as a culture we are continuing to foster a schizoid response in people. There is no way to eliminate sex outside of marriage in our open society. We can either face it squarely and seek answers that make sense to us now, or we can continue to act with duplicity, dishonesty, and carry on with the patterns that have helped to create a world that is much less than humane in its effects on so many people. If persistence of the system is what it is all about, let us no longer talk of people as important. If, in fact, people and their needs are important, let us proceed with the realignment of the mores related to the social and legal definition of styles of marriage.

NOTES

1 The survey of a sample of 300 first-year students in Social Science classes was conducted in a Southern Ontario University, characterized by recent immigration; some students are marginals, many are educated in their pre-university training in separate schools (essentially Catholic). Thus the population is likely to be over-represented by those with conservative parental backgrounds (which may be reacted to by many degrees of rejection or acceptance by university youth).
2 Robert N. Whitehurst and Barbara Plant, "A Comparison of Canadian and American University Students' Reference Groups, Alienation, and Attitudes Toward Marriage," *International Journal of Sociology of the Family*, Vol. 1 No. 1, March 1971, 1-8.
3 Several books of recent vintage which make marriage appear as a readily soluble problem would include: Nena and George O'Neill. *Open Marriage*, M. Evans Co. New York: 1972. George R. Bach and Ronald M. Deutsch. *Pairing*, Avon Books, New York, 1970. Julius Fast. *The Incompatibility of Men and Women*, Avon Publishing Co., New York, 1972.
4 Jessie Bernard. *The Future of Marriage*, World Publishing Co., New York: 1972. Also see, Bernard, "Marriage, His and Hers" in Ms. magazine, Dec. 1972, pp. 46-49, 110-113.
5 Whitehurst and Plant, op cit.
6 Unpublished student paper, 1972, University of Windsor by Tom Rolfe and Cathy McCully. A study done under supervision of R. N. Whitehurst explored informal incest taboos and their violations in quasi-family settings in co-ed dorms.
7 Jessie Bernard, "Marriage, His and Hers," Ms. magazine, Dec. 1972, pp. 46-49.

17

STUDENT ATTITUDES TOWARD ALTERNATE MARRIAGE FORMS
Mervin White and Carolyn Wells

This chapter dealing with student attitudes toward alternate marriage forms investigates the range of life-styles of interest to students as well as their expressed willingness for themselves, friends and others to participate in such life-styles. The typology of alternate marriage forms which is discussed serves as a framework for the research. Ad hoc and contractual marriage forms received support and interest from a large proportion of the respondents, with communal, co-marital, and mate-swapping interests expressed by a lesser—but unexpectedly high—proportion of the respondents.

Of course, it is difficult to generalize from small-sample studies, especially when trying to understand trends leading to the future. Still, the authors cautiously suggest the conclusion that the greater interest in ad hoc marriage forms and the limitation of marriage by contracts is likely to have a long-lasting and possibly drastic effect on marital interactions in the future. The trend seems unmistakeably to favor increased awareness, permissiveness, and less emphasis on partner ownership and exclusivity. The ultimate outcome of all this is a predicted increase in equality between the sexes.

Introduction

It is now commonplace to observe that sociologists have been slow to recognize the significance or extent to which marriage is being transformed by the many nonconventional marriage-related practices emerging in the United States (Cuber, 1970; Greenwald, 1970; Olson, 1972; and Moore, 1968). These changes concern both the functions performed by the marital institution and, more importantly, the style of marriage being practiced. There are many indications which suggest that monogamous marriage, as conventionally practiced in our society, is not meeting the demands placed upon the institution by the larger society (Roy and Roy, 1971). First, divorce, separation, and desertion rates are very high and apparently are rising. The comparison of marriages and divorces occurring in the same year shows a current divorce rate of one in three. Nye (1973) suggests that a more accurate estimate of the divorce rate may be a comparison of marriages in one year with divorces occurring seven years later (the median year of divorce). Based upon this comparison, the divorce rate for marriages contracted in 1965 is 42 percent. Nye further estimates that the divorce rate for 1973 may be as high as 50 percent using this latter comparison. Second, Gebhard has recently estimated that almost two of every three married males (about 60%) and almost one of every two married females (about 40%) engage in extramarital sexual relations at some time in their life (Hunt, 1969). This estimate, made in 1968, is likely to have increased in the past five years. Unfortunately, no reliable data exist to either support or reject these estimates. The *Psychology Today* Survey (Athanasiou, Shaver and Tavris, 1970) shows that 40% of their male and 36% of their female respondents have had extramarital intercourse. It is unclear, however, whether these data indicate an increase in extramarital involvements, given the study's youth, higher educational and upper socioeconomic status biases.

Third, the current literature suggests that many marriage-related practices are evolving which amount to changes in the style or form of the marital arrangement. These practices include mate-swapping, communal forms of living together, homosexual marriages, heterosexual cohabiting of unmarried couples, and open acceptance of emotional and sexual alliances of marital partners with extramarital partners (Otto, 1970; Berger, Hackett and Millar, 1972; Ramey, 1972; Macklin, 1972; Karlen, 1971; Symonds, 1971; Denfield and Gordon, 1972; Bartell, 1971, 1972; Delora and Delora, 1972; Smith and Smith, 1970; Palson and Palson, 1972; Breedlove and Breedlove, 1964; Varni, 1972; O'Neill and O'Neill, 1972; Cuber and Harroff, 1965; Cuber, 1972; Roy and Roy, 1968). It seems particularly relevant to note that participants in these alternative forms of marriage frequently report doing so because traditional monogamy does not fulfill their needs. Fourth, the secularization of marital values, including changes in sexual morality, implies major changes in traditional monogamy as the only acceptable form of marriage (Cadwallader, 1971,[1] gives an excellent discussion of problems with monogamy).

There exists practically no research on the attitudes and values held by people related to these emerging forms of marriage (see Athanasiou, Shaver, and Tavris, 1970 for an exception). What little literature exists attempts to document motivations, consequences, and social characteristics of persons participating in these new forms of marriage (mostly mate-swapping and group marriages). Further, sometimes researchers have been interested in social behaviors which are only coincidentally related to the "form" of marriage being practiced (i.e., studies of "hippies," drug cultures, and communes).

The aim of the present study is to determine the attitudes and values of university students toward certain alternative forms or styles of marriage. In particular: (1) what alternative forms would be of interest to students? and (2) what alternative forms would they be willing to accept participation in by family members, friends, and other people? (While it would be in error to assume that attitudes and values held by college students are representative of the total population, it may not be amiss to suggest that these attitudes and values may well filter down the social structure to the larger population in time).

Definitions of Marital Forms

The forms of marriage we will be discussing are a combination of actual practices reported in the literature and forms theoretically derived by combining or altering certain structural elements in marital arrangements generally. The major axes along which these arrangements are described here are suggested by the literature on the topic. Five basic structural axes were selected which are intrinsic to marital relationships. These axes are as follows: (1) marital arrangements may vary along the heterosexual-homosexual axis of sexual involvement and companionship; (2) the sexual relationships of marital arrangements may vary along an exclusive-inclusive axis; (3) marital arrangements may vary according to the number of people recognized as participants; (4) the longevity of marital arrangements assumed at the beginning of the relationship may vary from some limited time period to the death of participants; and finally, (5) marital arrangements may vary according to the degree of closure of the marital arrangement itself, that is, the degree to which the participants, others, or both consider the arrangement "marriage." The reader should not assume that these are the only important axes along which a marital arrangement can vary. We would contend, however, that these axes are indeed basic ones and must be included in any description of alternative marriage styles or forms. All five axes need not be equally important in describing any given marital arrangement.

We will describe eight alternative marital arrangements utilizing this framework. Many of these are currently practiced in the United States although, it must be recognized that such practices may be very limited, especially in the case of certain forms (e.g., homosexual marriage). Contract marriage is the only form defined below which has no participants in our society. This form could not be practiced as we have defined it without legal recognition of the time-limitation contract which presently does not exist. The question of legality regarding any of the alternative marriage styles is not of concern here because in our society they are all seen as deviations from the accepted. The only legally recognized form of marriage is a monogamous one which has been solemnized (in some states, common-law marriage is an automatic legalization of the arrangement).

The following definitions of traditional monogamy and the eight alternative marital forms are based upon actual (reported) or assumed practices. Unless otherwise noted, the longevity of the marital arrangement is assumed to be permanent or until the death of the participants.

1. *A traditional monogamous marriage is a legalized, heterosexual, sexually exclusive, dyadic relationship in which both participants and nonparticipants consider the pair "married."* Hereafter we refer to monogamy in our society as "traditional monogamy."

2. *A contract marriage is a legalized monogamous arrangement for a limited period of time (e.g., five years) at the end of which the couple has the option to renew the contract.* The closest types of arrangements to this one are those proposed by Judge Lindsey (1927) and Margaret Mead (1970). These, however, are different because they do not specifically incorporate a time limitation. This type of marriage was introduced into the Maryland legislature by two legislators, Ms. Lee and Ms. Boswell, in 1971 and their proposal received some attention in the mass media (Editors, Time, 1971).

3. *An ad hoc marriage is an arrangement of two people living together for the advantages of traditional monogamy without being formally married (including common-law marriages).* It is assumed that this type of marriage would be more permanent than the heterosexual cohabitations described by Macklin (1972) and thus, approximating that described by Karlen (1971), Coffin (1972), and Wells and Christie (1972). The ad hoc marriage could allow for the transition to traditional monogamy (if desired), but the arrangement specifically avoids legalization either by ceremony or by default as in the case of common-law marriage.

4. *Homosexual marriage is a relationship of two individuals of the same sex who are committed to the relationship in a manner regarded by them as "married."* The sparse literature on the topic makes passing reference to homosexual couples who have lived together as "married" for long periods of time (Athanasiou, Shaver and Tavris, 1970; Leitsch, 1971). Manosevitz (1972:36) reports that 46% of the homosexuals in his sample were "married" or had been "married" to another homosexual. The essential characteristics of homosexual marriage would be similar to traditional monogamy, except that the pair-bonding would involve two persons of the same sex.

5. *A comarital relationship is an intimate arrangement, probably including sexual intimacy, with an extramarital partner, to which a monogamous, heterosexually married couple openly agree prior to the involvement.* This definition must be taken as an ideal. The term

"comarital relationship" has been utilized to refer to all those in which marital partners agree to extramarital relations whether openly or not, willingly or grudgedly, prior to or after the involvement. In its ideal, then, the comarital relationship would always involve the extramarital pair-bonding as an adjunct to the marriage of the dyadic pair. These involvements would always be on a unilateral basis and not involve the marital pair as a group activity.

6. *Mate-swapping is an arrangement in which monogamous married couples exchange partners for the purpose of sexual activity.* This marital form involves a heterosexual marital pair who becomes mutually and simultaneously involved in extramarital sexual relationships. In actual practice, singles are sometimes involved in this type of activity.

7. *A polygamous marriage is an arrangement in which an individual (male or female) has two or more partners of the opposite sex.* There are two forms of polygamous marriages: polyandry and polygyny. These group types of marriage are complex because they include multiple pair-bondings of mates within the marriage. The pair-bondings, however, revolve around the dominant mate, rather than all partners having equal pair-bonding rights (sexual rights in particular). While polygamous marriage is not unknown in American society, its practice has been explicitly outlawed (and thus given up by the Mormons) or practiced underground by several small ex-Mormon groups in Arizona (Editors, *Time*, 1952; 1953; Editors, *Newsweek*, 1953).

8. *A communal marriage is a group-living arrangement of sexually exclusive couples who are committed to the relationship in a manner regarded by them as "married."* This type of arrangement could be a solution to one of the major problems experienced by "group" marriages—jealousy. Research into group marriages almost invariably concludes that one of the most divisive influences in these types of marriages is jealousy (Ellis, 1970; Constantine, 1971; 1972). There is apparently an implied threat to the group marriage when preference coupling occurs in which the monogamous sexual arrangements begin to exclude other marital partners from sexual access to the preferencing pair. This is particularly a problem when the coupling is among the more attractive members of the group. It seems logical to conclude that this particular problem could be overcome when the marriage is composed of sexually exclusive couples entering into the arrangement on a bilateral sexual basis. The marriage would otherwise function as a group, sharing the roles and responsibilities for the common welfare.

9. *A multilateral marriage is a marital arrangement with three or more persons, including shared relationships, who are committed to*

the relationship in a manner regarded by them as "married." This type of marital arrangement would permit maximum sexual and emotional freedom to form pair-bonded arrangements with all members of the marital group (see Constantine, 1971; 1972). The research into these types of group marriage hint at the complexity of the relationships (primarily through the types of problems found) and at the wide array of subtypes which compose multilateral marriages. Problems in ideology (or lack of it), role differentiations, jealousy, equality of participants, child-rearing practices and so on, promote, if not create, high turnover in participants in these types of communal living arrangements (Ramey, 1972; Berger, Hackett, and Millar, 1972; Hedgepeth, 1972; Haughey, 1972; and Estellachild, 1972).

One of the problems in the literature on the topic is the lack of distinction between communes as opposed to group marriages living in a communal setting. Most of the communes described by researchers generally reflect arrangements in which marital and familial roles and responsibilities are assumed and performed. However, there is often the eschewing of these qualities in marital and familial contexts. That is, communal participants may come into the group and leave as they wish; have emotional, sexual and material access within the communal group; and yet, assume minimal responsibilities which go with a marital arrangement: commitment to pair-bonding; equality of participants; mutual sharing of roles and responsibilities and so on (Estellachild, 1972). Much more research is needed to differentiate communal living arrangements from what we have described here as multilateral marriage.

Methodology

Sample Selection Procedures

The data reported here are part of a larger study of student attitudes and values related to the alternative marriage styles defined above. The sample was a randomly selected five percent sample of the undergraduate population of an intermediate sized Northwestern state land grant university located away from larger urban areas. The sample was selected to meet the following requirements: (1) equal numbers of males and females were selected; (2) foreign students were not included; (3) all four class levels (year in school) and the marital status of students were proportional to the student population.

Data Collection Procedures

A pretested questionnaire, with almost exclusively precoded items was used. Although the questionnaire was relatively long, it was easily completed in 30 to 45 minutes. Respondents were contacted by telephone and their cooperation in the study requested. They were asked to come to the Sociological Research Laboratory where they were met by an interviewer and the study objectives were explained. The interviewer remained available to answer any questions respondents had while completing the questionnaire. Although most of the questionnaires were completed under the above conditions, there were a number of respondents who could not be reached by telephone and were contacted in person by an interviewer and requested to complete the questionnaire at the time of the contact. It is significant to stress that the data were collected under completely anonymous conditions. Further, participation was strictly voluntary and refusals were minimal (14%). An analysis of selected social characteristics of those who refused to participate reveal no major differences from the larger sample.

Characteristics of the Sample

One question of interest with the present data is how adequately our sample represents the larger population of college students in the United States. This question cannot be answered definitively here. However, it may be possible to indicate the beginnings of an answer by reviewing some of the basic social characteristics of our sample. First, there are 47% males and 53% females. Thus, males are slightly underrepresented. Second, there are 28% freshmen, 30% sophomores, 22% juniors, and 19% seniors. Therefore, well over half of our respondents (58%) are freshmen and sophomores. Third, the youth of the sample is further indicated by the age distribution which shows the mean age to be 20.8 years old. Fourth, the living arrangements of our sample conform to those of the university student population with 50% living in dorms, 19% living in Greek houses, and the remainder, 31%, living off-campus. Fifth, the rural-urban backgrounds of our respondents appear to approximate the population concentrations in the state. The data show that 16% come from residential areas of less than 2,500 population, 46% from areas of 2,500 to 50,000 population, and 38% from areas larger than 50,000 population. If anything, the large urban residential areas are slightly under represented in our sample. Sixth, the socioeconomic status (SES) characteristics show that 13.1% come from lower SES backgrounds, 34% from middle SES backgrounds, and 50% from upper middle and upper SES backgrounds. Seventh, 16% are Catholics, 57% are Protestants, 5% claim other religious preferences, and 18% claim no religious preference or classify themselves as agnostic or atheist.

On the basis of these social characteristics there is reason to believe that our sample of college students is roughly similar to that of the larger college student population of the United States. However, one must recognize that there are some important variations. First, our sample is composed of 98% whites. Thus, minority students in the United States are inadequately represented by our sample. Second, there may be variations of some importance related to the geographical distributions of the student population in the United States. These variations cannot be estimated by our sample. Third, students who attend the very large universities in major urban areas are likely to be more liberal than ours. Finally, students who attend small colleges, particularly the private, religiously affiliated ones, are likely to be more conservative. Given these differences, our sample should be roughly similar to the majority of college students in the United States.

Findings

As noted, the data reported in this study are part of a larger study of attitudes, values, and perceptions related to interest in, and acceptance of, alternative forms of marriage. Four items of data are reported. These deal with the amount of interest our respondents have in and whether they would accept family members, friends, and other people participating in the alternative forms of marriage. All four items are taken as measures of the acceptance of these forms of marriage by the respondents. We will first discuss the data related to the respondent's interest in the alternative forms and then their acceptance of the participation of others in them.

Interest in Alternative Marital Forms

Table 1 reports the percentages of our respondents who have an interest in the eight alternative forms of marriage both by the sex of the respondents and for the total sample. Interest categories have been collapsed into some interest and no interest for the sake of simplicity. In our discussion of the findings reported in Table 1, we will focus upon generalizations which can be drawn from the data rather than upon the specific alternative marital forms.

Table 1 Percent of Sample Indicating Some Degree of Interest in the Alternative Forms of Marriage

	Total Sample		Males		Females	
	No Interest	Some Interest	No Interest	Some Interest	No Interest	Some Interest
ad hoc	28	72	19	81	36	64
Contract	30	70	26	74	34	66
Communal	57	43	46	54	67	33
Comarital	62	38	47	53	75	25
Mate-Swapping	67	33	49	51	84	16
Polygamous	73	27	60	40	85	15
Multilateral	76	24	69	31	83	17
Homosexual	90	10	92	8	89	11
Sample Size	N = 308		N = 342		N = 651	

First, the proportions of respondents indicating at least some degree of interest in the alternative forms of marriage are unexpectedly high. If we assume that our respondents grew up believing in traditional monogamy and aspiring to marry in the traditional fashion of our society, the findings reported here are indeed surprising. Specifically, we note that the *ad hoc* and contract marital arrangements hold the most interest for our respondents (72% and 70%, respectively). These proportions are very high. The next three marital forms, communal (43%), comarital (39%) and mate-swapping (33%), rank far below the first two in terms of the proportions of respondents having interest in them. Even so, the proportions of respondents indicating at least some interest are quite high given that these forms explicitly permit some degree of emotional and sexual involvement outside the primary pair-bonding arrangement. The next two forms in preference are polygamous (27%) and multilateral (24%) marriages. Finally, homosexual marriage is at the bottom of the preference list with only 10% indicating some interest in it.

Second, we note that there are large differences in the proportions of males and females who indicate an interest in the alternative forms of marriage, with more males indicating an interest. There is one exception to this observation—more females indicate an interest in homosexual marriage. It is of particular interest to note that a much larger proportion of males than females are interested in the more complex forms of marriage. The proportions indicating an interest in comarital, mate-swapping, polygamous and multilateral marriages are two to three times higher for males than females. The proportions are much closer for the *ad hoc* and contract forms. These data strongly suggest a greater liberality on the part of males.

Third, there is a definite hierarchy of preferences for the alternative marital forms based upon the proportions of respondents who have an interest in them. The order of preferences for the total sample and for males is: *ad hoc*, contract, communal, comarital, polygamy, mate-swapping, multilateral, and homosexual marriages. This preference order is only slightly different for females. For the female, the order of preference is: contract, *ad hoc*, communal, comarital, multilateral, mate-swapping, polygamous, and homosexual marriages. The order of preference for the females indicates a greater conservatism than for the males.

The preferential hierarchal ranking is apparently based upon several factors. Five of these will be discussed here. First, generally speaking, greater interest is shown in marital forms which are structurally most similar to traditional monogamy. Thus, the *ad hoc* and contract marriages are at the top of the ranking and the more complex group and homosexual marriages are at the bottom. Several factors may be responsible for the interest in the forms of marriage that have greater structural similarity with traditional monogamy. It may be that the norm of sexual exclusivity within pair-bonding arrangements in our society is important here. In this respect, the effectiveness of socialization maintaining the exclusivity norm lessens interest in the more complex forms which provide greater sexual variety. The socialization processes within our society which stress traditional monogamy, may also have greater compatibility with the *ad hoc* and contract forms than with the more complex ones. Further, it may be that the dyadic pair-bondings of the *ad hoc* and contract arrangements are more easily contended with, whereas the complexity of the interrelationships in other forms involve an unfamiliar life style. The complexity of these latter marital forms are perhaps too demanding emotionally and require greater commitments than our respondents are willing to make. Finally, it may be that the scant exposure of the more complex arrangements in the mass media is another determining factor. Most of the information available to the layman deals with the extreme experimentation with these marital forms (i.e., drug and "hippie" cultures) resulting generally in them being portrayed in negative terms.

Second, the heterosexual-homosexual relationship within the marital arrangements apparently override everything else in determining interest in the marital forms for the sample. Thus, homosexual marriage is ranked below all of the other marital forms in terms of both the proportion of respondents indicating interest and the strength of that interest. Apparently the taboos our society places upon homosexuality are strong enough to preclude extensive interest in a marriage based upon this type of sexual arrangement.

Third, it is apparent that the degree of sexual variety permitted outside a monogamous pair-bonding arrangement is highly influential in determining interest in the marital form. Thus, the *ad hoc* and contract marriages rank very high while the group marital forms, which explicitly permit mutual, simultaneous, sexual pair-bondings, rank very low in the hierarchy. The sexual taboos related to sexual exclusivity in marriage are apparently still quite strong.

Fourth, there is the suggestion in the data that the explicit recognition of the equality of participants in the marital form may be an influential factor determining interest. Thus, polygamy is less often of interest than comarital, mate-swapping, and communal marriages. In this respect, it is of some interest to note that multilateral marriage which could ideally provide maximum individual freedoms and equality is ranked below the other group marital forms. It may be that the low interest in this marital form is related to certain negative public attitudes toward "hippie" and other communes. This cannot be determined here.

Finally, these observations about the preferential hierarchy for the total sample apparently hold for both males and females. In fact, the greater conservatism of the females probably underscores the greater extent to which these observations apply to them. Even so, it is of particular interest to note the relatively low proportions of females who have interest in the group marriages which permit greater variety in sexual pair-bonding arrangements and in the homosexual marriage. In all of these marital forms, less than seven percent of our female respondents indicate a strong to moderate interest, suggesting that females may feel these forms are less viable for meeting their marital needs.

One further observation can be made regarding the data in Table 1. The high proportions indicating interest in the alternative marital forms seem to underscore the significance and relatively widespread disenchantment of young people, particularly college youth, with traditional monogamy as the arrangement within which to find fulfillment of their marital needs. The particular significance of the findings reported above is further highlighted when it is recalled that over one-half of our respondents are under 20 years of age and are either freshmen or sophomores. Usually persons in these age and class categories are more conservative and their presence would normally be expected to depress the apparent liberality of older upper classmen. It can be expected that the older upper classmen are more liberal and thus more interested in the alternative marital forms than are freshmen and sophomores. This cannot be determined from the data in Table 1, however. If this is true, the disenchantment with traditional monogamy is greater than that indicated by the data we have presented.

One caution should be made explicit regarding the interpretation of these data. It is assumed that amount of interest is a measure of the degree of the respondents' acceptance of the alternative forms of marriage as legitimate alternatives for meeting their marital needs. The context within which this question was asked supports such an interpretation. However, the reader should be aware that interest does not necessarily indicate a readiness to participate in these alternative marriage styles. In some instances interest may simply mean the respondent wants to know more about the form. The reader is cautioned not to over-interpret these findings.

Acceptance of Others' Participating in Alternative Marital Forms

Interest is only one measure of acceptance of the alternative marital forms as possible arrangements within which marital needs may legitimately be met. Another measure is the degree to which one accepts the participation of others in these alternative forms of marriage. We asked our respondents whether they would accept family members, friends, and other people participating in these forms of marriage. Their responses to these questions are summarized in Table 2. In the following discussion we will summarize the findings related to these data.

First, the proportions of our respondents who report that they would accept the participation of others in the alternative marital arrangements are very high. More than 80% report that they would accept friends and other people, while almost three quarters are willing

Table 2 Percent of Respondents Reporting They Would Accept or Reject Family, Friends, and Other People for Participating in the Alternative Forms of Marriage

	Family			Friends			Other People		
	Accept	Tolerate	Reject	Accept	Tolerate	Reject	Accept	Tolerate	Reject
ad hoc	73	26	1	80	19	1	84	15	1
Contract	72	23	4	78	19	3	81	16	2
Communal	50	38	11	59	34	7	65	28	6
Comarital	37	49	14	48	47	5	57	37	6
Polygamous	38	43	19	46	40	14	54	33	13
Multilateral	38	44	18	46	41	13	44	32	13
Mate-Swapping	36	46	19	33	43	14	51	36	13
Homosexual	26	42	31	29	39	31	36	34	29

Sample Size = 651

to accept family members participating in *ad hoc* and contract forms. The lowest proportion of our respondents willing to accept participation in any of the eight forms is 26% for family members in homosexual marriages. Perhaps even more important, very small proportions of our respondents report that they would reject such participation. Only one to four percent report they would reject participation by anyone in the *ad hoc* and contract forms. The highest proportion who would reject participation by others is 31% for homosexual marriages. In this respect, our sample appears to be quite liberal.

Second, the acceptability of participation in the alternative forms is directly related to the degree of the structural similarity of these forms to traditional monogamy. That is, marital forms which are very similar to traditional monogamy, such as *ad hoc* and contract marriages have the highest proportions of respondents willing to accept others' participation, while forms such as multilateral, polygamous, and homosexual marriages which are most different, have the least acceptance of participation by others. This finding appears to parallel the finding reported earlier concerning interest in the forms and the observations made there appear relevant here also.

Third, the ordering of marital forms on the basis of respondents' willingness to accept the participation of others is almost exactly the same as that indicated for respondents' interest in these forms. Thus, willingness to accept the participation of other people in the alternative marriage forms is apparently related to respondents' interest in them. This observation holds for all three categories of others—family members, friends, and other people.

Fourth, the acceptability of participation by others is inversely related to the social distance of the participant to the respondent. That is, family members are accepted less often than friends, and other people are accepted most often. This is true of all of the alternative forms of marriage. It appears that the farther socially removed the participant is, the more likely he is to be accepted by our respondents. We note that in general the differences between the three categories of others (family, friends and other people) is quite small. These differences are most pronounced for the comarital, mate-swapping and polygamous marriages. The significance of this finding is difficult to determine from the data presented here. In general, however, it appears that our respondents are most conservative with participants socially close to them and most liberal with participants who are socially distant.

Fifth, perhaps the most surprising and unexpected finding in the data presented in Table 2 is the large proportions of respondents who report that they would accept participation in the alternative marital forms by family members. It is usually true that people are less accepting of norm-violating behavior within their own family. This is especially true of certain marriage-related behaviors which are sometimes interpreted as bringing social disgrace upon the family. The sexual and emotional permissiveness of the more complex marital forms would generally be expected to produce an unfavorable attitude toward participants. In this respect, then, the large proportions of respondents reporting they would accept participation by family members in communal (50%), polygamous (38%), multilateral (38%), and mate-swapping (36%) marriages is probably the most significant indicator of the liberality of our sample.

Sixth, the permissiveness in the sexual pair-bonding arrangement appears to be of crucial importance in determining the acceptability of participation. In this respect, the forms which permit sexual pair-bonding beyond the monogamous pair have relatively similar acceptability rates. This is especially evident in mate-swapping, multilateral, and polygamous marriages. Here, as with the data on respondents' interest, the norm of sexual exclusivity appears to be extremely important. Thus, the greater the variety of sexual outlets permitted within the marriage, the less acceptable it is as an alternative to traditional monogamy for meeting marital needs.

Possible Future Trends

The data suggest apparently increasing liberality on the part of our sample toward marriage. These data seem to suggest that a number of possible changes in our marital institution may be eminent. Several of these changes would appear obvious. First, we are likely to see greater youth involvement in the *ad hoc* type of arrangement which will specifically avoid the legal entanglements of traditional monogamy. Entering a legalized arrangement may well be delayed until the couple feels entry is warranted or necessitated, (e.g., for the sake of children).

Second, there appears to be a great deal of interest in developing a limited legalized marital form (e.g., a contract for five years). This type of arrangement would provide partners with maximum flexibility in terms of entering and maintaining the marriage. Proposals such as those by Judge Lindsey and Margaret Mead would, therefore, seem to have a great deal of viability. A marriage form permitting easier dissolution would seem to be desired by large proportions of young people.

Third, it is very likely that we will see emotional and sexual permissiveness more openly accepted in marital arrangements which characterize our society. These highly significant aspects of companionship and affectional needs will probably receive greater emphasis in outside relationships agreed to by marital partners prior to involvement. Adultery, or cheating, or the affair, as traditionally defined, is likely to go the way of the double standard, which is apparently on the way out—even though it has a long way to go before its ultimate demise!

Fourth, if our data are indicative, even in a very crude way, then it is likely that there already exists a great deal of social approval for certain alternative marital forms. If this is true, then it is very likely that acceptance will increase as practice and knowledge of these marital forms become more widespread. In particular, the group marital forms are quite likely to receive greater attention in the near future by the young, well-educated segments of our population.

Fifth, even though it was obvious that the sexual exclusivity norm strongly influenced the comparative acceptability of group marriages, there was a great deal of interest expressed in them. It may be expected that as participation in these marital forms becomes more socially visible there will be an erosion of the sexual exclusivity norm. We may, therefore, see greater social interest in nonexclusive sexual pair-bondings.

Sixth, as greater equality between the sexes develops within the society, we may expect to see increased emphasis on equality in the pair-bonding arrangements which constitute acceptable marriage styles. As noted earlier, explicit emphasis upon equality in pair-bonding may already influence interest in alternative marital forms. It can be expected that this trend will receive greater attention in the future.

REFERENCES

Athanasiou, Robert and Phillip Shaver and Carol Tavris. "Sex." *Psychology Today*, 1970, 4, 39-52.

Bartell, Gilbert D. *Group Sex*. New York: Signet Books, 1971.

Bartell, Gilbert D. "Group Sex among the mid-Americans." In Joan L. and Jack R. Delora, (eds.), *Marriage and Its Alternatives*. Pacific Palisades, Calif: Goodyear Publishing, 1972.

Berger, Bennett, Bruce Hackett and R. Mervyn Millar. "The communal marriage." *The Family Coordinator*, 1972, 21, 419-427.

Breedlove, William and Jerrye Breedlove. *Swap Clubs*. Los Angeles: Sherbourne Press, 1964.

Cadwallader, Mervyn. "Marriage as a wretched institution." In Judson R. Landis, (ed.), *Current Perspectives on Social Problems*, 2nd ed. Belmont, Calif.: Wadsworth, 1971.

Coffin, Patricia. "The young unmarrieds." In Joan S. and Jack R. Delora, (eds.), *Marriage and Its Alternatives*. Pacific Palisades, Calif.: Goodyear Publishing, 1972.

Constantine, Larry L. and Joan M. "Sexual aspects of multilateral relations." *The Journal of Sex Research*, 1971, 7, 204-225.

Constantine, Larry L. and Joan M. and Sheldon K. Edelman. "Counseling implications of comarital and multilateral relations." *The Family Coordinator*, 1972, 21, 267.

Cuber, John F. "Alternate models from the perspective of sociology." In Otto, *op. cit.*

Cuber, John F. "Sex in five types of marriages." *Sexual Behavior*, 1972, 2, 74-80.

Cuber, John F. and Peggy B. Harroff. *Sex and the Significant Americans*. Baltimore: Penguin Books, 1965.

Delora, Jack R. and Joan S. (Eds.) *Marriage and Its Alternatives*. Pacific Palisades, Calif.: Goodyear Publishing, 1972.

Denfield, Duane and Michael Gordon. "The sociology of mate swapping: Or the family that swings together clings together." In Delora, *op. cit.*

Editors. "Big raid, Short-Creek, Arizona." *Newsweek*, 1953, 42:26.

Editors. "More the merrier." *Time*, 1952, 59:22.

Editors. "Great love-nest raid, Short-Creek, Arizona." *Time*, 1953, 62:16.

Editors. "Renewable marriage: Bill before Maryland legislature." 97:43 *Time*, 1972, 97:43.

Ellis, Albert. "Group marriage: A possible alternative?" In Otto, *op. cit.*

Estellachild, Vivian. "Hippie communes." In Delora, *op. cit.*

Greenwald, Harold. "Marriage as a non-legal voluntary association." In Otto, *op. cit.*

Haughey, John C. "The commune—Child of the 1970's." In Delora, *op. cit.*

Hedgepeth, William. "Maybe it'll be different here." In Delora, *op. cit.*

Hunt, Morton. *The Affair*. Cleveland: World Press, 1969.

Karlen, Arno. "The unmarried married on campus." In Clifton D. Bryand, (ed.), *Social Problems Today*. New York: Lippincott, 1971.

Leitsch, Dick. "Interview with a homosexual spokesman." *Sexual Behavior*, 1971, 1, 15-23.

Lindsey, Ben B. and Wainswright Evans. *The Companionate Marriage*. Garden City, N.Y.: Garden City Publishers, 1927.

Macklin, Eleanor D. "Heterosexual cohabitation among unmarried college students." *The Family Coordinator*, 1972, 21, 463-472.

Manosevitz, Martin. "The development of male homosexuality." *The Journal of Sex Research*, 1972, 8, 31-40.

Mead, Margaret. "Marriage in two steps." In Otto, *op. cit.*

Moore, Barrington, Jr. "Thoughts on the future of the family." In Frank Lindenfeld, (ed.), *Radical Perspectives on Social Problems*. New York: Macmillan, 1968.

Nye, F. Ivan. Personal communication, 1973.

Olson, David H. "Marriage of the future: Revolutionary or evolutionary change?" *The Family Coordinator*, 1972, 21, 383-393.

O'Neill, Nena and George. *Open-Marriage: A New Life-Style for Couples.* New York: M. Evans, 1972.

Otto, Herbert A. "Introduction." In Herbert Otto, (ed.) *The Family in Search of a Future.* Meridith Corp., New York: 1970.

Palson, Charles and Rebecca. "Swinging in wedlock," *Society*, 1972, 9, 28-37.

Ramey, James W. "Emerging patterns of innovative behavior in marriage." *The Family Coordinator*, 1972, 21, 435-456.

Roy, Della and Rustum. *Honest Sex.* New York: New American Library, 1968.

Roy, Rustum and Della. "Is monogamy outdated?" In Lester A. Kirkendall and R. N. Whitehurst (eds.), *The New Sexual Revolution.* New York: Donald W. Brown, 1971.

Smith, James R. and Lynn G. "Co-marital sex and the sexual freedom movement." *Journal of Sex Research*, 1970, 6, 131-142.

Symonds, Carolyn. "Sexual mate-swapping: Violation of norms and reconciliation of guilt." In James M. Henslin, Ed., *Studies in the Sociology of Sex.* New York: Appleton Century Crofts, 1971.

Varni, Charles A. "An exploratory study in spouse-swapping." *Pacific Sociological Review*, 1972, 15, 507-522.

Wells, Theodora and Lee S. Christie. "Living together: An alternative to marriage." In Delora, *op. cit.*

18

NOTES ON MARRIAGES IN THE COUNTER CULTURE[1]
John S. Kafka, M.D.
and
Robert G. Ryder

Selected examples of unconventional marriages are portrayed with interpretations of the potential meanings for other marriages. The authors describe not only the process of separation from conventionality, but how some couples drift back into conventional life-styles. An important contribution in the chapter centers on the authors' discussion of altered conceptions of sexuality in the counter-culture; the comparison with more conventional marriages is also useful in describing differences in the approach to or avoidance of tension.

A portion of this chapter is devoted to changing social-sexual relations in a society characterized by a psychology of plenty. New sharing norms as an outcome of this changing scene are considered as part of an emergent ideology of the counter-culture which may create further changes in male-female relationships. It would appear that young people with a counter-culture orientation tend to face difficulty and complexity in relationships with rather different kinds of views of themselves and the world around them. While the indicators of change are easy enough to perceive, the strength of the trends and their ultimate meanings for men and women of the future remain more obscure.

In the course of an extensive study of early marriage (Raush, Goodrich and Campbell, 1963; Ryder, 1970a; Ryder, 1970b; Ryder, Kafka and Olson, 1971) a small minority of couples (less than 1%) were located who seemed to have serious allegiance to what has been called (Roszak, 1968) the counter culture or, more recently, alternative culture or "hip" culture, characteristics of which will be described below. These and other couples located by a variety of ad hoc means were interviewed in either individual or joint sessions, and in some cases were interviewed in informal group settings in which some interviewees casually entered or left while the interview was in progress. The kind of interview procedure employed makes it impossible to arrive at a well defined figure for sample size, but we estimate that we each spoke with upwards of 40 persons (Total N thus above 80) located mostly on the east and west coasts, and in particular around Washington, D.C., and San Francisco. To a certain extent participants were treated more like informants, in the anthropological sense, than like subjects, i.e., we were as interested in reports about other families known to an interviewee as in self reports. Most of the persons in the sample were in their middle twenties, with a range from the late teens to the late forties.

There can be little doubt that, as Roszak (1968) has emphasized, the expression "counter culture" refers to a poorly defined, heterogeneous and changeable set of phenomena, and yet, as Roszak also points out, it is a set of phenomena with a slippery but insistent reality. In the present study, for a couple to be included there had to be an explicit intention to avoid the "hangups" of conventional marriage: to maximize intimacy, minimize utilitarian aspects of a relationship, (c.f. Cuber and Harroff, 1965) and to eschew possessiveness and loyalty to conventionally acceptable cultural roles. The importance of money was generally minimized. Boundaries, as in separating what is inside a marriage or out of it, or inside one's living quarters or out of it, were deemphasized. Geographical mobility seemed high. Most participants, but not all, used "soft" drugs and often but not always indicated that they were comfortable with drug use. Many participants, but by no means all, wore their hair long, dressed casually and presented a manifestly "hippy" appearance.

All of the participants shared one anomaly in terms of a thoroughgoing counter culture orientation: they were all legally married, and were involved in primarily dyadic relationships.[2]

This group of couples, and the others described by them, seemed impressionistically to manifest several notable central tendencies. Briefly, these central tendencies were as follows:

1. While there was substantial overt unconventionality, there was also a consistent tendency toward a sometimes covert "return of the conventional."

2. While sexual activity was prominent in the lives of these people, there is a sense in which sexuality was given a reduced role; one contemporary way of putting it is that sexuality was "demystified."

3. The "demystification" of sexuality was related to the tendency of some couples of this group to actively approach emotional tension, and sometimes to go out of their way to create it.

4. Finally, there is the possibility that a psychology of plenty, as it were, led some couples to altered affectional and sexual patterns.

Return of the Conventional

John and Sally[3] lived downtown in a small flat. Sally and her family were somewhat more affluent and better educated than John. He was a poet, which is to say he generally slept during the day, spent the evening with his wife, and stayed up all night writing and playing with the couple's six-month old baby. Sally had a regular office job with a major insurance company, and provided the family's sole source of income. Certainly this was not a stereotypically conventional middle-class couple, even setting aside the fact that they lived downtown rather than in the suburbs. Conventionally, husbands have higher socio-economic status than wives, wives provide more baby care than husbands, and of course the more usual pattern has the husband working for money while the wife stays home. There was even a role reversal in the skills John and Sally attributed to each other, with Sally seen as having practical, instrumental abilities, and John seen as being good with feelings and emotional matters. Yet there is a sense in which all this overt unconventionality did not prevent the emergence of conventional sex roles. John was not a male housewife. He was a poet (or a guru), i.e., the performer of a highly valued activity. Sally was not seen as the head, or the mainstay of the family, but as the performer of meaningless work, i.e., earning money at a "straight" job. Again, John was not just the enactor of a socio-emotional role; John was the socio-emotional *expert*, while Sally performed the *merely* instrumental activities. In short, to the extent that sex-role conventionality means that the husband has the higher family status, and performs more valued activities, this couple and others like them were quite conventional.

Another way in which unintended conventionality appeared was through a gradual drift over time. John and Sally eventually rented a house in the suburbs, which they shared with several other people. John took a parttime job in the records section of a local hospital, and supplemented his income by occasionally stealing his friends' records. They bought a Volkswagen bus. For one reason and another, the several companions in the house moved out. Sally became pregnant again, and was forced to leave her job. At this point in time they had thus become a nuclear family living alone in the suburbs, with the wife staying home and the husband wondering how he could earn enough money to make the house and car payments.

Conventional patterns also sometimes reappeared suddenly and surprisingly, and caused interpersonal problems, most notably in the case of jealousy. Sometimes the wife, but more often the husband, was an articulate advocate of nonpossessiveness, including sexual nonpossessiveness. John and Sally boasted that they put a great deal of energy into honestly sharing their feelings and beliefs with each other. It turned out that this "sharing" largely consisted of John telling his wife about the various women he would like to sleep with, and advocating a permissive attitude toward sexual sharing, without jealousy. Jealousy, however, emerged abruptly and intensely when Sally told her husband that she had been putting his ideas into practice.

There are two serious qualifications which must be made with regard to the unexpected appearance of jealousy. First, there do appear to be couples in which serious jealousy simply seems not to be the case, or is resolved to the apparent satisfaction of the spouses.[4] Second, while jealousy itself is a conventional enough feeling, the attitude taken toward the jealousy is not. One might expect in a conventional marriage, in which John is jealous because of Sally's sleeping with another man, that Sally would be seen as misbehaving. If she kept it up, Sally might be perceived as having a "problem." In our sample, however, it was the jealous affect, not the sexual behavior, which was likely to be seen as the source of difficulty. It was John who was seen as having the problem, and who was faced with the task of somehow dealing with his unpleasant feelings. There was no question of Sally's right to sleep with whomever she wished.

Connotative Changes in Sexuality

One assumed feature of counter culture that has received much public attention has been not only a permissive, but an open and forward attitude toward sexual behavior and related matters. Among those who believe we are in the midst of a sexual revolution, it is probable that the counter-culture is perceived to be in the revolutionary vanguard. Marcuse (1969) speaks of this process in terms of "desublimation," and suggests that overt and blatant sexuality has a political effect, subverting not only conventional sexuality but also the psychic defensive structures which help to support contemporary political forms. It is perhaps in such a context that one is to understand newspaper reports of pornography in which performers insist on being identified by their correct (and well known) family names, and such publications as "Zap Comix," in which obscenity and violence are played for laughs, in a comic book format.

One would expect that those who live in the context of overt and "desublimated" or "demystified" sexuality would not esteem sexual behavior in quite the same way as people in a more conventional context, and such seems in fact to have been the case in our sample.

Harrison (1965) has suggested that technological innovations alter our experience of awe. Vast mountain ranges and oceans, for example, are seen in a more matter of fact way because of the invention of the airplane. The uncanny affect that perhaps used to accompany certain bodily sensations of movement is experienced no more by those who have grown up used to riding in elevators. We would suggest that by a similar process, a certain "awesomeness" which used to accompany the reality and the fantasy of sexual behavior has been much attenuated for persons like those in our sample.

Members of our sample appeared to be more sexually involved

than conventional persons, but to esteem it less highly, at least in the sense that sexuality was not the object of a reverential or fearful attitude, nor on the other hand did couples' social lives revolve around sex in the way that seems true for those couples who have been referred to as "swingers" (Bartell, 1971; Denfield and Gordon, 1970).[5] Awe and related feelings seemed to be found more in connection with mystical belief systems, "soft" drug use, and other similar ways of altering one's experienced world.

Approaching Tension

Many persons in this group seemed to feel almost an obligation to approach and face up to tension. The stance taken vis-á-vis jealousy is related to this, in that there was more tendency to deal with the jealousy as such than to terminate the jealousy by ending extramarital sexuality. For example, Donald and Connie joined together in trying to help one of Connie's girlfriends. When Connie discovered that Donald's "helping" included sexual intercourse she became furious. She "yelled and threw things." The extramarital sexuality continued, but Connie claimed to have largely mastered her jealousy, and that she then found pleasurable excitement in her husband's sexual sharing.

George and Betty traveled around the country a great deal. They used to hitchhike and seemed to enjoy the adventure of not knowing whom they would meet on the road. After their baby was born, they acquired a small van for their travels. They emphasized that at the beginning of each trip they would be quite uncertain as to whether they would be coming back, or coming back together, and seemed to enjoy the thrill of not knowing what would become of them.

Susan lived alone, and was therefore not really part of this sample; but her attitude toward her way of living is illustrative of the positive evaluation of tension. Susan felt guilty about living alone, because living alone was comfortable for her. She could be with people when she enjoyed it and avoid them when she wished, and thereby avoid the possibility of being caught in a difficult interpersonal situation. She therefore feared her behavior to be a "copout," and that it would prevent her from "growing."

On a more public level, encounter groups and related activities appear to be popular in alternative culture. In political confrontations other than racial ones the more dangerous barricades, so to speak, tend to be peopled by individuals from the counter culture. Even the valued ability to remain "cool" often is shorthand for the ability to remain comfortably in a situation of potentially disabling stress.

A conceptual connection is possible between the tendency to approach tension and the "demystification" of sexuality. Lichtenstein (1970) suggests that the problem of "how to affirm human beings in the emotional conviction of their existence" is central to the "alienation of our youth." While he states that "sexuality is . . . the most basic way

... to experience an affirmation of the reality of . . . existence," he adds that "in the course of ontogenesis, other methods, as yet poorly understood, of feeling affirmed . . . develop. . . . " We wish to suggest that in couples like those in our sample, the self-confirmatory function of overtly sexual experience may be altered and perhaps diminished, and replaced in part by the search for drug-related and other ecstatic experiences, and the general valuing of tension and intensity as such. That is, tension and intensity as such are valued because they serve the need for self-confirmatory experience.

A Psychology of Plenty

The idea of limited resources—of scarcity—seemed alien to many of the people we considered. Husbanding one's resources, saving up for the distant future, or in general denying oneself in the present for the sake of one's own long term benefit—these were not popular ideas. While one orientation toward the future was expressed in the saying, which seemed to achieve popularity for a while, that "When you are sailing on the Lusitania, you might as well go first class," there was also concomitantly an implicit orientation to the effect that in the foreseeable future satisfaction of one's wants would be readily available without a great deal of difficulty. In financial terms there was realistic support for this view in the form of money from parents, or welfare checks, and in the claimed discovery of some couples that they could be comfortable on $100 or $200 a month. One couple calculated that they needed to work for money on no more than one day out of thirteen, in order to be self-supporting.[6]

A psychology of plenty seemed if anything to be more accepted in social than in material terms. At one time, people like those in our group seemed to believe, with some apparent accuracy, that they could wander into certain neighborhoods in almost any major city, or hitchhike across country, and feel assured of being befriended and treated as comrades by nominal strangers. If not love, at least warmth, friendliness and comradeship were felt to be available on any street corner. This rosy world view was not so widely held currently in our sample as it once was, or at least it was not held in such an extreme form. But it was still believed that for a prudent and "together" person, companionship is plentiful and easily available. Sexual satisfaction as well was seen by many persons to be plentifully available with a minimum of effort.

To summarize, a psychology of plenty in terms of goods and services was supported by a dramatic attenuation of felt needs. A psychology of plenty in social terms was supported by social arrangements which in effect partially abrogated conventional boundaries between friends and strangers, and also between spouses and non-spouses.

Plentiful social resources were seen by some as making clinging and possessiveness irrelevant. It was one explanation offered for reduced jealousy in the face of extramarital sexuality or affection. In at least quasi-psychoanalytic terminology, one aspect of this point of view was that an anal-genital basis for object relations was partially supplanted by an oral-genital basis, i.e., affectional ties became less controlled and more diffuse. Some participants put it in terms of a "capitalist" model of relationship being replaced by a communitarian model. Still another way to put it, again in quasi-psychoanalytic terminology, might be in terms of relationships being, descriptively, less similar to an oedipal model, in which gratification is primarily dependent on one particular person, and more similar to a sibling model, in which many "siblings" may have some functional equivalence.

While it has been noted that the retention of pregenital capabilities may be adaptive (Kris, 1952; Weisman, 1966, 1967; Novey, 1955), the basic psychoanalytic position nevertheless traces a hierarchical and more or less linear development of object relations. Object choices progress from anaclitic to non-anaclitic, from part to whole object, from pregenital to genital phases, and from pre-oedipal to oedipal (or part oedipal), and each shift along this developmental scale represents a partial supplanting of more primitive characteristics by more advanced ones. Some of the people we have seen would regard any such hierarchical scheme as restrictive, and might suggest that in a situation of plentiful resources "supplanting" one relationship form with another might be senseless self denial—one can have both.[7] Whether on this kind of basis or some other, it did seem to be true that in some of our couples polymorphous perverse relationship aspects seemed to be tolerated or even valued in a de-differentiation of the usual developmental phases.

Overview

The several aspects of ideology and living patterns upon which we have commented fit together with a certain degree of consistency. The idea of plentiful resources supports and in turn is supported by a sharing orientation, which some of our participants would call communitarian. That aspect of sharing which is affectional or sexual directly creates bountiful resources (c.f. Slater, 1970, Ch. 4). It also tends to remove from sexuality a certain tinge of awe, a certain transcendental quality.[8] Perhaps this more matter of fact attitude toward sexuality leaves unfulfilled a kind of need for self affirmation, which contributes to a high evaluation of tension and intensity in general, which in turn relates not only to drug use and "up front" interpersonal relationships, but also to a confrontational political attitude, which again may contribute to openness and bluntness in some aspects of sexuality. It also means that sometimes people are to put up with potentially upsetting interpersonal events without simply changing their behavior so as to avoid them.

There are however flaws in this ideological-behavioral configuration, even apart from the degree to which it may oversimplify an extremely heterogeneous and complex set of phenomena. It is not true that the people in our sample were so confident of gratification that they eschewed all arrangements which might bring them security. They did, after all, get legally married, and their marriages did tend to include a "return of the conventional," in the form of conventional sex-role attitudes which were masked by overt sex-role reversals, occasionally in a gradual drift back into concerns with middle class economic security, and in the disvalued but real appearance of jealousy. One possible view, which we sometimes heard, is that these aspects merely represented unfinished business. Heightened awareness will gradually diminish sex role bias, and the disvaluation of jealousy along with increased appreciation of the availability of affection and sexuality will gradually eliminate jealousy. An alternative view might be that the character structure of people in our society simply does not support, for example, radically nonpossessive affection. It may also be that our society is simply not dependably enough bountiful, and is getting less so, and that the mutual relationship between sharing and plentiful resources is in the direction of less sharing leading to less plentiful resources, and so on.[9] Obviously we do not know which if any of these interpretations have any validity. We do not even know whether our small set of couples is representative of some significant portion of the vague entity called the counter culture, or whether it only illustrates aberrant and ephemeral phenomena, although we lean toward the former view. We do believe, however, that the ideologies, attitudes and living patterns observed in these couples provide useful and suggestive information as to what is possible in changing patterns of close personal relationships, and some idea of the complications which such changes might encounter.

NOTES

1   The writers wish to acknowledge their debt to the various colleagues who have contributed ideas, information and critical commentary in the course of completing this paper, and particularly so to David H. Olson, who has been closely associated with this project, and who has made many substantial and valuable contributions. We wish also to express our thanks to Raymond K. Yang, whose comments on various drafts of this paper have been most helpful.
2   While non-dyadic relationships occurred in this group, none was primarily non-dyadic, and there were no "multilateral" marriages of the sort described by Constantine and Constantine (1970).
3   Case material is presented to illustrate the writers' impressions rather than to provide evidence for them. Any given "case" may include a selection of material from several actual couples, and is in all instances disguised to protect couples' confidentiality.
4   We are deliberately refraining from discussing here various defensive, including counterphobic considerations, although information obtained often reached to some extent below a merely descriptive level (c.f. Ryder, 1972).
5   Young children of these couples also tended to be exposed to open and matter of fact sexuality, with consequences that are as yet unclear.

6 Compare the centrality of money and money problems among conventional couples suggested by Mitchell, Bullard and Mudd (1962).
7 Perhaps the "plentiful resources" ethos may be in more conflict with hierarchical formulations, than with less linear formulations such as that of Lichtenstein (1970).
8 For a more extended consideration of the implications of this kind of affect, see Kafka (1969) and Kafka (1971).
9 One is reminded in this context of the words of Mack the Knife, the pertinence of which is emphasized in a different but not unrelated context by Smith (1972): Erst kommt das Fressen, dann kommt die Morale.

REFERENCES

Bartell, Gilbert D. *Group Sex: A Scientist's eyewitness report on the American way of swinging.* Peter H. Wyden, Inc., N.Y. 1971.

Constantine, L. and Constantine, J. "Where is marriage going?" *The Futurist*, 1970, 4, 44-46.

Cuber, J. F. and Harroff, P. B. *The Significant Americans: A Study of Sexual Behavior Among the Affluent.* New York: Appleton-Century, 1965.

Denfield, D. and Gordon, M. "The sociology of mate swapping: or the family that swings together clings together," *Journal of Sex Research*, 1970, 6, 85-100.

Harrison, J. B. "A reconsideration of Freud's 'A disturbance of memory on the Acropolis' in relation to identity disturbance" *Journal of the American Psychoanalytic Association*, 1965, 13, 518-527.

Kafka, J. S. "The body as transitional object: a psychoanalytic study of a self-mutilating patient," *British Journal of Medical Psychology*, 1969, 42, 207-212.

Kafka, J. S. "Ambiguity for individuation: a critique and reformulation of double-bind theory," *Archives of General Psychiatry*, 1971, 25, 232-239.

Kris, E. *Psychoanalytic Explorations in Art.* New York: International Universities Press, 1952.

Lichtenstein, H. "Changing implications of the concept of psychosexual development: an inquiry concerning the validity of classical psychoanalytic assumptions concerning sexuality," *Journal of the American Psychoanalytic Association*, 1970, 18, 300-318.

Marcuse, H. *An Essay on Liberation.* Boston: Beacon Press, 1969.

Mitchell, H. E., Bullard, J. W. and Mudd, E. H. "Areas of marital conflict in successfully and unsuccessfully functioning families," *Journal of Health and Human Behavior*, 1962, 3, 88-93.

Novey, S. "Some philosophical speculations about the concept of the genital character," *International Journal of Psychoanalysis*, 1955, 36, 88-94.

Raush, H. L., Goodrich, D. W. and Campbell, J. D. "Adaptation to the first years of marriage," *Psychiatry*, 1963, 26, 368-380.

Roszak, T. *The Making of a Counter Culture.* New York: Doubleday and Company, 1968.

Ryder, R. G. "Dimensions of early marriage," *Family Process*, 1970a, 9, 51-68.

Ryder, R. G. "A topography of early marriage," *Family Process*, 1970b, 9, 385-402.

Ryder, R. G. "Describing variations among marriages." Unpublished paper, 1972.

Ryder, R. G., Kafka, J. S. and Olson, D. H. "Separating and joining influences in courtship and early marriage," *American Journal of Orthopsychiatry*, 1971, 41, 450-464.

Slater, P. E. *The Pursuit of Loneliness: American Culture at the Breaking Point.* Boston: Beacon Press, 1970.

Smith, M. B. "Ethical implications of population policies: a psychologist's view," *American Psychologist*, 1972, 27, 11-15.

Weissman, P. "Psychological concomitants of ego functioning in creativity," *International Journal of Psychoanalysis*, 1966, 49, 464-469.

Weissman, P. "Theoretical considerations of ego regression and ego function in creativity," *The Psychoanalytic Quarterly*, 1967, 36, 37-50.

IV

MARRIAGE: EMERGENT FUTURES

As the context in which social interaction takes place changes, so do the ground rules for marriage and other long-term intimate and sexual relationships. In this section we will consider some of the solutions that have been proposed and outlines that have been laid down for possible better ways of living and loving. We will in fact propose goals of: coming to terms with jealousy and the drives that cause it; being open and loving in a holistic way; exhibiting a balanced, considerate, aware kind of honesty in our relationships; allowing oneself to choose whatever life-style fits him best ("Dare to be different"); and extending that fight for freedom to all peoples in every area of their lives.

We have been talking about what is and what has been attempted. Now we are going to talk about what could be and what should be.

In a searching review of Erving Goffman's *Relations in Public*, Marshall Berman describes Goffman as the Kafka of our time. What he suggests is that the problem of identity in the context of interpersonal relations becomes intensified by various forms of instability in family life. As family members move into new life-styles, the family/community boundaries are challenged, its emotional certainties are shattered, its resources shaken. Berman suggests that as an outcome of the extreme changes of the 60's and the new perspectives that accompanied these changes:

> ... In every sphere, we 'refused to keep our place,' we broke boundaries, tore down walls, acted out what we felt, encouraged others to do the same. And where are

we now? Goffman's final version seems unrelievedly bleak. Life in the streets appears as a Hobbesian nightmare, life in the family an existential battleground. It seems terrifying both to go out and to stay in. And social life turns out to be far more fragile, more vulnerable than we thought.

Thus, when a so-called maniac and paranoid . . . 'gives up everything' that family and society have to offer, his behavior reminds us what our everything is and then reminds us that this everything is not much. . . . It is now possible for anyone to rationalize anything he wants to do to anybody as heroic resistance to oppression—and harder than ever to judge who is sincere and who is right. There is no honest radical who doesn't, at least in some moments . . . feel some responsibility and guilt . . . yet, if we remember the quiet degradations that so many people endured for so long, while they obligingly 'kept their place'—I think our nostalgia and regret will fade, and we will be willing to accept, in all its ambiguity, what we have done. . . . We will be worried . . . but not contrite. Tearing down walls does create ruins—for a while. But it also creates the space and chance to put up a new, a better building. And it can give people a sense of their own strength and beauty, of their power to build. [1]

This tribute to Goffman's work likewise expresses the authors' feelings of the desire to rebuild—to turn what are now essentially the ruins of a (destructive) family life into a relationship that will lead to the growth and fulfillment of the parties involved. Marriage in the context of human love can indeed use renovating.

NOTES

1 Berman, Marshall. Review of *Relations in Public* (Erving Goffman, 1971). In *New York Times Book Review*, Feb. 27, 1972.

19

CHANGING GROUND RULES AND EMERGENT LIFE-STYLES
Robert N. Whitehurst

This chapter dealing with changing ground rules discusses the potential range of alternative life-styles relating to marriage as a dominant form today. Among the most likely outcomes (seen by the author as modal forms) are: modified open marriages, post-marital singlehood, and extended quasi-kin networks. Whitehurst speculates about the probable impact of changing ground rules as evidenced by changes in youthful attitudes toward marriage and the relations between the sexes. Love, sex, jealousy, children, and privacy are considered as areas in which normative changes are occurring and which will have an impact on future relationships. Included is an incisive analysis of comparative roles played by wives and husbands as spouses and lovers which suggests reasons why EMS is seen as an enticing activity for ever-larger numbers. In summary, Whitehurst develops a suggestive hypothesis claiming that much about marriage (and its budding alternatives) can be understood in terms of the ways in which feelings of security and needs for autonomy are balanced by each individual. The conditions under which one would decide to enter a conventional marriage or modified open marriage, to remain single, or would remain ambivalent about marriage are arrayed into a typology.

The measurement and evaluation of social changes affecting male-female relationships continues to be a popular sport for futurists. This may in part be a reflection of the power of the media and its concern for saleable messages, but it most likely is as well a reflection of some real changes occurring in the lives of a great number of people. It is suggested in this paper that real social change affecting men and women is occurring and that the changes are as of this time poorly understood by our usual sociological conceptions. The standard works on the sociology of the family simply fail to depict underlying currents of change within male-female relationships—partly because of the framework and traditionalist mold in which they are cast, partly because some of the change is taking place underground. Usually, family sociologists ask their questions in terms of a closed-system functionalist model which implies stability. Our concern will be to develop some ideas about what relationships will be like in the future based on the observation of some more general indicators of social change than survey data. The paper is thus speculative, but it is an inductive effort to draw some tentative conclusions about change on the basis of limited knowledge. All futurists must do the same—so, without apology, but remembering the tentativeness of it all, let us look at what's happening now.

Some Alternatives

There is little evidence to suggest that in the foreseeable future, most people will not continue to opt for the conventional styles of marriage—that is, monogamy as usual, often with other people in clandestine relationships involved here and there. There is evidence, however, that a large (though as yet undetermined) number of people are opting for some alternative(s) to this older model. The reasons for this have been described elsewhere.[1] Extrapolating from current social trends, the following seem likely choices for significant numbers of people in the future—that is, as long as favorable political and economic conditions continue.

Modified Open Marriage

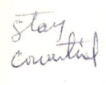

Since its publication, the O'Neills' *Open Marriage* has become a best seller—possibly because many North American marriages are in some kind of semi-desperate straits.[2] Instead of giving up totally on marriage, many people are attempting to work out some kind of non-restrictive relationship that would enable both partners to have something (such as more autonomy, freedom, time, privacy, and the like) each sees as desirable without totally breaking up the relationship. Attempts in this direction can be seen as a fairly straightforward extension of other North American values and habits. At this time it appears to be extremely difficult for most married people to extend the idea of non-exclusiveness in an open-ended relationship as far as the area of sexuality—a fact attested to by the O'Neills. But is a relationship genuinely open if one can have tennis and cocktails with someone who is a non-spouse, but one must stop short of sexual involvement with a non-spouse? As this problem now stands, it is a gray area, remaining undefined and ambivalently handled by many couples attempting to work out modified open marriages. Jealousy, although partly a result of cultural conditioning which can be modified, is still deeply related to the insecurities felt by almost everyone. Therefore, jealousy remains one of the areas in which it will take more effort to lessen the disparity between intellectual-normative commitment and the ability to follow through in actions and feelings the sense of commitment to new norms, such as non-jealousy.[3]

It is probably true as Jessie Bernard indicates in her recent work on women and marriage that women tend to be the losers in agreements made for open-ended marriages.[4] As women become better able to defend themselves from male put-downs, chauvinism, and manipulation, more true equality in working out satisfactory terms for such arrangements will become a possibility. In the meantime, many more couples will attempt to work out their own set of ground-rules governing their relationships. In the absence of older and more conventional guidelines (such as the Bible, local folklore, and the like) and of social control agencies, marriage in the immediate future is bound to become more difficult and problematic than ever before. Since the church, extended family, and the community no longer count on the old ways to keep us on to narrow paths, we will have to deal with our relationships on a more ad hoc basis.[5] On the negative side, this trend does lead inevitably to more ill-considered experimentation and probably to more disruption, but it also lends itself to innovation, creativity, and openness—values that are strongly held in this culture. It's a pity that we cannot get all this excitement, change, and suspense and keep the comfort of placid stability as well (a combination most of us long for), but unfortunately things don't seem to work out that way. Modified open type marriages which struggle with sets of rules to govern the relationships in some non-standard ways will probably become more of a modal response of younger marriages. How much success they will have in developing an ethic of sexuality in openness with others that still recognizes and supports the continued primacy of the original pair bond remains to be seen.

Post-Marital Singlehood

Increasing numbers of people are joining the ranks of the world of the formerly married.[6] Larger numbers of people are (mostly inadvertently) taking the advice of Bertrand Russell who suggested "get your divorce while you are young." Although there is little evidence as yet that large numbers of these individuals will not be returnees to the sea of matrimony, much more caution is now being exercised by those who married young, have undertaken divorces, and are not quite ready for another go at it. As the literature of women's liberation continues in its impact, as new freedom is experienced by more women (and some more men), marriage as an option becomes less appealing. A trend first described (at least in such detail and so vividly) by Toffler as "rentalism" may now be creeping into the people-specialization arena. Toffler described some of the current trends as ad hoc-ery, rentalism, transience, and novelty. All of these goals and adaptations can be seen in the lives of many young people who do not see how they could become committed to the older and more stable forms of marriage and family life that seem so dreadfully monotonous to them. As a result, many young and some not-so young people engage in a life-style that puts them in touch with a fairly large coterie of friends who can be called upon for a variety of experiences, depending on the need of the moment. One recently divorced young person recently related:

> Now, as a single female in my own apartment, I can organize my own life in ways that formerly were impossible with my husband— if I want sex now, I know exactly how to get it (and only when the mood is right), if I want good dinnertime conversation or to talk about intellectual things, I know who to call for this. The only problem is at times the hectic nature of life, as all these things do not work out so neatly as with one—but I am enjoying my freedom and ability to organize my life immensely and have no desire to go back to marriage. At some time in the future I may feel differently, but now the positives by far outweigh the negative things. My friends all respect my freedom and understand my needs. If life sometimes feels a bit fractionized, it is a small price to pay for the good things I am getting now as compared to the restrictive nature of marriage.

What is expressed most clearly here is the fact that this person feels that pair-bonding in monogamy is highly restrictive and that freedom to be oneself can be fully obtained only in the unmarried state. Others have explained to me how they feel that the options open to a pair in marriage—or even in an open-ended relationship—are always constrictive. Fairly obviously, the strength of freedom needs versus security needs will be an important factor in determining who chooses which of these two life styles—an open marriage or post-married singlehood.* In any case, it is predictable that large numbers will opt for one or the other of these two life-styles as they are the simplest extensions of available possibilities of life as we now know it.

Extended Intimate Networks

When these occur without extramarital sexual involvement, they will probably be like those described by Stoller.[7] These networks of non-kin intimates will often include activities involving children and weekend recreational activities. They will sometimes be concerned with cooperative ventures intended to solve some of the economic problems of families, and in some cases may include common housing. More clearly, families with common problems with children, problems involving a lack of clear sense of community, and some sense of need to cooperate with others outside of the nuclear family unit will be most likely to try out this kind of alternative. This is an area that has been investigated pretty much in terms of child-care services and some recreational patterns. There are not as many widespread adaptations

---

* See typology in summary.

designed for sharing of some household goods, cars, and other goods and services not commonly shared between members of nuclear families. Neither the extent nor the direction of this trend is well understood and its implications for more radical forms of family sharing are unclear. There is a clear potential to consider this as a radical alternative if families share cars, TV's, vacations, and other commodities formerly held to be in the domain of the single nuclear family. The implications for sexual sharing are certainly present in any arrangement which involves intimacy and sharing of so many *other* aspects of one's personal life. However, this kind of arrangement must necessarily involve so many factors and be so complex, it may be unrealistic to view this as a viable alternative for very many families.

Swinging

Swinging can probably be dismissed as a non-radical activity in North American society since it does not affect the nuclear structure of the family in any real way.[8] Children are usually brought up conventionally in families of swingers, thus the implications for change—at least as the term is now understood—are minimal. The fears of becoming affectionately involved, if continued as a norm of swinging, do not enhance the probability of creating true alternatives to the conventional marriage. It tends instead to simply translate the old-fashioned ephemeral affair into a game for everyone.

Triad and Group Marriages

This topic has been covered to date best in the work of the Constantines.[9] To date, the amount of talk about the formation of group marriages far exceeds the number of steps taken toward making the commitment to actually doing it. Some group marriages have survived for a considerable length of time, but these have involved only a select minority of the total population. This does not mean that the implications of group marriage for the future are unimportant, for the fact that there is now talk on a large scale appears to indicate a willingness to accept new ideas, and perhaps at some point in the future to consider some kind of alternate venture for oneself. The most important implication is probably for the development of a truly democratic set of alternate possibilities in terms of sex, marriage, and family styles. Legitimizing freedom to try something other than conventional monogamy must be seen as a radical change in North American culture. As a realistic option for a large segment of the population, restrictions of past socialization will make the choice an extremely difficult one for most people. Thus, until the system becomes more open, true group marriages will likely be a statistically unimportant development in the future. Simple recognition of urban sex ratios, when coupled with an emergent norm of non-jealousy, will create a tremendously enhanced potential for triadal arrangements as an alternate life-style.

Rural Subsistence Communes

This form is probably the most subversive alternate life-style of all, even though it calls for something approximating some old-fashioned virtues—especially those of making it on your own and getting by because of your own labour. The rejection, sometimes nearly total, of the technology and consumer package held out as desirable for urbanites must be seen as revolutionary.[10] The adaptation of the work ethic in subsistence farm communes likewise is radical. What seems to be lacking is a rational formula that would describe the optimum ratio of numbers of people (with some requisite skills), the minimum numbers of acres for survival, and the minimum level of technology needed to make it effectively as subsistence farmers. To the extent that some communes have worked some of these problems out and are still operating, this form can be termed to be a limited success. Their goals are very much at odds with the dominant culture's mores of acquisition, consumption, and the never-ending search for status accompanied with the gadgetry of a productive society. Work (if defined as less-than-pleasant tasks) is simply something to be done (celebrated) as a symbolic gesture of man's cooperation with the land. It only helps one survive—then leisure, recreation, crafts, music, dancing, and sex become celebrated as normal events. Although the life-style is romantic and holds a great attraction for large numbers of escapists who hold some kind of idyllic dream of returning to nature, few have enough of a sense of commitment to endure for long a return to the primitive condition required by most of the farm returnees. Thus, as a viable life-style alternate, it must remain for most in an unimportant realm of reverie and daydream. We are, at least most of us, so urbanized and used to technology that few can resist the temptation of the life of "ease," even though it is often accompanied with dis-ease.

Since the rural commune denies many of the major values necessary to the maintenance of corporate capitalism, it is probably the most destructive to it. The fact that the rural subsistence farm commune is pretty much ignored as an aberration probably means that few establishment-types take the movement seriously, or that they have not as yet figured out how to co-opt it. Since in its extreme form, the rural commune denies traditional norms of sexual behavior, child-rearing, consumption, religious practice, and occupational rules of conduct, the establishment may think it safer to ignore than to confront. In terms of current or prospective numbers, it is not likely to become a major social movement.

Changing Ground Rules

Some evidence suggests that there are a number of specific areas of intimate relationships which are undergoing restructuring.[11] Among the important norms that are changing, the following are more likely than some others to have an impact that creates greater awareness of alternate life-styles and possibly supports the trial of them.

Love

As an empathic response, the meaning of a sense of loving relation between individuals is dramatically changing. No longer do so many people believe in lifetime monogamous true-love as a possibility, even though it may be held out as desirable. Many feel that love by its very nature tends to be impermanent but life-giving and so should be enjoyed on those terms. Increasing numbers also feel that love can be shared and that it is possible to love any number of people simultaneously.

Jealousy

As a culturally-induced problem, jealousy tends to be regarded as purely the problem of the person experiencing the feeling, not the person who presumably produced the state. In marriage, if a husband and wife have agreed to a non-exclusive relationship, the problem of jealousy is one which each of them must grapple with and work through essentially alone. No longer is jealousy automatically seen as reasonable and as a sign that one partner loves the other. Jealousy more frequently is seen as a reaction to one's own immaturity and insecurity. Thus it is a problem to work out the best way one can; it less often means the "offending spouse" stops doing whatever it was the produced the jealous state (perhaps a distortion of the psychoanalytic view which holds that it is more often one's emotions that are out of line rather than the environment—or other people—who are provocative or destructive).

Sex

More often these days, sex is seen as an occasion to celebrate one's aliveness with another with whom one shares a loving relationship or at least has an understood sense of common attraction in which exploitation and gamesmanship have been minimized. Its central importance is receding and the symbolic meanings once attached to it appear to be diminishing. As the meanings change, the threat so often associated with sexual activity changes as well. The overall effect is to tend to make sexual activity a celebrated commonplace, much like eating, which can have many social connotations and varieties of expression. It (sex) is somehow becoming legitimized in the face of a still harshly punitive and repressed society. This may be due as much to the prurient interests of the majority and to the voyeurism of "the conventionals" as to the efforts of youth to construct new norms and new meanings surrounding sexuality. At least some of the implications of the changed attitudes on sex for marriage are rather obvious, as sex becomes something less than that magic which either makes or breaks a relationship in its total sense. When it is just one more lovely and loving activity that people do, and insofar as it becomes detached from the old order, humans stand to become enlarged as people.

If we could conceptualize extramarital sex (EMS) as a problem to be understood from the vantage point of role analysis, it might be clearer that more, not less, EMS should be expected in this kind of society. Looking at the respective roles of legal marriage partners as contrasted with lovers (extramaritally), it immediately can be seen that the content of the roles carries with it some relatively powerful portion of the explanation of the glamour of EMS activity (at least in the early stages of the development of EMS relationships).

At the onset of an EMS relationship, there is a flirting period in which all the romance and flashy verve of youth is recaptured, if even for a brief moment before the episode is either consummated or short-circuited. This initial encounter takes people back to more romantic days of their lives to situations replayed that are often forgotten or downplayed in the daily rituals of living as husband and wife. The role expectations for lovers are very similar to the situations in premarriage dating, in which topics of conversation, activities, and body preparations are the sort that tend to heighten romanticism and escape from boring daily realities. Thus it is likely that, given current North American values on newness and experience-seeking, we will continue to see a rise in EMS activity as long as opportunity structures remain open for participants.

After settling into marriage, wives less often have the opportunity (or may not as often make opportunity) to be shown off with husbands under the above described circumstances. Thus, in some combination of forces that impel males and females to stray from the conjugal bed, the following may be among the more important to understand: Given some doubts about current norms (or feelings of anomia—which means a sense that the rules do not apply to oneself or have no meaning), open opportunity, intelligence enough to engage in moral relativism, and a need for new experience (also aided by the contrast of daily dull routines), people are likely to seek EMS experiences more frequently. If this listing of predisposing factors is any indication, it is likely that many more North Americans may be at some level ready to consider the game.

A general hypothesis which may be tested by research also involves the changing nature of touching experiences in marriage. There is probably a decrease over the span of the marriage cycle of frequency of touching, fondling, and general caressing of partners; it may be that this is what people miss in relationships and are searching for in sexual situations. The basic content and meanings sought in EMS may then be sensual rather than sexual. However, due to our strong *expectations* of sexuality, much sexual interaction might occur as a substitute for sensuality. After all, in this culture it would almost be an affront to personal identity to engage in all the processes of beginning an 'affair' and then only engage in petting or body fondling; meanings get sexualized beyond their ordinary significance in the life of this kind of sex-obsessed culture and sexual acting-out is one result.

It is a growing norm that wives and husbands are not so much better or worse than each other, but simply different, and it is enough to experience the difference. However, since we are all extremely well conditioned to exercise a competitive framework in most of our activities, it will probably be some time before this emergent norm about the relative differences in people takes real effect. As siblings in families, we are compared favorably or unfavorably—not thought of simply as different human beings. Thus wives and husbands are similarly compared unfavorably (but apparently on second thought more often favorably) with paramours. Probably adopting such a norm would be extremely humanizing to all social contacts, but its acceptability is made less likely by the fact that it runs counter to what all North Americans seem to use as a perceptual base of experience—namely that there are good guys and bad guys out there and one's task is to simply sort them out, attach labels, then act on the premise that these categories are reality. Perhaps the norm is in part changing in response to a need of so many to avoid the bad-guy label for engaging in EMS. If so, the change must be welcomed as a more sophisticated reaction to all people, finally abandoning the witch-hunt process which separates people in favor of a more positive approach which enhances human interaction.

Children

Offspring are no longer seen as an unalloyed blessing to create the fabric of a solid marriage. They are less often seen as extensions of parents, as status objects, or as things to manipulate and control to our own liking. Children are, in counterculture families, less often prisoners of the family, are more likely to be treated as autonomous persons much earlier and kept in positions of dependence less long.[12] As both men and women take responsibility for contraception, both marriage and children will continue to be redefined in terms of the ecological and economic strategies felt to be appropriate for the coming world. Clearly, the meaning of having and rearing children is not the same as in times past.

Privacy

Jessie Bernard has shown that when people marry, there is a marriage that is *his* and one that is *hers*.[13] Quite obviously, if a woman's work is taken at all seriously (and it must be, given its level of professionalism) we might conclude that women will soon be demanding something like equal opportunity. This notion will no doubt extend to cover such exigencies as *her* study, *her* conventions attended, *her* own private sphere in which she can act with impunity and freedom as an agent of her own free will. This does not mean that home and family, husband-wife, and mother-child relationships will be non-existent. It simply means that wives and mothers will probably gain the same (or nearly the same) freedoms to pursue their own private and personal interests in much the same way as men have done for some time. Sports, corner-tavern drinking, and extended liberty from home as privacy spheres will no longer likely be the sole province of men. The future in this area looks as though it will become as good for women as for men—and a reasoned analysis should suggest no reason why this should not be.

Summary

Some alternatives to conventional monogamous marriage have been discussed in the light of changes now occurring in North American society. The two adaptations held to be most prevalent as potential alternatives to monogamy in its usual sense are modified open marriages and post-marriage singlehood. These are viewed as most probable in terms of the extensions of values and structures now available as options today. Open sexuality remains problematic in the near future for large numbers of people in male-female relationships. Although the norms governing jealousy are changing, some difficulties remain in closing the gap between stated ideals (intellectual commitment to a norm of non-jealous behavior) and actual behavior. Other adaptations such as extended intimate networks, swinging or comarital sex, triad and group marriages, and rural communes were discussed as having a lesser potential as viable options for many people. Changing male-female relationship ground rules involving love, jealousy, sex, children, and privacy were discussed as real changes having a potential effect on all men and women.

Earlier in the paper, it was suggested that people will opt for alternate life-styles in terms of a balance of their needs for freedom and autonomy as related to their sense of personal security or needs to be succored and emotionally supported constantly by one significant other. The following oversimple typology depicts these relationships and provides some suggestive hypotheses for research on the problem. In general, it is hypothesized that in cases of high personal security and high need for freedom, persons would be more likely to either resist marriage in the first place or wind up in the post-marriage single portion of the typology. If high security is found to coexist with a low freedom need, the result may be an expected outcome of marriage, possibly an open-ended style of relationship. Given a low sense of security and a high need for freedom, one would expect to find the usual condition of men in marriage today—that is a deep sense of ambivalence and commitment to the idea of marriage.* This is probably the case in which marriage is most disparaged and most participated in

---

* This is not meant to imply that were women provided with an equivalent structure of freedom and equal opportunity to express autonomy in their socialization experience that they would not be very similar to men in this respect.

by the average married man. It is probable that many married men want the security and good aspects of marriage but still prefer the freedom of singlehood. In the last case, given both low security and low need for freedom, one would expect more conventional marriages in this cell. There are, of course, many implications other than these to be drawn from such an exercise in typologizing, but it is instructive as a means of beginning to look at these relationships anew. There would probably be sex and age differences in the frequency in which each of the cells would locate the indicated responses. Other variables may be of equal or greater importance. Such a typology can be defended if it produces either thinking or research actions leading to verification, substitution, or alteration in terms of the purported realities.

Marriage Orientations as an Outcome of the Relationship Between Sense of Personal Security and Need for Freedom and Autonomy

Sense of Personal Security*	Need for Freedom and Autonomy	
	High	Low
High	A. Singles or open-ended marriage	B. variously open or modified open marriage
Low	C. deeply ambivalent (but married)	D. conventional marriage

Rank order of probability of occurrence of cases in cells:
(from highest or most frequent to least-often occurring)

        C. Ambivalents
        D. Conventionals
        B. Modified open marriages
        A. Singles and open-marriages

---

*Security, as used here, might be indicated by any or all of the following:
Ability to be alone,
To make decisions easily,
Feeling good about oneself while alone,
Feeling complete when alone,
Not needing to compulsively seek company,
Ability to face life cheerfully without need to scapegoat or blame others, i.e. accepting responsibility.

NOTES

1. Whitehurst, Robert N. "Violence Potential in Extramarital Sexual Responses," *Journal of Marriage and the Family*, Nov. 1971, pp. 683-691.
2. O'Neill, Nena and George. *Open Marriage*. New York: M. Evans Co., 1972.
3. Whitehurst, Robert N. "Jealous Wives and Adaptation Potential," to be published in 1972 by *Medical Aspects of Sexuality*.
4. Bernard, Jessie. *The Future of Marriage*. New York: Grune and Stratton, 1971.
5. Toffler, Alvin. *Future Shock*. New York: Random House, 1970.
6. Hunt, Morton. *The World of the Formerly Married*. New York: McGraw-Hill, 1966.
7. Stoller, Frederick H. "The Intimate Network of Families as a New Structure," in H. Otto, (ed.) *The Family in Search of a Future*, Merideth Corp., New York: 1970, pp. 145-160.
8. Whitehurst, Robert N. "Swinging into the Future: Some Problems and Prospects for Marriage," presented at the Midwest Sociological Society, April 21, 1972. (Available on request.)
9. Constantine, Larry L. and Joan M. "The Group Marriage," in Michael Gordon (ed.), *The Nuclear Family in Crisis*. New York: Harper and Row, 1972, pp. 204-222.
10. Whitehurst, Robert N. "Back to the Land: The Search for Freedom and Utopia in Ontario," presented at the Canadian Sociological and Anthropological annual meetings, Montreal, P.Q., May 29, 1972. (Available on request.)
11. Whitehurst, Robert N. and Barbara Plant. "A Comparison of Canadian and American Reference Groups, Alienation, and Attitudes toward Marriage," *International Journal of Sociology of the Family*, Vol. 1, No. 1, March 1971, pp. 1-8.
12. Smith, David E. and James L. Sternfield, "Natural Childbirth and Cooperative Childrearing in Psychedelic Communes," in Michael Gordon (ed.), *The Nuclear Family in Crisis*. New York: Harper and Row, 1972, pp. 196-203. Also, see chapter by Bennett Berger, et al. in Skolnick and Skolnick (eds.), *The Family in Transition*. Boston: Little Brown and Co., 1971.
13. Bernard, Jessie. Ms magazine, Dec. 1972, pp. 46-49.

20

BEYOND JEALOUSY AND POSSESSIVENESS
Ronald Mazur

In the following chapter, we first are exposed to an analysis of jealousy, showing how sharing can enrich human relationships rather than destroy them. Mazur begins this chapter with a discussion of the Biblical foundations of jealousy, moving on to look at the various forms of jealousy and how they add to destructiveness of relationships and reflect problems in the person having the jealous feelings. To go beyond jealousy, Mazur has included some suggestions that enable small groups to begin to cope with these problems in a setting that can be instrumental in breaking down old views of jealousy meanings. His contention is basically that as we learn these behaviors, we can likewise—in a supportive setting—unlearn them and relearn more adaptive ones. His chapter then continues with a critique of the usual modern marriage, showing us that being aware of the pitfalls in conventional marriage, when coupled with the means of coping with jealousy, can lead to an examination of a more realistic basis for non-jealous—more open and fulfilling—relationships in marriage.

The J and P Exercise: Before you read the following chapter, "Beyond Jealousy and Possessiveness," take a sheet of paper and write a paragraph about your last remembered experience of intense jealousy. Think about it for awhile, and try to recapture what you thought and felt the last time you had an experience which you could call "jealousy." Put aside your paragraph (or more) after you have finished it and read the chapter, returning to your paper as the last paragraph of the chapter.

"I the Lord your God, am a jealous God" (Deut. 5.09, RSV)
"Love is not jealous or boastful" (I Cor. 13.04, RSV)

To those who are not familiar with the complexities of Jewish and Christian theology, it certainly looks as if St. Paul one-upped God in wisdom. The transposition of the above biblical sentences implies that the boastfully jealous God is without love, and provides an interesting example of the varied and confusing meanings of "jealousy."

It is astonishing that so little has been written in recent years about such a universal and powerful emotion; an emotion which has triggered horrendous violence in human experience. Religious mythology, the theater, and the classics are suffused with themes of jealousy and its consequences. In the ancient Greek pantheon, Hera is the prototype of the jealous bitch who constantly nags husband Zeus about his incurable and outrageous philandering. The second-century Latin writer Apuleius contrives the gripping story of a vengeful mother who is bitterly jealous of Psyche, her son Cupid's lover. And among Shakespeare's gory tragedies, Othello, whose insane jealousy drives him to murder his faithful wife, Desdemona, is an unforgettable characterization. And yet, in works of psychology, sociology, anthropology, and philosophy, scant attention is given to the analysis and significance of jealousy. Perhaps jealousy has simply gone underground to allow a superficial social accommodation of changing marital partners.

Jealousy is a critical clue to models of marriage. It is an emotional response which is situational and learned. Its primary function has been to reinforce the sexually exclusive factor in traditional monogamy. But as models of monogamy change, the expression of jealousy loses its value and may even be considered inappropriate behavior and a sign of emotional immaturity. In 1958, for example, David Mace could write: "Jealousy can be a very destructive force in a marriage. Yet we won't understand it aright unless we recognize at the start that it is essentially quite natural and, in its right place, good and useful. We are all endowed with certain protective emotions.... Jealousy (is one of them)—it makes you watchful over the relationships upon which your security and happiness depend."[1] In 1972, the husband and wife authors of *Open Marriage: A New Life Style for Couples* state forthrightly: "No matter how little or how much, jealousy is never a good or constructive feeling. It may show you care, but what you are caring for is too much for yourself, and not enough for your mate."[2] Which viewpoint is correct? Possibly both. Something has happened to marriage in the fourteen-year interval between those two statements. With greater equalitarianism, and new covenantal or contractual options within marriage, the function of jealousy is changing if not disappearing. Sociologist Jessie Bernard clearly understands the process when she asserts: "If monogamous marriage as we have known it in the past is in process of change, there may be less and less need for jealousy to buttress it, and less and less socialization of human beings to experience it or move to control it."[3] In traditional monogamy, jealousy may be attributed a positive value; the lack of it, for example, being interpreted as indifference, uncaring, or unloving. In open-ended marriage, however, jealousy has no positive function and is not valued; it is at best, a symptom of tension and poor communication in the relationship.

For those who are strongly motivated to outgrow jealousy, three questions are critical: what is the nature of jealousy; can jealousy be totally and permanently eradicated from a person; and how do persons go about understanding and deconditioning jealous feeling and behavior patterns? Before answering such questions, it is helpful to assume a casual and positive attitude toward jealousy in persons: it's there; it's something to deal with; somebody is experiencing deep feelings, and the task is to understand them in the context of what that person is trying to learn or communicate. Joan Constantine and Larry Constantine, in their research and work with multilateral or group marriages, make observations about jealousy applicable to other alternative lifestyles. "If all jealousy is simply rejected as undesirable or immature, the affect goes underground and interferes with group functioning and the exchange of other feelings. If jealousy is lauded or facilely accepted, growth in important dimensions can be hindered. Thus it is necessary for participants in group marriages to differentiate among various forms of jealousy. Jealousy, if approached properly, becomes an opportunity to discover new information about individuals and their relationships."[4] Jealousy must be recognized, admitted, and worked with if it is to lead to personal growth and relational enrichment.

What, then, is the meaning of jealousy and how can it be recognized? While nineteenth-century American dictionaries clearly indicated both negative and positive meanings of the word, it is interesting that the 1970 paperback edition of *The American Heritage Dictionary of the English Language* gives predominantly negative denotations of "jealous." To be jealous is to be "1. Fearful of loss of position or affection. 2. Resentful in rivalry; envious. 3. Possessively watchful; vigilant." What seems clear is that the word itself has borne the burden of too many meanings; there is a great deal of legitimate difference and semantic confusion surrounding its historical usage. The trend also seems to be to use it only in a negative way. Regardless of how contemporary lexicographers define it, jealousy is more than a word; it is usually a gut-feeling experience filled with anxiety, resentment, threat, fear, and other hurtful emotions. It comes like a flash flood, undoubtedly causing various physiological manifestations. Jealousy is a complex emotion, and perhaps the only way to understand it and to control it—not eliminate it—is to analyze its various forms. Perhaps, if we analyze its various forms, we will find that jealousy can be defused of its demonic potential.

The following is a typology of jealousy which does not include the archaic positive usages, or the classifications of "healthy" or "romantic" jealousy. It is intended for use by all those who are disturbed by unwanted feelings of jealousy—who want to work toward eliminating it in relationships. In the open-ended marriage, jealousy has no creative purpose. This is to recognize, however, that in a lengthy transitional period, persons conscientiously experimenting with OEM and other lifestyles will already be conditioned to be jealous under various circumstances and will have to relearn new emotional and behavioral patterns. The task, then, is to recognize, understand, and deal openly and creatively with whatever kind of jealousy is experienced. It must also be emphasized that the forces of jealousy are interrelated with some common causes and consequences.

Envy-Jealousy Versus Reality Living

While some scholars make a case for differentiating jealousy from envy, it is more fruitful to consider enviousness as a variety of jealousy. The terms are often used synonymously and defined as such in contemporary dictionaries. Although an 1886 American dictionary states that "Envy is a base passion, and never used, like jealousy, in a good sense," it is quite probable that of all the forms of jealousy, most persons can easily empathize with envy. Early American lexicographers were clergymen or theologically astute scholars who understood and accepted biblical morality. They knew that the "jealous God" of Scripture was zealous for the righteousness of His people, that the quality of that jealousy was commitment and caring. They also knew the biblical commandment against covetousness—desiring wives or cattle not lawfully theirs. To be envious, therefore, was to break the Commandments.

To feel envy, however, is not actually to steal anyone's wife, livestock, or other possessions—it is wishful thinking. Everyone experiences it countless times. Someone else is always better-looking, more personable, more talented, richer, luckier, more intelligent, more courageous, happier, more lovable, or loved, or more valuable for the human race. What one envies reveals not simply what one would like to have, but often what one would like to be. But if envious wishful thinking is not soon transcended by realistic, dedicated work toward desired goals, or by honest, possibly humorous rejection of the specific source of envy, it can lead to crippling resentment and self-pity. A Boston newspaper interview with a young couple living an open-ended relationship probed the difficulties of such a lifestyle. The young husband was enthusiastic and self-assured but did admit to one difficulty. He admitted to being jealous on occasions when a male friend of his wife's would take her to restaurants he could not afford. Although the husband used the word "jealous," what he was more specifically feeling was envy-jealousy. He wanted to have the money to provide experiences as enjoyable for his wife as any other male could provide. The nature of envy, as well as other forms of jealousy, is that it always needs more to satisfy it. The young man seemed to be able to express his wishes honestly, without rancor or self-defeating pride. But if he had lacked the ability to be in touch with his feelings, to deal with them openly, he would have set conditions for the failure of his marital relationship.

Perhaps certain types of personalities are prone to certain types of jealousy, but everyone at times has reflected on his/her given life-situation and looked with envy on greener fields. If one faces the reality of one's own limitations and circumstances, however, anger and/or aspiration will be appropriately directed rather than deflected inwardly causing depression and/or debilitating self-pity.

Possessive-Jealousy Versus Autonomy

Emotional space for each partner to be autonomous is a necessary condition for any type of creative marriage or intimate relationship. For the recognition and growth of our own self—our integrity or wholeness—we need emotional space. Poet Kahlil Gibran advises lovers: "Love one another, but make not a bond of love. Rather let it be a moving sea between the shores of your souls," and he speaks of "spaces in togetherness." This is startling for young lovers to hear, for they think of their love as an eternal bond. But Gibran jars the thoughtful into serious consideration of unspoken realities. Very few couples, however, consider the meanings of a traditional pronouncement of marriage: "I now pronounce you man and wife." Man and *wife*? Apparently men, clergy and grooms, are loath to create such a binding role as husband, for why not say "husband and wife?" Clergymen would sound ridiculous saying, "I now pronounce you Man and Woman," though such a declaration has intriguing possibilities. In any case, such a pronouncement would grant the Man nothing—which is not what traditional marriage was created for. It is the woman who is *given* in marriage by her father or other male kinsman. The traditional wedding service, deceptively elegant and sentimental, is the ritual wherein the father of the bride pays his property tax and transfers the title of ownership. It is no wonder that people cry at weddings—there are a number of profound reasons why tears are appropriate.

Possessiveness is culturally sanctioned but is nevertheless a dehumanizing process. The possessive person does not know the inherent value or even the identity of the person possessed. The possessor is also possessed by private versions of reality—a reality requiring order, reassurance, and respect from without, and a sense of power and control. This allows for predictability, homage, and manipulation, but negates the qualities of spontaneity, authentic self-esteem, and mutuality of relationship. By perceiving the other merely as an extension of one's own life—even when romantically intended—that other person is deprived of dignity, individuality, and freedom to be and become with integrity. Possessiveness can, of course, be symbiotic in the sense that both spouses build their lives around it and feed off each other. This is so much the case that possessive marriage has superseded religion as the "opiate of the masses"; it is a stupefied security without joy, enthusiasm, or adventure.

The double-standard reinforces the sanctions for possessiveness in accordance with the best interests of males. When the male is possessive-jealous, the female is supposed to feel proud and grateful. When the female is possessive-jealous the male flaunts it as a sign of his desirability and attractiveness as long as the female doesn't push too hard. But when the female becomes too demanding she is demeaned as being nothing but a castrating bitch.

Possessive-jealousy is perhaps the most raging and wrathful form of jealousy, leading to acts of cruel vengeance and even murder. "You belong to me and if you cross me I'll get even with you. If I can't have you nobody is going to have you." That sentiment sounds as if it comes from one of those unbelievably trite movies. Yet, the sentiments of possessive people *are* unfortunately trite, and potentially destructive.

Is it possible to be monogamously committed to someone without possessiveness? We pose the question because many couples seem to confuse commitment with belonging to. Possessiveness is commitment without trust. Conversely, commitment with trust celebrates the autonomy of the other; rejoices in the uniqueness of the other; is aware of the privacy needs of the other. There need be no contradiction between mutual commitment and the mutual allowance for emotional space.

Exclusion-Jealousy Versus Sharing

The most painful type of jealousy is exclusion-jealousy: being left out of a lovely or critical experience of a loved one. While it's true that *every* experience is unique to the person undergoing or feeling it—since no two persons will ever see, feel, understand and value a shared experience in precisely the same way—it is nevertheless true that there is something beautiful and important about a couple going through something together. For those who seek to live a joyous open-ended marriage, exclusion-jealousy will be the most difficult interpersonal barrier they must overcome. It is a formidable hurdle which occasions the most sublime exhilaration once cleared. Over the long course, it reoccurs at intervals but it becomes easier to take and soon becomes a pleasurable challenge.

It's easy to feel jealous when you are excluded. It's not a matter of wanting to deny one's partner a new or enjoyable experience with someone else. Rather one wants to be included in the experience. It is also not a matter of possessiveness as such. For one can be genuinely nonpossessive and yet be overcome by exclusion-jealousy. It can happen for two reasons: being shut out of a good time and/or not having similar pleasure with another while the spouse is involved elsewhere. It sometimes comes down to a matter of, "Damn it, how come you have all the opportunities while I seem to be stuck in a rut?" Or it could be something like, "Why did you go there with your friend when you never like to go there with me?" Exclusion-jealousy is especially intense when a partner feels—or is—neglected in comparison to the time, finances, interest, and enthusiasm the spouse is lavishing upon someone else. Then there are those inevitable disappointing conflicts in plans when one partner says, "Oh, by the way, I'll be out with so-and-so on next Thursday evening" and the other replies, "Hell, I was hoping we could do something special together that evening." That "something special" is usually quite specific and it means changing plans with the friend or disappointing the spouse. With a little practice, however, couples can avoid such conflicts.

Couples living an open-ended marriage will handle the problems of exclusion-jealousy in various ways, including an attempt never to exclude each other. Some couples, for example, feel strongly that they can always include the spouse, even when the spouse is not present, by sharing their experiences verbally and by having their friends always meet the spouse. This inclusive approach might possibly work for couples with similar needs who are able to verbalize experiences and always enjoy meeting each other's friends. Other couples, however, will not find this a satisfying solution—their needs for privacy and emotional space may be strong, they may find verbal analysis of their experiences superficial. Such couples would rather confront the fact of exclusion directly. They are willing to say, "Yes, it's true we have experiences with others from which our spouse is excluded. We don't experience all of each other's intimate friendships, but we rejoice in the persons we are and in the richness of our relationships. We simply have to learn to live with the freedom to have partially separate lives—and we really wouldn't want it any other way." Ultimately, it is not so much a question of just sharing each other.

Competition-Jealousy Versus Specialness

Marriage partners who are self-actualizing may at times be jealous of each other's achievements and will compete for recognition and success. At its best, this can be creative tension; at its worst, undercutting oneupmanship.

The arena of competition, however, is not restricted to status and success. This is not to say that this contest is unimportant or trivial. On the contrary, it's imperative for women to refuse being consigned to supportive roles, to unleash their full creative potential for the benefit of themselves and for all people. If this kind of competition makes men uncomfortable, that's *their* problem. Women for too long have apologized for bruising frail male egos, and such men are just going to have to grow up and stop expecting their wives to be their mothers.

Negative forms of competition stem from a lack of self-confidence or self-esteem leading to jealousy of the partner's achievements, attractiveness, friends, or sexual performance. Behind competition-jealousy is the attitude: "You think I'm not good enough for you, but I'll show you!" This projection of inadequacy demands constant reassurance from the partner, but the reassurance is always suspected of being mere condescension. What is needed to overcome this form of jealousy is the development of self-esteem in combination with the sense of being essentially *special* to one's lover. This sense of specialness rests on the attitude: "Sure, I'm aware you know some fantastic people who also think you're great, but that makes me happy for you because I also know I'm uniquely special to you, that the quality of our relationship is one of the highest shared values in our lives." To be glad for the other without feeling like a second-rate person does indeed require a high degree of self-esteem. And, ironically, that self-esteem is easier to develop when two people lovingly help each other to be special through mutual respect, sensual pleasuring, admiration, approval, support, and sometimes forgiveness.

Egotism-Jealousy Versus Role Freedom

Role flexibility or interchangeability is a new personal freedom and a new feature of contemporary interpersonal relationships. The rigid stereotypes of masculinity and femininity have already been shattered, opening new avenues for self-realization and interpersonal openness. There are, to be sure, casualties of this shattering of sex stereotypes, and there are those who defensively hide from its impact. A time of transition is confusing and difficult for many. Nevertheless, the change is relentless and there is no turning back to the comforting absurdities of conformist man-woman, woman-woman, or man-man relationships. There is a new role freedom for all persons who will no longer allow themselves and their potentialities to be defined by cultural conformity or the insensitive expectations of others. This freedom also allows problems to surface: men who become enraged or embarrassed because their wives challenge them in public; women who become enraged or embarrassed because their husbands seem openly affectionate to other males. Examples of anger or embarrassment over a conflict in role expectations are endless.

Egotism-jealousy is a denial of role freedom. It is, in a sense, wanting a girl/boy just like the girl/boy that married dear old dad/mom. Rather than see the crisis of role interchangeability as an opportunity for growth, some people are ashamed of their "unfeminine" wives or "unmasculine" (note that the word is usually "effeminate") husbands and are jealous of other people who have "ideal" husbands/wives.

Egotism-jealousy can also be turned against the spouse with the ability for role flexibility who exposes the rigidity of the less flexible partner.

Egotism-jealousy is similar to envy-jealousy but is more specifically related to one's ability or inability to expand one's ego awareness and role flexibility. When both men and women can be persons in whatever ways that make them happiest regardless of what and how tradition defines them sexually, they will invest less of their egos in social roles and status. Can you imagine a time when baby boys and baby girls will be born free?

Fear-Jealousy Versus Security

Jealousy can be just plain fear: fear of losing someone special; fear of being lonely, of being rejected. To the extent that one's own value depends upon a partner's devotion, one will be vulnerable to the fear of desertion. If there is a classic form of jealousy, this probably is it, although an equally strong case can be made for possessive-jealousy. Fear-jealousy doubts the commitment of the other; it breeds on insecurity. It torments with anxiety and anguish. "What if my lover finds someone else better than me? What will happen to me?" Underlying such fearful feelings is the assumption that one is satisfying to the lover only as a desirable product—when something "better" comes along one will be abandoned. It's a hell of a way to live, but fear-jealousy is the foundation on which most marriages precariously endure.

The only security in a healthy relationship is to be a person, not a product. None of us is desirable or enjoyable in every way on every day, and if our relationships depend on the fear of having our lovers discover the attractiveness of others, then we do indeed shape dull and emotionally crippled lovers. Let your lover look at you with all of your blemishes and shortcomings and let your relationship be a dynamic exploration in life and becoming rather than a wedding exchange of personality packages. The strongest and most joyful relationships are those in which partners are not afraid to let each other go; attempting to control the duration of a relationship because of insecurity sacrifices the magnificence of every *now*. Bless and celebrate each moment of joy and loving with thankfulness, and let the future take care of itself.

The Durability of Jealousy.

Jealous behavior continues to be socially sanctioned in "appropriate" forms, but there are reasons to believe it will diminish as it ceases to serve a useful function in interpersonal relationships. Jessie Bernard believes: "If it is true that marriage is indeed moving away from the old monogamic format in the direction of some as yet unclarified form, jealousy in the classic form would no longer be required to support it and we could expect its gradual diminution. But until we know with more certainty the nature of the model—or models—of marriage we are moving toward, jealousy in some form or other may continue to crop up in the clinician's office."[4] It is probable, also, that even as models of marriage are clarified and become culturally accepted, forms of jealousy will be experienced by most people to some degree some of the time. Whether one believes that jealousy is inevitable or eradicable, normal or neurotic, is ultimately not the most important issue. What is important is to ask the most helpful question: "What kind of jealousy affects my relationships?" It is of no practical use to try to decide once and for all whether or not one is a jealous person. But if one understands the various types of jealousy something *can* be done to control and minimize it—to disarm it if not dissolve it. Simply expressing jealousy is a copout in a relationship—it is not being honestly open to one's self or to the special other. So much more of the expectations and satisfactions of a relationship could be understood, communicated, and creatively acted upon, if couples could understand the specifics of jealousy. What is it that you *really* resent? Are you afraid? Envious? Excluded? Competitive? Possessive? Does your ego hurt? What do you *really* want to communicate to each other? It doesn't help merely to say "I'm jealous." Jealous how? Can we *do* something about it? Should we renegotiate our expectations of each other? How can we grow from here?

Jealousy Inventory Exercise

A couple or a small group may gain insight into the specific meanings of jealous feelings by analyzing jealousy experiences according to the six types of jealousy described above.

A couple can simply write out or relate to each other their last remembered jealous experience and then try to rephrase the feelings more directly in terms of the six kinds of jealousy.

In a group of six or more, each person could write about a jealousy experience anonymously (without age, name, or sex). Shuffle papers and redistribute with each person reading the paper in hand and offering some possibilities for more direct expression of the experience: e.g., "this person felt left out"; "this person isn't aware of his/her partner's need for privacy"; "this person seems envious and unhappy about what he/she doesn't have"; etc.

If it doesn't feel right or comfortable to share a jealousy experience with a partner or a small group, use the following four examples for discussion. They were obtained in a small group and are shared as written. Were the writers male or female? How could they have expressed themselves directly and honestly to the person who occasioned the jealousy? What could each person *do* to improve the relationship or situation?

Question: When was the last time you felt jealousy and how do you remember the experience?

Example 1

My last experience with jealousy took place when the person with whom I'm involved chose to spend a weekend vacationing without wanting to have me along. My feelings were very intense because for me there could be no real pleasure in a vacation without bringing this person. I was angry, hurt, rejected totally out of proportion to the occasion.

Example 2

I feel jealousy to *a limited* extent when my partner or I discover relations *as deep* as ours that were had before our present relationship.

I feel a *twinge* of jealousy when friends in a "family network" relationship have a tactile relationship with partner.

Example 3

Although I felt, and feel, that the sensual/sexual experience need not be confined exclusively to the mate or partner of the moment, I became extremely jealous, insecure, annihilated when this led to my partner's acute emotional involvement. By losing the partner's primary commitment to me, I was losing much of my identity.

Example 4

When I felt my mate was able to express feelings completely (not necessarily sexual) and I was not able to do so I felt jealous of this ability. This was not a threat on the part of my mate, but rather a feeling of a lacking on my part. My mate's warmth, concerns, fears, and hopes were able to be expressed and experienced but mine were hidden both to me and others.

NOTES

1. David Mace, *Success in Marriage*, p. 11 (Abington Press, 1958)
2. Nena and George O'Neil, *Open Marriage*, p. 246 (M. Evans Inc., 1972)
3. Jessie Bernard, "Jealousy in Marriage," *Medical Aspects of Human Sexuality*, p. 209, (April, 1971)
4. Jessie Bernard, same as footnote number three.

21

BEING IN BED NAKED WITH YOU IS THE MOST IMPORTANT THING IN MY LIFE
Robert H. Rimmer

Robert Rimmer outlines a philosophy which he has been developing over the years and which is epitomized in the title of this chapter. Rimmer's contention is that man's spiritual side must be placed in the perspective of the Godness in us all. He does not believe in what is often called 'free sex.' Instead he believes that we can probably handle no more than three relationships and that it is possible to maximize joy in life by becoming open and sexually freed with that expanded kind of awareness and togetherness created and described in his four novels described in the chapter. The Rebellion of Yale Marratt, The Harrad Experiment, Proposition 31, and Thursday My Love are the taking-off point for a discussion of the next-step potential in real people adapting (in their own particular ways) to the life-styles he proposes. Rimmer, no utopian dreamer, claims that it is possible to live and find fulfillment in the adaptations of the life-styles he describes and advocates. These are only next-step possibilities, standing in the wings of the near future, ready to be activated by creative and courageous people who find conventional life-as-usual too unfulfilling. Although time will be the judge of this, Rimmer is an undoubted herald of some potential futures and has gained a large following because of his creative, thoughtful and positive approach to loving.

As you read the title of this essay are you smiling or frowning? If you're between sixteen and twenty-five years of age, of either sex, and have had a reasonable loving and protected early life, I hope you are smiling. Maybe even in agreement. Because you still have some wonder left in your life, and the possibility of snuggling and warm body contact with a loving human being of the other sex is high in your order of personal priorities.

But, alas after thirty, the wonder and the joy and the amazement of this other person, naked in bed with you (Oh, hell I've done this so many times!) is often replaced by genital priorities or how-to-do-it-techniques, or a complete lack of spontaneity. The sexual merger for many humans has about the same significance as the singing commercial—"You deserve a treat today"—and the physical blending and ultimate orgasm is as familiar and as about as inspiring as the one billionth look-a-like hamburger. "Now that's over with—do we turn on television, or do we go to sleep?" For humans who have arrived at this point in their lives being-naked-with-you is more an embarrassment than a joy, and certainly not the most important thing in life!

Because I believe that human sexual loving in simultaneous combination with mental surrender can actually induce altered states of consciousness, and humans have an innate necessity to experience the world in different dimensions—stoned thinking as distinguished from straight thinking—(terminology used by Andrew Weil in his book *The Natural Mind*) I have written a quartet of novels all of which basically try to convince the reader of this essential premise. Being naked with you (the convenient location often being bed, but not necessarily so) is the most important thing in my/your life!

In July 1943, in a paper titled *A Theory of Human Motivation*, Abraham Maslow proposed historically that man passed through a hierarchy of human needs, and at any epoch in human life on this planet different cultures could simultaneously be on different levels on the ladder of personal development. Man can only begin the climb to the next peak when he has his feet firmly placed on the plateau below.

The first needs which must be satisfied are physiological—basically the hunger and sex needs followed by the safety needs (the needs of freedom from pain or fear). Third are the love needs—the necessity of being a part of a world that cares about you, and finally are the needs for esteem, followed by the top of the pyramid—the need for self-actualization—in Maslow's words "the need to become everything one is capable of becoming."

It seems to me that the fourth and fifth needs—all of which make a sharp demarcation between man in control of his environment and animal-man who is a prey to the unpredictable world—are encapsulated in the third needs—the love needs. Additionally, I am convinced that most human beings can *learn* a complete awareness of their humanity and these completely human love needs—as distinguished from the primal needs—have no direct connection with our descent from the apes.

If there ever was a "territorial imperative," or we have innate tendencies toward "human aggression," these childish hedonisms can be easily "conditioned" out of us in the learning and growth process of living.

Men and women who have already arrived at this level of humanity are able to blend their personal selves with others without loss of identity. They may even be able to surrender themselves with deep intimacy with several persons of the other sex, and make the discovery that finding ones' self is the ability to lose oneself. Thus the concept of being naked with you is both a sexual need, and a need for alternate consciousness that becomes the road to Nirvana. This is an almost ineffable peak that can be experienced as one learns to surrender oneself with another human being. And as a true Buddha, you do not go alone to Nirvana but remain to bring the world of humans with you.

The surrendering of course, at this time in human history (even for those well advanced in the hierarchy of human needs) is a more daring adventure than most people are capable of, basically because nowhere in the advanced technology of the western world, where it should be possible, are our religious or educational systems making any effort to train young people in the vast potential of human interrelationships. In fact, just the opposite. Our strong Christian-Judeo conditionings still motivate our actions and despite the decline of interest in week-end religion, while most of us may agree that we are created in the image of God, few would agree with me that you and I are the only God we'll ever know. The split between God out there—(not God as you)—coupled with the Anglo-Saxon certainty that work and Kantian duty are the salvation of man, plus the meritocracy structure of capitalism all combine to destroy our natural childish wonder, and we are afraid to admit need to experience the world upside down (as youngsters do by looking head-down through their legs, or by whirling). So the average human being, confirmed in the ego-centric behavior of his early years, actually fears surrendering or disclosing himself and is unaware that "being naked with you" could save him from vast loneliness and the interpersonal muddles most of us live in.

About fifteen years ago when I was approaching forty while the inward rebellion against the hoked up morality and ethics and sheer shuck of my world (yours, too) was only a smouldering fire—one about which, like most of us, I presumed that there wasn't much I could do personally—I tried to evoke the feeling of being naked with you in the form of Ten Commandments which became an integral part of the novel *The Rebellion of Yale Marratt.*

Commandments, of course, is an overblown word for a basic philosophy of life. Like any proselytizer worth his salt, I was trying to convince a largely disinterested world that there was a saner departure point for human relationships. Here are the foundations for a new kind of religion which Yale Marrat tried to introduce into the world via his foundation Challenge, Inc.

1. Challenge believes that Man is God.
2. Challenge believes that men must be taught to challenge and excoriate any concepts that deny the ultimate divinity of Man.
3. Challenge is not concerned with the immortality of Man. Man must be taught to seek his salvation on this earth and in this lifetime through the Love and Understanding of all men.
4. Challenge believes that the only destiny of Man is the pursuit of knowledge, and every Man of sound mind and body should actively pursue his destiny.
5. Challenge believes that no Man is preconditioned to act by metaphysical fate or man-conceived determinism.
6. Challenge believes that Man is the measure of all ethical and moral values, and the test of validity in Man's ethics and morals and written laws should be that they exalt and confirm the dignity of Man.
7. Challenge believes that any human problem (hence, all problems known to Man) can be solved in the atmosphere of Love, and that the existence of hate as an emotion should be extirpated from Man's relationships and be considered the greatest evil confronting civilization.

Now here is the first statement of the being-naked-with-you philosophy which I still believe is quite valid.

8. Challenge believes that in the sexual union of Man and Woman, all humans regardless of language, race, or creed become deeply aware of the Beauty and Goodness inherent in each Man and Woman, and that through proper instruction from childhood can learn to transfer this Ultimate Insight into their daily commerce with each other.
9. Challenge believes that its beliefs are so honestly right for today's civilization that if men everywhere would accept them and teach them to their children for several generations, eventually a crusade would result that would wipe tyranny and oppression from this world.
10. Challenge will never cease to challenge. No thing . . . no belief, not even the Commandments of Challenge are sacred or inviolable.

The Tenth Commandment could well be the most important one because, in addition to the Eighth Commandment, it embodies an entire philosophy of life, suggesting that even the ego of the Commander is not sacred, and that human beings with a cosmic consciousness, and hence a sense of humor can be their own *doppelganger*, and stand aside and chuckle at themselves, and their own pretentiousness.

The story of Yale Marratt is essentially the search of one man (myself) for the roots and meaning of living. Why am I here? What's this life all about? Does it really matter? The potential answers all of us have experienced are either optimistic—God's in heaven, all's well with the world—or a parallel cynicism which uses the daily reality to disprove such foolishness, or a shrugging, hopeless hedonism which seems to be typical of the past few decades in American life.

In this framework, Yale Marratt marries two women, both American girls, one in a Hindu wedding ceremony, and one later by a justice of the peace. Cynthia, the second girl he marries, is the first woman he ever loved. At the time he married her, he had been unable to locate Anne, his first wife. Cynthia is pregnant, not by him, but by the man who took her away from him and who has died in an automobile accident. Shades of Peyton Place and the morning television soap operas!

But Yale Marratt is not a conventional book—nor am I interested in the kind of morality that would resolve this situation in a divorce court. In 1960, about three years before the beginnings of the present sexual breakthrough in fiction, thirteen publishers read the manuscript of Yale Marratt and rejected it because it was obviously a thesis book. Women who read ninety-nine percent of all fiction presumably don't like thesis books, nor would they approve of a man who openly shared his sexual life with another woman. For the modern American woman bigamy was the most detestable idea ever conceived. Look what happened to the Mormons! Worse, Yale Marratt believing firmly in the Sixth Commandment of Challenge—man is the measure of all ethical and moral values—had the effrontery to challenge the law, and proclaimed his right to live in a responsible bigamous marriage.

Obviously if the author of such a book had any sense he would have resolved the problem by having one of the girls die, or, more romantically—one of them could have her own man! But rebellion in the title of this book means something. The book concludes with "the Lady or the Tiger" ending—with Yale Marratt defending his right to live with Cynthia and Anne. It leaves the reader with the question whether people of the State of Connecticut will take action to change the outmoded laws on bigamy.

Twelve years later, Connecticut (as well as 49 other states) has continued to let sleeping dogs lie. But many menages á trois are flourishing sub rosa. From hundreds of letters I have received I'm sure that this form of marriage, whether it be two men and one woman, or two women and one man, because it tends to act out monogamy, by revolving around the lone representative of one sex as the leader, is surprisingly viable and long lasting. Today, many marriage counselors believe that a legal three-person relationship should be available to older people who could pool their resources, and their social security and live much fuller lives. The stress is placed on economics however and not being naked with you! On the other hand, since older men particularly in their seventies revert to a childhood demeanor more than women of the same age do, it opens the possibility of a male finally discovering ego-displacement with two women of his own peer group especially if they offered him sympathetic ears and comforting arms and breasts. Unfortunately, aged males and females cling to their ego-image training with a tenacity that belies their need to be Thou as the most valid part of their remaining existence.

Such is the speed of change and future shock in our world, not only does bigamy seem a rather tame idea today, but alternative living-styles of every description are now emerging into the sunlight. Many religious leaders, suddenly aware that being naked with you can be embraced without the necessity of denying that God is out there somewhere, are now accepting the fact that while monogamy will continue as the prime basic interpersonal encounter, marriage in the future will offer much looser structures in the area of companionship, family, and sexual fidelity.

Group marriage, wife swapping, and communal living, all quickly latched onto by the popular press in the past few years, are now giving way to the panacea solution—the hot, new, swinging marriage which the O'Neill's have labelled "open marriage" and then proceeded to define in terms of better interpersonal relationships in monogamy. But the O'Neills, though they offer the possibility of companionship with the other sex, sidestepped the day to day interaction of a monogamously married couple trying to cope with a second or third love relationship.

The plain truth is that despite the O'Neills' book, *Open Marriage*, or Carl Rogers' fascinating excursion into this area in his new book, *Becoming Partners: Marriage and Its Alternatives*, or *John and Mimi*, by John and Mimi Lobell, written by a young couple in their twenties, who use their own names and freely reveal to each other in separate chapters their numerous sexual encounters in their particular brand of open marriage—despite my book *Adventures in Loving* which will be published in the Spring of 1973, and has more than twenty articles by people between twenty-five and forty-five attempting different life-styles from bigamy to group arrangements, to orgies, and triads and open marriages—the plain truth is that most of these experimenters or adventurers, as I call them, only have the faintest idea of how to make alternate life-styles which incorporate multiple sexual involvements really work on an emotional interpersonal basis.

Most of the marriage counsellors writing books, whether they be Gina Allen and Clement Martin in their book *Intimacy*, or Joyce Brothers in her book *The Brothers' Approach to a Liberated Marriage*, or *The Marriage Grid* by Jane Mouton and Robert Blake or *Total Sex*, by Herbert and Roberta Otto (there are numerous others, and new ones monthly, plus all the ladies' magazines and many of the so-called intellectual magazines like *Harper's* and *Atlantic* flooding the market with new versions of a jet-set liberal philosophy) sadly give lip service to an unreal, impossible world of sexual freedom coupled with I-gotta-be-me interpersonal relationships. And most of them seem to be unaware that sexual hedonism as a way of life may be possible in the animal world but won't work for human beings.

Typical of the confusion in the minds of many of the sexual popularizers (and I suspect it is deliberate—to cash in on those who believe, evidently along with Masters and Johnson, that good sex is physical first and mental second) is some of the work by Helen Gurley Brown. Here is a quote from Cosmopolitan's *Love Guide*, which sells for a dollar-fifty and is a bedside companion for the confused young female.

"Here," Helen says in the introduction, "we hope is the ultimate *love* book . . . it is not a sex text—although it *will* revolutionize your sex life if you really do all we tell you. Sexuality is *not* a mechanical thing. If an orgasm were your only goal, an electric vibrator would help you achieve that, *technically*. But what any woman *really* wants is so much more . . . more human, more beautiful, more fulfilling, more magical, more supportive. She craves intimate sharing between two people."

The emphasis is Helen Gurley's. Few females or males would disagree with the last two sentences. But do those sentences jibe with the contents of the book? Here are the chapter titles—and the sheer shuck that you get for your money: "*Awakening Your Sensuality . . . Sexual Muddles and Fallacies . . . The Erotic Senses . . . Know Your Body Nude . . . How to Excite Yourself . . . How to Make a Man Want You . . . Know His Body Nude . . . Losing Your Virginity without Losing Your Cool . . . That First Night with a New Man . . . Ways to Sustain Passion . . . How to Make Him a Better Lover . . . Sick Sex . . . Continuing to Live Sensuously . . .* topped off with *Your Zodiac Seduction Book.*"

Contrast the introduction with the contents and you have the typical guide to what can be the ultimate physical contact any of us can experience in interrelationships. "Being naked with you as the most important thing in one's life," I'm sure would be regarded by Helen Gurley Brown as sheer pollyannaism. It's obvious that *Cosmopolitan's* advertising revenue and circulation is much higher on her order of priorities. But picking on Helen Gurley Brown isn't fair. I'm sure even Helen has once or twice experienced the ultimate sensuality of letting go of her ego . . . surrendering herself. If she or any female would dare to convey the how-to of that mental-sexual involvement in print it would be a more valuable guide than *Sex and the Office Girl.* The first question that needs to be answered is why can't we recapture our childhood wonder?

In *The Rebellion of Yale Marratt* I took the first tentative steps toward identifying the being naked approach to life with the following statement that Yale makes to Cynthia whom he has just married. Previously, Yale has told Cynthia that he is married to Anne, but he doesn't know where she is. On the day of his marriage to Cynthia he discovers that Anne has his child. Here's a portion of their conversation:

"You don't have to say that," Cynthia tells him. "She has your baby. You have to love her. What have I got? Another man's child in my belly! Yale, why didn't you just leave me alone? I'd have made a life for myself. O God, I should have known better. Of course, Anne would turn up. I really knew it in my heart. You can't recapture the past. There have been too many years between. Can't you see that? You're not the same, Yale. I know that. I'm not the same person you knew, either. For a few weeks it seemed possible, but I should have known better. If it weren't Anne, it would be your father. Pat would never be happy or just stand by and let you go your way." Cynthia turned away refusing to look at him. "Your father will approve of Anne."

"Listen," Yale said, angrily, "my life, so far, has been conditioned by people making tragedies where there is no tragedy. If you had come to me and told me what Pat had said to you, I would have told him to go to hell. I would have married you. We would have found a way somehow. I doubt very much if, faced with our marriage, he would have attempted any old-fashioned vengeance on your father. It would have gained him nothing except further alienation of me. Cindar, did you ever stop to think of how most people live life with a suicidal complex, a masochistic drive to hurt themselves? That's what I mean by making tragedies where there is no tragedy. Look at my father. He could make a tragedy out of my love for you simply because you are Jewish. He multiplies tragedy by trying to make me something I'm not. My sister is making tragedy where none need exist. Anne has a tragic complex evidently; or else she would have tried to find me. Everywhere you turn people have twisted their lives out of perspective over some human failing."

Now here is the first being naked with you approach. Yale continues:

"Some person or persons fail to measure up to some idiotic idea another person has of himself, and boom you have the seeds of self-destruction. Look at the world around you. What is the basis of all the hatred but a deluded idea of the importance of 'self'? Look at the murders in the morning papers, the divorces, the man-made scandals. What does it all amount to but a form of ego-mania? A feeling that the I is so damned important that it must justify itself at all cost. Do you know, I'll wager ninety-five percent of the novels written or the plays produced each year would have no basis for existence if it weren't for making tragedies where no tragedy should ever exist. There is only one tragedy in the world, and that is this terrible delusion with the importance of self."

Cynthia had stopped crying. She listened to him in silent wonder. "What has this to do with us?" she asked, thinking Yale hasn't really changed. He could still run wild with words.

"It means simply, I love you! I love Anne. Your solution for that situation is for you or Anne to withdraw in lonely resignation, wishing the winner good luck in the best jolly-old-cricket tradition—while the unseen audience wipes away the tears; because of course that is the only thing to do. That's the way they want the world to end," Yale said bitterly, "not with a bang . . . but with a whimper. Man must love the idea of whimpering idiots; there are so many of them."

Later in *The Harrad Experiment* I proposed as an integral part of the Harrad approach to life, entirely new interpersonal experiences based on a self-disclosing style of human interaction that likewise proposes that learning a new perspective on one's ego, vis-a-vis other human beings, is possible for most youngsters. Here is an example in a conversation between Phil Tenhausen, who is the guiding light of Harrad College, and an undergraduate student, Harry Schacht.

"I was never demanding of Beth," Harry said angrily.

Phil chuckled, "You expected because you loved her that she would love you in an identical way, didn't you? That's an extremely demanding idea. It can lead to the following conclusions. You either blame yourself, telling yourself that Beth didn't love you because you are ugly or you are Jewish or any of a host of masochistic ideas that you may dream up to whip yourself with; or you take a more positive approach and tell yourself that Beth is really not a good person because she didn't respond to your good love. The first approach will destroy your identity and probably lead to insanity; the second approach which is more typical, will ultimately bring you to the following: 'I really dislike Beth. She is promiscuous and will never love any one except herself.'

"Depending on how strongly you react, it is a simple stop to move from her apparent rejection of you to your rejection of her. This makes life simple. You reduce your problems to black and white. In this case: 'I hate Beth.' All of this is extremely unrealistic thinking. You are planning to be a doctor, aren't you, Harry? In our opinion many of the illnesses that you will encounter will have been triggered by this type of thinking. Hating is a self-indulgence that eventually leads to self-destruction. Where are you at the moment, Harry?"

Later, Beth tells Harry, "From each person I've made love with, I've learned something . . . mostly that the act of sexual congress is simply not so damned death-defying, all encompassing serious. It is not the alpha and omega of love or marriage. It's fun. The really wonderful thing about it is, if you come to the act of love defenseless, willing to give your self to another person, and the other person shares this feeling, then for a few moments in your life it's possible to be wholly and completely the real you. If two people make love this way, and stop playing roles with each other and can enjoy and accept each other for the frightened little people they really are . . . then sexual intercourse becomes a way of saying 'I am for a moment no longer me, I am you!' "

Thus basically Beth is stating the concept of being naked with you, expressed as the ultimate key to deeply involved interpersonal relationships. Just in case you think I only mean this figuratively, let me refer you to the quartet of my novels. Being naked in these books is a literal way of life, too, and accompanying it is the *continuous wonder of you*—your flesh, your physical processes, your contingency as a human being (you will die) that makes me aware of the unending mystery of life. Thus the literal and figurative act of being naked together combine in a *simultaneous mental-sexual surrender*—a letting go which carries overtones of Eastern philosophies in its re-structuring of human values, and lets you, the lover, discover beyond any shadow of a doubt that the third priority of human life is what makes us human. We do not live by bread alone. Everything else, assuming that you are not starving or in danger of physical extermination, is way down the ladder of human needs. Bypassing the third priority for the shuck values will ultimately leave you feeling sick and poisoned.

In *The Natural Mind* Andrew Weil establishes a potential educational and religious approach to life that is in distinct contrast to the popular philosophy embodied in the songs, "I'll do it my way" and "I gotta be me." A style of hedonism which ultimately one can't live with and has produced the age of the shrink, sensitivity training and encounter—most of which insist on being true to one's self, doing one's thing, as a much higher priority than being naked with you.

In the novel *Proposition 31*, I have suggested many times through the action of the characters that ability to lose one's ego, even to the point of playing at the role of a chameleon and taking on the other person's coloration, will not endanger one's personal identity, but opens the possibility of an exchange for a cosmic identity and a world of warm laughter and objectivity about one's self, and one's petty problems. Corporate marriage as proposed in *Proposition 31* (a merger of the lives of two to three families) or as proposed in *Thursday, My Love*, synergamy (two co-existing monogamous marriages) can exist only if most of the participants achieve this kind of interpersonal interplay. And this is true, likewise, of the million or so monogamous marriages each year that wouldn't end in divorce, if the individuals knew how to surrender their egos.

In *Thursday, My Love*, temporarily putting aside the exploration of a two-couple or three-couple group marriage, I have suggested that a parallel relationship, co-existing with the monogamous marriage might be easier to cope with (especially at the outset) than the complications of learning the being naked with you approach that is a *sine qua non* of humans interacting together in a group relationship.

Most people who have been married for any length of time are aware that "the one-and-only" aspect of monogamous marriage is a romantic concoction of the nineteenth-century writers and theologians. At some point in their married lives, many spouses actually discover another human being with whom they might have been just as happy (or miserable?). Why isn't it conceivable that this second relationship, which is at present considered adulterous, could be structured into a committed involvement which would be approved by the original spouses? The second relationship would not necessarily be an economic one. The important aspect of it would be that a man or woman involved in this second dyad could adjust to it separately without feeling guilty. Unlike the group or corporate marriage which I have proposed in *Proposition 31*, synergamy (a word I have coined) would allow the learning experience of functioning in two separate relationships to proceed without the additional cross-relationships that make group living under one roof traumatic for those who have had no training in interpersonal relations.

The being naked with you aspects of synergamy which ultimately might create the groundwork for a group marriage (but not necessarily so) are expressed in many places throughout the book. Here is Father Jesonge Lereve, in *Thursday, My Love*, and portions of his ceremony wedding Angela Thomas to Jonathan Adams who have been previously married for many years in a synergamous marriage.

"Angela and Jonathan . . . as lovers you have come to this humble church to consecrate your love in a form of marriage which has no sanction in the law of the State, nor of the Church. Yet the truth is that the marriage or commitment of two human beings to care for each other has neither strength nor stability because of any divine origin nor sacramental quality, nor pronouncements of man, but rather because the individuals dare to transcend their own ego and in the process be each other. Such a commitment is something one gives out of his own desire. Duty, obligation, responsibility may be contained in the word commitment, but these states of being tend to be outer-induced . . . pressured into existence by society. Such feelings tend to define love in terms that are self-destructive. A marriage of the kind you are entering into, ideally, should be witnessed and approved by your present spouses, and in view of the prior giving of oneself the limitations of the new commitment informally agreed upon. One day we may be able to offer this open strengthening of the family by a responsible process of accretion and blending of existing family units."

Father Lereve smiled as he noted that Angela and Adam were holding hands. "There is no ring in this ceremony. The words I ask you to repeat after me are only as strong as your joy and love for each other as interacting human beings. Repeat after me this synergamous bond you willingly assume. 'I, Angela . . . I, Jonathan . . . with no less love for my present spouse and my family, do accept the commitment to love and to cherish . . . You, Jonathan . . . you . . . Angela. I am aware that my love for you does not modify my prior commitment to my husband . . . to my wife. While our relationship to each other is supportive, it should also grow and gain strength because it reinforces and strengthens and adds perspective to the nature of our love both for each other and for our first spouses and children.' "I pronounce you man and wife. May God love you!"

Common to all the life-styles I have proposed and even in the "fun" novels I have written, *That Girl From Boston* and *The Zolotov Affair* as well as the non-fiction, are these six basic beliefs:

First, being naked together is a hetero-sexual, mental-sexual, surrender. The quality of this surrender may be possible in homosexual or lesbian relationships but I am deliberately not going to go into that or even the potential of bi-sexual surrender.

Second, this mental-sexual surrender is a one-to-one relationship—or to use sociological lingo it is dyadic. While the insights and the loss of ego experience inherent in such a relationship can be recalled and used to broaden the scope of *all* interpersonal experience, it cannot be attained in group sex or in casual wife-swapping. My feeling is that these cannot be labelled either good or bad activities, and they might have one advantage—they could (but not necessarily do) provide some experience in learning how to live in a life-style that involves several intimate dyadic experiences occurring alternately in one's life.

This brings me to the third belief that seems to shock more people than anything else I write—and that is that some people are able (and millions could be trained) to maintain several dyadic relationships with members of the other sex on a committed basis over a lifetime, and thus enhance the quality of their lives beyond what would be possible in an exclusively monogamous situation. But such relationships won't work as secret adulterous relationships, nor as post-facto comparison indulgences where the original monogamous couple have separate sexual flings, and then regale each other, presumably to jazz up their own sex lives, with the re-telling of their new sexual satisfactions and encounters.

How many of these separate dyadic hetero-sexual relationships can be maintained in the average person's life? I don't know. Two, I'm sure of—three might be even better—particularly if the three couples lived under the same roof, and had common purposes and goal directions for their lives. Of course, if there were a Harrad type undergraduate training available, the couples who had this training could easily embrace this kind of mental-sexual surrender with more than one member of the other sex.

But I doubt whether more than three couples could interrelate their lives on this level. The human time factor is against them. And there can be no surrender if you are climaxing with a dozen different human beings. Group sex may be better for you and more fun than jogging, and many medical experts are in full agreement that a really active sex life will keep you in good physical shape . . . but on the other hand since an orgasm only takes as much energy as climbing two flights of stairs, if there isn't mental surrender too it probably won't give you much satisfaction. And it could leave you puffing!

Whenever I categorically state my fourth premise to a live audience it isn't long before half the hands are waving in vast indignation.

Many of the younger generation believe that right now they have a kind of Harrad situation, since the dormitories are pretty open, and many couples live together off campus—and as for marriage, why get married? But no matter—the premise is—and I am certain about it—that hetero-sexual relationships function more effectively when there is commitment—and that commitment, whatever variety *it may be*,is a *defined*, accepted part of the social structure. All of our past Western social structures have emphasized monogamy, and offered very little approved pre-marital experimentation except perhaps bundling or hand-fasting which is mentioned by Sir Walter Scott in his novel *The Betrothed*, as a one year introduction to monogamy without the bells necessarily tolling in a wedding ceremony.

I don't think there will be a Harrad type pre-marital education in 1974. Nor will there be legal structures that permit bigamous marriages or synergamous marriages. But I believe all of these proposals including Harrad will be actualized in the next twenty years. Because *they are not Utopian*—and, despite Ecclesiastes, all we have to do is dare and there could be something new under the sun.

The fifth belief that I will never cease championing is that this new kind of interpersonal behavior could be taught to young people from birth, but it is not too late for an effective beginning at seventeen and eighteen no matter what the youngster's previous family conditioning has been—*if* the teaching could occur in an undergraduate life style and environment similar to that I proposed in *The Harrad Experiment*. The nature of the living environment, the opportunity to experience more than one member of the other sex on a deeply involved intimacy coupled with a continuing seminar in human values taught by teachers who were capable of entirely new approaches to interpersonal relationships, embodied in the being naked with you approach to life, would be eagerly embraced by young people out of high school, most of whom amazingly, still hang onto much of their idealism.

And finally, if we dared to consciously condition a new generation and make this approach to education a human birthright in the United States, so that every young person could be exposed to a warm, humorous *de-conditioning* from the moral, ethical and shuck values that dominate much of our total lives, we would give every human being the opportunity to climb the final steps on Maslow's hierarchy of human needs. The need for self-esteem and the need for self-actualization would emerge like a butterfly from its previous incarnation as the need to be naked together.

And the goal can be summed up in Soren Kirkegaard's key to living "Learn to be objective toward one's self and subjective toward others"—Being naked with you is the first step.

22

MARRIAGE, HONESTY AND PERSONAL GROWTH (Reflections on upper middle-class, urban marriages)
Lonny Myers, M.D.

Dr. Lonny Myers, a woman physician with many years experience in dealing with the world of male doctors and married couples, bends her energies toward development of a view of marriage which recognizes the complexities of styles of relationships. A description of the variable conditions under which sex takes place at-home, away, with spouse or with others make for a deeper understanding of these complexities. These variants are compared with the oversimple textbook version of marriage as a simple monogamy, happiness-for-life ideology. Her forceful discussion reveals the point of view only a dedicated feminist and liberated woman could produce. Her discussion of honesty in marriage leads her to the conclusion that there are conditions under which our traditional concept of honesty could have a destructive impact on relationships. Her ultimate conclusion is that it is laudable to work for the kind of open and honest relationship described so frequently by writers commending working together in this kind of atmosphere, but that one's ultimate sense of honesty and loyalty must lie within the self. Her arguments demonstrate that if we can live with ourselves in easy honesty, whether in fact we completely achieve the social ideal in relationships, we will have succeeded in creating an atmosphere in which growth and development can occur.

Traditional views on marriage in our society severely limit the types of activities in which either partner to a marriage may engage without the other. Because of this, many people find themselves in conflict, torn between their desires for personal growth and the restrictions imposed by these traditional views. This conflict becomes more severe when it involves the question of extra-marital intimacy. Here also, the problem of honesty becomes most acute. This chapter will discuss the restrictions imposed by marriage, the problem of honesty within marriage, and the possibilities for personal growth which exist in various kinds of marriages.

Personal growth may involve big decisions regarding an entire life-style, or little decisions about how to make today more meaningful—plus all the variations in between. Much has been written about how marriage robs millions of women of personal growth (no *man* has to choose between medical school and marriage). And much more will be written about how the pressure on men to make money and support a family thwarts personal growth. I have chosen to discuss extramarital relationships because they are the most threatening and the most controversial of all possible routes to personal growth. If I discussed growth through music, theater, meditation, astrology, sports, or anything else, when I was all through the question would still remain "what about sex?" But in discussing intimacy with another person, I can establish a principle that will apply to the less frightening sources of personal growth as well.

Marriage

Marriage means different things to different people. Thoughts and tasks connected with marriage can take up 80% of the wife's time, energy and emotion, while taking only 30% of the husband's time. One couple may get most of their satisfaction in togetherness, thus making their occupational, social, and political lives far less important. Another couple may enjoy their most rewarding experiences outside of the marriage, while their relationship with each other is more a matter of comfort than of excitement. There are low-key/low-energy people who do not find life very exciting either inside or outside marriage. There are high-energy/high-key people who take an exuberant joy both in marriage and in outside activities. There are all possible combinations of these. There are couples for whom playing traditionally defined social roles is important: the wife does wifely things and the husband does husbandly things. There are couples for whom even the basic roles of breadwinner and housekeeper are reversed. There are couples for whom traditional sex roles are unimportant—whoever has the energy does the job. There are highly structured marriages with well-defined rules. There are casual marriages which are defined as they go along. There are marriages with children; marriages without children; marriages with in-laws; marriages with no in-laws; marriages with serious financial problems, serious drinking problems, serious health problems; marriages with no easily identifiable serious problems; and marriages with no apparent problems at all.

Marriage also means different things to the same couple at different times. The importance of a good sexual relationship at the age of 25 is certainly different from the importance of sex at 80. The importance of doing things together may change greatly as education, jobs, and children influence the activities of each partner. Possessiveness may gradually become far less important after an intense marriage has developed into a comfortable one. And then again, time may have little to do with possessiveness. One couple may remain possessive for forty years while another may not be possessive even at the start.

One of the primary sources of confusion about extramarital relationships is found in the temptation to think about them without reference to the different kinds of marriages from which they stem. Yet it should be obvious that in a marriage which is perfectly satisfying and fulfilling without outside relationships there is no temptation to develop them. But in many marriages there is not even mutual appreciation—much less gratification—of each other's needs and wants. The difficulties involved in working and managing a household tend to interfere with intimacy and sensitivity. Although it is possible for some marriage partners to achieve communication and simple joy from being together, often it is much harder to achieve inside marriage than outside it. Outside of marriage interaction and intimacy often flow easily, whereas inside the marriage it may take complex preparations and dedicated effort to make it happen. Even when there is mutual respect, love, and admiration within the marriage, many people find that the excitement and freedom possible in an extramarital relationship cannot be duplicated at home. At home may be "better"; away may be a supplement, not a substitute.[1]

Another thing that is often assumed is that most couples are enjoying at least a reasonably satisfactory sexual relationship. The reality is that many couples have miserable sexual relationships, while others are making love joyfully and almost daily after 35 years of marriage. Whatever the pattern, chances are that one of the partners is having sex either more often or less often than they would choose. It would seem exceedingly rare that two people over a period of 20 years would continually have the same appetite for coitus with each other, year after year. When the differences are slight, the reasonable adjustment to the needs of one's spouse may be easy. But my educated guess is that millions of men and women are forced into a pattern of infrequency or abstinence at times when sex is very important to them. For many persons this means years of frustration with solitary masturbation as the only legitimate sexual outlet, while for some, even this is excluded.

At the same time, these couples may behave quite "normally" in social situations. They may even seem quite affectionate. But this outward display may bear little resemblance to what happens when they go home to bed. An apparently affectionate couple may not have had coitus in five years, while a bickering pair may make passionate love as soon as they arrive home.

Moreover, social conformity demands that both halves of a couple be invited together. So parties usually end up including only those couples that neither the host nor hostess have any objection to. The fascinating Mrs. X and the notorious Mr. Y may never get invited because their spouses don't fit in with the other invited guests. Seldom is either member of a couple invited to attend on his/her own merits. They almost always come as half of an institution. Millions of people accept this partial loss of personhood along with many opportunities for personal growth when they get married.

Both of these assumptions—the idea that extramarital affairs all relate to the same kind of marriage, and the idea that all marriages are at least partially satisfactory—are usually implicit in discussions concerning the desirability of intimate relationships outside of marriage. And both assumptions are false. To speak of the institution of marriage is to refer to a wide spectrum of very different relationships with outward images that are much more in conformity with social expectations than are the actual interactions of the couples. The only thing that *all* marriages share is a certain legal status.

Textbooks, journals, and magazines, however, tend to depict a model marriage and expect people to accommodate themselves to that mold. Until recently, almost everyone speaking publicly about "marriage" was referring to the traditional marriage, i.e., a social image of a compatible couple. Paradoxically, the very people who encourage the traditional marriage are usually the ones who emphasize that "marriage is hard work." There is no claim that it is *easy* to satisfy all one's needs within the marital relationship. But the idea presented has been that most people, if they work hard enough, will be able to capture at least part of the turn-on so noticeable when they got married. For years, no mention was made of the possibility of a vacation from all this work. If indeed marriage is work, won't people need a vacation from time to time? Regarding parenthood, a more lenient attitude is currently being taken. Professionals are suggesting that women do not have to be mothers all of the time. (Fathers of course were never expected to be eternally on duty.) Getting away from one's children occasionally is now accepted as an option within the category of responsible motherhood. What about getting away from one's spouse?

There should be nothing new or startling about this idea. In many marriages both people enjoy activities without the other. But for the vast majority there has to be a specific reason. If the men are going fishing, the women may be left at home. If a woman is going to visit her sister, she may leave her husband at home. But there is a tendency to avoid leaving simply for the purpose of being apart for a while. Convention demands that we invent rationalizations to camouflage an honest motivation to be separated for awhile.

Less conventional couples may allow for separate vacations and talk freely about the usefulness of temporary separation. But what about dating? This is usually very different. A man can opt to go fishing rather than be with his wife. A woman can choose to go visit her sister rather than be with her husband. But neither of them can elect to go out on a date rather than be together. Both of them must sustain the illusion that night after night, year after year they would prefer each other's company to that of anyone else. Married people are not allowed under the traditional rules to go out merely because they seek to relate privately to another human being (potential sex partner).

There is no scientific proof for the common assumption that dating is destructive to a marriage. We don't know that. What evidence has been collected comes solely from the dating habits of "patients" and "clients," who bring their "problems" to "experts." No one studies the dating habits of people who find it satisfying. Only when dating behavior becomes a problem does it come to the attention of experts who then incautiously write about the problems created by dating.

Again, there are no scientific data to prove that sexually monogamous couples are happier or healthier than couples who have explored extramarital sex. But again, we have some "experts" in psychiatry who deliver opinions based only on the dating behavior of their clients with problems and who feel no responsibility to study the effect of extramarital relationships on non-patients. This is similar to using patients in a tuberculosis sanitarium to study the effect of hospitalization on respiratory functions.

The ban on extramarital dating is so thoroughly imbedded in popular wisdom and "expert" opinion that even to challenge it verbally is to invite retaliation rather than discourse. Anti-dating messages have come through so strongly for so long that any married person who seriously considers dating probably has enormous independence of mind, or is desperate. For people who have reached the point of desperation in their marriages divorce becomes likely even without dating. This situation provides enough examples of dating followed by divorce to draw conclusions of cause and effect. Yet all of these conclusions violate common scientific practice because there are no comparable data about dating not followed by divorce.

Also, since the social sanctions against dating are so severe, married people who arrange dates are likely to become both fearful and guilty. Thus an element of self-fulfilling prophesy enters with all but the most secure individuals. When all the "experts" condemned masturbation and warned of its horrible consequences, millions of people suffered agonizing guilt over a harmless, enjoyable, and very human activity. Most marriage partners suffer the same kind of guilt, and probably for just as little good reason, if they spend an evening with a "date."

Almost all the "experts" say that dating will destroy marriages. And most married people seem to accept that it is evil and wrong. It is believed to violate the sanctity of marriage. It is thought to be the result either of insane desires or of hopeless inadequacy. Most people seem to simply accept the highly dubious axiom that any healthy adult can, with reasonable effort, find all the intimacy necessary within a marriage. But what is "necessary"? And why not expand beyond "necessity"?

In relationships that remain marriages in name only, for economic or social reasons other than good companionship, the lack of permission to date is truly pathetic. There are too few adults who can face the situation squarely, admit that they do not enjoy each other's company, and allow each other a private life. Even in marriages in which there is no sexual relationship at all, the partners may deny each other the right to enjoy sex with someone else. And even this restraint may receive the blessing of the "experts" who equate self-denial with strength.

The publication of *Open Marriage* by the O'Neills in 1972 was one of the first breakthroughs toward sanity on the subject. The O'Neills specifically accept dating in their concept of open marriage. The unfortunate aspect is that, like the traditional marriage model, they are describing an ideal situation. They state that one's dating experiences must be of the variety that can comfortably be related to one's spouse. They de-emphasize the role of sex. The assumption is that if the marriage is great, the marital sex both exciting and abundant, there is little need for sex on the outside. Thus dating can be used to enhance and enrich the lives of two happily married adults, without the complications of romance or coitus.

When the O'Neills finally do confront the problem of sex, they concede that these relationships can, on occasion, include coitus and still be helpful rather than harmful to the marriage. But they do not deal with extramarital sex as fun or casual sex as a source of personal enrichment.

Their system is fine for a marriage in which the two partners grow at relatively even rates. But a marriage that started out as a successful open marriage might come under a great strain if one partner began having much more fun and dating much more than the other. The less popular one might well decide to close up the marriage and cut off the freedom. This could happen even though the freedom was continuing to fulfill the partner.

It is probably more common for a marriage to start off as traditional and closed, then develop to a point at which one partner wants to open it up, while the other refuses. Ideal marriage is a fine goal. But there is an implication that if you don't attain this state, you are a failure. Since the vast majority of people will never develop an ideal marriage (traditional or open), a model limited to perfect relationships promotes feelings of inadequacy, guilt, and frustration. It is my belief that to impose a sense of failure upon the millions who cannot attain the ideal is destructive and an obstacle to personal growth. On the other hand, to hold that divorce is the solution for every couple who cannot attain the ideal is to advocate the end of marriage as a dominant social institution. My special concern is with the personal growth of millions who are caught in mediocre marital relationships—but it extends further to the enrichment of people lucky enough to enjoy a good marriage.

Honesty

Honesty is a fascinating subject because it means so many different things to people. For some, honesty means being unashamed to share any fantasy. For others, it means only that one does not knowingly make a false statement. Most of us probably mean something in between these two extremes. Few people would believe that honesty required them to reveal their worst thoughts about their spouses.

Honesty may also mean different things to the same couple at different times during their relationship. Early in marriage it may be possible to be almost completely honest. But as the peak of fervent attraction gradually subsides into deep caring, the partners may either consciously or unconsciously put consideration of each others' feelings above "honesty."

There are many times when honesty may be synonymous with cruelty. Should a person pass on gratuitous slander? Isn't it "moral" to leave something that is unimportant unsaid if it would cause pain? Isn't it even possible to confuse revenge with honesty, or disguise punishment as honesty? My conclusion is that to be completely honest is a valid concept only when applied to oneself.

To hide an irrelevant truth from a loved one may be good. Even to hide a relevant, but harmful, truth may be acceptable. Many people hide their extramarital experiences from their marriage partners. Some I have interviewed have stated that they would love to tell their spouses about these experiences but cannot because they do not believe that this information would be accepted in the same spirit it was given. The spouses could not understand how adultery could possibly be a positive growth experience, and they would be terribly threatened. People who find themselves in this position may be as honest as possible within the limits of their spouse's capacity to understand. And these limits are easy to find because as they are approached, negative feelings become strong. Yet this reluctance to be completely open is clearly not hypocrisy. It is remarkably different from the person who agrees that adultery is wicked and then secretly takes a lover. The first is being as honest as possible—until one reaches the point of knowingly hurting someone very dear. The second is clearly not being honest at all.

Another kind of qualified honesty makes a distinction between feelings and physical behavior. This kind of honesty would demand the truth about stolen kisses or actual adultery, but not about fantasies. So, if confronted by suspicious questions a person could be honest about their physical behavior without describing their emotional involvement.

Honesty in all serious matters has usually been regarded as a requisite for a good marriage. The only time that dishonesty has been recommended is after the fact. Some professionals may suggest that it is better not to reveal everything about the past. But few would endorse embarking on a new venture that demands withholding the truth from a spouse. Withholding the truth about fantasies—out of loving concern—is often acceptable. But to act out the fantasy in order to eliminate the frustration is usually regarded as a weakness and rarely thought of as being honest with oneself.

Yet in millions of marriages, fantasy, frustration, and dishonesty are already a reality. The honest conflict is between obeying the rules or not. And until a person accepts the possibility of breaking the rules as a personal option, he/she rarely can give any honest consideration to the real possibilities inherent in extramarital relationships.

Personal Growth

Most of us could not grow ("succeed") without a fairly significant amount of dishonesty. In politics, to get the power to be able to do what you believe in usually means some large compromise of honesty. In order to advance within a company, most people find it necessary to hide many of their negative—but honest—reactions to their superiors. Whenever a person has a vested interest in a relationship they usually find it best to temper their honesty with demonstrations of respect and/ or affection. In marriage, there is an enormous vested interest. Unlike their employers, people choose their mates *because* they feel they can share themselves. The conflict arises when fantasies or desires are not easily shared. And the conflict greatly increases when the possibility of acting out one of the unshared fantasies is considered. As long as a person feels that they are growing and enjoying life while sharing everything with their spouse, there is no problem. But for millions, the rules of marriage prohibit activities that would greatly enhance personal growth.

I am still referring to intimate extramarital relationships as a source for personal growth because these are the most difficult for most people to handle. But I want to emphasize that personal growth often involves other activities, hobbies, sports, job changes, music, art, travel, and the like. In each of these there are various degrees of restriction depending on circumstances and attitudes. But extramarital relationships are usually surrounded by maximum restrictions and are given the minimum of serious consideration. For people who merely accept the idea that extramarital relationships are forbidden, serious discussion is precluded and nothing is learned about this resource for personal growth.

Consider some generalized examples. Mary is having an affair. She tells her friend Alice about it. Alice's reaction is: how can you deceive your husband like that? But the deception did not begin with adultery. Even Alice, who would never make love with anyone but her husband, is deceptive and dishonest in many ways. She has flirted in safe group situations, and she has dreamed of exciting dates with several attractive men, even though she would never meet them alone. Her dreams were like wishes for a million dollars—so far from reality that they never even became a source of serious anxiety or decision. So Alice was not dishonest in the same way that Mary was, but she deceived her husband in her own way.

Now consider Joan. She is somewhere in between Mary and Alice. She has never had an affair, but she has flirted and occasionally met men for lunch or a drink after work. She got to know one man very well. They often had long talks on the phone. They shared a fantasy of sex together. But they were both married and never allowed themselves to be caught anywhere that they could not explain. It was fun, but also frustrating. Joan was tempted, yet her conviction that extramarital sex was wrong always won out. So perhaps it could be said that Joan, Alice and Mary had specific and different kinds of deceptions—the biggest difference being the amount and kind of risk involved. Mary risked being caught physically, Joan risked rumors about being seen with "X"; Alice took no risks at all. The real point, however, is what each of them got from their "dishonesty."

Mary went through many Alice-type experiences of simple flirtation, and one Joan-type experience of secret phone calls and clandestine meetings. Then she met Bill, the man with whom she was having the affair. Bill was a gentle man with great sensitivity. He talked about enrichment, about responsibility, about remaining concerned with both his wife and Mary's husband. Mary had been exposed to all the conventional wisdom concerning extramarital sex: it breaks up families, it is disloyal, it is the worst act you can have on your conscience. But Bill was so nice, and he treated his wife so thoughtfully. Even with Mary he could talk about what a wonderful woman his wife was and how much he loved her. The idea was tearing Mary apart—it all went contrary to everything she had ever heard. She asked him how he could deceive his wife if he loved her. And he replied that for twenty years he had supplemented sex at home with responsible extramarital relationships. He said that if he had not, he would have resented the restrictions that the marriage placed on him. He said that he would not have been able to love his wife as well or as long as he had, without taking the freedom he needed to meet other women and be with them occasionally. He said that he still made love with his wife four or five times a week, but that he needed variety. Mary reflected a great deal about Bill's wife. He was kind and loving to her and their daughters. He brought her presents unexpectedly. He was always surprising the girls with some unusual plans. He was a beautiful husband and father. But how could that be possible?

Mary's husband was rather cold and authoritarian. She loved being with Bill who was warm and sensitive. Yet it was an agony. And

Bill was very realistic. He did not want her to get involved beyond the point where she could take care of herself. He wanted his first priority of wife and children to be clear. He sincerely cared for Mary and did not want to hurt her. Before she decided on extramarital sex he wanted her to be certain that it was a decision that she could live with and find helpful. He simply told her that it was a life style that worked for him, and that if she believed she could handle it it would probably enrich her life. But he also said that if she had too many conflicts then they should just let the relationship cool and remain friends.

Mary and Bill are certainly not typical. But they do represent real people I have interviewed at length. The reason I chose this case is that it separates extramarital sex from all the irresponsibility, lack of love at home, and other negative associations which are usually attributed to it. If a marriage is strong and healthy concurrently with extramarital sex, why condemn adultery when we do not even know whether the success is "in spite of" or "because of" extramarital relationships?

Apart from the conditioned religious responses, the answer is usually that it is wrong because it involves deception. That is the answer Joan might give. But perhaps it is actually a fear of risking confrontation rather than a distaste for deception. Joan did not tell her husband about the phone calls, the dreams, or the mutual fantasies. She did not reveal that she often seriously considered meeting the other men or that she was rapidly changing her attitude about adultery. She did not explain that if there was a next time she might make a different decision. She did not discuss these intimate and important developments with her husband because she did not want to risk his adverse reaction.

Although Joan's aborted affair did in fact involve considerable dishonesty and deception, she might still insist that the reason she gave it up was that she could not "deceive" her husband. She did not risk serious guilt or serious trouble, but she also experienced a giant step in her own growth that will stay with her forever. (It is totally unnecessary for me to list Susan, Janet, and Sally who got hurt and regretted that they ever followed through on their attraction—every advice column and most medical books are filled with this kind of case history.) My point is not to compare the number of affairs which have been helpful with the number which are harmful—the data for such a study have never been collected. What I wish to point out is that "honesty" is never a simple thing, and that the dislike of "deception" may only be a rationalization for one's actions. Tangible evidence of deep separation between two people's philosophies may be the real cause for apprehension. Mary gradually began to accept extramarital sex as a valid experience, whereas her husband feared and hated it, thought of it as evil and the work of the devil, and to be punished. Perhaps the thing most often in the way of enhancing extramarital relationships is the fear of the clash that will occur when one partner accepts what the other still finds unacceptable.

As soon as a person drifts from fantasies to serious consideration of clandestine communications, the traditional ideal of marriage has already been violated. One way of dealing with this change is to keep the conflict a secret and work hard toward phasing it out. The effect of this is to bury the growth temptation as though it had never been discovered. This usually means a decrease or cessation of phone calls, an end to meetings, and a residual of *unshared* fantasies and frustrations that may remain for days, months, or years. Along with these negative aspects there is often a distinct feeling of pride, of loyalty, of self-esteem at having done the right thing for the marriage. The effects on the marriage may vary from an increased appreciation for the comforts it affords, to a strong hostility because of the limitations it involves. In some cases, the attraction can be mentioned and dismissed casually without revealing the degree of emotional involvement. This technique is very helpful in carrying out the decision to cut off a relationship, for once the attraction is admitted, every phone call or meeting, every glance becomes suspect. In some cases the third person may become a friend of the family and fantasies may be shared between potential intimates with a tremendous number of precautions to keep their true feelings secret.

The vast majority of married people have experienced some problem like this. When solutions to these problems are worked out intelligently, a sort of emotional cost/benefit ratio is considered. The sacrifice of personal growth may well be a bargain. The cost of the extramarital relationship may far outweigh the expected benefits.

In other cases the "secret" becomes known but never openly dealt with. Sometimes after many years have elapsed, the secret will lose its frightening potency so that older couples can talk about their fantasy lives of the past. They may, from a position of safety established in their relationship over the years, look back humourously on their youthful foibles and smile. And in fact, they may well be happier with their clear consciences and rich fantasy lives. To have pursued their fantasies might have led to years of guilt and anxiety because of experiences they were afraid to share. I have interviewed many people who felt that the cost of squelching a potential sexual relationship was worth it. They were happy with their decision. Most people I talked to, however, admitted that they were never completely honest with their partners about dreams and fantasies.

To be completely honest would demand that each person share not only fantasies but all of their conflicts with their partners. It would mean admission not only of clandestine meetings, but even consideration of such meetings. It would mean confessing to moments of wishing to be free and single. The cost of stretching honesty that far is often exorbitant. Few persons find that the benefits of sharing this kind of conflict even worth thinking about. This is often regarded as a decent departure from honesty. When dealing with inner conflicts, it is generally regarded as unselfish and virtuous to be selective and to keep certain things to oneself. Thus extramarital relationships are often sacrificed not in order to maintain total honesty, but to preserve the image of togetherness.

A Proposal: The Compartmentalization of Marriage

Traditional marriage tends to thwart the personal growth of one or both partners. Even so-called "open marriage" depends on equal growth and does not deal with the realistic possibility that one partner may have far more imaginative fantasies than the other. Dating may be accepted by both, but are both partners in agreement that a date for the whole week-end, or a month in Europe with a lover, will leave the marriage still viable?

For millions who enjoy companionship, loyalty and a good sex life within their marriage, the sacrifice of extramarital intimacies in exchange for years of mutual support, trust and gratification may well be a good bargain . . . at least the best one to be made. But for millions of other married persons who do not even enjoy comfort and understanding within their marriages, the restrictions against extramarital intimacies is an exorbitantly high price to pay for maintaining a proper image.

What choices are open to allow for more personal growth within the institution of marriage? I suggest that life for the married person can arbitrarily be divided into compartments. Compartment I is the time/energy spent with one's spouse; Compartment II is the time/energy spent on "family" matters (with or without children) but specifically not with one's spouse. Compartment III is non-family time; time/energy spent at work, community projects, entertainment with friends, sports, and so on, when one is not accompanied by spouse or children, but time that is completely "open" to inspection: your spouse can know exactly what you are doing and with whom. Compartment IV is energy devoted to private time—time that according to traditional standards is "cheating" or at least "deceiving." It is the opportunity to do something that you do not want your spouse and/or your boss and/or your neighbor and/or your children to know about.

The important thing is that you are not proposing to rob your family of compartments I and II—or rob your job or community obligations of compartment III. You are taking private time, and instead of doing something conventional . . . being daring and allowing yourself to explore new experiences . . . without your usual identity; you are just you: not Mr. Brown or Mrs. Smith; not president of the P.T.A. or circuit court judge; not mother of Jane; not son of the bank president . . . just you, acting according to your conscience and with *no accountability for your time/energy*.

During the early phase of marriage, the need for compartment IV may appear not to exist; for most people it is there, but dormant. For most people (involved in a traditional marriage) after the totality of "in-love-ness" ceases to dominate all other pursuits, all other relationships, often one or both partners harbor a desire for compartment IV. Compartment IV is based on the premise that it is possible to remain close, loving, caring and passionate even when you have secrets from your loved one ... *providing each understands that part of her (him) self did not get married.* With this realization, neither remains permanently "melted" in to an institution (relationship)—both remain individuals voluntarily teaming up to share most of their lives together and developing a trust that allows each to follow his/her own conscience. Each gives the other the right to a certain amount of time/energy that can be used completely independently; each respects the compartment IV of the other without censorship. A mature kind of trust is maintained because each remains bound by conscience. Living within rules diminishes the responsibility of conscience. Freedom from rules demands the exercise of conscience. Thus developing an intimate extramarital relationship (or smoking pot, or attending a gay party, or anything else) is not something that one automatically may or automatically may not do. It is a matter for independent decision.

This is an alternative to the traditional dogma that everyone should give up independence in marriage and share everything, making the merger of two persons as complete as possible. This is an alternative to possessiveness in human relationships.

The traditional ideals make all sex outside of marriage evil, and all intimacies outside of marriage irresponsible. These ideals are built into our culture and our personalities at an irrational level. In terms of personal growth, the price of striving for these ideals is often extremely severe. A married person is forbidden to learn about people, about life, or about sex through extramarital intimacies.

The traditional possessiveness which our society inculcates may remain entrenched for generations, but even now the acceptance of compartment IV can allow spouses to accept the possibility of extramarital relationships without demanding to know the degree of intimacy or sexual involvement. It can avoid direct confrontation with something that our traditional values uniformly condemn. It can help to eliminate irrational compulsions either to give or withhold information. It can allow each person to decide for her (him) self when everything or nothing may be communicated to the marriage partner.

This changes the level of trust between two people from, "I trust you not to do anything I don't approve of," to, "I trust you to act according to your conscience. You do not have to pass my list of do's and don'ts when you make a decision. I do not want to restrict your growth. I do not want you to restrict mine. Let us agree to be faithful to our marriage, to remain motivated to help each other achieve maximum fulfillment and growth."

The limitations of this philosophy, as applied to extramarital intimacies are great. As indicated in the introduction, the use of extramarital sex as a source for fulfillment and personal growth depends on available time, energy, and space where discreet meetings can take place. It is also necessary that other obligations and responsibilities are fulfilled. For years, the public has been bombarded with images associating intimacy outside marriage with irresponsibility. There are enough cases "proving" this to keep the campaign going for many years more. But there is another side to the coin. Many responsible people do in fact use extramarital intimacy as a source of personal growth. This was verified by Kinsey over 25 years ago. Under most marriage contracts, this means that a person must either cheat or go underground.

Cheating occurs when a person feels that they are doing something wrong, but want to do it enough so that they accept the guilt, or else find the compulsion so strong that it seems they cannot help themselves. Going underground occurs when a person believes what they are doing is right, but understands that the "occupation army" has power over their job, the custody of their children, their status in the community, and their future opportunities.

Many hundreds of thousands are a part of the sexual underground. These people believe that their life-styles are best for them, even though unacceptable to the community and often to their spouses. Untold thousands of homosexuals and bisexuals are in the underground. They are not ashamed of their sexual orientation, but they simply must keep their behavior secret or suffer dire consequences. With them are hundreds of thousands of persons enjoying extramarital sexual relationships which they feel good about, which are positive experiences for them. I am referring to responsible persons who are highly motivated to cause no harm, with the result that most of their relationships are positive and fulfilling.

To date, there is little choice for someone who is far more imaginative than her (his) mate. The options are: (1) frustrate personal growth, (2) cheat, or (3) join the underground. If the concept of a private sector were accepted, there would be a built-in escape valve, an opportunity for the conscientious withholding of selected information without breaking the rules. It is a matter of making the rules fit people's needs rather than trying to fit people's needs into rules already proven to be inadequate.

Summary

I propose the following *options for those interested in a less restrictive form of marriage:* 1) that dating after marriage (with or without sex) be accepted on its merits as a legitimate source of personal fulfillment and growth; 2) that persons contemplating long-term pairing incorporate the concept of compartment IV; 3) that those already involved in a bond that restricts fulfillment and personal growth seriously consider putting loving concern above honesty to others, and putting honesty to oneself above all.

NOTES

1. It should be noted that in some circles, the monogamous norm of being jealous is being supplemented with the idea that 'others' outside of one's marriage can be seen as merely different, not better or worse.

EPILOGUE
Roger W. Libby

This book has attempted to make readers more aware of emerging sexual life-styles and the potential for renovating marriage. It is assumed that some can engage in monogamous, sexually exclusive marriage and merely endure, while others may be more happily monogamous. However, it is increasingly clear that options to monogamy will continue to develop in the form of experiments with living, and that they will become more visible through the mass media. It is also probable that social scientists will take counter-culture definitions of the male-female relationship more seriously as they carry out studies on the varieties of marriages. Alex Comfort aptly recognizes these options:

> The adult of today has all three options—sex as parenthood, sex as total relationship, and sex as physical pleasure accompanied by no more than physical affection. . . . The fantasy-concept of total one-to-one sufficiency has let us down. Since sex is now divorced from parenthood, there are many more relationships into which it can enter if we choose (1972b:12).

While Comfort's observations are considered to be realistic by some, and inappropriate by others, the publicity his comments are receiving in the mass media is bound to have an effect on some readers. Comfort, Carl Rogers, and many others are openly encouraging experiments with alternatives to sexually exclusive pair-bonds, as with the "satellite relationships" labeled by the Francouers, or the closely related "intimate network" of complementary, nurturant co-marital relationships envisioned by Frederick Stoller (1970). We have attempted to present an overview of potential marriage concepts in the 70's. There is little doubt but that other variations of the dyadic and group marriage concepts will be experimented with in the coming years; we do not know how much social support experimenters will receive from the larger society. Those who take risks to be different must have a protective shell to withstand social pressures to conform to traditional definitions of marriage. It is obvious that adventures in loving and living sexually will initially remain a part of the "secret society," but as these styles of interaction become visible through the writing of journalists and the research of social scientists, the social and legal institutions will likely make necessary adjustments.

Jessie Bernard summarizes her view of human desires and the need for security:

> Human beings want incompatible things. They want to eat their cake and have it too. They want excitement and adventure. They also want safety and security. These desiderata are difficult to combine in one relationship. Without a commitment, one has freedom but not security; with a commitment, one has security but little freedom.
>
> In the past the desire for security, though present in both marital partners, has tended to be stronger among women than among men, and the desire for outside—especially sexual—adventure greater among men than among women. There is no assurance that this difference will survive the decline in the importance of motherhood in the future, or in the increase in labor-force participation by women, or the lengthened years of sexual attractiveness in women. My own observation of young people convinces me that in the future the emphasis among both men and women may well be on freedom rather than on security, at least to a far greater extent than today. Conceivably to a too great extent (1972a:81).

So the quest for both freedom and security is closely related to the way we approach experiments with new sexual life-styles.

An Approach to Experiments with Intimacy

As has been outlined in detail in this book, there is already a range of alternatives to the exclusively monogamous heterosexual relationship available if one desires another life-style. There is a wide range of ground rules possible within open marriage, from the O'Neills' rather limited view in terms of sexual freedom, to the views of many of the contributors to this volume. It seems that most if not all of the alternative sexual life-styles are based on equality between the sexes, and the encouragement of individual growth and developing the uniqueness of a private identity. This is well conceived in Frederick Perls' major theme:

> *I do my thing, and you do your thing.*
> *I am not in this world to live up to your expectations*
> *And you are not in this world to live up to mine,*
> *You are you and I am I,*
> *And if by chance we find each other,*
> *It's beautiful* (1969:i).

Perls' philosophy replaces for some the monogamous "I am you, and you are me, and we are one" ideal.*

We have stressed marriage as a process, rather than a static entity incapable of change. It seems too much to expect that two individuals will share all of the same interests and needs for an entire lifetime. While this reality is increasingly recognized in many areas of marriage, the sexual seems to be the last arena of acceptance of change and confrontation.

Sex is, among other complex things a language—a communication. But, as John Wilson (1965) indicates, it is too often treated as a *possession* in the Acquisitive Society where materialism and competition are stressed. Many fear touching adults of either sex in a loving or a sensual way, conscious that in our culture such gestures are automatically construed as sexual foreplay. Unfortunately, to many women sex is a bargaining point to be used, rather than a natural desire to be expressed. As Wilson indicates, we tend to barter sex for love, or he might have added, the illusion of love! Wilson contends that we should explore our desires and proceeed to obtain them, as he elaborates:

> None of us know what we want, or think we know: but we lack the moral courage to try to achieve it, because we are beaten down by life. We over-value things like security, we become timid and resigned, and perhaps we create for ourselves a morality or a meta-

---

*The ideal of doing one's own thing may have come to be an ideal which involves some oversimple (and perhaps distorted) interpretation of Gestalt theory—placing more emphasis on the individual than may be warranted. There is always a need to be aware of the balance of rights, obligations, and needs of the person in relation to himself and others. Past socialization practices have no doubt overemphasized social responsibility; the new emphasis may have gone too far in the other direction (emphasizing autonomy and self-approving freedoms. A more desirable situation would be to emphasize a balanced awareness of how people communicate their desires and wishes to each other. This latter aspect of Gestalt theory seems to have been somewhat neglected by some youth today in their haste to become more fully autonomous.

> physic to prop up our resignation. We compromise too soon. Others of us, uncertain what we want, still lack the courage to try out new experiences and new forms of living...(1965:252)

Wilson continues:

> Whatever our sexual objectives—and no doubt these will be substitutes for earlier objectives—there are good reasons for saying that we ought to pursue them if only in order to find out the precise nature of our own wants. We may be forced ... to *work through* certain desires in order to understand our own natures. The tragic side of human sexual activity is that most people seem either to work *at* satisfying their desires without gaining any understanding, or else to deny themselves satisfaction, equally without any increase in awareness of their own natures (1965:253)

It appears that many parents view maturity as conformity to their values, rather than accepting or tolerating alternative values about sex and marriage, and viewing maturity as whatever is effective for each individual in his or her communication with others. But, since maturity is a value judgment, and since values are facts to each individual, we often have trouble accepting those who are "different." Wilson aptly identifies the meaning of being "sensible" or "reasonable" about sex:

> A 'sensible' attitude to sex usually means thinking about it but not doing anything. This is directly contrary to the empirical or experimental attitude I... advocate. 'Don't do anything you may regret' is one of the stupidest pieces of advice ever given. If one took it, one would never learn anything at all; to learn something, you have to start by making mistakes and doing it badly—and of course you will regret this later. But this is how one learns.
>
> On the other hand, you know what some mistakes are already; you have your own criteria of what is sensible. It is not sensible (in this society) to have illegitimate children, seduce minors, bring up children before you know that you and your wife (or husband) can produce a happy family, and so on. (1965:260-261)

In the book we have assumed sexual choice as the legitimate right of each human being. It is important to ask oneself: "Does this relationship make me happy?" (as well as to consider the consequences of the relationship to others). Additionally, one should realize that if one person in a relationship either cares less and/or knows more about the other person's social script (what motivates them, what they fear, how they want to be seen, and the like), that person who cares less and knows more is in a position of power—power which can be used to exploit the other. However, if one does know more about the social scripts in a relationship and also cares about the relationship, that person is also in a position to further the intimate growth potential of that relationship. As Wilson puts it, we must say "yes to life", rather than being reluctant to extend ourselves to others, or sitting on the fence and watching life go by while we nurture our security.

We feel that humans need more laughter and joy and self-awareness through personal and interpersonal growth from creative experiments in living. This involves taking risks and trying out new things; it involves being in touch, rather than *fearing* touch communication. We need a variety of experiences. We need to be willing to discuss openly, to reappraise our values and our behavior, to introspect, to relate, to care, and to *enjoy!*

If we have added in any small way to the potential for joy to the reader, we have succeeded. This does not gainsay the fact that potential joys are just that—potentials that must be acted upon and courageously attacked with as much of our own good sense as we can muster. It was nicely put by Jessie Bernard in the summary of her great book dealing with communications among the sexes:

> There are many casualties in the process of working out relationships suitable for this day and age, many experiments that prove lethal. Coping with challenges new to the human species is, we repeat, not easy. But whoever said the human condition was painless? Who ever said it was easy to be a human being? Of either sex? (1972b:332)

Casualties occur in "normal" as well as in unconventional marriage; we cannot help but find life limiting when we refuse to take up the challenge. The attempt to *renovate* marriage may yet be one of the 20th century's notable achievements—and we are only on the threshold of change.

As we go to press (August, 1973), a few additional observations are in order. First, Morton Hunt has been writing a research report funded by the Playboy Foundation which will appear in a series of articles beginning in the October, 1973 issue of *Playboy* and culminate in a book entitled *Sexual Behavior in the 1970's*. Since our book will appear about the time of the October issue, permission has been granted to cite a few of the findings on EMS. Hunt's data indicate an increase over those of Kinsey twenty years ago in reported EMS for both sexes in the 18-24 age group. The increase is especially pronounced with young married females. It is not known how much of the increase in EMS is based on co-marital, open marriage agreements amongst spouses, or how much is merely "unfaithfulness." While the sample may not have included an adequate representation of emerging marital styles, about two percent of the spouses reported engaging in swinging at least once before or after their marriage. The increase in active incidence of EMS in the under-25 age group suggests a future increase in the *accumulative* incidence of EMS over a lifetime.

A further indication of changing mores may be seen in the relatively new terms (or old terms used in a new way) "old man" and "old lady" used to describe the partner in an *ad hoc* marriage relationship.

The term is a "hip" way of saying "I'm not available; I have a partner." "Old man" is used much more commonly than "old lady," indicating continuance of the double standard. The unmarried woman may have to report to her "old man," but the "old man" generally feels no compulsion to communicate that he is possessed by an "old lady." Thus, even though we have discussed emerging sexual life-styles, it is apparent that many young people have dressed up monogamy in new terminology. While wanting to avoid the stereotype of being "married," they are apparently creating new but similarly limiting images.

The 1970's are exciting times in terms of the changing attitudes and visibility of alternative sexual marital life-styles. The mass media reflect the range of attitudes about open marriages. A few semi-traditional publications are slowly considering possible virtues in open marriages. For example, Erica Abeel's "Beyond Monogamy" in *Cosmopolitan* (June, 1973) is a step beyond that magazine's more typical frown at alternatives to sexually exclusive marriage. But the most courageous plunges into the emerging options are evident in *Couples*, in a special issue by the editors of *New York Magazine*, and in each issue of what is probably America's most liberating magazine for both sexes, *Ms*. People's Liberation, including the freedom to explore more flexible concepts of masculinity, femininity, and sexuality has been notably advanced through Gloria Steinhem's success with the new journalism. Perhaps the increasingly active roles of today's social scientist and journalist will encourage further experimentation and evaluation of sexual life-styles. Such has been the goal of this book.

REFERENCES

Bernard, Jessie. *The Future of Marriage*. New York: World Publishing Co., 1972a.

Bernard, Jessie. *The Sex Game*. Atheneum, New York: 1972b.

Comfort, Alex. "Sexuality in a Zero Growth Society." *Center Report*, The Center for the Study of Democratic Institutions. 1972, 12-14.

Perls, Frederick. "The Gestalt Prayer" in *Gestalt Therapy Verbatim*. New York: Bantam, 1969.

Stoller, Frederick. "The Intimate Network of Families as a New Structure." In Herbert Otto, ed., *The Family in Search of a Future*. New York: Appleton-Century-Crofts, 1970.

Wilson, John. *Logic and Sexual Morality*. Baltimore, Md.: Penguin Books, 1965.